外贸函电写作

段 婕 编

西北工业大学出版社

西 安

【内容简介】 本书将国际贸易知识、商务技能知识与英语语言知识融为一体,系统介绍了外贸函电中常用文体的基本知识,包括各类商务信函的格式、常用语句和拟写技巧,还附有外贸业务磋商过程中各个环节往来函电的示例,诸如建立贸易关系、寻盘、报价、推销、还盘、支付、装运、保险、申诉、索赔、代理等环节函电示例。

希望本书能够帮助读者快速熟悉各种函电格式和常用句型,了解不同商务活动的具体操作规范及程序,从而提高业务能力。

图书在版编目(CIP)数据

外贸函电写作 / 段婕编. — 西安:西北工业大学出版社,2022.12
ISBN 978-7-5612-8538-1

Ⅰ.①外… Ⅱ.①段… Ⅲ.①对外贸易-英语-电报信函-写作-高等学校-教材 Ⅳ.①F75

中国版本图书馆 CIP 数据核字(2022)第 229067 号

WAIMAO HANDIAN XIEZUO
外 贸 函 电 写 作
段 婕 编

责任编辑:李 欣		策划编辑:李阿盟	
责任校对:李文乾		装帧设计:李 飞	

出版发行:西北工业大学出版社
通信地址:西安市友谊西路 127 号　　邮编:710072
电　　话:(029)88491757,88493844
网　　址:www.nwpup.com
印 刷 者:西安五星印刷有限公司
开　　本:787 mm×1 092 mm　　1/16
印　　张:27.5
字　　数:722 千字
版　　次:2022 年 12 月第 1 版　　2022 年 12 月第 1 次印刷
书　　号:ISBN 978-7-5612-8538-1
定　　价:68.00 元(全三册)

如有印装问题请与出版社联系调换

前　言

随着我国对外开放水平的进一步提升以及经济全球化的发展，国际商业往来日益频繁。尤其是在国际贸易中，买卖双方通过洽商就各项交易条件达成一致后，磋商环节即告完成。买卖双方当事人在订立买卖合同、明确交易关系的同时，也完成了整个交易过程中最重要的一个环节。在实践中，交易可以通过口头方式达成，但大都通过商务函电的方式进行。在涉外经济活动中，外贸函电写作将国际贸易业务与英语写作融为一体，具有联络业务、沟通交流的作用。它不仅是洽商国际买卖合同的手段，而且是签订国际买卖合同的主要形式之一。掌握好这些实用的英语写作技能，从事对外贸易活动的人员就能更好地拓展国际市场，建立对外贸易关系，发展贸易伙伴，从而促进对外贸易发展。

外贸函电英语作为国际商务往来经常使用的工具，是开展对外经济贸易往来和从事有关对外贸易经营活动的重要工具。通过学习外贸函电写作，学生可以掌握较为系统的外贸函电基础知识，了解国际贸易实务流程，熟悉国际贸易中的英语表达方法，掌握国际商务往来中不同类型函电的写作模式及单证制作知识，提升在外贸活动各个环节中使用英语的能力、胜任外贸业务工作的能力。

根据目前教学和实践需求，本书在介绍外贸活动表达方式、特殊用语、缩略语和写作技巧等的基础上，主要按对外贸易磋商的一般程序提供各环节贸易函电的书写实例，具体包括建立贸易关系、询价、报价、还盘、订单、支付、装运、保险、索赔、代理等相关业务，以期培养具有扎实语言基本功、宽广知识面、丰富专业知识，在学习中了解、宣传我国对外经济贸易政策，掌握外贸日常业务用语及国际规则的复合型人才。

本书既吸收了以往教材的优质内容，又根据新形势、新环境更新了相关内容，主要目的是让学生能系统地学习、掌握外贸函电英语，其中包括书信体的行文结构、专业词汇及语言文体等特点，提高在日常对外经贸工作中正确地使用英语语言和进行各项对外业务联系和通信活动的能力，以适应对外经济贸易发展的需要。

本书可作为本科、高职高专等学校国际经济贸易、国际商务等专业的教材，亦可供国际贸易从业人员培训、进修与自学使用。

在编写过程中参阅了一些文献资料,在此一并向相关作者表示深深的谢意!

由于水平有限,书中难免存在一些不足之处,敬请读者批评指正。

编 者

2022 年 9 月

目 录

Unit One　Overview 概述 ·· 1

    Section 1　Background ·· 1

    Section 2　Business Letters Introduction ··· 3

    Section 3　Introduction to the Course ·· 8

    Section 4　Features of Business Letters ·· 8

    Section 5　Business Letters' Categories ··· 10

Unit Two　Basic Knowledge of Business Letters Writing 商务信函写作基础 ············ 12

    Section 1　Introduction ·· 12

    Section 2　Purposes and Importance of Business Letters ································ 13

    Section 3　How To Create Effective Business Letters ··································· 15

    Section 4　8 Cs of Business Letters ··· 20

    Section 5　Tone of Business Letters Writing ·· 33

    Section 6　Preparation Before Writing ·· 34

    Section 7　Rules of Good Writing ··· 35

Unit Three　Structures and Styles of Business Letters 商务信函的结构与格式 ·········· 39

    Section 1　Introduction ·· 39

    Section 2　Structures of Business Letters ·· 40

    Section 3　Principal Parts of Business Letters ·· 44

    Section 4　Optional Elements of Business Letters ······································· 49

    Section 5　Styles of Business Letters ··· 51

    Section 6　Spacing, Margin and Envelop Addressing ··································· 67

Unit Four General Tips for Modern Business Writing 现代商务写作技巧 … 70

Section 1 General Tips … 70
Section 2 Grammar Focus … 82

Unit Five Establishing Business Relations 建立贸易关系 … 92

Section 1 Introduction … 92
Section 2 Examples of Establishing Business Relations Letters … 93

Unit Six Inquiry and Quotation 询盘与报盘 … 111

Section 1 Introduction … 111
Section 2 Examples of Inquiry and Replies … 113
Section 3 Examples of Quotation and Replies … 115

Unit Seven Counter Offer, Firm Offer and Non-Firm Offer 还盘、实盘与虚盘 … 121

Section 1 Introduction … 122
Section 2 Examples of Counter Offer … 123
Section 3 Examples of Firm Offer … 127
Section 4 Examples of Non-Firm Offer … 129

Unit Eight Orders and Acknowledgements 订单与接受 … 132

Section 1 Introduction … 132
Section 2 Examples of Orders … 134
Section 3 Examples of Acknowledgements … 137
Section 4 Different Types of Orders and Replies … 138

Unit Nine Payment Option 支付方式选择 … 157

Section 1 Introduction … 157
Section 2 Examples of Letter of Credit … 158

Unit Ten Insurance 保险 … 176

Section 1 Introduction … 176
Section 2 Examples of Insurance Letters … 177

Unit Eleven　Packing and Shipping 包装与装运 ············· 184

　　Section 1　Introduction ············· 184
　　Section 2　Examples of Packing Letters ············· 186

Unit Twelve　Complaints and Claims 申诉与索赔 ············· 202

　　Section 1　Introduction ············· 202
　　Section 2　Examples of Complaints and Claims ············· 203

Unit Thirteen　Agency 代理 ············· 219

　　Section 1　Introduction ············· 219
　　Section 2　Examples of Agent Letters ············· 220

Unit Fourteen　Contracts and Agreements 合同与协议 ············· 230

　　Section 1　Introduction ············· 230
　　Section 2　Example of a Contract ············· 233
　　Section 3　Examples of Agreements ············· 237

Unit Fifteen　Invitation for Bids and Advertisements 招标和广告 ············· 241

　　Section 1　Introduction ············· 242
　　Section 2　Examples of Invitation for Bids ············· 242
　　Section 3　Examples of Advertisements ············· 245

附表 ············· 248

　　附表 1　外贸函电常用词汇 ············· 248
　　附表 2　外贸函电常见词组搭配 ············· 250
　　附表 3　商务贸易类型词汇及其解释 ············· 262
　　附表 4　进出口业务常见流程及词汇 ············· 263

Unit One　Overview
概述

◆ *Learning Objectives*

a. Know the basic knowledge of business letters writing;
b. Master the features and categories of business letters.

Section 1　Background

In the 21st century, countries are inextricably linked to one another in trade, taking advantage of exchange rates on import and export with maximum profitability. The international market is huge, making it an essential part of any company's expansion strategy. The most well-known American companies, such as Coca-Cola, Nike and McDonald's, all have significant overseas footprints. Multiple free-trade agreements now exist between global participants that help fuel the rapid pace of globalized businesses. Organizations such as the WTO and cross-country agreements such as *North American Free Trade Agreement* (NAFTA) and *General Agreement on Tariffs and Trade* (GATT) reduce and eliminate trade barriers and tariffs, which are seen as detrimental to global corporate growth. Participating countries benefit from importing goods by acquiring a wider variety of available products, which increases local competition and in turn improves quality and decreases prices. This ideally produces a self-sustaining system in which only the best quality products sold at the lowest price survive, forcing companies to refine their production capabilities repeatedly to remain competitive.

As we know, the global economy is around our daily life. Almost everyone is engaging in international business. International business refers to the performance of trade and investment activities by firms across national borders. Firms organize, source, manufacture, market, and conduct other value-adding activities on an international scale. They seek foreign customers and engage in collaborative relationships with foreign business partners. While international business is primarily carried out by individual firms and governments, international agencies also engage in international business transactions. Firms and nations exchange many physical and intellectual assets including products, services, capital, technology, and labor.

While international business has been around for centuries, it has gained much speed and complexity over the past two decades. Today firms seek international market opportunities more than ever before, influencing the lives of billions of people around the world. Daily lives such as shopping, and leisure activities such as listening to music, watching a movie, or surfing the Internet, involve international business transactions that connect people to the global economy. International business gives people access to products and services from around the world and profoundly affects people's quality of life and economic well-being.

The growth of international business activity coincides with the broader phenomenon of globalization of markets. The globalization of markets refers to the ongoing economic integration and growing interdependency of countries worldwide. While internationalization of the firm refers to the tendency of companies to systematically increase the international dimension of their business activities, and globalization refers to a macro-trend of intense economic interconnectedness between countries. In essence, globalization leads to compression of time and space. It allows many firms to internationalize and has substantially increased the volume and variety of cross-border transactions in goods, services, and capital flows. It has also led to more rapid and widespread diffusion of products, technology, and knowledge worldwide, regardless of region.

With the further expansion of China's opening to the outside world, the development of economic globalization has made international business exchanges more and more frequent. Especially in international trade, after the buyer and the seller reach an agreement on the terms of the transaction through negotiation, the transaction is reached, and the buyer and the seller have a contractual relationship. The negotiation of international sales contract is the most important link in the whole transaction process. Although it can be carried out orally, in practice, it is mainly carried out by letter and telegram. Correspondence is not only a means of negotiating international sales contracts, but also one of the main forms of signing international sales contracts.

English business correspondence refers to English letters, faxes and E-mails. It includes foreign trade (and domestic trade) of course. International business correspondence is not simply writing or information exchange. It is something that you want others to know about you, to know about your business and the way you deal with business transactions. It is by the way you create your letter that your reader can identify whether you are friendly, rude, or you just simply want to do business. Your letter shows an attitude. This is one reason why it is important to consider your way of writing. Write professionally and with courtesy. Success of business transactions is not only dependent on your ability to talk and communicate verbally, but also the way you communicate in letters.

Business letters writing skill is a kind of practical English writing skill which integrates international business and English. In foreign economic activities, international correspondence has the function of business liaison, communication and exchanges. As a common English applied tool, it plays an important role in promoting international traders to further international markets and develop foreign trade.

Section 2 Business Letters Introduction

Recently with the globalization of economy, international business has become more and more frequent and business English is playing an increasingly vital role in the international community.

Business English is a variety of English concerned with such economic affairs within or outside a country as international trade, international marketing, economics, finance, accounting, law, administration, and so on. As an applied style, business English has its own stylistic characteristics. It is very useful to study the International business letter writing techniques for success in a globalized marketplace.

1. Write Your Way to Success in International Business

Business people need to communicate with their suppliers, customers, and other stakeholders. Mastering the techniques of writing good international business letters helps to prevent misunderstandings and deliver messages effectively, so as to increase responsiveness and the chances of success.

The success of any business depends on effective communication, and letter writing constitutes an integral and indispensable part of business communications. When writing international business letters, make sure to understand the established conventions in the recipient's land, what a word or phrase means in the recipient's culture and languages, the importance of considering time zone differences, and address the letter properly.

(1) Culture

Effective business letters always comply with the recipient's cultural sensitivities. For example, some cultures stress the need for very formal business letters, a stark contrast to the often casual and conversational tone of some business letters in America. For instance, applying for a license to do business or open a bank account in India requires a formal introductory letter that does not digress from the accepted style and pattern.

In many bureaucratic cultures such as the government in India, people higher up in the echelons of power consider a letter starting with "Dear Mr. XXX" as an insult and expect a salutation of "Sir" instead.

The recommended approach for marketing pitches in America involves listing out potential uses of the product for the customer. Japanese culture, however, considers one person suggesting what another person should do inappropriate.

It is also polite to wish the recipient success at a local festival underway. Although not a mandatory requirement, it may make the recipient more responsive.

(2) Languages

Use standard and consistent grammar that employs simple words with clear-cut meanings. Similarly, avoid using slang and phrases that international recipients would remain clueless in deciphering.

A major manifestation of problems related to grammar and word usage is the different meaning or connotation of some words and phrases in British English and American English. British English is in vogue in most of the Commonwealth countries.

Consider the following examples that illustrate the dangers of not understanding what a word means in the recipient's country.

While the United States requires people to drive a car on the "pavement", Britain makes it illegal to do so. The reason is that "pavement" means the "surface of the road" in American English, but means "a path with a hard surface beside the road" in British English.

A "moot" point in traditional British English is the "point to discuss". In American English, "moot" means "null and void". Thus, if an Englishman writing a business letter to an American stating, "The moot point is shipping the goods over the Atlantic.", he is stressing the need to discuss shipping logistics which is an important part of the deal. His American partner will interpret this sentence to: "The issue of shipping is of no consequence to the deal."

An Englishman once messaged his American girlfriend, "I'll give you a ring tomorrow." All he meant was that he would call her by telephone the next day. The American woman, however, thought this sentence meant that her boyfriend would offer the betrothal ceremony. The lack of understanding of the subtle difference in word meaning led to the relationship breaking off.

Even when the word's meaning is the same, the local context can make a world of difference. There is a famous story of a former minister from India on a visit to the U.S. wanting a modest bite to eat. He requested some sandwiches from a New York hotel. "How many do you want?" the room service waiter asked. The former minister, imagining small triangles of thinly sliced bread that he associated with sandwiches, replied, "Half-a-dozen." Six sandwiches arrived soon enough, each measuring a foot (about 30.48 centimeters) long and four inches (about 10.16 centimeters) high.

Another critical issue relates to translations. Many countries with English as a second language may interpret words differently from what the sender intends. For instance, an English movie in which a cop commands a motor cyclist to "pull over from the road" once had Italian subtitles that mean "the cop asking the driver for his sweater". Web based translation software may help in a big way, but it does have limitations. The better approach is to use simple words and sentences that leave no room for dual interpretations.

(3) Time Zone

Most people underestimate the importance of considering time zone differences when writing international business letters. Considering time zone differences becomes relevant in instances, such as greeting a person "Good Morning" when it is evening or night in the recipient's local time such as E-mails ending with the phrase "Waiting for your immediate response" when the recipient's local time is 2 am.

Proposing voice chat, video conferencing, or any other mode of real-time engagement also need to consider time zone. For instance, proposing a daily review meeting at 5 pm EST (Eastern Standard Time) in a business letter would require the Indian staff to tune in at 3:30 am in the dead of the night.

Make sure the E-mail or other mode of communication reaches the recipient preferably in the morning or well before close of business hours in the recipient's local time. Considering the recipient's time zone is a sure way to increase responsiveness.

(4) Address

Another concern is the use of correct postage stamps and addresses. The basic address requirements in most parts of the world are the recipient's name, building number or name, street, city, and zip code or its equivalent. However, never assume this is always the case. For instance, United Arab Emirates Postal Service does not offer door to door delivery service and the only way to reach out to a person there by government mail service is through a Post Box number.

When in doubt, cross check the Postal Service which has a wealth of information on postal rates, standard postal article sizes, and other information for all international destinations. Not adhering to such specifications will result in delayed delivery, or worse, no delivery at all.

No one can anticipate every potential miscommunication problem, but it is still a good idea to brush up on your international business letter etiquette from time to time. If nothing else, the recipient may notice your efforts and appreciate the time and courtesy—that alone can result in a more favorable response to your letter.

2. Business Letters in English

Business letters are formal paper communications between, to or from businesses and usually sent through the post office or sometimes by courier. Business letters are sometimes called "snail-mail" (in contrast to E-mail which is faster). This part concentrates on business letters but also looks at other business correspondence, which includes memo, fax and E-mail.

(1) What is a business letter?

The business letter is the principal means used by a business firm to keep in touch with its customers; often enough it is the only one channel that customers get their first impression of the firm from the tone and the quality of the letter.

Good quality paper and an attractive letterhead play their parts in this, but they are less important than the message they carry. Business does not call for the elegant language of the post, but it does require people to express themselves accurately in plain language that is clear and readily understandable.

Writing plainly does not mean that letters must be confined to a mere recital of facts, in a style that is dull and unattractive. When we write a letter, we enter into a personal relationship with our reader. Like us he/she has feelings and we cannot afford to disregard them. This is a necessary reminder because many people who are warm and friendly by nature became another sort of person when they sit down to write or dictate a business letter. They forget that they are "holding a conversation by post" and make use of impersonal constructions that produce a cold and aloof tone.

(2) Who writes business letters?

Most people who have an occupation have to write business letters. Some write many letters each day and others only write a few letters over the course of a career. Business people also read letters on a daily basis. Letters are written from a person or group, known as the sender to a person or group, known in business as the recipient. Here are some examples of senders and recipients:

business↔business
business↔consumer
customer↔company
citizen↔government official
employer↔employee
staff member↔staff member

(3) Why writes business letters?

There are many reasons why you may need to write business letters or other correspondence: maybe to persuade, to inform, to request, to express thanks, to remind, to recommend, to apologize, to congratulate, to reject a proposal or offer, to introduce a person or policy, to invite or welcome, to follow up, to formalize decisions.

One reason is that a great deal of business is conducted via writing. With the wide use of fax and recent development of EDI (electronics data interchange), more and more writing is involved in every part of business. Another reason is that effective business letters writers can use their writing skills to help increase their company's sales and profits by building up good relations with customers, employees, and the public. In addition, proficiency in writing gives the man or woman in business a personal advantage over less capable writers and contributes substantially to his or her self-confidence, which is a necessary quality for business success.

Example:

Dear Ms Jana,

We understand from *The Swiss Business Guide for China* that your organization is helping Swiss firms in seeking opportunities of investing in China and business cooperating with Chinese partners. To establish business relations with your organization and attract Swiss companies' investment here in XX, we write to introduce our city, the city of XX, as one of the open cities in XX Province, China and also ourselves, Foreign Economic Relations & Trade Committee of XX, as a XX government initiative to facilitate business relationship with foreign companies.

Our committee provides advice and assistance to XX firms seeking to export their services, goods to foreign areas and import goods and services abroad. We also assist XX firms in establishment of joint ventures and carry the procedures for examination and approval of joint ventures and foreign sole investment firms. Our committee can provide XX companies with information on the world market and specific commercial opportunities as well as organize trade missions, seminars and business briefings.

Our committee facilitates and encourages investment from other countries into targeted sectors of XX economy and maintains active promotion of XX through its network of contacts in domestic and abroad areas.

Nowadays, we are seeking foreign investment in the field of capital construction, such as improving of tap water system and highway construction. Also, we are setting up a tannery zone in XX County, the largest leather clothes producing and wholesaling base in North China. We invite Swiss companies with most favorable polices to set up their firms in any form on tanning, leather processing and sewage treatment.

Any information on investment projects into XX and on business cooperation with firms in XX is highly appreciated and will be pass on to everyone who have approached us with interest in similar project. You are also invited to our city for investigation and business tour.

Should you have any questions, please feel free to contact us. Thank you for your attention and I am looking forward to your prompt reply.

Sincerely yours,

XX
Commercial Assistant

Of Foreign Economic Relations & Trade Committee of XX

Section 3　Introduction to the Course

Business correspondence or business letter is a written communication between different parties. Students are supposed to know the means through which views are expressed and information is communicated in writing in the process of business activities. The students are supposed to learn both the language and the professional knowledge (in other words, to learn the language you are going to use when you work).

1. Course Description

Business correspondence is one of the most important courses (a compulsory course) for International Business Trade major. It is designed to help students to accomplish the transition from general English learning to specialized English learning, aiming at preparation for the future business career.

2. Course Objectives

After the completion of the whole course, students are supposed to:

a. Comprehend and master the basic writing skills for various types of business correspondence.

b. Be familiar with the general conventions as well as main procedures in international trade practice.

c. Conduct business, make quick and correct reactions to the business information and do business concluded in real life situations.

3. Learning Guide

In order to write good business correspondence, students should:

a. Achieve balance between language-learning and business-learning.

b. Achieve balance between input and output of what have been learned.

c. Achieve balance between course-book learning and simulated practice.

d. Focus on various writing patterns and writing skills of business correspondence.

e. Master commonly-used business vocabularies and make good use of them.

Section 4　Features of Business Letters

Even before, the business letter was one of the most circulating papers around the world. The business world has continued with its communication and business transaction successfully using business correspondence. From announcement, to information relay, to placing of orders, acknowledgements, payment, complaints, adjustments, insurance, shipping and transportation, are all doing processing and communication and along with them are the business letters. Business letters have been widely used. Skills and sometimes, training are required for writers in order to write effective letters. Here are some of the things to remember about when dealing with business letters.

1. Letters Are Permanent

Whatever is written or said in the letter will be permanently remembered or it can even be retrieved even if it has already been passed in many years. That's why a lot of letters can be used as permanent documents.

2. Letters Are Powerful

Letters can be used as an authority. Sales transactions, agreements, legal documents and the like are made sure to be written in black in white. Words said verbally can be changed and can be revocable but not what is written and signed in a black and white paper. Letters can change one request, confirm what has been agreed upon, give authorization to in-cash cheque, and stop business communication once it is not done properly. Letters are powerful.

3. Letters Are Evidence

Letters are proof that has been said or has been agreed to be done. Even in legal matters, the documentation can be used as evidence and secondary proof of what a certain person has done or has agreed on. Same is through with business, letters are evidence that something has already been forwarded and received, or something has been agreed to be done within a specified period of time, or certain adjustment has been approved and promised to be given on the date mentioned. Businesspeople prefer written agreements rather than merely verbal words.

A certain firm cannot deny something that has been written and signed in the business letter. That's why a written letter is usually sent after a meeting is done, that is, to confirm all that has been discussed and agreed upon during the meeting. Then, their signatures and written acceptance are requested to be given so as to make the written letter or document to be a binding agreement between them.

4. Letters Reflect Communication Level

A business letter reflects its writer's communication level. That's why it is very important to consider a guideline in making a business letter. A business letter will not only represent your company, but it will also represent you as a person and your character. It reflects how well you manage to communicate. Time has changed and so is with business letters.

From long letters to shorter ones, from questionnaires to filling of forms, from longhand to word processing using computers, communication technology changes but to produce an effective business letter is still the same goal people need to achieve and same good relationship people need to maintain. Even with the advancement of technology and enhancement of methods, international business trades continue to exist.

Business letters will continue to exist, and continue to circulate, to be powerful, to act as evidence. Business letters will still play a big role in the business world in the future.

Section 5　Business Letters' Categories

There are nine kinds of business letters that will be discussed in this section.

1. Sales Letter

"Turning words into profits." That's what sales letters do. Sales letters find new customers for you and persuade them to give you a chance. A sales letter also keeps your existing customers connected to you and buying more. It brings back customers who have stopped from communicating with you and encourage them to buy from you again. Understanding how sales letters work can give you the power to create a successful business. The sales letter is also used to set-up or confirm appointments, to make announcements regarding sales promotions or store openings, to congratulate sales persons, and to introduce new products. The sales letter is in itself a sales tool.

A sales letter is used to sell, so it should be specific, complete, informative, believable, friendly, and personal. It must direct to the right audience, and appeal to the reader's needs. Paragraphs in a sales letter should be short and contain simple, everyday language. You can enclose a brochure or product sheet if you want to provide further details or add credibility of your product.

2. Inquiry Letter

Inquiry letters at some instances may also be referred to as request letters. Most inquiry or request letters are short. They can be sent by mail, telex, fax, or E-mail. It may be written as an initial contact in a business transaction. Its objective is to introduce the writer and to ask a question or to express concern that needs any specific response. A letter of inquiry seems quite simple to write, but in actual practice it is not so. Sometimes it is so confusing that the recipient is almost embarrassed. Hence, be precise, direct and straightforward, otherwise the recipient might have to write back to ask you to explain things, or it is just possible your letter won't be read at all.

3. Order Letter

Order letters deal with orders. Business deal with orders almost every day, may it be for merchandise, for services or supplies. Communications are done through letters to place an order or to acknowledge and order. In this communication between a seller and a buyer, they take it as an opportunity to establish a relationship, then eventually, loyalty that will build your company's name and will generate more revenues.

4. Complaint Letter

Errors are unavoidable occurrences in business. These usually lead to complaints. May it be a misunderstanding of the orders or delivery, or errors in the address or delays, these may lead to complaints. This is where the complaint letter comes in.

5. Adjustment Letter

The claim letter or complaint letter is the prerequisite of an adjustment letter. Granted that the complaint is justifiable, an adjustment will be made, otherwise there will be no adjustments to be made, but a letter of rejected claim.

6. Payment Letter

Issues regarding payment are what the payment letter for. There are five major methods of payment for international trade: cash-in-advance, letters of credit, documentary collections, open account, and consignment. During business transactions, there could also be some issues regarding payment like payment may either be too much, short, or delayed. Some payments are lost and are not acknowledged.

7. Transportation and Shipping Letter

Letters involved here relate to freight handling agents and companies involved in the transport. Some instances may be companies that may send a letter informing the customer about the goods to be transported or rebooking the transport. There are times where circumstances happened like damaged goods reached the customer, then a letter to inform the company is forwarded. There's several documentation involved in transport activities. There are mainly four means of transporting goods. These are by road, rail, sea, and air.

8. Insurance Letter

Insurance has a big part in the business world. It is a means of protection for individual or companies from financial losses. To understand insurance better is to put it in a perspective where there is a risk. The primary reason of having insurance is to give payment for those who experience loss or damage. Risk is one big factor why insurance must be undertaken. Insurance will help to protect both people and business against a possible risk that will produce losses. Initially, the insurance was only for rich people who would want to protect their fellow businessmen and was only given a few rules to maintain. However, due to globalization, enlargement and development of trade especially, internationally, insurance was considered to be one important factor. The increase in the number of companies applying for insurance opens an opportunity for an insurance market. Now, the insurance business is one of the fast-rising services in business trades.

9. Banking Letter

Banks may simply be known as storage of money where bank staff looks after it. But aside from that, banks offer other services like credits, debits, inter-banking and others that may be related to money. There are also correspondence involved in banking and they are usually business-related letters. Bank supervisors use letters to build relationships with banking officials that may be able to help them in their business. Some letters serve as reminders, applications for an account and others.

Unit Two Basic Knowledge of Business Letters Writing
商务信函写作基础

Learning Objectives

a. Master the principles of business letters writing;
b. Become acquainted with the general layout of business letters;
c. Skillfully write structural parts of business letters with proper styles.

Section 1 Introduction

Business communication is very important. One of the most used business communication before and now is the business letter. The business letter continues to circulate locally and overseas for its purpose. A lot of areas in business are using the business letter, may it be for placing of orders, acknowledgements, adjustments, payment, insurance purposes, or even banking transactions. International business communication continues to grow, especially this time where the market is open globally. Business firms aim to be competitive. In order to do this they will not only try to conquer the market in their area, but also need to be part of the global market. One of their means to convey their messages and purposes is writing international business letters. It is then safe to say that the business letter is inevitable in the business world.

Small, medium or large business reaches success at some point. There are factors to consider in order for that success to come. One of which is the use of business letters. To start with a promotion, to announce an opening, to communicate your products available, to negotiate, to close a sale, and so on, these are just some of the areas where business letters are involved. The proper use of business letters will give an affirmative feedback for the company. These letters serve as the representative of your company.

A business letter is a recognized way of communication between people or companies who deal with trading, may it be for goods or in service. The trade between the two entities is built and progresses as they communicate through the business letter. The business letter is considered as an official document. It is not like any other thank-you letters or postcards. This letter is issued with authority. A business letter is also an effective and influential communication tool in order to have a systematic and structured flow of information between two transacting entities. This is a letter used for essential communications. A wrong impression placed on a letter may result to a negative feedback from a reader. That's why writing a business letter needs some skills. Any person dealing with business letters is seeking for guidelines in order to convey the correct message.

A business letter is an essential document because it deals with trade concerns. It shows how professional the writer is in conveying what the writer wants to inform the reader and how the receiver react on the writer's concern. An international business letter is then defined as a business letter that deals with communications not only in one particular country, but also internationally. To start a business letter, you have to note that the first thing the reader would like to know is, "What is the letter all about?"

Business communication is a process through which the parties involved establish partnerships or relationships, negotiate terms, and complete transactions. Every company, big or small, communicates with many different firms and companies everyday. Although new information technologies are increasingly used, business letters are still the main channel and medium of business communication. Even though the way of transmission of business letters is changing, the essential act of sending a message from one person to another remains the same. Therefore, it is necessary to be aware of the importance of business letters writing. In business world, words are as important as figures. By words we make sales, create goodwill, win customers and hold old ones. Words can let us obtain credit, get bills paid, report on new ideas and products, and launch sales campaigns. So success in writing is a key to success in business.

Business letters can be roughly grouped into three categories in terms of their purposes: to get action; to build goodwill; to furnish information. If you want to write successful business letters, always keep in mind that you are going to have a talk with your reader. The most effective letters are messages from one real people to the other. They should be easy to read, easy to understand, and they must be friendly and courteous.

Section 2   Purposes and Importance of Business Letters

1. Purposes and Importance of Business Letters

There are several purposes and importance of business letters.

The primary purpose is to communicate to your reader about important facts. You must take note that to communicate in an accurate and precise manner. These facts may affect your reader's schedule or activity. For example, there is a delay in delivery. You must provide the accurate reason for the delay and when the delivery will be received. Your letter may contain the following phrases:

Please accept our apologies for the delay in the delivery of your order. There has been a miss communication between our dispatch department and the shipping agency. We are currently doing our best to fix this problem. Please expect your delivery to come in your area in a week. You should be receiving it on the 20th of this month. Again, we apologize for the inconvenience that may cause you because of this delay. We assure you that this kind of problem will not happen again in the future. Thank you for your understanding.

The second purpose of a business letter is to prompt the reader regarding an action to be done. The reader is given an instruction that needs to be replied with an action. Here is an example:

With reference to our previous meeting on last 19th of June, we have agreed to place a discount of 10% from the total amount of our orders. We are now sending you the order form which needs to be filled-out. Please send this form back to us before the 25th of June so we can arrange the shipment by the 2nd of July.

The third purpose is to make a decent impression on the reader. A business letter serves as an ambassador of the company who sent it. "A good letter is a master key that opens the locked doors." So if your letter gives a good impression on the readers, they would most likely be communicating back to you. But if your letter does not even give interest to the reader then, you lose your chance to build a relationship or a trade. Your letter must form a positive image in the reader's mind.

Here are other purposes and importance of business letters.

a. To build the business;
b. To sell products or services;
c. To build relationship and friendship;
d. To catch new customers;
e. To open new markets;
f. To win back lost customers;
g. To solve problems and issues between two conflicting organizations;
h. To bring more finances or profits;
i. To collect unpaid debts;
j. To build confidence between two transacting people or organization.

2. Important Points to Consider in Writing Business Letters

In writing a business letter, there are also some things to be considered in order for this letter to serve its purpose. Here are some points:

A. Consider the relationship.

Know your relationship with the receiver of the letter. Are you his/her customer? Or employer? Or supplier? Or just an acquaintance? By this you would know how to start the letter and what the contents should be. Create a goodwill with your reader. A goodwill is a friendly feeling or feeling of confidence. Many people will not respond or may not talk to you because their impressions and attitudes are formed out of reading your letter. As earlier mentioned, your letter acts as an ambassador. It represents your company.

B. Consider the timing.

Is this the right time for you to send the letter? For example, your customer is declared to be bankrupt and they still have an outstanding balance. Is it the right time to send a letter demanding for the payment? Or would you rather send a letter that will comfort your customer and reminding them of the outstanding balance in a polite manner? Consider the timing for sales and promotion. This will help you get a positive feedback. Use a tone that is suited to the occasion.

C. Consider your reason for writing.

Your letter must be clear enough to be understood. You should also use an active voice to ask for a particular response. Your request should be reasonable and legal. Know the purpose of your letter and use this as a guideline in writing your letter. Inform the reader what he/she needs to know and don't let him/her guess between the lines.

D. Consider your reaction if you were the receiver.

If you were to receive the letter, will you be pleased? Or will you be irritated? Will you understand right away what you request or written in the letter? Is it politely done? Put yourself in the shoes of your reader and see if your letter is clear enough to be understood and politely done to be accepted. Don't use jargon that your reader is not familiar with. Consider the format.

Section 3 How To Create Effective Business Letters

Writing a letter indicates a mirror of who we are and how we perform business transactions. The letter we make helps us to catch customers, maintain customers, communicate with subordinates or colleagues, coordinate with associates and so on. This is not the same letter that is lengthy or giving sugarcoated words, but it is a professional letter written to let your reader provide a response. You don't need to write to impress your reader but you write to give your point, what you need and what is needed to be done. This letter will deal with the situation that requires response. This may even create a series of letters just to finish one transaction and this letter communication may continue to maintain good business relationship. This is a business letter.

1. Plan

One important factor in the success of any business is planning. Preparation and foreseeing all the possible areas of risks, income, and losses are all included in planning. Business letters are also part of it. A business letter without any consideration and plan will surely come to failure. Planning is also a key factor in creating a business letter.

(1) Research the facts

It is always an advantage to do a little research before making your letter. Have a chance to check on previous correspondence and find out everything you need to know about your reader. This will help you to get away from creating a poor letter. Going through a little research in the previous correspondence, you can list down some things that will help you know your reader. You may be able to know about your reader if they are committed to a business relationship, or know how to separate professional and personal relationship, or offer ideas to help improve business relationship and customer services, or are interested to reduce cost rather than waste money.

After seeing these things, try to imagine and have a visual concept of your reader. After that, have an attention to the topic you want to relay. Another important point is to make your letter simple and understandable, direct but courteous, short but complete.

(2) Consider the subject and the reader

After the research, you now have an idea of your reader. With this, you can also have an idea of what topic you are going to talk about in the letter. The facts you've gathered from your research will allow you to organize the best letter output. Making an outline is a good method to see the logical order or the idea in general. Here is an example:

Paragraph 1: (i) Say "thank you" for the meeting held.
 (ii) Be grateful for new ideas shared that can be used for business.
Paragraph 2: (i) Present the details of the meeting and present the actions to be made.
 (ii) Verify some corrections or additional topics missed out.
Paragraph 3: (i) Appreciate their support and hope for reply.
 (ii) Suggest another meeting if needed.

One good point to consider is also the interest of the reader. It is good to open your letter with a topic that will attract the interest of the reader. The letter you sent must give a good impression to the reader. In order to do this, you can imagine yourself to be the reader. How will you feel or what will be your impression upon reading your letter?

Give emphasis on the "You" attitude rather than the "I" or "We". The "You" attitude must be worked out in order to bring the best approach to your reader. One principle to remember here is writing letters to a person from a person. Write a letter to a person. Don't just merely write a letter to answer a letter. Another area to consider about your reader is, "What is your relationship with the reader?" An employer? A supplier? A customer? A subordinate? These questions will help in the way you make your letter.

One good letter is difficult to write because not all people are the same. One apology letter may be accepted by a person because he/she understands the situation. One may reject

Unit Two Basic Knowledge of Business Letters Writing 商务信函写作基础

the letter because what he/she cares the most is the business, and no mistake is acceptable. That's why the planning and research are very important so that you can send a letter that will really cater to the person who will be reading the letter.

2. Set Your Objective and Make Sure to Accomplish

A good letter has an objective. Your research will help you find out about your reader and the company. Your outline will give you an idea of the letter as a whole. Your objective will keep you on track and will guide you while creating the letter. Stay focused on your goal and make sure to accomplish it. Your objective should lead you to the answer, "What is the letter all about?" The reader wants a clear answer to the question. This will be enhanced by the details you will include in the letter. One general objective for all business letters is to avoid confusion, cliché, technobabble, phraseology, and inadequate conclusion that will fail to move the reader to action.

3. Components of Effective Business Letters

Aside from planning, an effective and successful business letter should aim to consider that its content corresponds to the proper components of an effective business letter.

(1) Language

One cause of misunderstanding is the "language barrier". You have to understand that it is not enough that you have given your message; it is also important that your reader understands the message. It is significant to consider that the language you use is also the same language your reader uses. This means that what words you use in your letter should be understandable to the reader. Do not use jargon that they are not familiar with, nor write a letter that your reader does not even have any idea what you are talking about. Your line of communication should be at the same level in such a way that you both understand what you are dealing with. It is not necessary to exaggerate with the use of words, nor decorate the letter in a way that you are moving away from the actual message. Your reader may feel overwhelmed by the use of words. Use simple and plain words. Here are some examples (See Table 2.1):

Table 2.1 Examples

Avoid these	Use these
will you be kind enough to	please
come to a decision	decide
express a preference for	prefer

Avoid cliché in order to have more focus on the message of your letter. Consider saying things in a more natural way.

(2) Tone

Another factor to consider in your letter is the tone. The tone is the sound of the writer's voice, and this will propose something different from the literal meaning. The writer's words may imply contrast to the literal meaning of the words. A pleasant tone can be accomplished if you are natural, friendly and courteous. Your letter must be personal. Show your reader that you are not only giving statistics, but you are writing as a person. The tone of your letter should show that the writer is a human being. The letter has a human touch. If your reader feels that you are sincerely concerned not only about the business, but also personal relationships, it is most likely that you will receive a response. One point already mentioned above is the relationship between the writer and the reader. This will also have an effect on the tone of your letter. A boss or an employer who is sending a letter to his/her subordinate will sound different from the supplier sending a letter to his/her customer. Different letters are written for different purposes. Because of this reason that tonal component is important. With proper use of tone, you can make negative news as positive. But ignoring your tone, even positive news may come out to be negative. Here is an example:

The competition in this position is very tough, with many outstanding candidates. Your credentials are very impressive, but we regret to inform you that they did not match with the current position we need. We hope that you will be able to find a position that will match with your skills and experience.

(3) Focus

The focus of your letter should be on the reader. This is having the "You" attitude. The "You" means you are putting yourself from the standpoint of the reader. With this, you see clearly what your reader's skills are, what he/she loves to do and hates to do. This gives a human touch on your letter. There are instances where the writer thought he/she is focusing on the reader and assumes that his/her interests and likes are the same with the reader. But the truth is not. Here are some guideline questions that you need in order to know that whether you are following the "You" attitude or not:

a. What motivation will you include for the reader to react positively with your letter?

b. What will give interest to the reader?

c. What can be the reader's perspective with regards to the topic you detailed in your letter?

At first glance, you may not know the answers to these questions. But if you will do some research and planning, take time to sit down and check in these areas, you will be able to draw clear answers. You must let your reader feel that your letter is of personal value.

Here is an example of a letter with a "You" attitude:

Unit Two Basic Knowledge of Business Letters Writing 商务信函写作基础

Dear Mr. Brown,

Thank you very much for considering our agency for your insurance policy.

As your line of service is not covered in the current insurance policy program we have, we are keeping your application on-hold for future reference and further processing once our policy program is updated. We are currently working on this service to be approved. Once the approval is given after six months, we will surely exclude your application.

Should you request to pull out your application from us, we would appreciate if you will inform us immediately. We would like to inform you that your application is valuable to us. We hope that you will still consider to start a partnership with us. We appreciate your patience and your understanding on this matter.

Yours sincerely,

XXX

(4) Length

"The shorter, the better." This is one of the most common rule of thumb, as long as the components of your letter are included. Different letters have different purposes. The purpose of your letter will help you in deciding how long or how short your letter will be. Here are some examples (See Table 2.2):

Table 2.2 Examples

Avoid these	Use these
Please see that an inquisition is conducted to ascertain the source of the fault.	Please find out the reason.
We would like to express our regret for being unable to …	We are sorry to inform you …
Fill in your orders at this time considering your prompt that …	We cannot meet your present request order immediately.

"Come right to the point." This is another point to consider. Most businesspeople are busy and they will not read a very long letter. As much as possible, limit your letter to one page. Put your main topics in the first paragraph. So your reader will know what the letter is all about. Planning will help you limit your letter.

(5) Stationery

In writing a business letter, it is also good to consider the materials you will be using in making your letter presentable and easy to recognize. You are selling your company by your letter address. The paper to be used should always be of the best quality. It is plain and not full of unrecognizable designs. The paper colors vary, and some may use shades of gray, brown, or blue. Some may use different colors of paper for different departments. But the best one to use is the white paper. Before, the paper size used the 8.5 inches×11 inches, but now as the computer age has governed the business world, A4 size becomes popular. Most printers today are designed for A4 papers. But this does not eliminate the use of the 8.5 inches × 11 inches. The letterhead varies from one business to another. But the most commonly used is designed with business logo, business address, E-mail address, contact number, fax number, website address. If the company has a trademark or distinctive symbol, it is advisable to place it on the letterhead. This trademark should also be placed in every paper transaction of the company like the bills and invoices. Normally, letterheads are printed at the top of the paper. Some companies place some other information at the bottom of the paper aside from their letterhead details on top.

All business letters should be type-written. Proper spacing is important. The font size ranges from 11 to 12 depending on the font. Your font should be formal like Times New Roman or Arial. Do not use decorative fonts. The envelope is also important. This is the first part that your reader will see. It again, leaves an impression. The address should be properly placed horizontally and vertically. Also, the address printed on the envelope should be exactly the same as the address printed in your letter. There is no restricted color of the envelope but light colors are preferable. The envelope size that is normally used is the 9 inches×4 inches. Others may use the smaller size, 3.5 inches×6 inches.

Section 4 8 Cs of Business Letters

In the business world, business letters are widely used and are commonly circulating between transactions. It is known that business letters serve many purposes. Business letters are used for selling, apologizing, seeking explanation, introducing a company or new product, expressing complaints, rejecting, providing an adjustment, organizing, and so on. Your letter must serve its goal and objective and aside from that, you also need to differentiate the good letter from the bad. You have to understand that a business letter is formal and it involves proper information and documentation. There is a way to measure the quality of a letter. The benchmark to use is the 8 Cs or eight characteristics of a business letter. An effective and successful letter must seek to include all these substantial qualities.

1. Clarity

Vague and unclear letters will only lead to confusion or doubts. To clear any doubt or confusion, the letter should be created with the use of precise and familiar words, as well as, the sentences and paragraphs should be constructed coordinately and supporting each other. The following paragraph in your letter should support the first and main paragraph. If you will be talking about another topic in the second or third paragraph, you fail to accomplish "clarity". Clarity is considered the cornerstone of effective communication. The writer should consider the reader's level of understanding. The letter should be logically and coherently arranged in a way that one idea will not be covering the other. Instead, each idea should stand out, but complementing each other. A good letter will bring a good result. The message of your letter must be understandable without any interpreter or translator. The language you use must be the language that everyone understands. It is important to choose the right words to use in your letter. You may have the correct idea and precise thoughts that you want your reader to know, but using inappropriate words will give another meaning to what you meant to say. Some business letters use general words instead of specific words. Most of the time, the general words only create cliché (which you need to avoid). Here is an example of using general words:

We believe that if you will implement the use of the Inventory Automation System, it will have a considerable effect on your inventory problems.

You will notice that the writer has used three general words: considerable, effect, problems. The reader will then ask what is considerable, what could be the effect, and what are the problems you are talking about. Now, this is the best time to use specific words. Specify what considerable effect that the system will have. For example, it will make the counting of materials faster, or it will lessen the possible mistake of miscounting. Will it automatically update the inventory every time a new material will come? Mention the specific benefit and effect. And the problems should also be specified, for example, problems on human miscounting, or problem with the number of hours doing the inventory because it is still manual.

You'd better say it as:

We believe that if you will implement the use of the Inventory Automation System, you can experience the following benefits:
Fast and efficient materials counting;
Automatic update of the inventory when new materials arrived;
Computer-generated monthly report.
And eliminate the problems on:
Error of human counting;
Extra hours added for new materials to be counted and updated in the inventory;
Volume of paper works to check for monthly report.

A point that is ambiguous in a letter will cause trouble to both sides. In this way, clarity is often considered to be one of the main writing principles and language features. To achieve clearness and clarity, you must first have a clear idea of what you wish to convey in the letter, such as the purpose, the attitude, and the matter concerned.

Clarity tells the reader exactly what he or she wants and needs to know, using words and a format that make your writings totally understandable with just one reading. To achieve this, you should include illustrations, examples or visual aids to convey your information, and, above all, use simple, plain language and avoid business jargon. Basically, the writer should keep off anything that might be misleading, or avoid using words and sentences that are equivocal in meaning. To meet such an end, the writer should follow the following rules.

(1) Try to use concise and accessible expressions

Let us look at the following sentence:

As to the steamer sailing from Shanghai to Los Angeles, we have bimonthly direct services.

The basic meaning of this sentence is "we have direct sailings from Shanghai to Los Angels", but the word "bimonthly" has two meanings, one of which is "twice a month" and the other of which is "once every two months". You'd better not use the word like "bimonthly" of double meanings, but use the words that can express your idea clearly as follows:

a. *We have a direct sailing from Shanghai to Los Angeles every two months.*
b. *We have a direct sailing from Shanghai to Los Angeles semimonthly.*
c. *We have two direct sailings every month from Shanghai to Los Angeles.*

(2) Pay attention to the position of modifier

The basic principle for using modifiers is simply to put them as close as possible to the word or words they are modifying. Naturally, if you want to discuss a potential market, you will want to talk about the market directly; you will not put the modifier in some distant part of the sentence.

The idea of keeping related words together—and as close together as possible—is probably the "whole idea" behind studying modifiers. Adjectives should be placed right next to the things they describe, and adverbs should be placed right next to the action or the other modifiers they describe.

Let us look at the following sentences:

Your proposal for payment by time draft is acceptable to us under Order No.115.

This sentence is poor in that "under Order No.115" is too far away from payment by time draft.

Pay attention to the position of modifiers:

a. *We shall be able to supply 10 cases of the item only.*
b. *We shall be able to supply 10 cases only of the item.*

The modifier "only" in the above sentences modified two different words, so the two sentences have different meanings.

(3) Pay attention to the object of the pronoun and the relations between the relative pronoun and the antecedent

Whom or what the pronoun refers to and what is the relation between the relative pronoun and the antecedent? These should be paid attention to. Generally speaking, the pronoun and relative pronoun are used to refer to the nearest noun from themselves and should be identical in person and number with the noun referred to or modified.

Let us examine the following sentence:

They informed Messrs. Smith & Brown that they would receive a reply in a few days.

In this sentence, what does the second "they" refer to, the subject "They" of the main clause or the "Messrs. Smith & Brown"? This can't be explained clearly.

It will be clear if you change the sentence into:

They informed Messrs. Smith & Brown that the latter would receive the reply in a few days.

(4) Pay attention to the rationality in logic

At first, you must pay attention to the agreement of the logical subject of the participle and the subject of the sentence.

For example:

Being a registered accountant, I'm sure you can help us.

In this sentence, the subject of the sentence is "I", but the logical subject of the participle "being" should be "you" according to inference. In order to keep the logical subject of the participle in agreement with the subject of the sentence, the above sentence should be rewritten as the following:

a. *Being a registered accountant, you can certainly help us.*
b. *As you are a registered accountant, I'm sure you can help us.*

(5) Pay attention to the sentence structure

Compare:

a. *We sent you 5 samples <u>yesterday</u> of the goods which you requested in your letter of May 25 <u>by air</u>*.

b. *We sent you, <u>by air</u>, 5 samples of the goods which you requested in your letter of May 25 <u>yesterday</u>*.

(6) Paragraph carefully and properly

Commercial letters should be clear and tidy, and easy to understand the content. So a writer should paragraph a letter carefully and properly. One paragraph for each point is a good general rule.

2. Conciseness

"Time is gold" is a saying that businesspeople always consider. So, you must consider it too. Conciseness is very important for busy buyers and sellers. You can save time and effort by being concise. Using too many words will only delay decision making, so just put in the appropriate issue. But note that in using few words, you should consider not to lose the clarity or courtesy. Conciseness is a quality style. To produce a concise letter, use only the necessary information and words for efficient communication. You should not confuse conciseness with being brief. A brief letter means a short letter. But a concise letter will only use many words as needed in order to deliver the message accurately and efficiently. And note that, it includes words that will keep you on track, reaching your objective.

Another key to achieve conciseness is you know how to begin and how to end your letter. If you will just beat around the bush and don't know where to start or end, then your letter will be a long uninteresting letter. Note that the opening of the letter is either to announce or to acknowledge. If your letter is not a reply, then you are announcing or informing your reader about your business. If it is a reply, then acknowledge your correspondent's letter. Once you know the purpose of the letter placed in the opening part, you can add details to explain it further but briefly. Don't waste too many words on unimportant matters. Your ending part is also an important part of your letter. The ending is the most likely part to be remembered. Aside from thanking or appreciating your reader, make sure that you leave your correspondent with a message that he/she will remember.

Conciseness is considered the most important principle in business letters writing as we now live in a world where time is money. Conciseness means to write in the fewest possible words without sacrificing completeness and courtesy. To achieve conciseness, you should avoid wordy statement and fancy language, use short sentences instead of long ones, and compose your message carefully. To achieve this, the following guidelines must be adhered to.

Unit Two Basic Knowledge of Business Letters Writing 商务信函写作基础

(1) Make a long story short and try to avoid wordiness

Make it a rule, to use no more words and pithy sentences to express your meaning clearly and concisely. Try to use a word or phrase to express your idea as much as possible instead of using long sentences or clauses. For instance, use a word to replace a phrase (See Table 2.3):

Table 2.3 Use a word to replace a phrase

You shouldn't use	You'd better use
at this time	now
express a preference for	prefer
enclosed herewith	here
from the point of view	as
in view of the fact that / due to the fact that	because
a draft in the amount of $1 000	a draft for $1 000

(2) Avoid the unusual or out-of-date words or jargons, and try to express your ideas in modern English

You can use usual words or phrases to express your ideas in modern English (See Table 2.4):

Table 2.4 Express your ideas in modern English

You shouldn't use	You'd better use
consummate	complete
terminate	end
remuneration	payment
converse	talk
inst.	this month
attached hereto	enclosed is/are
acknowledge receipt of	thank you for ... I received ...
awaiting the favor of your early reply	we are looking forward to your reply
up to this writing	so far
take the liberty of	omitted

(3) Build effective sentences and paragraphs

Generally speaking, the average length of sentences should be 10 to 20 words, not over 30 ones. Usually a paragraph consists of no more than 10 lines, because short paragraphs encourage the readers to finish reading.

Let us look at the following sentence:

We would like to know whether you would allow us to extend the time of shipment for twenty days and if you would be so kind as to allow us to do so, kindly give us your reply by fax without delay.

This sentence is a bit lengthy, and is too courteous in expressions, which sounds unclear in meaning, in order to express the main idea better, this sentence may be abbreviated as follows:

Please reply by fax immediately if you will allow us to delay the shipment until April 21.

Conciseness is often considered to be the most important writing principle and language feature. It enables both parties to save time. Conciseness also means you should clearly express what you would do in a short and pithy style of writing as possible as you can. To achieve this, the following guidelines must be observed.
    a. Avoid unnecessary repeat;
    b. Build effective sentences and paragraphs.

3. Consideration

Consideration gives emphasis on the "You" attitude rather than the "I" or "We". Effective communication is having an impression that you care about people and at the same time giving your best in the business you are dealing with. Interaction is important. If letters are just communicated for business reasons and no human natural interaction, then it will increase the percentage of losing a customer or supplier. Make your letter conversational. You can write in a casual way and not too strict. It is easier to understand if the letter is conversational and friendly rather than strictly business-oriented. One way of being considerate is to pay attention to letters that need immediate replies. If you cannot deal the problem or issue at the moment, explain why and inform them you will be writing them back again. Try to understand and respect the letter sender and don't react negatively as if you will never make any mistake. Instead, answer him/her with courtesy and with consideration.

Consideration means thoughtfulness. So you should always put yourself in your reader's place, which is what people now emphasize, i.e. "You" attitude, and avoid taking the writer's attitude, i.e. "We" attitude. Therefore, you should always keep in mind the receiver you are writing to, understanding his or her problems and take the positive approach.

Let's make a comparison between the following two groups of sentences.

"We" attitude:
    a. *We allow a 5% discount for cash payment.*

b. *We won't be able to send you the brochure this month.*

"You" attitude:
a. *You earn a 5% discount when you pay cash.*
b. *We will send you the brochure next month.*

In addition, we should try to discuss problems in a positive way rather than in a negative way. Make a comparison between the following groups of sentences and you will find which is better. Focus on the positive approach.

Compare:

a. *We do not believe that you will have cause for dissatisfaction.* (Negative)
b. *We feel sure that you will entirely get satisfied.* (Positive)
c. *Your order will be delayed for two weeks.* (Negative)
d. *Your order will be shipped in two weeks.* (Positive)

4. Courtesy

Consideration and courtesy work together. Courtesy will nurture the goodwill and friendliness. Courtesy is as important as being clear and concise. Most effective and successful letters are done with courtesy. Some business people may tend to be cold and jargon when they create a letter. They tend to enclose themselves in the idea of "business writing". Saying "please" and "thank you" is not enough to be courteous. You have to reflect it throughout your letter. Any reader will not be interested to continue reading if he/she feels the letter is discourteous. Always consider how your reader will feel when he/she reads your letter. Avoid negatives in writing as much as possible. Negatives will make a connotation of what not to do. But in business writing, it is best to suggest positives, what to do. A letter with friendly conversation will not only be clear, but also sincere.

Courtesy plays a considerable role in business letters writing as in all business activities. It is not mere a way of showing politeness. By courtesy we mean treating people with respect and friendly human concern. In order to make a business letter courteous, try to avoid irritating, offensive, or belittling statements. To answer letters promptly is also a matter of courtesy.

Review of actual business correspondence reveals that special attention should be devoted to assuming the courtesy of business communication. Effective writers visualize the reader before starting to write. They consider the reader's desires, problems, circumstances, emotions and probable reactions to their requests. Let us compare the following sentences.

a. *We are sorry that you misunderstood us.*
b. *We are sorry that we did not make ourselves clear.*

In sentence a, the author is to put the blame on the customer for something, but in sentence b, the author takes the initiative to bear the responsibility.

There are a lot of language styles or ways to express courtesy, some of which will be presented here for your reference as follows:

(1) Change the commanding tone into requesting tone

Change the imperative sentence into general question with the word "will" or "would" at the beginning.

For example:

a. *Will you tell us detailed information on your requirements?*
b. *Will you please tell us more detailed information on your requirements?*
c. *Would you please tell us more detailed information on your requirements?*

(2) Use the past subjunctive form

For example:

a. *Would you send us your latest catalogue and price lists on cotton piece goods?*
b. *We would ask you to make a prompt shipment.*
c. *We wish you would let us have your reply soon.*

(3) Use mitigation and avoid overemphasizing your own opinion or irritating your partner

In order to avoid overemphasizing your own opinion and irritating your partner, you should use mitigation, such as "We are afraid that ...", "We would say ...", "It seems to us that ...", "We would suggest that ....", etc.

(4) Passive voice should be adopted accordingly

In some cases, passive voice appears more courteous than active voice because it can avoid blaming the doer of the act.

For example:

a. *You made a very careless mistake during the course of shipment.*
b. *A very careless mistake was made during the course of shipment.*
c. *You did not enclose the price list in you letter.*
d. *The price list was not enclosed in your letter.*

(5) Try to avoid using the words with forcing tone or arousing unpleasantness

Some words or expressions such as "demand", "disgust", "refuse", "want you to" will arouse unpleasant feeling in audience, therefore they should be avoided or changed into some forms to express. Let us look at the following examples.

a. *demand prompt shipment from you*

b. *request prompt shipment from you*

c. *We must refuse your offer.*

d. *We regret that we are unable to accept your offer.*

(6) Use expressions about joy and willingness, thanks and regret, etc.

For example:

a. *It is with pleasure that we have reached an agreement on all the terms.*

b. *It is a pleasure for us to sign such a sales contract.*

c. *Thank you for your letter of July 9th, 2020.*

d. *We are extremely sorry that we could not answer your letter in due time.*

5. Correctness

Correctness deals with the accuracy of the figures, facts, grammar, spelling, punctuation marks and the format of the letter. The correctness of your letter can be done by using a grammar and spell check software or proofreading. Proofreading can be done by other people so as to check the other items you might have missed while proofreading your letter. Make sure that you will correct all the errors after checking and proofreading. The final version of the letter should be free from errors.

Correctness not only refers to the correct grammar rules, contents, and forms, but also accuracy in style, language and typing. To choose the right words that can most closely convey the meaning of your thoughts is one of the ways to improve the readability of your business writing. At the same time, the right tone is also significant. Usually, mistakes with tone can be avoided by using the following techniques:

a. Place more emphasis on the reader than yourself;

b. Avoid extreme cases of humility, flattery, and modesty;

c. Avoid condescension;

d. Avoid lecturing.

Correct spelling, proper grammar and punctuation will give your letter a good appearance, but they are not all the factors that correctness comprises. In business letters, you should attach great importance to this writing principle, especially when you are giving information regarding dates, specifications, prices, quantities, discounts, commission, units and figures, etc. A minor mistake in this respect sometimes means you will make no profit or even lose out. Let us look at the following sentences to see if there is anything improper.

All offers by fax are open for 5 days.

The above sentence does not clearly explain or account for specific 5 days, and should be changed into:

All offers by fax are open for 5 days inclusive of the date of dispatch.

This contract will come into effect from Oct. 1.

The above sentence does not clearly explain whether Oct. 1 is included or not and should be changed into:

This contract will come into effect from and including October 1, 2019.

This product is absolutely the best one on the market.

This is the overstatement of the fact, and the sentence should be changed into:

This product is the best one we can supply.

We assure you that this error will never occur.

Similarly this sentence can be changed into:

We will do all we can so that we may not repeat such an error.

Correctness refers not only to correct usage of grammar, punctuation and spelling, but also to standard language, proper statement, accurate figures as well as the correct understanding of commercial jargon.

(1) Avoid grammar mistakes
a. With pronouns.

Our competitors' prices are 2% lower than us (ours).

b. With verbs.

It is one of the machines that was (were) delivered last week.

c. With conjunctions.

This fridge not only is attractive (is attractive not only) in proper price, but also in good quality.

d. With subjects.

While studying the report, the telephone rang. (Wrong)
While I was studying the report, the telephone rang. (Right)

(2) Avoid using overstatements

We are well-established exporters of all kinds of goods made in Sweden. (Wrong)

We are well-established exporters of Swedish sundry goods, such as toys, buttons and stationary. (Right)

(3) Use accurate numbers

5% up to 10% both inclusive
up to $40 inclusive
on or after July 10
from the 1st to 15th of March both inclusive
for five days exclusive of the day of dispatch
for 15 days exclusive of Sundays
Stg. £445.00 (Four Hundred and Forty-Five Pounds Sterling only)
£15.01 (Fifteen Pounds and One penny)
5 ft. 10 in (five feet ten inches)
1/4 in pipe (pipe measuring 1/4 inch)
120 sq. ft. (120 square feet)
40 c. ft. (40 cubic feet)
28 in × 30 yds. (28 inches in width, 30 yards in length)

(4) Use capital letters

Business correspondence has its special capital letter writing regulations besides the ordinary rules.

A. North, South, East, West.

When they are used for districts or areas but not for orientations:

South-West Africa
North America
West Europe

B. The name and the brand of a commodity.

"Great Wall" Electric Fan
"Three Stars" Calf Shoes
Chinese Cotton Piece Goods

C. The name of documents.

Price List
Letter of Credit

D. The name of the transportation tools.

the S.S. "Merry Captain"
the S.S. "Lucky Prince"

6. Character

This principle will make your letter special and more interesting. A writer has his/her own personality and it is unique. Each person has individuality. If your letter is written in your own style, considering of course the necessity of business letter, this will add interest to your letter. Rather than simply copying or stereotyping, your own style as a writer shows your character, your strong points and how confident you are in what you are saying in your letter. This principle will help you to be more positive in writing and in reaching your objective. Just bring out that distinct personality.

7. Concreteness

In creating a business letter, you also need to consider the words you used within the letter that appeals to the reader's senses. If your letter is dull and uninteresting, the reader may just skim through it and missing the important points. This will give you a negative response, and you may end up waiting for nothing. Aside from that, concreteness also includes the proper use of codes, ratios, and numbers in order for your reader to identify which of the transactions you are referring to. Definitely, there are hundreds of business transactions going on each day, it will help if you can specify the shipping code or any reference number that will point to a specific transaction.

A practical English writing is very successful and highly effective only when it contains all the necessary information to the readers (the counterpart or the public) and answers all the questions and requirements put forward by the readers. See to it that all the matters are stated or discussed, and all the questions are answered or explained. For instance, when the

Unit Two Basic Knowledge of Business Letters Writing 商务信函写作基础

buyer writes a letter to accept an offer that the seller made, the buyer must state his/her condition of acceptance in detail or quote the evidences of the offer.

In order to verify the completeness of what you write, five "Ws" (who, what, where, when and why) and one "H" (how) should be used. For example, if what you write is a letter of order, you should make it clear that who wants to order, what he/she wants, when he/she needs the goods, where the goods to be sent and how payment will be made. If some special requirements should be presented, you could explain why you would do so.

A business letter should include all necessary information. It is essential to check the message carefully before it is sent out. As you work hard for completeness, ask yourself these questions: Why do you write the letter? What are the facts supporting the reasons? Have you answered the questions asked?

Business writing should be vivid, specific and definite rather than vague, general and abstract, especially when the writer is requiring a response, solving problems, making an offer or acceptance, etc. You need to use specific facts, figures and time to stress concreteness. Try to heed the following tips:

a. Complete with the 5 Ws+1 H: Who, What, Where, When, Why, How.

b. Concreteness in action: using specific language to make the information more concrete and convincing;

c. Use concrete words.

Let us look at the following sentence:

We wish to confirm our fax dispatched yesterday.

Like "today" and "tomorrow", the word "yesterday" is a vague and general concept, which allows possibility for misinterpretation.

8. Cheerfulness

Writing a business letter is not just simply writing a letter in order to receive a response. But, you need to demonstrate a positive attitude and express joy in your letter. If your reader feels that your letter will only be a burden, then the reader will just ignore it. Let your reader feel that you are glad to have a business transaction with him/her. Reflect cheerfulness in your letter. Cheerfulness should already start in the opening of your letter. Remember that you need to leave a good impression to your reader. Everything that will be detailed in your letter is build from the opening.

Section 5 Tone of Business Letters Writing

1. Conversational Style

A good letter should reflect the personality of the writer and needs to be pleasing to the reader. In a good letter a conversation is held. People who write with a sense of personal contact have a better chance to make what they say interesting and convincing than those who feel they are writing letters. Whatever you talk about in a letter, the language you use should be the same as if you met the person on the street, at home, or in the office. Such a language is warm and natural. It is also the language we use most and understand best.

But when faced with a writing task, many of us tend to be different. Instead of writing in friendly, conversational language, we write in stiff and stilted words. There is a misconception that big words and difficult words are preferred in business letters, but the result of such words is a cold and unnatural style—one that does not produce the goodwill effect you want your letters to have.

2. Avoid the Archaic Language of Business

Early English business writers borrowed heavily from the formal language of law and from the flowery language of the nobility. From these two sources they developed a style of letter writing that became known as the "language of business". It was a cold, stiff, and unnatural style, but it was generally accepted throughout the English-speaking world, for instance, "wherein you state as per your letter", "take the liberty of", "acknowledge receipt of", etc. Obviously the tone is cold, out of date, and a good writer should take care to give up such stale expressions.

3. Use Positive Language and Avoid Anger

People enjoy and react favorably to positive messages. A positive tone builds the reader's confidence in the writer's ability to solve problems and strengthens personal and business relationships. Positive words are usually best for letter goals, especially when persuasion and goodwill are needed. Positive words emphasize the pleasant aspects of the goal and tend to put the reader in the right frame of mind. They also create the goodwill atmosphere readers seek in most letters.

When confronted with frustration, writers sometimes may lose temper and get angry, but rarely is anger justified in letters, because it destroys goodwill. Most of comments made in anger take many forms like sarcasm, insults and exclamation, and do not provide needed information.

The effect of angry words is to make the reader angry. With both writer and reader angry, the two are not likely to get together on whatever the letter is about. A tactful writer can refer courteously to the subject matter to avoid jeopardizing goodwill. But when pleasant, positive words have not brought desired results, negative words may be justified.

Section 6　Preparation Before Writing

As a writer, you should make preparation for your creative works before writing. Generally speaking, the following should be borne in mind.

1. Studying Your Reader's Interest

It means that you should think of what your reader thinks.

To achieve this, you should put yourself in your reader's shoes and try to imagine how he/she will feel about what you write. Ask yourself constantly, "What are his/her needs, his/her wishes, his/her interests, his/her problems to be solved, and how can I meet his/her requirement?" "What would be my own feelings, if I were to receive a letter of the kind I propose to write?"

Try to imagine that you are receiving rather than sending the letter and emphasize the "You" attitude rather than "I" or "we" attitude.

2. Planning What You Will Write

In order to plan what you write better and to write effectively, you should draft an outline before writing. Every language has its own features. For Chinese students, English is a foreign language. They should learn to think and write directly in English and draft an English outline before writing.

3. Writing Naturally

Writing naturally is to reveal your true feelings between lines, make sure that what you write would sound sincere and natural, and try to avoid the affected words and florid style with little content. In addition, as a writer, he or she should also lean to use polite language and be considerate to the readers.

Section 7 Rules of Good Writing

1. Adopt the Right Tone

If a letter is to achieve its purpose, its tone must be right. Before beginning to write and think carefully about the way in which you want to influence your reader, ask yourself, "what do I want this letter to do?" and then express yourself accordingly, being persuasive, apologetic, obliging, firm and so on, depending on the effect you want to produce.

2. Write Sincerely

When you write or dictate a business letter, try to feel a genuine interest in the person you are writing to and in his/her problems. Say what you have to say with sincerity and make sure that it sounds sincere. Express your thoughts in your own words and in your own way. Be yourself.

3. Avoid Wordiness

Make it a rule to use no more words than are needed to make your meaning clear. Businesspeople today have many letters to read and welcome the art of letter that is direct and to the point.

4. Write Clearly and to the Point

First be quite clear about what you want to say and then say naturally and with frills, in language your reader will understand just as if you were in conversation with him/her. For the most part, keep your sentences short and avoid the over frequent use of such conjunctions as "and", "but", "however", "consequently", the effect of which is to make sentence long.

5. Be Courteous and Considerate

Courtesy consists, not in using polite phrase (your kind inquiry, your esteemed order, your valued custom, and so on), but in showing your consideration for your correspondent. It is the quality that enables people to refuse to perform a favor and at the same time keep a friend, to refuse a customer's request for credit without killing all hope of future business.

Deal promptly with all letters needing a reply. Answer them on the day you receive them if you can. It is discourteous to keep your correspondent waiting for an answer. If you cannot deal promptly with a letter seeking information, write and explain why and say when you will write again. This creates an impression of efficiency and helps to build goodwill.

Try to understand and respect your correspondent's point of view and resist the temptation to reply as if you could not be in the wrong. If his/her suggestions are stupid and his/her criticism unfair, reply with restraint and say what you feel tastefully and without giving offense. If he/she sends you a rude or sharp letter, resist the temptation to reply in similar terms. Instead, answer him/her courteously, and lower your dignity if you allow him/her to set the tone of your reply.

As the buyer and the seller have both common and contradictory interests, it is very important to keep in mind the distinction between certain overlapping concepts—courtesy overdone may amount to obsequiousness. In short, any virtue overdone will bring with it some undesirable effect, and propriety is the undesirable effect, and propriety is the watchword in distinguishing the right course from the wrong.

6. Avoid Commercial Jargon

Avoid using state and roundabout phrases that add little or nothing to the sense of what you write. Such phrases were at one time common, but they have no place in modern business letters.

7. Write Effectively

In business letters writing you should use simple language, which calls for a plain style—a style that is simple, clear and easily understood. Use plain, familiar words and prefer short words to long ones if they will do just as well. Wherever possible, prefer the single word to the elaborate phrase. Express yourself in simple language so that your message is clear at first reading.

Be consistent in writing a business letter. Avoid repeating in the same sentence. But in your efforts to avoid repetition don't make the apposite mistake of confusing your reader by using different words to express exactly the same thing. Don't say the same thing. Don't say in the same letter that goods have been sent, forwarded, and dispatched, and if you begin your letter by referring to a firm, don't change it as you go along into a "concern" or a "business", or an "organization". If you do, you will have your reader wondering whether something different is intended.

Preciseness is also required in a business letter. Use expressions with precise meanings. When acknowledging a letter, refer to it by date, subject and reference number (if any). When referring to dates mention the month by name and avoid using "instant" or "inst." (for the present month), "ultimo" or "ult." (for the past month), and "proximate" or "proxy." (for the next month). Avoid using vague expressions but concrete words.

8. Avoid Monotony

In a business letter you should use either loose sentences or sentences which will make your message vivid. Short sentences are preferable to long ones because short sentences are easily understood. A succession of short sentences, however, has a disagreeable jerky effect and the best letters are those which provide a mixture of sentences of different length. Sometimes you wish to emphasize the sentence. Emphasis is also achieved by using "it is" or "it was" to introduce statements:

Unfortunately, the goods did not arrive in time. (normal order)
It was unfortunately that the goods did not arrive in time. (emphatic order)

9. Plan Your Letter

Many business letters are short and routine and can be written or dictated without special preparation. Others must first be thought about and planned. First jot down all the points you wish to cover and then arrange them in logical order to provide the plan for a letter that will read naturally and fluently. If your letter is in reply to one received, underline those parts which seek information or on which comment is necessary. This will ensure that your reply is complete.

10. Pay Attention to First and Last Impressions

If your letter is one sent in reply to another, refer in the opening paragraph to the letter you are answering, but avoid the sort of old-fashioned phrases, such as "we are in receipt of your letter …", "we have to acknowledge that your letter …". Although they are grammatically correct, they tend to be dull and monotonous.

If a letter has been well planned and follows a logical sequence, a brief observation will usually be enough to provide the kind of ending introduced by a participle. "Thanking you in anticipation" and similar endings are no longer used in modern letter-writing. They mean nothing and serve no useful purpose.

11. Check Your Letter

Be careful to create a good first impression with your letter. Before signing, check it for the accuracy of its contents, and test its general suitability against such questions:

a. Is its appearance attractive? Is it well laid out?

b. Is it correctly spelt and properly punctuated?

c. Does it cover all essential points and is the information given correct?

d. Is what I have said clear, concise and courteous?

e. Does it sound natural and sincere?

f. Does it adopt the reader's point of view and will it be readily understood?

g. Is its general tone right and is it likely to create the impression intended?

h. Is it the kind of letter I should like to receive if I were in the reader's place?

If the answer to all these questions is "yes", the letter will take the first step in creating goodwill and you may safely sign and send it.

Unit Three Structures and Styles of Business Letters
商务信函的结构与格式

◆ *Learning Objectives*

a. Know different structures and styles of business letters;
b. Master principal parts and optional elements of business letters.

Section 1 Introduction

Because at present many business messages are sent by way of fax or E-mail instead of traditional post, and the language and styles used in the fax or E-mail messages are almost the same as those used in the letter by post, letter-writing is again regarded as quite important in international trade communicating.

In today's highly developed and competitive society, communication between individuals and groups is becoming frequent and important. It serves to pass on information, to express ideas or to exchange feelings. Generally speaking, the function of a business letter is to get or to convey business information, to make or to accept an offer, to deal with various businesses.

When we write a letter we enter into personal relationship with our readers. A business letter is a formal letter corresponding with other parties in regard to a particular concern or objective. There are many different types of letters, because every individual business has its own aims and interests. However, all business letters are similar in styles and formats.

1. Types

The sort of business letters depends on the aim of the person writing it. For instance, a bank manager may write a letter informing a client of an opportunity for a loan or a missed payment on their mortgage. A very common type is the cover letter to go with a CV or resume when someone wants to gain employment.

2. Language Style

No matter who the audience of the business letter is, be clear and concise. This is because the person receiving it is likely to only have time to scan over the letter; if they misunderstand anything, it may jeopardize further correspondence. This can be done by

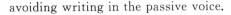

avoiding writing in the passive voice.

3. Main Parts

The main parts of a business letter are the date, sender's address, recipient's address, salutation, body, closing and signature.

4. Form

The form will always be by E-mail or a typed and printed document sent in the mail. An E-mail is more likely to be written in a casual tone, whereas the printed one is more likely to be formal.

5. Power of Persuasion

A business letter is often used to persuade the recipient in some way, such as an unemployed person trying to convince a manager to hire him/her or a lawyer trying to negotiate terms of an agreement on behalf of a client. No matter what the aim is, think of all the relevant points the reader will need to know when writing the letter.

Section 2 Structures of Business Letters

A business letter is one of the vital tools of communication in business organizations. To make a business letter effective we should give attention to structures of a business letter. An effective/good business letter may have the following parts:

1. Letterhead

The following information is highlighted:

a. The full name of the firm or individual sending the letter;

b. Address of the sender;

c. Reference number;

d. Date of drafting the letter;

e. Telephone, telex, Fax, and E-mail address of the sender.

For example:

Commerce Publications
37, Banglabazar, Dhaka-1100
Phone: 02-7170495
Cell: 0176-190865
Web:WWW.com.Pub

Ref. 110 Dx

15th, November 2017.

Unit Three Structures and Styles of Business Letters 商务信函的结构与格式

2. Inside Address

The address of the receiver is given here as would appear on an envelope. It helps the outward clerk to write the same address on the cover. It is also a record on the copy which serves to identify the letter for filling a purpose. For example:

BANI BITAN LIBRARY
40, Sadar Road
Barisal.

3. Attention Line

The person who can take prompt action for the letter, his/her name, and department are stated here. For example:

Mr. Mahabub, Sales Manager

4. Subject Heading

The main theme of the letter is highlighted here. For example:

Sub: Confirmation of Order for 100 GT Television.

5. Salutation

It is the complimentary greetings with which the writer opens his/her letter. It should be written below the inside address. The salutation is made according to the status of the receiver. For example:

If the name is unknown, use *Dear Sir or Madam*.
If the name is known, use *Dear Mr. XX*.
If he/she is a close friend, use *My Dear XX*.
If there is a large number of people, use *Dear Customers* or *Dear Subscribers* or *Dear Members*.

6. Body

It is a part of the letter which contains the message or the information to be communicated and therefore the most important part. It must be natural, and simple with logical sequence. It should be stated considering "You" attitude.

7. Complimentary Close

The complimentary close is a polite way of ending a letter. There are various styles to write a complimentary close, which are given below:

Yours faithfully,
Yours truly,
Truly yours,
Yours very truly,
Yours respectfully,
Yours sincerely,
Sincerely yours,

8. Signature

It is the assent of the writer to the subject matter of the letter and is a practical necessity. It is usually handwritten and given below the complimentary close.

9. Sender's Name and Address

The person who is sending the letter, his/her name and address should be given for proper identification. Such identification is placed just after the signature. For example:

Jack Hossain

Deputy Manager, Sales & Distribution

10. Enclosure

Sometimes other papers such as price list, catalog, prospectus, order, invoice, railway or lorry receipt, cash memo, check, draft, bill, etc. are enclosed with the letter. In such a case, a mention should be made of these enclosures in the letter. For example:

Enclosures:

Proforma Invoice
Bill of Exchange
Bill of Lading.

11. Carbon Copy

Sometimes copies of a letter have to be sent to some people other than the addressee. In such a case, the names of those persons should be mentioned. For example:

Copy:1. Mr. Hasan
 General Manager, Administration.
 2. Mr. Salam

Deputy Manager, Sales.

12. Identification Mark

The person taking dictation of the letter and the person typing or composing the letter should be identified by their initials to the end of the letter, e.g. T, & A, etc.

13. Postscripts

Postscript (P.S.) is something written after the letter is closed, writing P.S. indicates that the writer had forgotten to include something important in the body of the letter. It is a bad practice to write a P.S. and it should preferably be avoided.

Structures of a business letter which are mention above create a good business letter. See Figure 3.1 for the layout example of different parts of a business letter.

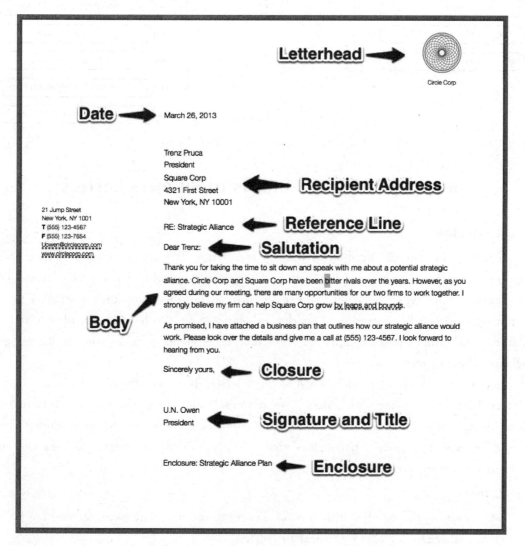

Figure 3.1 Business letter layout example

See Figure 3.2 for the structures of business letters, which display the basic and additional components respectively.

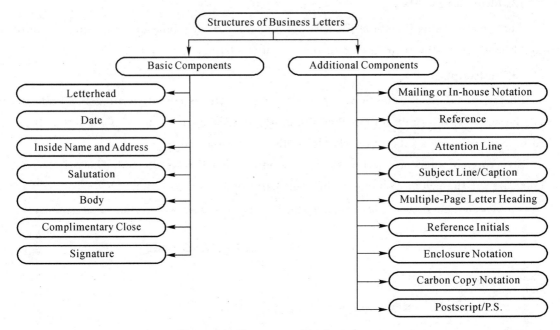

Figure 3.2 Structures of business letters

Section 3 Principal Parts of Business Letters

1. Letterhead

The letterhead is the heading at the top of a letter. It usually consists of the name, address, telephone number and fax number of a company who delivers the letter. The letterhead can be typed out, but is usually printed on the companies stationary (such stationary is also called letterhead) in the up center or at the left margin of a letter. In addition, the printed letterhead may also include other items such as the company logo, website, E-mail address, etc.

Letterhead can also be called heading of a letter. It is usually placed on the top of a letter. Besides the name and address, sometimes it also gives the relevant information about the sender's company, such as telephone number, fax number, internet address, etc.

It includes the essential particulars about the writer's name, postal address and zip-code, telephone and facsimile numbers.

2. Date

The format of the date line differs from country to country. The common ones are M/D/Y (typical American), D/M/Y (typical British).

Unit Three　Structures and Styles of Business Letters 商务信函的结构与格式

e.g. *02/12/2020*

This form in Britain could be taken as December 2, 2020, but in American and some other countries it would mean February 12, 2020. So the month written in letters is preferred because figures may create confusion.

The date is typed a few lines below the last line of the letterhead. Different from the place in a Chinese letter, the date in an English letter should be put above the inside name and address.

In business letters, date line is very important. You can decide from the date line whether an order is fulfilled, a contract or an agreement is in effect, or a bill is paid. Therefore, it should not be wrongly written or omitted.

Generally speaking, there are two ways in writing the date. You can write it in the logical order of day, month, year, for instance, 12th Dec., 2020. Or you can write the date after the month and use a comma between the day and the year, e.g. Dec. 2nd, 2020. You had better use ordinal numbers for the day.

The date should be placed two or four spaces below the letterhead to the right for indented style or the left for the blocked style. The date should be written in full and not abbreviated. The preferred order of the parts that make up the date is: the day of the month, the month, the year.

3. Inside Address

The reference may include a file name, departmental code or the initials of the signer followed by that of the typist of the letter. Many letterheads provide space for references.

e.g. *Your ref*:
　　Our ref:

The inside address is the recipients address, which should be identical to the delivery address on the envelope. The inside address serves as the delivery address. It is typed at the left hand margin two lines below the date. The information should be given in a way like this: The address of the organization receiving the letter is typed single-spaced at the left margin. This part usually refers to the recipient's name and address. The information should be given in a way like this:

　a. Receiver's name or his/her official title;
　b. Company's name;
　c. Number of the house and name of the street;
　d. District, name of the town or city;
　e. State or province, ZIP code;

f. Name of country.

Here is an example:

President
Shanghai Foreign Trade & Economics Training Center
89, Fuzhou RD.
Huangpu District, Shanghai, 200003
P.R.C.

Sometimes "Messrs.", which is the plural form of "Mr.", is placed as a courtesy title before the name of a company which includes a personal element. For instance:

Messrs. Evans & Sons Co., Ltd.

It consists of the correspondent's name and address. It appears exactly the same way as on the envelope.

4. Salutation

Courtesy titles, such as "Mr.", "Ms.", etc. are commonly used to address one person. Use "Ms." if you do not know whether a lady is married or not. If there is any official position of that person, his or her official position should follow after the name.

e.g. *Mr. Smith, President*

For most letter styles, place the letter greeting or salutation two lines below the last line of the inside address or the attention line (if used). If the letter is addressed to an individual, use that person's courtesy title and last name, e.g. "Dear Miss Helen". The salutation varies according to the writer-recipient relations and the formality level of the letter. "Dear Sir", "Dear Sir or Madam" or "Dear Sirs" and "Ladies and Gentlemen" can be used to address a person of whom you know neither the name nor the gender.

Sometimes some special titles may be used as the salutation. They are preceded by "Dear" and followed by the surname only, e.g. "Dear Dr. Watson", or "Dear Prof. Young". Be sure to add a colon or a comma (not a semicolon) after the salutation. Examples of typical salutations are as follows:

Dear Mr. XX (Men),
Dear Mrs. XX (Married women),
Dear Miss. XX (Unmarried women and girls),

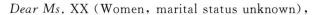

Dear Ms. XX (Women, marital status unknown),
Dear Dr. XX (Physicians, PHD. holders),
Dear Prof. XX (Professors and any holder of a professional rank),
Dear Sir(s)/Madam (No specific reference, formal),
Gentlemen (No specific reference, formal),
Ladies and Gentlemen (No specific reference, formal),
To whom it may concern (You do not know yet who is the recipient),
(Dear) First name (Only close friend, informal),

The salutation is the polite greetings with which a letter begins. The customary formal greeting in a business letter is "Dear Sirs" or "Gentlemen".

5. Subject Line

The subject line is placed one line below the salutation. It helps both the sender and the recipient identify the subject matter. It is used to attract readers's attention, therefore, you may underline it or make it in boldface letters. Below are some samples of the subject line:

Subject: Order No. 12345
Subject: S/C No. 345
Re: Invoice 567
Re: Your L/C No. 678

6. Body of the Letter

This is the most important part of every business letter. It is typed two lines below the salutation or subject line. Whether your letter is long or short, it usually consists of three paragraphs: the opening paragraph which is to give a subject introduction of the letter; the middle paragraph to discuss the details of the transaction; and the closing paragraph to end a letter in a way of summation, further request or suggestion. And when writing a letter, you should attach great importance to these principles: Clearness, Conciseness, Consideration, Courtesy, Correctness, Concreteness and Completeness. It is advisable to keep the following tips in mind:

a. Write simply, clearly, courteously, grammatically, and to the point;

b. Paragraph correctly, confining each paragraph to one topic;

c. See that your typing is accurate.

This is the most important part of a letter in which you convey the real information. Before you write it, you must consider two points as follows:

a. What is the purpose to write this letter?

b. How to present the letter in the best way?

7. Complimentary Close

This part is like bidding farewell to someone with a handshake, a wave of hand, or a kiss. Like the salutation, the complimentary close has various styles: formal, semi-formal and informal. The style shall match that of the salutation.

The complimentary close is merely a polite way to bring the letter to an end. If the salutation is "Dear Sirs", "Dear Madam or Sir", you can use "Yours faithfully", "Faithfully yours" as complimentary close.

If the salutation is "Gentlemen", "Mr./Mrs./Miss/Ms. White", etc. you can use "Yours sincerely", "Sincerely yours", "Yours truly", "Truly yours", "Best wishes". Or "Best regards" can also be used in less formal letters.

It is often given from the second line below the closing sentence of the letter.

The complimentary close is mere a polite way of ending a letter. It should match the form of the salutation. The most commonly sets of salutation and complimentary close (See Table 3.1) are:

Table 3.1 Salutation and complimentary close

Salutation	Complimentary close
Dear Sirs	Yours faithfully
Gentlemen	Yours truly
Dear Mr. XX	Yours sincerely

Some samples of the complimentary close (See Table 3.2) are:

Table 3.2 Complimentary close

Formal	Semi-formal	Informal
Yours sincerely	Sincerely yours	All the best
Yours very truly	Cordially yours	Cordially
Yours respectfully	Faithfully	Best regards

8. Signature

The signature is generally placed two lines below the complimentary close. It consists of a handwritten signature (by hand and in ink, usually illegible), the typed out name and a title. It usually consists of lines like:

a. Manual signature of the writer;

b. Typed name of the writer and his or her job title.

For example:

Unit Three Structures and Styles of Business Letters 商务信函的结构与格式

Yours faithfully,

The NATIONAL TRANSPORT CO.

(signature)

Zhang Wei
Manager

Section 4 Optional Elements of Business Letters

Optional parts of a letter are the references, the attention line, the subject line, the enclosure, the carbon copy notation, the postscript, and the identification line.

1. Attention Line

If you send your message officially to an organization, an attention line allows you to send it directly to a specific individual, officer, or department. However, if you know an individual's complete name, it is always better to use it as the first line of the inside address and avoid an attention line.

2. Subject Line

A subject line helps identify the subject of a letter. The subject line is often inserted between the salutation and the body of the letter to invite attention to the topic of the letter. Although experts suggest placing the subject line two lines below the salutation, many businesses actually place it above the salutation. Use whatever style your organization prefers. Using a subject line will alert your reader to the content of your message and enable him or her to decide whether the letter requires immediate attention. So a subject line is often underlined or typed in capitals. For example:

RE:Claim Number XXX
Re:Tool
Subject:Order XXX

3. Enclosure

When something else is sent together with the letter, you add the enclosure to inform the reader what is enclosed. For example:

Enclosure: Sales Contract

Encls:
Packing List
Commodity Inspection Certificate
Insurance Policy

If an enclosure or attachment accompanies the letter, a notation to that effect should be placed four or five lines below the signature. The word "Enclosure" or shortened "Encl." followed by a period or colon should be written. For example:

Enclosure: Bill of Lading
Encl.: Commercial Invoice
Enclosures: 3

If something is enclosed with the letter, you may type one of the following examples at the left bottom.

Enclosure:
Enclosures:
Enclosures: 2

Encl.:
Encls.: 2
As Stated
Encls.: 2 Invoices
Encls.: 1 B/Lading
       1 Photo
       1 Certificate

4. Copy Notation

If copies of a business letter have been made for other individuals, a copy notation is typed one or two lines below the enclosure notation (if used). A colon following is optional. Most people prefer to use notation like CC., cc, Cc, C.C. (all mean carbon copy). Since most

Unit Three Structures and Styles of Business Letters 商务信函的结构与格式

copies are now photo-copied, some people use the notation CX (xerox copy), PC (photo copy), or C (copy). However, if you do not want the addressee to know that someone else is receiving a copy, do not include this notation on the original copy.

When copies of a letter are sent to others, you may type "C.C." below the signature at the left margin:

C.C.: *The Bank of Osaka, Ltd., Kobe*

The Osaka Chamber of Commerce & Industry

5. Postscript

The postscript (P.S.) is used to add an afterthought, aiming at the drawing of the reader's attention to a point you wish to emphasize or something you forget to mention. The note of a P.S. should be avoided as far as possible, since it may suggest that you have failed to plan your letter well. It is strongly advised to rewrite the letter instead of using the afterthought when you forget to mention something important.

As a special device, the postscript is placed two lines below at the left margin.

As a special device, the postscript has two legitimate functions.

a. Some executives occasionally add a postscript to add a personal touch to the typewritten letter.

b. Writers of sales letter often withhold one last convincing argument for emphatic inclusion in a postscript.

e.g. *P.S. ... to see you at the annual sales meeting on October 16.*

Section 5   Styles of Business Letters

There are several styles for writing professional letters, such as indented style, modified block form with indented style, full block style, semi-block style, modified block style, and so on.

Many word processing programs will have templates available that will make it easier for you to format the letter appropriately. Take advantage of those templates so you can focus on the content of your letter instead of the formatting. Whichever format you choose, make sure to single-space the letter and skip a space between every paragraph and section.

1. Indented Style

An indented letter style is a letter-writing style where the paragraphs are indented.

When writing a letter using indented form, indent each paragraph. First include your name, address, phone number, and the date. These information should be located at the top of the page, either in the center, or indented on the right side of the paper. You then include the name and address of the person to whom you are sending the letter.

The paragraphs are typically indented by half an inch.

The indented letter format is not popular in modern business correspondence. Using the indented format can be an indication that the letter sender or the firm he/she is representing is traditional. However, someone thinks that the format does not look elegant. For a modern and sophisticated appeal, someone recommends the use of the full-block with no indention letter style.

In a composition, an indentation is a blank space between a margin and the beginning of a line of text.

The beginning of this paragraph is indented. Standard paragraph indentation is about five spaces or one-quarter to one-half of an inch, depending on which style guide you follow. In online writing, if your software doesn't allow indentation, insert a line space to indicate a new paragraph.

The opposite of first-line indentation is a format called hanging indentation. In a hanging indent, all the lines of a paragraph or entry are indented except the first line. Examples of this kind of indentation are found in resumes, outlines, bibliographies, glossaries, and indexes.

The main feature in this style is that each line of the inside name and address should be indented 2–3 spaces, and the first line of each paragraph should be indented 3–5 spaces.

Sample 1

THE EASTERN SEABOARD CORPORATION
350 Park Avenue, New York, 10017, USA
Telephone:2252788 Fax:2252780
E-mail:ESCO.@CA.com

January 4, 2021

Our Ref:QW9807
Your Ref:UI 87
Kanto Mercantile Corporation
2-1 Nihonbashi
Tokyo 89, Japan

Unit Three Structures and Styles of Business Letters 商务信函的结构与格式

Dear Sirs,

<u>Price List</u>

  Here is the price list you asked about. You will be happy to know that all of the items listed on pages 5 – 7 will be marked down 30% between February and March. If you would like to take advantage of this special opportunity, please fill out the enclosed order form and return to us by the end of January.

  Thank you for writing.

Yours faithfully,

THE EASTERN SEABOARD CORPORATION
James Baton
Vice President

Sample 2

Date

Dear XXX,

  I hope you are doing great in the new country. I am missing you a lot here. However, I am quite aware of the fact that this opportunity is going to be great for your future. The weather is excellent on your side as well.

  I have decided to resign from the current job as I have a great opportunity to apply at XXX Company. There is a vacancy for the post of administrative assistant and as you know I had been interested in this post since the beginning of my career.

  I am fine and my married life is going great.

  I am looking forward to seeing you in the summer vacation. Send me a message before coming so that I can make some arrangements. I have planned to have so much fun this summer.

  Till next time.

LMN

2. Modified Block Form with Indented Style

In this form with indented style the sender's address is typed (or printed) in the up-middle part. The receiver's address starts from the left margin. The complimentary close as well as the signature is typed from the middle little towards the right.

Sample

                                Carol Taylor
                                28251 Clinton Keith
                                Murrieta, California 92563

                                14 August 2008

Joan Smith
4256 Adams Avenue
San Diego, California 92129

Dear Mrs. Smith,

Ah, there are block formats, and indented formats, modified block formats … To simplify matters, we're demonstrating the block format on this page, one of the most common formats. For authoritative advice about all the variations, we highly recommend *The Gregg Reference Manual*, 11th ed. (New York: McGraw-Hill, 2010), a great reference tool for workplace communications. There seems to be no consensus about such fine points as whether to skip a line after your return address and before the date: some guidelines suggest that you do; others do not. Let's hope that your business letter succeeds no matter which choice you make!

                                                Sincerely yours,

                                                Carol Taylor

3. Full Block Style

This is the most popular business letter layout nowadays. It is the easiest to format as everything starts at the left margin. Letterhead is laid out in the center of the letter, while the rest elements of a business letter start from the left-hand side of the sheet neatly.

Open punctuation is adopted for the inside address, which means that both sender's address and recipients' address must avoid using more punctuation.

The body of the letter has double spacing between the paragraphs. Typists generally prefer the full block format, for it has a simple appearance, and is quicker to type.

In the full block form, every part of a letter is typed from the left margin. It is convenient to be typed with a typewriter but the layout is not so beautiful. So some businesspeople use a modified block form with indented style.

When you use the block form to write a business letter, all the information is typed flush left, with one-inch margins all around. First provide your own address, then skip a line and provide the date, then skip one more line and provide the inside address of the party to whom the letter is addressed. If you are using letterhead that already provides your address, do not retype that information; just begin with the date. For formal letters, avoid abbreviations where possible.

Skip another line before the salutation. Then write the body of your letter as illustrated here, with no indentation at the beginnings of paragraphs. Skip lines between paragraphs.

After writing the body of the letter, type the closing, followed by a comma, leave three blank lines, then type your name and title (if applicable), all flush left. Sign the letter in the blank space above your typed name.

Sample 1

456 Anyplace City
Zip Code

Date

Mr. XXX
XXX Corporation
Place
City
Zip Code

Dear Mr. XXX,

My friend and your former employee informed me about a job vacancy of Office Manager at XXX Corporation. I have a five-year experience of Administrative Assistant and it would be a great opportunity to work for your company.

As you can see from my resume that I had been taking the different tasks at XXX Company. I had been involved in the workflow management of the company.

Thank you for considering my application.

Truely yours,

Mr. JKL

Sample 2

Cleôn M. McLean
Department of English
Ontario High School
901 West Francis Street
Ontario, California, 91762

September 14th, 2015

Chaffey Joint Union High School District
211 West Fifth Street
Ontario, California, 91762

To Whom It May Concern:

A full block letter format is the most formal of the three letter formats, i.e. full block, modified block, and semi-block. With the full block format, everything except the letterhead begins at the left margin.

The date of the letter, the name and address of the receiver, the salutation, all paragraphs, the complimentary close, and the signature block all begin at the left margin. Fewer keystrokes and other adjustments are required with full block.

Some writers prefer full block because they see it as a crisper, cleaner look. In some cases, these writers will also choose right margin justification as a personal choice, although it is not required for the full block format.

Cordially,

Cleôn M. McLean

Unit Three Structures and Styles of Business Letters 商务信函的结构与格式

4. Semi-Block Style

A semi-block style letter is a less formal version of a block or a full-block letter with the differences being the sender's address, date, reference or attention line and complimentary closing. In addition, the signature lines are located direct center or slightly right of center, along with indented paragraphs.

Depending on the purpose and content of the letter, a semi-block format may be more desirable for less formal business correspondence, such as thank you messages or announcements of events. Letters to, and dealing with, smaller businesses with less corporate oversight and formality should use the semi-block style to create a more personalized correspondence than a standard corporate business letter.

Sample 1

              Cleôn M. McLean
              Department of English
              Ontario High School
              901 West Francis Street
              Ontario, California, 91762

              September 14th, 2015

Veronica Partida
Chaffey Joint Union High School District
211 West Fifth Street
Ontario, California, 91762

Dear Mrs. Partida,

  A semi-block letter format is the most personal and old-fashioned of the three letter formats in business today. Oftentimes the semi-block format is used for more social notes than for common business purposes.

  With the semi-block format, the date, the complimentary close, and the signature block begin near the center of the page or a little to the right. In addition, all the paragraphs are indented approximately one-half inch. Only the inside address, the salutation, and the reference notes begin at the left margin. As with the modified block format, make sure that the date, the closure, and the signature block line up with each other, beginning in the center or a little to the right of center.

  With all three letter formats, position the letter in the visual center of the page. A short letter should begin lower on the page to create a pleasant visual effect. Do not use right margin justification with the semi-block format because it is contradictory to the style.

              Sincerely,

              Cleôn M. McLean

Sample 2

Dear Mr. Smith,

 I enjoyed my visit to Company XXX today and hope to expand our business-to-business relationship in the near future. The factory tour answered many of my questions regarding production of Widget 1, but as we discussed, there are additional areas where I would appreciate greater insights into production.

 My administrative assistant will be scheduling a follow-up appointment for one of our design supervisors during the week of October 8. His or her job will be to obtain additional information regarding streamlining the Widget 1 production process through improved design.

              Sincerely,

              Mark Jones

5. Modified Block Style

 Modified block style business letters are less formal than full block style letters. If you are corresponding with someone you already have a good working relationship with, the modified block style letter is a good one to use.

 Modified block layout is quite common in business letters. It is traditional and quite popular. Modified block business letters use a slightly different format from the full block business letters. In the modified block style, the return address, date, complimentary closing and the signature line are slightly to the right of the center of the paper. It is recommended to tab over to the center of the letter and not use Ctrl-E which would distort the block.

Unit Three Structures and Styles of Business Letters 商务信函的结构与格式

Sample

Cleôn M. McLean
Department of English
Ontario High School
901 West Francis Street
Ontario, California, 91762

September 14th, 2015

Veronica Partida
Chaffey Joint Union High School District
211 West Fifth Street
Ontario, California, 91762

Dear Mrs. Partida,

A modified block letter format is the most common of the three letter formats in business today. Most people prefer it because it has more visual balance than the full block format and is easier to work with than the semi-block format. With the modified block format, the date, the complimentary close, and the signature block begin near the center of the page or a little to the right.

All other elements, the inside address, the salutation, the paragraphs, and reference notes all begin at the left margin. When you use the modified block format, be sure the date, the closure, and the signature block line up with each other. You do not want one beginning three inches from the left margin and the other beginning four inches to the right. Avoid aligning the date and closure with the far right margin and creating a ragged left line.

If you are unsure about which format to use and you have no handy example of the receiver's style, use the modified block format. Right margin justification is a personal choice and is not required for any of the letter formats.

Respectfully,

Cleôn M. McLean

6. Standard Format

Standard format business letters are quite formal. Because they include an optional subject line, they are ideal for situations in which you need to create a formal response or communicate about an account number or case number.

At the bottom of this template, you'll see something other business letter templates don't contain. Below the signature block are three lines of text indicating that a secretary or assistant typed the letter for the sender, that a copy was sent to another recipient, and that there are enclosures. In other business letter formats, "Enclosures:" is written out. In standard format, the word is abbreviated.

Sample

Your Name
Address
Phone

Today's Date

Recipient's Name
Company Name
Address

Dear XX(Recipient's Name),

SUBJECT: Type the Subject here and Underline It.

This standard business letter format looks very much like the block letter format. Notice that everything is left justified.

You will notice that this template contains some elements that are different from those in other business letter formats in this unit. First, there is a subject line. This element is optional, and can be replaced with a "RE:" line that is used to reference something specific like a previous communication or an account number. Be sure to underline this so that it stands out.

Additionally, this template has three other elements. On the line located beneath the signature block, you will notice the initials in upper case letters. A colon separates them from the assistant's initials, which are written in lower case letters. This indicates that the assistant typed the letter. If you type a standard business letter yourself, you do not need to include this element.

Beneath the initials, you will see "cc:" followed by the business partner's name. This indicates that a copy of this letter has been sent to the partner. If you write a letter like this one but don't "cc" anyone, there's no need to include this element.

Finally, you will notice the letters "encl" followed by a colon. This indicates that there are enclosures. Interestingly, the standard business letter is the only one in which you use "encl" instead of writing "enclosure" to show that a brochure, application, invoice, or other item(s) are enclosed. As you may have already guessed, you can skip the "encl" if you haven't included anything with the letter in the envelope.

Sincerely,

Your First name, Last name, and Title

cc:Business Partner, Other entity
encl:Business letter template

7. Open Format

The open format business letter has a clean, formal look just as the block format letter does. It is suitable for all business communications.

There is one major difference between this format and the other business letter formats in this unit. It contains no punctuation after the greeting, and no punctuation after the closing.

Summary

Depending on the purpose of your business letter, there are several formats from which you can choose. The most widely used business letter formats are full block and modified block. You can also use the memo format, which is a form of business correspondence used mostly within an organization. Remember, the format of the letter helps to establish its tone and presentation.

(1) Components of business letters

A. The heading includes the date the letter is written. If you do not use letterhead stationery, you need to include your address above the date.

B. The address above the salutation is the letter recipient's full address. This address should match the address on the envelope.

C. The salutation is the line that begins "Dear ...". Place a colon or comma at the end of the salutation. Use "Mr." for men and "Ms." "Mrs." for women. Try to obtain a name to which you can address your letter. If you cannot obtain a name, you should address the letter to the person's position, e.g. "Admissions Officer" as a last resort, and you can use "To Whom It May Concern" as a salutation. You can also include an attention line two spaces down from the recipient's address and a subject line (if necessary).

D. The body of your letter contains your message.

The first paragraph of a typical business letter should state the main purpose and/or subject of the letter. Begin with a friendly opening, then quickly transfer to the purpose of your letter. Use several sentences to explain your purpose, but do not go into detail until the next paragraph.

The second paragraph states the specific information regarding your purpose. This may take the form of background information, statistics, or first-hand accounts. A few short paragraphs within the body of the letter should be enough to convey your message.

The closing paragraph briefly restates your purpose and why it is important. If the purpose of your letter is employment related, consider ending your letter with your contact information. However, if the purpose is informational, think about closing with gratitude for the reader's time.

E. The complimentary close should appear two lines below the last line of the body. Capitalize only the first letter of the first word and you can end the line with a comma. You can use a variety of closures: Sincerely, Sincerely yours, Yours truly, Regards, Best regards, or Best wishes.

F. Your signature should be in blue or black ink. Allow four vertical spaces for your signature.

G. The identification line contains your typed name, and, if you have one, your title, placed below your typed name. Depending on the purpose of the letter, you can position your phone number or E-mail address in place of your title.

H. Enclosure (Encl.)—attached document(s), or distribution (cc)—copies sent to another party, is placed two vertical spaces below the identification line.

(2) Letter formats

Sample 1   Full Block Format (See Table 3.3)

Unit Three Structures and Styles of Business Letters 商务信函的结构与格式

Table 3.3 Full block format

Heading (your address and date)	20 - 54 Jackson Avenue Brooklyn, NY 11352 June 28, 2020
Address (of the person you are writing to)	Ms. Jennifer Esposito John Doe Fellowship 595 Park Avenue New York, NY 10021
Salutation	Dear Ms. Esposito,
Body	The John Doe Fellowship has always loomed on the horizon for me. Ever since I decided to major in history, I have wanted to participate in your program. From the research that I have done, I believe that your program provides its participants with an extensively detailed look at the history of the world through hands-on experience with fossils, artifacts, and other remains that compose the blueprint of our existence. I am applying for the John Doe Fellowship because I believe that it would benefit me throughout my career and allow me to further understand the ideas behind history and how it is constructed. I am a very committed and goal-oriented person with excellent interpersonal skills. My background in history involves studying many different eras and time periods. My specialty, though, is the archeological study of the ancient world and its history. During the summer of 2019 and 2020, I interned at the Metropolitan Museum of Art as a tour guide. Both times, I not only utilized my knowledge of art and history, but I also learned a lot about how that history was constructed. This experience has influenced me to intern as a tour guide at the American Museum of Natural History, where my love for the origins of history and learning from the tactile experience with artifacts increased. In the future, I would like to participate in historical research and eventually become a full-time professor of history.

Continued Table

	I believe my skills, experience, and goals make me an excellent candidate for your program. Thank you very much for considering me for the John Doe Fellowship. I am looking forward to hearing from you.
Complimentary Close	Sincerely yours,
Identification Line Title or Phone Number	Bill Lurie (419)352 – 5425
Signature	
Enclosures or Distribution	Enclosure

In a full block business letter, every component of the letter (heading, address, salutation, body, salutation, signature, identification, enclosures) is aligned to the left. Also, first sentences of paragraphs are not indented.

Sample 2　Modified Block Format (See Table 3.4)

Table 3.4　Modified block format

Heading (Your address and date)	123 Corona Blvd. Flushing, NY 11235 July 3, 2020
Address (of the person you are writing)	Dr. Steven Serafin, Director Reading/Writing Center Hunter College 695 Park Ave New York, NY 10065

Continued Table

Salutation	Dear Dr. Serafin:
Body	My name is Sally Eisner. I am writing this appeal to request a 4th chance to take the CUNY Proficiency Exam in June of 2020. I have taken the exam twice and missed it once. The first time, I feel that I was simply unprepared. I did not realize that I should have attended CPE workshops offered at the Reading/Writing Center. The second time, I attended the workshops and learned more about the exam; however, my Task 2 score was unsatisfactory, so I failed again. Finally, I registered for CPE tutoring at the Reading/Writing Center and studied very hard for the third time. However, on the Saturday of the exam, I had a family emergency, which caused me to miss the date. I had forgotten that I could defer the test date until after I missed it. Now, I am working hard to build on my academic skills. After a consultation with a CPE advisor at the Reading/Writing Center, I have a clear vision of what I should do in order to pass the exam. Again, I have registered for a semester of CPE tutoring at the Writing/Reading Center that I plan to attend weekly. I would really like to have a 4th chance to pass this exam because I am confident that if I work hard, I can do it. Thank you very much for considering my appeal. I hope to hear back from you soon.
Complimentary Close	Sincerely,
Signature	Sally Eisner

In a modified block business letter, the heading, complimentary close, the signature, and identification are aligned to the right. Address, salutation, the body, and enclosures are aligned to the left. First sentences of paragraphs are indented.

Sample 3 Memo Format (See Table 3.5)

Table 3.5 Memo format

Heading	
Date:	Date: July 5, 2020
To: Name of person addressed	To: Sophia Halley, Director, Public Health Engineering (DOHMH)
From: Your name	From: Pat Godowsky, Database Manager
Subject: The purpose	Subject: Database Format Changes Update
Text	I have made the expected changes to the database. Right now, the problems that the field inspectors experienced when they transferred their observations from their hand-held devices to the database have been resolved. A survey of the new changes shows that the field inspectors are very happy with the new system. Let me know if you need me to make any more corrections to the program.
Enclosure	Enclosure

In a memo form of business correspondence, every component of the memo is aligned to the left.

The following items should appear in the order listed below:

Unit Three Structures and Styles of Business Letters 商务信函的结构与格式

Date:
To:(*Name of the recipient*)
From:(*Your name*; *initials of sender added in ink*)
Subject:(*Briefly explains the purpose of the memo*)
cc:(*If applicable*,*copies sent to another party*)
Text:
Enclosure:(*Optional*)

(3) Proofread and check your letter

A. Remember to proofread your letter for these items:
- Spelling of the receiver's name
- Spelling of the receiver's place of business
- Spelling elsewhere—including your own name and business
- Typing errors
- Correct dates
- Subject-verb agreement
- Pronoun reference and form
- Punctuation

B. Checklist:
- Did you type in a date to validate the letter as a record?
- Did you place a colon after the salutation?
- Did you place a comma after the complimentary close?
- Did you sign the letter below the complimentary close and above your typed name?

Section 6 Spacing, Margin and Envelop Addressing

1. Spacing

Most business letters are single-spaced with the exception of extremely short and one-paragraphed letters, which are usually typed with double spaces between lines. However, there should always be a double space line between paragraphs. As for the spacing between such parts as the date line and the letterhead, the signature and the complimentary close, they are described respectively in the layout of a business letter.

2. Margin

No business letters should be typed without margins, which are as necessary as the frames of a picture. The simplest method is to leave at least a one-inch margin at the left side of the letter and to keep the right margin roughly the same. The margin at the bottom of the page should be at least one and one-half times that of the side margins while the same is applicable to the top margin of plain paper without a letterhead.

3. Envelope Addressing

Envelop addressing calls for accuracy, legibility and good appearance. Like the inside address, the address on the envelope can be written in two forms: the indented form and the blocked form. Usually no punctuation is used on the envelope. No matter in which way the address on the envelope is written, it should conform to the inside address in both style and content. Generally speaking, the address of the envelope should be written in the following order:

a. Name of the addressee;

b. Number and street;

c. City, state and zip code;

d. Country.

Here are some samples of envelopes (See Figure 3.3, Figure 3.4, Figure 3.5):

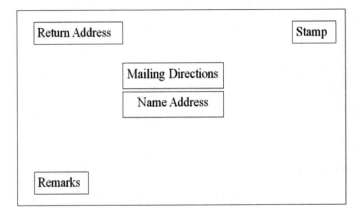

Figure 3.3 Envelope 1

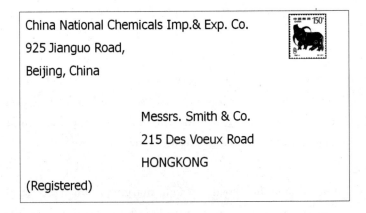

Figure 3.4 Envelope 2

Unit Three Structures and Styles of Business Letters 商务信函的结构与格式

Figure 3.5　Envelope 3

　　Business envelopes ordinarily have the return address printed on the upper left corner. The receiver's name and address should be typed about half way down the envelope.

　　The postmark or stamps should be placed in the up right-hand corner, while the bottom left-hand corner is for post notations such as "Confidential", "Secret", "Printed Matter", etc.

　　It is important to include the postcode (or zip code) in order to facilitate mechanical mail-sorting.

Unit Four General Tips for Modern Business Writing
现代商务写作技巧

◆ *Learning Objectives*

a. Master eighteen general writing tips;
b. Master some basic knowledge of English grammar.

Section 1 General Tips

1. Avoiding Wordy and Redundant Phrases

商务信函的措辞应简洁明了,若用过多词语来表达一个或两个词就能表达的意思,显然会使写作的内容拖沓冗长、观点模糊,更会浪费读者的时间。以下分别从 wordy(拖沓冗长)和 redundant(累赘重复)两方面举例说明(见表 4.1 及表 4.2)。

表 4.1 wordy 举例

Wordy	Concise
There is no existing system that can do this.	No system can do this.
The regulations are provided in the booklet.	The regulations are in the booklet.
as you may or may not know	as you may know
at all times	always
at this point in time	now
in compliance with your request	at your request

商务写作中应尽量多用简洁的话使传达的信息直接、一目了然。此外,诸如 free gift、foreign imports 等词语也过于累赘,有重复感。gift 本身就是免费的,不需要加 free;同样 imports 也是来自国外的,无须再加上 foreign。请看以下例子,左边累赘重复,右边则简洁明了,符合现代商务英语写作标准。

Unit Four General Tips for Modern Business Writing 现代商务写作技巧

表 4.2 redundant 举例

Redundant	Concise
actual experience	experience
advance plan	plan
a great honor and a privilege	an honor
as a general rule	as a rule
basic essentials	basics
current status	status
different varieties	varieties
close proximity	near
continue on	continue
absolutely perfect	perfect
final outcome	outcome
first and foremost	first
goals and objectives	goals
group meeting	meeting

2. Using Small Words

初学商务英语写作时,很多人都会认为用词越难越好,越正式越好。殊不知,现代商务英语写作要求多使用简单的小词。一封措辞复杂、晦涩难懂的商务信件的效果只会适得其反,对方可能会因看不懂而将信件"扔进垃圾箱"。在商务活动中,商务写作的目的是沟通、传达信息,并尽量说服对方,而非向对方炫耀自己的文采。请看以下例子(见表 4.3)。

表 4.3 使用简单词语

Big words	Small words
We will <u>ameliorate</u> the quality soon.	We will <u>improve</u> the quality soon.
The <u>aggregate</u> cost of the three projects <u>amounts to</u> $786,000.	The <u>total</u> cost of the three projects <u>is</u> $786,000.
This is the <u>optimum</u> method.	This is the <u>best</u> solution
We will study the price-list you <u>furnished</u>.	We will study the price you <u>sent</u>.
ascertain	find out
assist	help
commencement	start

3. Avoiding Sexist Language

现代社会中，含有性别歧视的字眼不宜使用。商务写作中尽量避免使用有性别歧视的词语，对沟通双方都有利。以下例子中，左边不可取，右边符合现代商务写作的趋势（见表4.4）。

表4.4 避免使用含有性别歧视意味的词语

Improper	Proper
businessman	businessperson（businesspeople）
postman	mail carrier
fireman	firefighter
policeman	police officer

在实际商务写作中，可采取多种办法来避免性别歧视，如：

1）使用具体名词，不用代词，如"Typically, a manager will call a meeting."。

2）使用名词的复数形式，如可说"Employees must decide for themselves."，而不说"Each employee must decide for himself."（性别歧视）。

3）用第二人称代词"You"代替有性别歧视的词语，如可说"You must sell three cars every month."，而不说"All salesmen must sell three cars every month."（性别歧视）。

4）采用 he or she 的形式，如"A manager must make sure that he or she do the right job."。

4. Using Modern Business Language

一直以来，商务英语写作中充满过于正式或陈旧的表达，如"As per your request" "Pursuant to our conversation"等，不符合现代商务写作的原则。商务写作旨在传达信息或说服对方，并非去赢得对方对你的写作水平的赞叹。因此，在商务写作中，应用现代的商务语言取代过时的或过于正式的表达。以下是不同类型的表达的对比（见表4.5）。

表4.5 使用现代表达

Old-fashioned	Modern
I am not in a position to recommend you.	I cannot recommend you.
Kindly send us the booklets.	Please send us the booklets.
We deem it advisable for you to wait.	We suggest you wait.
I am sending you the price list under separate cover.	I am sending you the price list separately.

5. Using Less Clichés and Jargon

陈词滥调（clichés）指的是那些由于使用过于频繁而失去原有新鲜感和魅力的词语，如 first and foremost、last but not least 等。类似的表达还有 beyond the shadow of a doubt、bury the hatchet、state of the art、hit the nail on the head、run it up the flagpole、take the ball and run with it 等。

行话（jargon）指某一特定行业人群使用的语言。几乎每一行业都有自己的行话。在商务写作中,应尽可能使用同义词来取代商业行话,避免产生误解。以下是一些常见的商业行话及其同义表达(见表 4.6)。

表 4.6 常见的商业行话及其同义表达

Jargon	Synonymous expressions
deplane	get off the plane
in-service	provide on-the-job training
interface	talk with

6. Avoiding Vague Expressions

商务信函中,有时会有一些模棱两可的词或短语。这种表达无疑会影响商务沟通。因此,商务写作的措辞应具体化,结构清晰,内容清楚。使用特定、具体的表达能让读者在大脑中形成一幅形象、生动的画面,而含糊其词只会使读者不识庐山真面目。有些商务人士由于图方便常使用一些笼统、模糊的词语,导致商务沟通障碍。譬如"Our contract will be finalized next week?"中的 finalized 意思不够明确,合同下周签好,还是合同下周将拟定好,或是下周同意签约,让读者百思不得其解。商务写作中,类似表达应杜绝。以下列举了一些模糊表达及简洁表达(见表 4.7)。

表 4.7 模糊及简洁表达

Vague	Concrete
Does wholesale have a positive impact?	Does wholesale increase our profits?
This will give us enough time to reach some meaningful conclusions.	This will give us enough time to determine our budget.

7. Avoiding Negative Wording

人们经常在生气或抱怨时使用否定的词或短语。这种表达常隐含对读者的批评或责备,因此不利于商务沟通。商务写作中应采用具有积极肯定意义的词语,尽量避免使用否定的表达。即便是想批评对方,也不应在措辞上表露出来,应采用委婉或积极的语气和语言,以便对方更好地接受。商务沟通的目的不是批评或责备对方,也不是故意让对方感到内疚,而是提供信息或劝说对方采取有益的行动,以便解决问题等。

譬如"You did not send us your L/C at the end of last month."一句中的 did not 就含有责备的语气。再如"Your lack of carefulness is the cause of the problem."中的 lack of 则传达了对对方的严重不满。这两个例句可分别修改为:"Could you please send us your L/C by the end of this month?"和"We would appreciate it if you could solve the problem for us."。下列句子分别是否定与肯定表达的对比(见表 4.8)。

表 4.8 否定与肯定表达对比

Negative	Positive
This letter is concerning your inability to remit payment on our invoice.	Did you receive our invoice?
This kind of unfortunate incident will not occur in the future.	Future transactions will be handled with great care.
The pricing scheme you suggested for this product is not practical.	If we can increase the profit by 10 percent, the pricing scheme you suggested could work.

8. Knowing the Proper Use of Commonly Misused Words and Phrases

商务写作中,有些词语很容易混淆,经常被误用。这些词语的发音和拼写类似,如 hopefully 这一词在商务写作中经常出现,但经常被误用。以下列举一些容易用错的词语,并进行比较。

ability   the state of being able or the power to do something
                    e.g. *He has the ability to write a 600-word essay within one hour.*

capacity   the power of receiving or containing
                    e.g. *The computer has the capacity to hold 7 plug-in boards.*

advise   to offer counsel and suggestions
                    e.g. *I advise that you buy a MP3.*

inform   to communicate information
                    e.g. *He informs us that our shipment hasn't arrived yet.*

affect   to change or influence

effect   to bring about; result or outcome
                    e.g. *The report will have a satisfying effect.*

because of   by reason of
                    e.g. *The meeting was delayed because of heavy traffic.*

due to   attributable to
                    e.g. *Her promotion to president was due to her managerial skills.*

beside   at the side of

besides   in addition to
                    e.g. *Besides the fees from advertising, we need also to spend a great deal of money on new office equipment.*

convince	to cause someone to believe something
	e.g. *The statistics convinced me that improved quality controls are necessary.*
persuade	to cause someone to do something
	e.g. *My secretary persuaded me to drink tea, for she thought that it was good to my health.*
disinterested	impartial
uninterested	not interested
	e.g. *He is uninterested in this kind of business as it is not concerned with his major.*
hopefully	in a hopeful manner or filled with hope
	e.g. *The phrase "hopefully the situation will improve" makes no sense because the situation cannot be filled with hope.*
practicable	which appears to be feasible
practical	used to indicate that a thing or activity is useful
percent	per hundred
percentage	a proportion of share in relation to a whole
	e.g. *My company has a small percentage of this market.*
presently	soon
at present	now
	e.g. *At present, we are expanding our foreign market especially in Germany and France.*
principal	head of a school, a main participant, a sum of money; first or highest in rank, worth, or importance
principle	a basic law or truth

9. Using Active Voice More

商务写作中,多使用主动语态会使信件语言直接有力,句子结构简洁明了。比较以下例子,看看哪一种更直截了当(见表 4.9)。

表4.9 被动与主动

Passive	Active
It was felt that the budget was too large.	Mike felt the budget was too large.
The findings were analyzed by Jack.	Jack analyzed the findings.
When your order is received, your goods will be sent.	When we receive your order, we will send your goods.

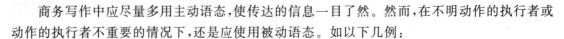

商务写作中应尽量多用主动语态,使传达的信息一目了然。然而,在不明动作的执行者或动作的执行者不重要的情况下,还是应使用被动语态。如以下几例:

a. *The company was founded in* 1998.

b. *Do you know when the meeting will be held?*

c. *The memo was sent yesterday.*

此外,有时生意人故意使用被动语态作为逃避责任或含糊其词的一种方式。如在"The status of your account will be checked and confirmed."此句中,账户谁来核对并确认,没有说明。但若改成"I will check and confirm the status of your account.",很明显责任由说话人来承担。

10. Using More Short Sentences

何为长句,何为短句,只能相对而言。一旦一个句子长到影响他人理解,则该句太长,需断开,如表 4.10 所示。

表 4.10 长短句对比

Lengthy	Shorter
I suggest that we change our service and supply fast food to give our customers what they seem to want so we can better compete with our main competitor.	I suggest that we change our service and supply fast food to give our customers what they seem to want. That way, we can better compete with our main competitor.

上例中,左句显然太长,读起来吃力;右句意思更为清晰,符合商务写作风格。当然,强调商务写作中应多用短句,并不是一味追求短小的简单句,否则会使句子结构太单一,显得孩子气。譬如表 4.11 中左边句子就不如右边句子流畅、自然。

表 4.11 长短句对比

Shorter	Lengthy
I went to the Conference Center on Wednesday. Soon I met the instructor on Wednesday. We had lunch. Then we started the class.	After going to the Conference Center on Wednesday and meeting the instructor, we had lunch and started the class.

11. Using a Natural, Conversational Style

现代商务英语写作的文体不同于其他文体,有着自身的特点:语言自然、流畅,如同面对面的口头交谈。这种写作的优势在于能使读者见信如见其人,富有亲和力,符合人性化商务发展趋势。

然而,在商务信函中经常可以看到这种句子:"Pursuant to our discussion, I am forwarding the book."及"We acknowledge with thanks the receipt of your letter dated 6th July."。当与客户交谈时,我们会这样说话吗?显然,这种表达过于正式,属于早已过时的商务套话。它们不仅可能使读者产生误解,甚至费解,还会疏远读者,不利于商务沟通。以上两例可改为:"As we discussed, I'm sending you the book."及"Thank you for your letter of 6th July."。为了进一步说明,以下分别对比不自然与自然表达(见表 4.12)。

Unit Four　General Tips for Modern Business Writing 现代商务写作技巧

表 4.12　不自然与自然表达对比

Unnatural	Natural
Upon receipt of your payment, further attention will be given to your order.	When we receive your payment, we'll begin to process your order.
Should you require further information, you could contact Mrs. Jane Lee.	If you'd like more information, please call Mrs. Jane Lee.
Please favor us with an early expression of your view.	Please let us know your opinion soon.

当然，提倡在现代商务写作中采用自然、口语化的风格，并不意味着要使用俚语或习语。商务写作者应像避开商务陈词滥调及商业行话那样避免使用俚语、习语。俚语和习语只适用于某些非正式社交场合，在大多数商务沟通中，尤其是书面沟通中不宜使用，因为有时俚语和习语会产生某种负面效应，甚至会冒犯对方。下列例句中，左边过于口语化，令人费解，不妥；右边的表达意思清楚，符合现代商务写作规律（见表 4.13）。

表 4.13　正式与非正式

Improper	Proper
Let's not drag this out.	Let's finish this as quickly as possible.
Keep your shirt on.	Please be patient.
It's asinine to blow our chances by being late.	It's foolish to lose the account by being late.
Jack's been canned.	Jack has been fired.
It's fourth down and goal to go.	This is our last opportunity to make the sale.

12. Using Courteous Expressions

礼貌是商务写作中的基本原则，无论何时，只要有必要，别忘了说"Thank you""Would you please …""We would appreciate it …"。但是，商务写作中的礼貌不仅仅是对以上所列举之例子的适时运用，还应注意其他几点，以下分别举例说明。

(1) Avoiding suspicion

诸如"if what you said is correct …""if that is what you claimed …"等语句往往让人觉得你是在怀疑对方的可信度，不利于双方的信任。试比较下列例句，右边比左边更妥当（见表4.14）。

表 4.14　避免不信任

Improper	Proper
If the commodities were damaged in transit, as you alleged, we will be responsible for them.	As you mentioned the commodities were damaged in transit, we will be responsible for them.

(2) Avoiding blaming

无论何时，切忌指责对方。如"you neglected""you forgot""you omitted"等语句都会给对方带来不愉快，甚至冒犯对方。试比较下列例句（见表 4.15）。

表 4.15 避免指责

Improper	Proper
Obviously, you forgot to send us the report by registered mail.	We did request that you send us the report by registered mail.

(3) Avoiding talking down

商务沟通中,合作双方是在平等互利的基础上进行合作,若任何一方凌驾于对方都会遭到失败,失去商业良机。试比较下列例子(见表 4.16)。

表 4.16 避免居高临下

Improper	Proper
In a company as large as ours, we seldom take an order of less than 2,000 items.	Please notice that it is not our common practice to take an order of less than 2,000 items.

13. Using YOU Attitude

商务写作中,切记要考虑读者的态度。在商务写作中,要时刻考虑对方的需求,应淡化 we 而强调 you,要暂时忘掉自己,为对方着想。如果不充分显示对对方的重视,对方可能不会感兴趣。比较以下例句,显然右边比左边更符合商务文体的要求(见表 4.17)。

表 4.17 不同的态度

We attitude	You attitude
We would very much like to have your regular order.	When you order our products regularly, you will surely benefit from increased profits.
I would like to have you consider me as a potential applicant for the position you advertised in the newspaper.	My M.A. degree in engineering at the Jiaotong University and two years' work experience should prove to be valuable in the position you advertised.

虽说商务写作中应使用 You attitude,但并非千篇一律,有时在指出对方的过失或答复对方抱怨时,为了不惹怒、冒犯对方,尽量少用 You attitude。这样也是为对方着想,如表 4.18 所示。

表 4.18 少用 You attitude

Improper	Proper
You did not send your payment on time.	We did not receive the payment on time.
If you are late four times with no justifiable reason, you will be dismissed.	Staff members who are late four times with no justifiable reason will be dismissed.

14. Using More Paragraphs

将一个商务主题分为几个小话题,然后每个小话题都用一个段落来阐述,保持每个段落短小精悍。使用小段落便于读者阅读,以及把握所读的材料的主要内容。相反,若将所有小话题用一大段来阐述,则会花费读者更多的时间来理解写作的内容,并不符合商界快节奏的规律。比较以下两封信,不难看出右边那封信更容易为读者所接受(见表 4.19)。

表 4.19　不同的段落安排

Poor paragraphing	Better paragraphing
Dear Mr. Wilson, As you will remember from our telephone call, we have recently been experiencing a number of difficulties with several large customers. This has resulted in unfortunate delays in paying outstanding accounts. We are extremely sorry that your company has been affected by these developments. We are doing everything to rectify the situation. Indeed we hope to be able to settle our debts within the very near future. I would very much appreciate it if you could bear with us patiently, as I am sure that liquidation on our part would not be in your interest either. Yours sincerely, William Becker Chief Clerk. Accounts	Dear Mr. Wilson, As you will remember from our telephone call, we have recently been experiencing a number of difficulties with several large customers. This has resulted in unfortunate delays in paying outstanding accounts. We are extremely sorry that your company has been affected by these developments. We are doing everything to rectify the situation. Indeed we hope to be able to settle our debts within the very near future. I would very much appreciate it if you could bear with us patiently, as I am sure that liquidation on our part would not be in your interest either. Yours sincerely, William Becker Chief Clerk, Accounts

15. Shortening or Deleting Warming Paragraphs

　　日常生活中,人们常常在进入正式谈话之前寒暄一番,同样书面沟通的开始往往也会有充当类似角色的段落,以便读者更好地接受正文。此外,寒暄段落还用来提供背景知识,但一般不涉及正题,故属于非重要段落。

　　商务写作有其特定的文体要求,即避繁就简,开头就应切入正题,以唤起读者的兴趣与重视。当然,也并不是说商务信件应杜绝寒暄、问候之类的语句,但没有必要用段落来充当该类角色,如表 4.20 所示。

表 4.20　删除多余段落

Improper	Proper
I enjoyed meeting you and your staff last Monday. Jack was wonderful, and other people have also showed great enthusiasm for this marketing program. I know that Mark and his team can do this job. I also trust that this project will bring great benefits to your company. 　　I have assembled and enclosed the documents which you requested as they concerns the project …	I enjoyed meeting you and your staff last Monday. Here's the information you requested concerning the marketing project we discussed.

以上为一封商务信件的开头,左边的开头段拖沓冗长,皆属无关紧要的信息,应予以删减。其实该信的目的主要是提供与市场营销项目相关的一些资料,故信的开头段就应阐明这目的,寒暄应点到为止。具体修改内容参考右边。

16. Identifying the Purpose of the Writing in the Beginning

前面提到商务写作的首段应切入正题,以唤起读者的兴趣与重视。那么何谓正题?顾名思义,正题就是写作的目的。无论是商务信件还是商务报告,都应开门见山地阐明写作的目的,然后才是正题的具体内容。一般来说,可用一句话或一个段落来表明商务写作目的。以下是常见商务信件的开头,让读者看完信件的第一句话或第一段便知道这封信的意图。

Letter of introductions: *This is to introduce Mr. Jackson, a business associate for many years.*

Letter of recommendations: *I am pleased to recommend Mr. Jack Lee, who has provided excellent training on business management for our staff over the past three weeks.*

Letter of invitations: *We are pleased to invite representatives of China National Textile Import and Export Corporation, Shanghai Branch, to visit the United States during May.*

Letter of thanks: *I am writing to thank you for the hospitality you extended on my recent visit to your country.*

Letter of inquiry: *We have noticed your advertisement in the September 15 issue of the Sweater World Journal. We would appreciate it if you could send us a pamphlet as well as the catalogue and price list of your products.*

Reply to an inquiry letter: *Thank you for your inquiry of 21st June, in which you expressed an interest in our hand-made leather gloves.*

Letter of order: *We would like to order the following goods.*

Letter of apology: *First of all, we must apologize for having not given you any news about your present order.*

同样,商务报告的首句或首段也应阐明报告的目的,便于读者阅读。例如:

• *Mr. King, our Marketing Manager, has asked me to write this report on a proposed incentive scheme offering rewards, possibly financial, to members of staff for money-saving ideas or ways to improve work practices.*

• *Following is the annual report you requested for the year …*

• *In this report I will explain how the sales program for the previous season worked, and what impact it will exert on the sales of this season.*

• *The objective of this report is to summarize the achievements we've made as well as the setbacks we've experienced in the past quarter.*

17. Basing Your Opinion on Facts

总体而言,商务写作的目的可分为提供信息(to inform)和劝说对方(to persuade)两种。

以提供信息为主要目的的商务写作,其内容主要为事实;而以劝说为主要目的的写作则要分清观点与事实,观点应以事实为基础,事实必须准确无误,而且不能脱离观点,方能更有效地劝说对方。

例如"I think interest rates will fall to 7 percent by the end of the year."这句是一个观点,不论说话者在经济学方面是如何权威,预测利率永远做不到绝对正确。要想尽量精确,只能提供更多的事实,才能提升说服力。

商务报告一般分为以下几部分:介绍(introduction)、调查手段/背景(proceedings/background)、调查结果(findings)、结论(conclusions)以及建议(recommendations)等。前面三部分主要属于事实部分,而后面两部分为观点部分。观点来自于事实,事实与观点都不可缺,否则报告就无意义。此外,将事实与观点分开,可使信息一目了然,可读性更强。下面列举一些常见的提出观点的语句:

I would like to point out that ...

It is recommended that ...

It is suggested that ...

In my opinion, the machine can ...

Personally, I think ...

My opinion is that ...

The point is ...

As I see it, ...

18. Crossing Out Unnecessary Closings

写作者有时不知道如何结尾,常常重复前文讲过的内容,易造成累赘感。商务写作的结尾如同开头应受到同等的重视,结尾可能影响整篇写作效果。在结束之前,想好要说的话,一次说清,无须再三重复。譬如,若你想与读者面谈,可用"I'd like to get together with you to discuss this matter in more detail."或"I am looking forward to seeing you Wednesday."等类型的语句结束。

实际商务沟通的信件中,不乏一些多余或不恰当的语句,如"Thank you in advance."。该句言下之意是作者已假设对方已经接受或同意信中所说的内容。作者一般在不确信自己的观点有充分的说服力时常常使用这类句子,认为不论对方是否接受先感谢对方总是对自己有利的。殊不知,这样的结尾常常起着相反的效果。

"If you have any questions, please call us."这句话在商务信件中用得过多,反而不妥。它常常会掩盖写作者的真正目的,从而给读者带来理解上的不便。最好是开诚布公,表明真正目的,以免对方产生误解。例如,你想要对方回寄一份签过的销售合同副本以存档,可用"Please send us a copy of the signed sales contract for our file."来结束,不必使用"If you have any questions, please call me."等语句。

总之,商务写作尤其是信件的结尾,应直截了当,切忌拐弯抹角。

Section 2 Grammar Focus

1. Sentence Construction Ⅰ

(1) Basic sentence patterns
- Subject+Verb:
  He retired.
- Subject+Verb+Object:
  The auditor will examine the numbers.
- Subject+Verb+Indirect Object+Object:
  He gave me an interview.
- Subject+Linking Verb+Predictive:
  The conference was successful.
  (Other linking verbs are smell, feel, sound, look, taste, remain, appear, etc.)
- There and Here Sentences:
  Here are some tips for you.
  There are many candidates competing for this position.
- Commands and requests:
  Stand up.
  Would you please send us the order by the end of the week?
- Questions:
  What are your views on this?

(2) Expanding basic sentence patterns

1) Using single words (adjectives, adverbs, etc.).
Our large shopping center has continually received a great number of customers.

2) Using word groups.
- Verbal phrases:
  The computer having the greatest versatility processed the data.
- Infinitive phrases:
  We processed the data to write a report.
- Prepositional phrases:
  The computer processed the data from the HR department.
- Appositive phrases:
  The computer, a special IBM model, processed the data.
- Adjective phrases:
  The only computer ready for use processed the data.
- Dependant clauses:
  The computer processed the data that the other ones cannot handle.

2. Sentence Construction Ⅱ

A simple sentence has a single subject+verb combination.

Mary works in her husband's company.

Many people have lost their life in the air crash.

Jackie's words and performance moved the audience.

Manny, Jack and Linda lubricated my car, replaced the oil filter and cleaned the sparked plugs.

A compound sentence is made up of two or more simple sentences, usually connected by a comma plus a joining word (and, but, for, or, nor, so and yet). A compound sentence is used when you want to give equal weight to closely related ideas.

Frank wanted to work in a large company, but Mary preferred to work in a small company.

The heavy rain started suddenly, so we stopped planting the trees.

A complex sentence is made up of a simple sentence (a complete statement) and a statement that begins with a dependent word. It is used when one wants to emphasize one idea over another in a sentence.

Because I forgot the time, I missed the meeting.

The compound-complex sentence is made up of two (or more) simple sentences and one (or more) dependent statement.

After I returned to work following a long illness, I found my position was no longer existed and I felt being left out in this company.

(1) Compound sentences (and, or, for, but, so, nor)

My secretary can type you an extra copy, or you can go across the street to a copying machine.

Mr. Cox did not go ahead with the merger with Smith and Company, nor did he have another one in mind.

(2) Complex sentences

You are requested work overtime if you get this job.

They received a bonus because they had worked so diligently.

1) Adjective/relative clauses.

The gains in stock value that we had anticipated did not materialize.

The Sales Manager who was promoted last week had to work abroad for a period of time.

2) Adverbial clauses.

I haven't seen Mr. Jones since he came back from Europe.

The workers are experienced and their morale is good, although the machinery is outdated.

Martha retyped the letter because she wanted it to be perfect.

3) Nominal clauses.

He cannot deny the fact that he is always late for work.

The reason is that the machine is really old.

I think that we can meet your deadline on time.

It is very important that we finish selling the stock by the end of the year.

(3) Avoiding primer-level (too short) sentences

Look at the following two paragraphs. The second one is acceptable in sentence structure.

Beauty aids take a big bite out of your personal budget. You can cut your costs in many ways. Use mayonnaise as a hair conditioner. Soften your hands with a mixture of glycerine and rose water. Brush your teeth with a paste of bicarbonate of soda, salt and water. Shampoo your own hair at home. Save from $10 to $20 on salon costs. Volunteer to be a model at a hairdressing school. Volunteer to be a model at a cosmetics demonstration. You can learn to live without other highly advertised products. They are essentially unnecessary.

If beauty aids take a big bite out of your personal budget, you can cut your costs in many ways. Use mayonnaise as a hair conditioner, soften your hands with a mixture of glycerine and rose water, and brush your teeth with a paste of bicarbonate of soda, salt and water. Shampoo your own hair at home, and you save from $10 to $20 on salon costs. Volunteer to be a model at a hairdressing school. Volunteer to be a model at a cosmetics demonstration. You can learn to live without other highly advertised but essentially unnecessary products.

(4) Avoiding overloaded (too long) sentences

Look at the following two paragraphs. The second one is acceptable in sentence structure.

My brother wished to become a court reporter, so he went to a community college for two years and obtained a degree, but then he realized he needed more training, so he took specialized courses at a business college for two more years, and now he is working on important civil cases and earning good money.

My brother wished to become a court reporter. He went to a community college studied hard for two years, and obtained a degree. Then he realized he needed more training. He took specialized courses at a business college for two more years. Now he is working on important civil cases and earning good money.

3. Avoiding Awkward Constructions

(1) Fragments

A word group that lacks a subject or a verb and that does not express a complete thought is a fragment. They are dependent-word fragments, ing and to fragments, added-detail fragments and missing-subject fragments.

1) Dependent-word fragments.

Some word groups that begin with a dependent word are fragments.

After I arrived in Chicago by bus, I checked into a room. Peter sat nervously in the dental clinic, while waiting to have his wisdom tooth pulled.

2) Ing and to fragments.

When an ing or to word appears at or near the start of a word group, a fragment may result.

Trying to find a garage to repair my car. Finally I had to have it towed to a garage in another town. I plan on working overtime. To get this job finished.

3) Added-detail fragments.

Added-detail fragments lack a subject and/or a verb. They often begin with one of the following words: for example, also, such as, including and especially.

The class often starts late. For example, yesterday at a quarter after nine, instead of at nine sharp.

He failed a number of courses before he earned his degree. Among them, English 1, Economics, and Biology.

4) Missing-subject fragments.

Sarah looked with admiration at the stunningly attractive model. And wondered how the model looked upon waking up in the morning.

(2) Run-together sentences

Two sentences are run together without a period to end the first one and a capital letter to begin the second one. This kind of error will confuse the reader, who will not be able to tell where one thought stops and the next begins. For instance,

Rita decided to stop smoking she did not want to die of lung cancer.

The exam was postponed the class was canceled as well.

The correct sentences are:

Rita decided to stop smoking because she did not want to die of lung cancer.

The exam postponed, and the class was canceled as well.

In other run-on sentences, a comma is placed between the two complete thoughts. The comma alone is not enough to join two complete thoughts. For example,

I took lots of vitamin C, however, I still came down with the flu.

The correct sentences are:

I took lots of vitamin C; however, I still came down with the flu.

The ways to improve run-on sentences are: use a period and a capital letter to mark the break between the thoughts; use a comma plus a joining word (and, but, and for) to connect the two complete thoughts; use a semicolon to connect the two complete thoughts.

(3) Lack of parallel structure

Parallel structure is a principle that requires the expression of ideas of equal importance in the same grammatical constructions. It lends our writing a sense of rhythm or rhythmic flow of sounds in language. Placing two or more ideas of equal value in the same grammatical form will enable us to express these ideas clearly and emphatically. However, to position parallel ideas properly, we must pay close attention to the logic of grammatical relationship.

1) Faulty coordination.

She works diligently and at night.

The correct sentences is:

She works diligently at night.

I was told to report to the supervisor and that I should bring my tools.

The correct sentences is:

I was told to report to the supervisor and bring my tools.

James Joyce's Ulysses, *a long and complicated novel and which is on our reading list, has been banned by the school board.*

The correct sentences is:

James Joyce's Ulysses, *a long and complicated novel on our reading list, has been banned by the school board.*

2) A faulty series of parallels.

When we arrived home, we unpacked our suitcases, took showers, and then we went to sleep after eating our lunch.

The correct sentences is:

When we arrived home, we unpacked our suitcases, took showers, and then went to sleep after eating our lunch.

Many people choose air transportation because it is fast, offers convenience, and it is not very expensive.

The correct sentences is:

Many people choose air transportation because it is fast, convenient and not very expensive.

3) Incorrect omissions.

He always has and always will compete for the highest honor. I always have and always shall practice diligently.

The correct sentences are:

He always has competed and always will compete for the highest honor. I always have practiced and always shall practice diligently.

4) Wrong use of "than" or "as".

The students attending our school are more intelligent than your school. His learning is as extensive as Paul.

The correct sentences are:

The students attending our school are more intelligent than those in your school. His learning is as extensive as Paul's.

(4) Misplaced modifiers

Misplaced modifiers are words that, because of awkward placement, do not describe the words the writer intended them to describe. For instance,

Tony bought an old car from a crooked dealer with a faulty transmission.

The correct sentence should be:

Tony bought an old car with a faulty transmission from a crooked dealer.

(5) Dangling modifiers

A dangling modifier is a phrase or an elliptical clause (a clause without a subject or verb or both) that is illogically separated from the word it modifies. Thus it appears disconnected from the rest of the sentence. For instance,

Going through a red light, the traffic police on duty stopped him.

The correct sentence should be:

Going through a red light, he was stopped by the traffic police on duty.

(6) Ambiguity

Ambiguity means the meaning of a sentence is vague, or it can be interpreted in more than one way. For example, "The lamb was too hot to eat." can be explained from two perspectives: The lamb felt hot, so it didn't want to eat food; The lamb (mutton) was too hot for people to eat.

4. The Use of Punctuation

Punctuation marks are the "traffic signals" of language. They tell us to slow down, notice something, take a detour, or stop. If we ignore these signals, we can cause an accident just as if we ran our car through a red light. Look at the following example and you will find the power of punctuation.

Dear Jack: I want a man who knows what love is all about. You are generous, kind and thoughtful. People who are not like you admit to being useless and inferior. You have ruined me for other men. I yearn for you. I have no feelings when we're apart. I can be forever happy—will you let me be yours? Jill

Dear Jack: I want a man who knows what love is. All about you are generous, kind and thoughtful people who are not like you. Admit to being useless and inferior. You have ruined me. For other men I yearn. For you, I have no feelings. When we're apart, I can be forever happy. Jill

5. Rules of Capitalization

(1) A capital letter is used in the following situations

- The first word of every sentence.
- Every word or phrase used as a complete thought (Are you going? No.).
- The salutation of an E-mail (Dear Mr. Lee).
- The complimentary close of an E-mail (Sincerely yours).
- Independent clause of following a colon (In conclusion, let me say this: Attractive packaging greatly increases sales.).
- Every important word in the titles of books, magazines, stories, paintings, essays, speeches, radio and television programs, and the like (*The Scarlet Letter*, Profits and

Profits Sharing).

(2) A capital letter is used for every proper noun or adjective derived from a proper noun

• Geographical names (Mt. Everest; Sweden; Colorado)

• Parks, schools, streets, churches, buildings (Zhongshan Park)

• Points of the compass used to name regions (We live in North Carolina.)

• Names of individuals (Michael Jackson)

• Family titles (Uncle Tom)

• Names of organizations such as companies, clubs associations, political parties (Ikea, IBM)

• Names of languages and nationalities (Japanese, Chinese)

• Nouns with letters or numbers (Act 1, Schedule A)

• Titles of office or ranks directly related to a person's name (President Bush, Professor Lee)

• Trademarks and brand names (Pepsi-Cola)

(3) Other points for attention

• Do not capitalize a geographical term used before or after a name when it is not a part of the name (the valley of the Mississippi); do not capitalize a geographical term that is used in the plural (the Missouri and Mississippi rivers).

• When the common-noun element (company, school, corporation) is used as a substitute for the full name, it should be capitalized. (The Company entered the Chinese market in April. The "Company" refers to "Warren Manufacturing Company".)

• The first and last words of a title are always capitalized. Prepositions, articles (a, an, the), and conjunctions are not capitalized except when they are the first and last words in a title. It is permissible to capitalize prepositions of six letters or more, or of more than one syllable. ("Man Against Darkness", "The Road Before Us")

7. The Usage of Prepositions

A preposition is a word or unit of several words that takes a noun or pronoun as its object and shows a relationship between the object and some other words in the sentence. The main reason for studying prepositions is to learn how effectively they can be used as joining words that establish logical connections between one part of a sentence and another part.

(1) Common prepositions

above the poster	outside the fence
after the injury	over the river
along the road	over the last decade
around the table	since last May
behind the desk	through the report
beneath the tree	to the store
beyond the hills/one's understanding	toward(s) the greater remuneration

Unit Four General Tips for Modern Business Writing 现代商务写作技巧

but (except) me	under control
down the pipe	until midnight
during the fall sales	up the creek
except him	with your approval
for the weekend	without her consent
in the group	according to the report
like a fool	because of the fire
near you	in front of the building
of the majority	before the event
off the truck	in regard to your question
on the freeway	in line with the principle

(2) Prepositional phrases

A preposition is never incorporated into a sentence by itself; it must always introduce a prepositional phrase (PP), a group of words beginning with a preposition and ending with a noun or pronoun.

The change in the schedule presented a problem in logistics.

The itinerary for your trip has been modified.

The compromise on the plans was approved.

A ship without a full cargo means a loss of profit.

He received a box of cigars.

The plane will depart at ten o'clock.

The agreement was made with your knowledge.

We should look into the future.

The meeting was canceled because of her illness.

The buyers have postponed their decision for a week.

By May the reorganization will have been finished.

(3) Prepositional phrases placed effectively

Be certain to place a prepositional phrase where it will function most effectively and convey the precise meaning intended. The placement of a preposition phrase affects the meaning of a sentence. For example:

The office for the new managing director has been refurbished.

The office has been refurbished for the new managing director.

(4) Prepositions used idiomatically

Many prepositions have acquired fixed, conventional uses in combinations with other words, especially verbs.

accompanied by (a person)	convenient for (a purpose)
accompanied with (an object)	convenient to (a person or object)
agree to (terms)	deal in (merchandise)

agree with (an opinion/somebody)　　deal with (a subject)
agree on/upon (a plan)　　　　　　　differ with (an opinion)
angry with (a person)　　　　　　　　differ from (in quality)
angry at (an object or situation)　　　different from (not than)
buy from (somebody)　　　　　　　　enter in/on (the record)
compare to (things of unlike class)　　enter into (an agreement)
compare with (things of like class)　　independent of (not from)

8. Paragraphs

(1) What is a paragraph?

A paragraph is a group of sentences that develop one central idea. It may be a part of a paper or it may stand alone like a mini essay. It may be long or short. Whatever the length is, a paragraph should be complete in itself and provide adequate information for the reader.

An effective paragraph must be unified, coherent, specific, and adequately developed. These features run through the entire paragraph. A good way to learn to achieve the purpose is to start with the paragraph structure. A standard paragraph has two very important components: a topic sentence often appearing at the beginning of the paragraph, sometimes at the end, and sometimes in the middle and supporting sentences.

(2) Topic sentences

"Writing an outline is an aid to organizing a composition." This sentence names the topic "writing an outline", and it contains a controlling idea: "is an aid to organizing a composition." The topic sentence of a paragraph does the following tasks:

• It names the topic in the paragraph, telling the reader what the paragraph is about.

• It contains a controlling idea that commits the paragraph to a specific aspect of the topic. A controlling idea is a key word or phrase that expresses the basic point of paragraph.

• It tells the reader what to expect in the paragraph.

• It is usually the most general and most important statement in the paragraph.

(3) Supporting sentences

Supporting sentences back up and explain the main idea—providing the reader with specific evidence and reasons. They present facts, figures, thoughts, observations, examples and personal experience. After this specific and adequate information is provided, the central idea of your paragraph becomes clear and meaningful.

(4) The unity of a paragraph

An effective paragraph achieves unity: all the sentences within the paragraph must be related to the main point. A unified paragraph is in which every sentence is devoted to providing the controlling idea in the topic sentence. In short, unity is sticking to your subject.

(5) The coherence of a paragraph

An effective paragraph achieves not only unity, but also coherence. Both are indispensable. While unity is concerned with ideas or content, coherence is concerned with the form of expression. Coherence refers to the smooth moving from one sentence to the next. If the sentences are well connected, the paragraph is coherent. To ensure the smooth flow of ideas within a paragraph, you can use pronouns, repeat key words or phrases, avoid pronoun shifts, and resort to transitional signals. These are the most commonly used connective devices.

(6) Sentences in a paragraph

1) Vary the lengths of sentences.

The paragraph looks and sounds better if sentences vary in length. The feeling of the paragraph can be partially determined by the length of sentences: Use short sentences for emphasis; in long sentences the beginnings and the endings are the most emphatic positions.

2) Vary the patterns of sentences.

To avoid monotony, use a mixture of simple, compound and complex sentences. Establish fluency through the use of transitional elements, such as the following words (however, therefore, thus, etc.), phrases (on the one hand, on the contrary, etc.), and clauses (I think, you will remember, I believe, etc.).

(7) Short paragraphs in business communication

• The main idea is more evident in a short paragraph.

• A concise message saves the reader's time.

• The first and last paragraphs should contain, as a general rule, no more than three or four lines.

• Paragraphs of more than six or seven lines often tend to be confusing and boring to the reader.

Unit Five　Establishing Business Relations
建立贸易关系

◆ *Learning Objectives*

a. Know the importance of establishing business relations;

b. Comprehend different ways to build business relations;

c. Grasp useful expressions used in business letters.

Section 1　Introduction

Establishing business relations with prospective dealers is one of the important measures to maintain or expand business activities in doing foreign trade. Customers are the basis of business expansion, therefore, it is a common practice in business communications that newly established firms or firms that wish to enlarge their business scope and turnover write letters to new customers for the establishment of relations.

To establish business relations with prospective dealers is the base of starting and developing of business. It is vitally important for both a new dealer and an old one. But by what means can a businessman secure all the necessary information about a new market and a new customer?

Well, we may establish business relations with other parties through the following channels or with the help of:

a. the advertisements in newspapers;

b. the introduction from his business connections;

c. the introduction from his subsidiaries or branches, agents abroad;

d. the market investigations;

e. attendance at the export commodities fairs;

f. visit abroad by trade delegations and groups;

g. self-introductions or enquiries received from the merchants abroad;

h. the banks;

i. the Commercial Counselor's Office;

j. the chambers of commerce both at home and abroad;

k. company's web;

Unit Five Establishing Business Relations 建立贸易关系

l. yellow page of telephone.

When having obtained the desired name and address of the firm from any of the above sources, one can write a letter or a circular to the other party. Generally speaking, this kind of letter includes the following ones.

a. The source of the information, i e. how and where the writer gets the name and address of the receiver's company.

b. The intention or desire of writing the letter.

c. Self-introduction, including the business scope, branches and other necessary information.

d. The references as to the financial status and integrity of the writer's company.

e. Expectation of cooperation and an early reply.

Traders must do everything possible to consolidate their established relations with the existing customers and also develop and revitalize the trade by searching for new connections. If they are to buy some products, they may ask for samples, price lists, catalogue or other reference materials. The letters should be written politely, clearly and concisely. As regards the receiver of such kind of letter, he or she is recommended to answer in full without any delay to create goodwill, leaving a positive impression on the other party and possibly expand the trade.

Section 2 Examples of Establishing Business Relations Letters

1. Self Introduction

Dear Sirs,

This is Water from SHV Company. I've been working in PPC (panel personal computer) field for more than five years. Hope that I can serve you with my professional experience from now on. Please feel free to study our offer as below.

First of all, I would like to introduce you some information about our factory. SHV Company is a professional manufacturer in producing portable panel personal computer, covering 7′,8.5′,9′,10.2′. And SHV got the supports as below.

Staff Number: over 300
Production lines: four lines
Monthly capacity: 60,000pcs
Quality control: FCC, CE, EMC, CCC, ROHS
Factory management: ISO9001 International Quality Management System and ISO 14000 International Environment Management System.

Markets: XXX from Spain, XXX, XXX from Italy, XXX from Germany, XXX from Ukraine, XXX from Bulgaria, XXX from Russia, XXX from Israel, XXX from Iran, XXX, XXX from India, XXX from Middle East, XXX from Paraguay, XXX from Panama, etc.

Now I would like to offer you the fast sale item with best price for your reference first.

Model: Item A701, 7′swivel screen with TV tuner, USB & Card Render
Offer: FOB Shenzhen US＄50
MOQ: 1,000pcs

Samples and more information are available for your study anytime. We appreciate your kind reply soon.

We are looking forward to our cooperation in near future.

Best regards,

Water

Notes
(1) 第一次主动联系客户,需要介绍本公司在行业内的经验和成绩,让客户产生信心。
(2) 介绍公司的产品和实力,以增加客户信心。
(3) 根据客户所在国家目前的产品销售情况,向客户推荐适当的产品。
(4) 报价时要包含产品的重要信息,比如,产品的主要功能、报价条款、价格、订单起订量等。
(5) 最后,提出合作的愿望。

2. Contact Customer After the Fair
Sample 1

Dear Sirs,

Thank you for your kind visit at our booth 2F18 during Canton Fairs. This is Water from SHV Company. I hope you could feel free to study our offer about Portable PPC.

SHV Company is a professional manufacturer in producing Portable PPC. The products are spreading the countries and regions including Asia, Europe and America, products covering

7′, 8.5′, 9′, 10.2′. We've been investing US＄38 million to set up a high-tech industry zone named SHV Technology Co., Ltd in Zhejiang Province, which covers 82,014 square meters and 201,400 square meters of building. With our strong R&D and workmanship, believe we can become your good partner and friend.

According to the memo during Canton Fair, we would like to list the following offers for your record.

  Model：Item A903,9′swivel screen with TV tuner,USB & Card Reader
  Offer：FOB Shenzhen US＄50
  MOQ：1,000pcs

Samples and more information are available as requested. We appreciate your kind ideas about our cooperation.

We are looking forward to our initial cooperation soon.

Best regards,

Water

Notes

(1)参加展会是很多公司推广产品的一种很重要的方式。在展会之前,通常都要向所有的老客户和潜在的客户发邀请函。这也是向客户展示公司实力的一次机会。通常邀请函都会做成图片的形式,方便发送给客户参考。邀请函的内容包括参展公司名称、参展日期、展位号、主展产品等重要信息。

(2)展会之后,联系客户时应提及展位号。这样客户更容易记起自己。

(3)开门见山地说明本公司销售的产品,容易抓住客户的注意力。

(4)简短的公司和产品介绍可以让客户在短时间内熟知公司的实力和优势,以拉近合作的距离。

(5)根据展会上的笔记,正式向客户报价。

(6)最后,提出合作的期望。

Sample 2

Dear Claus,

It was nice to meet you in Hong Kong, and hope you had a good trip.

Thanks for your kind visit to our showroom. It's a little pity that your schedule is so tight. If possible, we'd like to invite you to our office next time and show you around our three factories.

The follows are our meeting memo for your reference.
- For 5.1CH standard PPC (panel personal computer), US＄21
- DivX version, add US＄1 per set
- Nero function, add US＄0.5 per set

For PPC-T and new project MD-2720, it is still under consummating. When it is completed, we'll inform you immediately. Also we'll arrange PPC-591/PPC-592 sample for your test.

Even though we met a lot of problems by first cooperation, now it's OK and the second container will be dispatched next week. I think we can run more smoothly by the following days. Both sides know each other better. And also we learn a lot from your professional, cautious and serious working style.

I do hope you could share some of your proposals of our next step cooperation. Your ideas for our whole year plan will be helpful. Please try to offer me some minds, we'd hope we could expand our business, work more strategically, and support you by our best service.

Best regards,

Aaron

Notes

(1) 客户通常都会参加展会。一方面是考察现有的供应商，面谈订单计划，落实新订单的价格或者跟进进行中的订单情况；另一方面是获取更多的产品信息，包括市场新价格、同类产品的新供应商等。

(2) 展会后，对与客户面谈的内容进行总结，主动发给客户会议记录。

(3) 再次提及洽谈的内容，更为详细地说明这些内容的具体情况。特别是确定关于样品或者订单进行的时间等。

(4) 进一步充实内容，包括对彼此之间合作的评价以及对未来的展望，还有对客户运营方式的了解等。对问题点到即可，重点是期待合作以及未来服务质量的改进。

(5) 提出自己的希望，同时也提醒客户，随着合作的深入将来可以为客户提供更优质的服务，以增强客户的信心，这样可以加深合作。

Unit Five Establishing Business Relations 建立贸易关系

3. Inquiry from Customer

Sample 1

Dear Julia,

I hope you are doing well. My name is Marcelo. I represent R&S Corp., from Buenos Aires, Argentina. We met each other at the Las Vegas' CES, last January. At that time we talked about your products. Actually we are WalMart's Argentina traders, relating to PPC, FPD (flat-panel display). I remembered that during our meeting you informed me about some prices that were suitable for us. So, as this moment, I'd like to know your quotation of prices—FOB China—of the following articles, for WalMart's Argentina.

PPC 5.1 full size
PPC 5.1 1/2 size with display
FPD 10.1 full size
FPD 10.1 full size with USB

This request is for WalMart's order, which will be around 20,140 pcs of each article. Please, I'll appreciate you will send me your products pictures and price. If those are different from the catalogue you gave me at the CES, or just let me know which catalogue's articles you are quoting.

Please answer me as soon as possible. Thanks a lot.

Hope to hear from you soon.

Best regards,

Marcelo

Reply to the above

Dear Marcelo,

Thank you very much for your kind inquiry to us. Your detailed company and market information impressed us deeply. Glad to see that there is a chance for both R&S and Mizida in entering into some projects cooperation in near future.

Further to the enquiry, we would like to make you the offer as below. Photos are as attached.

PPC 5.1 full size, PPC-592, US $21

PPC 5.1 1/2 size with display,PPC-558B,US＄20
PPC 5.1 full size with USB,PPC-602/561,US＄23

The whole offer is upon FOB Shenzhen price.
And base on your potential quantity 20,140 pcs per item.Wish they could meet your request. We are ready to provide more information and samples as requested.

We appreciate your comments and looking forward to working together with you soon.

Best regards,

Julia

(1)展会之后或者通过网络联系的客户在一段时间内没有订单,一方面说明由于市场销售和客户的推广计划等原因,在当时确实没有订单需求,另一方面说明客户当时已经有较为稳定的合作伙伴。但客户往往也会将同等品质的供应商列为备选对象,当有合适的产品或者新项目的时候,客户也许会主动联系。因此,需要不间断地跟进,比如更新价格、更新产品或者进行信息交流。

(2)分析客户的邮件。邮件中客户陈述说明相识于何处、客户的公司和产品介绍以及销售的场所,还有关于产品的规格等较为详细的要求。这类有实质性内容的邮件说明双方合作机会往往较大。

(3)回复邮件。要根据客户的市场特征、订单数量、价格要求等,为客户推荐最合适的产品,报出最有竞争力的价格。客户喜欢和实力相当的公司合作,但需要产品质量过关以及有竞争力的价格。

(4)报价的内容要清晰,比如价格条款、起订量和相关的单价、产品的主要规格或者功能说明等。这些内容一定要清晰,不能模糊,以免引起误解。同时,附上精美的图片,让客户可以更直观地选择。

(5)期望合作,表现诚意和热情。

Sample 2

Dear Sirs,

Thank you very much for your kind enquiry to us. This is Alice. From now on,I will help to follow up your orders and hope my 5 years experience and hard work can serve you better.

Regarding your enquiry,please find our reply as below.

Our products are fast sales in EU countries and America. Especially we already had steady partners in those places. And the cooperation has been lasting more than 5 years.

Regarding American market, our customers prefer healthy sleeping, so they would like to buy the mattress to protect their backbones. For example, memory mattress, independent spring mattress, surely the reel mattress you mentioned is also fast sale. Please refer to the attachments, I would like to introduce some suitable items for your market.

Currently our company is applying for the American prevailing rules CFR1633 which is standard fire protection and becoming effective in July 1st, 2016. As we know that in Los Angeles they would apply for the standard fire protection rule TB603. But now they upgrade to CFR 1633. We think you might require for it, too. Please refer to the CERTIFICATION as attached.

Payment term:
- 30% deposit T/T in advance, 70% balance T/T before shipment.
- 50% deposit T/T in advance, 50% balance by irrevocable L/C at sight.

Leading time: 15 days upon deposit received

MOQ: 1×20GP, FOB ShenZhen

If you have any enquiry and need our help, please don't hesitate to contact me.

Best regards,

Water

Notes
(1) 行业内的客户一般比较关心产品的质量、公司产品的市场销售情况、公司的质量认证书等。这些都直接影响客户对公司产品的认识,因为不同的市场,质量要求是有区别的。
(2) 体现个性化的服务。
(3) 回复客户的问题,着重突出公司的优势和实力。
- 有稳定的客源,和客户合作超过5年,充分体现公司实力,并保证产品质量。
- 分析最终消费者的实际要求和特点,体现个人的丰富知识及专业水准。
- 分析客户市场对质量的要求,展现公司的实力与时俱进。
- 内容环环相扣。回复围绕客户问题的同时,也向客户说明了公司其他方面的操作程序,方便客户更深入地了解公司。

Sample 3

Dear Sirs,

I am the purchase manager of Sound Master Company in South Africa. We are planning to import mattress. The quantity may be around 200 sets at the first time. And our boss Mike and I will visit China next month. We would like to talk to you in your factory. In order to get the visa from Chinese Embassy, can you send an invitation letter to us?

We are looking forward to hearing from you soon.

Sincerely yours,

Anson

Reply to the above

Dear Anson,

Thank you very much for your kind enquiry to us. My name is John. From now on, I will follow up your orders and offer best sales service with my professional experience.

Because we don't have your ideas about target item, I would like to offer you some fast sale items in South Africa for your easy reference first. The details are as attached. We are also inviting you to visit our website at www.shvfurniture.com to know more details about us.

Regarding the invitation letter, we would like to share some information with you. Normally we have to submit application form and relative necessary information to our government for approval first. As we didn't start cooperation before, the application period may be longer. In order not to affect your schedule, I would like to advise that if you have other business partners here, you'd better ask them to help you. So you may get the visa within one week. Please take our suggestion as reference. Surely we are pleased to apply for you if you need our help. But please send us the details about the people who will come.

To catch the visit schedule and run the business soon, shall we exchange some important ideas first? We may conclude some agreements before you visit in China.

We welcome your coming and visiting. And looking forward to our cooperation soon.

Sincerely yours,

John

| Notes |

(1) 有些国家的客户如果要到中国访问，申请签证时需要工厂提供邀请函。申请时需要向相关政府部门提供详细的资料，比如到访人的个人资料、双方业务往来的资料，包括发票、报关单以及工厂的营业执照等重要文件。申请的程序比较复杂，申请的时间也比较漫长，需要一个月左右。

(2) 类似的询盘，回复时要抓住重点词语，比如 import mattress、visit China、invitation letter 等，分析客户的需求，尽快给出有针对性的回复和建议。

Sample 4

Dear Water,

We are currently looking to expand our product line including memory foam mattresses and pillows.

I will come to china next month. In the meantime, I would like to collect as much information as possible on prices and specifications.

Please advise us at your earliest convenience.

Sincerely yours,

Michael

Reply to the above:

Dear Michael,

We are glad to know that you will expand your business line on memory foam mattress & memory foam pillow. Believe we can serve you better and better in near future.

First, please refer to the attachments for your reference.

It is great that you will come to China for business. Please kindly arrange your schedule to visit our factory. We hope we can have a close talk face to face. Then we could show you our production lines and sample room. We are confident that if will make our cooperation smoothly.

When your visit schedule is available, please kindly let me know.

Sincerely yours,

Water

Notes

(1)客户计划扩展业务,对公司的产品表示感兴趣或者看好公司产品的前景,表示要访问中国,并参观工厂。

(2)针对这样的询盘,主要是分析客户的目的和要求,抓住重点词和主要意思。根据获取的信息,有步骤、有的放矢地回复邮件。

(3)在邮件中,对客户表示出诚意,同时要展示公司的实力,以增加客户对公司的了解,增强合作信心。

4. Take the Information from Other Colleagues

Sample 1

Dear Maitance,

Good day.

Nice to contact with you. This is Echo from CABC (Hong Kong) International Industrial Limited. And it is my great honor to serve you in the future.

Our boss Mr. Jason, just came back from the MIDO SHOW, and I learned that you are interested in our swimming products. Here attached our updated price list for your reference. Also, please take your time to visit our website at *www.cabe.com* for pictures and more details.

Mr. Jason had quoted you two models in MIDO, and here we list a gain as below for your easy reference.

Unit Five Establishing Business Relations 建立贸易关系

Swimming cap：CAP800 USD 2.0 (according to your quantity of 200 pcs)
Earplug with strap：EP-200 USD 0.8 (including package)

Please contact us freely if you have any question. We are looking forward to building business relationship with you in the near future.

Sincerely yours,

Echo

Notes

(1) 参加展会是一个公司推广产品的重要渠道,但是公司的投入会根据实际情况而定。一个公司的业务员一般都有两个或者两个以上。由于国外展会的费用较高,对于规模不是很大的公司,业务员参加展会的名额也是有限的。在展会之后,公司会把展会上取得的名片进行分发,每个业务员可以自己去联系客户。

(2) 先说明信息来源,并向客户表示友好。

(3) 在展会上,客户或多或少都对公司进行了一番了解。由于业务员没有直接和客户交流,所以要有适当的过渡,侧重说明自己将会提供个性化的服务,让客户满意。

(4) 提出合作期望。

Sample 2

Dear Marcus,

How are you doing? This is Water from ABC Company, Ms. Grace's colleague. She already left the company some time ago. It's been a long time no contact with you and your company. We are glad to contact you again about external battery pack for Mobile Phone and Notebook.

I would like to update you some latest model and new offers for your reference. We hope we can enlarge our business scale. Please find the details as attached.

Looking forward to hearing from you soon.

Sincerely yours,

Water

Sample 3

Dear Andy,

This is Tina, sales representative of ABC Electronic Company. Thanks for Eden's assignment, I'm pleased to have the opportunity to contact you and take charge of our cases directly. Hope we can set long-term business relationship and expand business it the future.

Now I'm taking up your first order—2015 (PPC), all the specifications and other details will be followed by me. Therefore if you have any problem, please feel free to contact me.

Further to your new order, please refer to the attachments for our quotations, we are waiting for your confirmation. Surely we will get a good delivery date for you.

Thank you for your good cooperation and your early reply will be appreciated.

Sincerely yours,

Tina

Notes

(1) 对已联系或者已合作的客户,撰写商务函电主要体现服务,不让客户感觉到突兀。

(2) 和暂时无合作、曾经联系密切、有邮件阅读回执的客户要保持联系,在某个特定的时间提醒客户产品的报价,以及产品的市场销售情况等。假如知道对方公司和自己公司生产的产品相符,要多参考客户公司的网页,根据网页上的信息不断向客户展开猛烈的"攻击"。另外,适当的电话联系也是必需的,或者以传真的方式,或者直接给客户发邮件。尝试不同的方式反复联系,提高成功合作的可能性。

5. Contact Customer by B2B Web Information

Dear Sirs,

I got your business information online. We would like to cooperate with you on CARDS, and become your good partner in near future.

With more than 12 years experience in manufacturing all kinds of PVC cards, paper cards, metal cards and smart cards in China, we've grown up into a main supplier in Italy, Germany, Sweden, France, Denmark and New Zealand, etc. The daily output can reach millions of cards. Including PVC blank and printed cards, paper cards, scratch cards, magnetic cards, IC cards, game cards, gift cards, member cards, pokers, playing cards, metallic cards, phone cards, irregular-shaped cards, ATM cards, IC cards, ID cards, RFID tags, etc. We welcome your ODM projects. All sizes and thickness can be done here.

We welcome your enquiries. Please visit our official website at http://www.ucard.biz. It will be appreciated that if someone from your company could contact me freely. My E-mail is: water@ucard.biz.

Please let us become partners and start the initial cooperation soon.

Looking forward to hearing from you.

Yours sincerely,

Water

Notes

(1)利用搜索引擎获取客户信息。首先应直接说明信息来源和目的,为客户节省时间,使客户一看便知道产品是什么。

(2)公司产品种类和市场情况的简短介绍。

(3)第一次联系的人也许不是直接的对口人。提出如果有人联系自己,也是一种很好的联系方式。

(4)最后,提出合作的愿望。

6. Importer Writes to Exporter

Dear Sirs,

We have obtained your address from the Commercial Counselor of your Embassy in London and are now writing you for the establishment of business relations.

We are very well connected with all the major dealers here of light industrial products, and feel sure we can sell large quantities of Chinese goods if we get your offers at competitive prices.

As to our standing, we are permitted to mention the Bank of England, London, as a reference.

Please let us have all necessary information regarding your products for export.

Yours faithfully,

Notes

(1) 写信建立贸易关系。

(2) 第一次联系客户，无论是通过何种方式获取客户的信息，撰写信函时都有一些必须要注意的事项，如主客要分清，句子不要零碎，结构要对称，要便于理解。

7. Introduced by One of Business Partners

Dear Sir or Madam,

Your company has been introduced to us by one of our business partners as a prospective purchaser of china. As this item comes within our business scope, we shall be pleased to into business relations with you at an early date.

To give you a general idea of the various kinds of china now available for export, we are enclosing a brochure and a price list. Quotations and samples will be airmailed to you after receiving your specific inquiry.

We are looking forward to your early reply.

Yours sincerely,

Dear Sir or Madam,

Your letter of 9th March addressed to our sister corporation in Beijing has been passed on to us for attention and reply as the export of pottery falls with the scope of our business activities.

However, as we are already represented by the Olong Corporation for the sale of this commodity in your area, we would like to advise you to get in touch with them for you to get in touch with them for your requirements.

If you are interested in other items, please let us know and we shall be pleased to make you a direct offer.

Yours sincerely,

8. From the Commercial Counselors's Office

Dear Sir or Madam,

We have learned your name and address from the commercial counselors's office of the Chinese embassy in the United Kingdom. We would like to inform you that we specialize in both industrial and pharmaceutical chemicals and shall be delighted to establish business with you.

To give you some idea of our products, we are enclosing a complete set of leaflets, which show various products being handled by our corporation with detailed specifications and means of packing. Quotations and samples will be sent upon receipt of your specific inquiries.

We will conclude the business transaction on the basis of shipping quality and weight, while testing and inspection will be made by the Shanghai Commodity Inspection and Quarantine Bureau before shipment. Necessary certificates about the quality and quantity of the shipment will, of course, be provided.

We look forward to your early reply.

Yours sincerely,

9. Credit Information

Sample 1

Dear Sir or Madam,

We have received an important order from Terry Derry & Co., of Hong Kong, who has give us your name as reference. We would be much obliged if you could give us some information respecting their commercial position.

It would give us great pleasure to be able to provide you with a similar service if we should have such an opportunity.

Yours sincerely,

Sample 2

Dear Sir or Madam,

In reply to your inquiry of the 16th of March, I am pleased to inform you that the firm you inquired about enjoys the fullest respect and unquestionable confidence in the business world.

They are prompt and punctual in all their transactions. I am sure that if you open an account with them, you will find them most straightforward people. Personally, I should have no hesitation in according them a credit of several million yen. However, this is without obligation on my part.

I hope I have been of some use to you in this matter.

Sincerely yours,

Sample 3

Dear Sir or Madam,

We have received your letter of 8 August, concerning the credit standing of Eastern Bank in this city. We regret that we have to reply an unfavorable communication to you.

Since the bankruptcy of the Kanto Bank, the house has been experiencing great difficulties. Though they are still struggling to survive the hardships, they will be unable to stand their ground long. The house is expected to stop payment in any time.

Unit Five Establishing Business Relations 建立贸易关系

We hope you will take this information into consideration with great care and not to our detriment.

Yours sincerely,

本章句式

1. Opening

(1) Through ..., we learn that you are interested in ....

(2) We owe your name and address to ... through which we learn that you were seeking partners in China for selling your ... products.

(3) Your company has been introduced to us by ... as prospective buyers of ... goods. As we handle these goods, we shall be pleased to enter into direct business relations with you.

(4) Your firm has been kindly recommended to us by ... as a large importer of furniture.

(5) On the recommendation of ..., we have learned with pleasure the name of your firm.

(6) We understood after contacting your trade delegation that you are one of the leading importers of ... goods in your area and wish to enter into business relations with us.

(7) We have been put in touch with you by your embassy here.

2. Introducing One's Own Company or Line of Product

(1) We would like to introduce ourselves to you with the hope that we may have a good chance of cooperation with you in your business extension.

(2) We would like to establish business relations with you.

(3) We have been in the line of ... for many years.

(4) Our competitive prices, superior quality and efficiency have won confidence and goodwill among our business clients.

(5) With reference to your letter of ... addressed to ... we are glad to inform you that it has been duly forwarded to us for attention and reply.

(6) Our market survey informs us that you have a keen interest in the import of ....

(7) Specializing in the export of ..., we wish to express our desire to trade with you in this line.

(8) We would like to write to you to enter into business relations with you.

(9) Your letter expressing the hope of establishing business connections with us has been received with thanks.

(10) We are writing to you in the hope that we can open up business relations with your firm.

3. Asking for Information and Ending

(1) Please let us know by return what your experience has been in your dealings with them.

(2) The above information is given confidentially and without responsibility on our part.

(3) Our mutual understanding and cooperation will certainly result in considerable business between us.

(4) It is hoped that by our joint efforts we can promote business as well as friendship.

(5) We shall be grateful if you will reply at an early date.

Unit Six Inquiry and Quotation
询盘与报盘

Learning Objectives

a. Understand that inquiries are usually made by the buyer and are integrated with letters establishing business relations;

b. Master basic writing principles of inquiries and basic points of quotation.

Section 1 Introduction

1. Inquiry[①]

Inquiries are made when a business person intends to purchase certain goods or obtain desired services. The buyer usually sends an inquiry to invite a quotation or an offer from the seller, therefore inquiries mean potential business for both the buyer and the seller.

Based on the inquired contents, inquiries can be divided into general inquiries and specific inquiries. The writer of a general inquiry asks for general information, a catalogue, a price list, or a sample book, while that of a specific inquiry focuses on the detailed information about the specific target goods or services.

There are two kinds of inquiries. One is called general inquiry, a request for a price list, catalogue, sample or quotation of price and other terms. This kind of letter should be simple and direct in content. Another kind of inquiry is specific inquiry, an inquiry for goods of a certain specification. It is made when a buyer intents to conclude some business with the seller. When this is to be sent, many firms use a printed form for the purpose of omitting the trouble of writing a letter. Inquiry should be addressed to the company instead of an individual, only in this way, prompt attention will be received.

Inquiries can also be classified into first inquiries and inquiries for repeat orders by the relationship between the writer and the recipient. A first inquiry is employed when the letter is sent to a seller with whom the buyer has not previously done business, and inquiries for

---

① inquiry,即询盘、询价,是买方对所要购买的商品向卖方做出的探询。其内容并不仅限于价格,还可兼问商品的规格、性能、包装和交货期等。询问的目的主要是从卖方即出口商方获得具有竞争性的价格,然后从几家报价中选择最佳者。因此对于同一商品的询盘,往往不只向一家公司发出询盘,而是向不同国家的、在经营某种商品有名气的且是相互竞争的若干家公司同时发出。外贸行业常说的"货比三家"就是这个意思。

repeal orders are mostly for acquainted customers. As for the latter one, the inquiry may be very simple and most often a printed inquiry form will be enough. Our focus of this chapter will be on the writing of a first inquiry.

In a first inquiry, it is useful for the writer to tell the recipient some information about his or her own business, the kinds of goods he or she needs, and the reasons for the inquiry to win trust from the other party. Besides, the writer needs to mention how he or she obtained the seller's name and address, the market analysis of the demand for the seller's goods or services, and the materials and information that he or she wants to receive. Mostly, the writer has interest in a catalogue, a price list, the seller's discounting policy, method of payment, delivery time and samples.

Inquiries should be addressed to the company because, in this way, your letter will receive quick attention. If you address the inquires to an individual, your letter many have to wait while he is away. Or you may make a mistake and address it to the wrong individual, and this will also mean delay

The following tips are of great value in guiding the preparation of letters of inquiries.

a. State concisely and exactly the request.

b. Enumerate the questions when there are many.

c. Make a request for reply and let the seller feel the value of the information to you.

d. Show courteousness and politeness.

e. Give the seller some hope of substantial order or continued business.

The reply to inquiries should be prompt, courteous and cover all the information asked for. If you can not satisfy the inquirers' demand at the moment, you should acknowledge the letter immediately, giving the reason and assuring that you will do all you can to meet his requirement. If the inquiry is from an old client, express your appreciation of his interest in your products. If it is from a new customer, say you are glad to receive it and express the hope of lasting friendly business relation so as to create goodwill and leave a good impression on the reader.

2. Quotation

It is well known that there four major steps in business negotiation: inquiry offer→counter offer→acceptance→contract.

Quotation is not an offer in the legal sense. An offer is a promise to supply goods on the terms and conditions stated, while a quotation is merely a notice of the prize of certain goods at which the seller is willing to sell. However, when sending an offer, the seller must not only quote the price of the goods he wishes to sell but also indicates all necessary terms of sales for the buyer's consideration. But, if a quotation is made together with all necessary terms and conditions of sales, it amounts to an offer.

When a seller prepares to export, he or she quotes the customer the price of the goods on receipt of the inquiry. A quotation is a promise to supply goods on the terms stated and it generally includes all the necessary information requested. The prospective buyer is under no

Unit Six Inquiry and Quotation 询盘与报盘

obligation to buy and the seller is not bound to sell. In brief, a quotation is not legally binding if the seller later decides not to sell. A satisfactory quotation will include the following:

a. Thanks for the inquiry if there is any;
b. The answers to all the information requested;
c. Details of prices, terms of payment, and discounts.

Section 2 Examples of Inquiry and Replies

1. General Inquiry for Export Commodities

Gentlemen:

We learn from ABC & Co. Ltd, New York that you are a leading exporter in your country.

We are, at present, very much interested in importing your goods and would appreciate your sending us catalogues, sample books or even samples if possible.

Please give us detailed information of CIF Guangzhou prices, discounts, and terms of payment. We hope this will be a good start for long and profitable business relations.

Truly yours,

Reply

Gentlemen:

We welcome you for your enquiry of March 21 and thank you for your interest in our export commodities. We are enclosing some copies of our illustrated catalogues and a price list giving the details you ask for. Also under separate cover, we are sending you some samples which will show you clearly the quality and craftsmanship. We trust that when you see them you will agree that our products appeal to the most selective buyer.

We allow a proper discount according to the quantity ordered. As to the terms of payment we usually require L/C payable by sight draft.

Thank you again for your interest in our products. We are looking forward to your order and you may be assured that it will receive our prompt and careful attention.

Truly yours,

2. Specific Inquiry for Dyeing Machines

Gentlemen:

We learn from your letter of July 2 that you are manufacturing and exporting a variety of textile machines. As there is a demand here for high-quality dyeing machines, we will appreciate your sending us a copy of your illustrated catalogue, with details of your prices and terms of payment.

Yours truly,

Reply

Gentlemen:

We warmly welcome your enquiry of July 15 and thank you for your interest in our dyeing machines.

We are enclosing our illustrated catalogue and pricelist giving the details you ask for. As for the payment terms we usually require confirmed, irrevocable Letter of Credit payable by draft at sight.

We have already sold some of those machines to China and are now represented there by The Engineering Export Ltd, Bering. May we suggest that you contact the company directly? We think the firm may supply you with more details of our machines. We feel confident that you will find the goods are both excellent in quality and very reasonable in price.

With best regards.

Yours sincerely,

Unit Six Inquiry and Quotation 询盘与报盘

Section 3 Examples of Quotation and Replies

Sample 1

Dear Sirs,

We thank you very much for your letter of October 17, asking for our washing machines Model HTW 11 and Model HTW 14. We, as being requested, enclose our latest price list of this month and details of our conditions of sales and terms of payment. We have examined your proposal to place an order for a minimum number of our washing machines in return for a special allowance, but we feel it would be better to offer you a special allowance on the following sliding scale basis.

On purchases exceeding an annual total of:
    US$10,000 but not exceeding US$20,000 .... 1%
    US$20,000 but not exceeding US$30,000 .... 2%
    US$30,000 but not exceeding US$40,000 .... 3%
    US$40,000 and above... 4%
No special allowance could be given on annual total purchase below US$10,000.

We feel that the above arrangement would be more satisfactory to both of us and can assure you that these goods are very popular in the European markets, of which we have had much experience.

We look forward to your acceptance of our proposal and to your orders.

Yours faithfully,

W. H. Ausman

Reply

Dear Sirs,

We have received your offer of October 21 for 500 sets of washing machines Model HTW 11 and Model HTW 14 at US$35,000 with 3% discount.

In reply, we regret to inform you that the prices you quoted are found too high. We trust the quality of your produces and would welcome the opportunity to do business with you. May we suggest that you give us more discount, say 5% on your quoted price of US $ 35,000? We believe that would help to introduce your goods to our market. Should you be prepared to grant us that rate of discount, we would be pleased to come to terms and place with you an order.

We are anticipating your early reply.

Yours faithfully,

W. Philips
Business Manager

Sample 2

Dear Sirs,

We thank you for your enquiry of August 22 and are pleased to send you our quotation for the goods you required as follows:

Commodity: "White Rabbit" Brand Woolen Mixed Blanket No.3
Size: 74×84 inch
Weight: 4 lbs
Color: yellow, brown, green assortment
Quantity: 1,000 pcs
Price: US $ 40.00 per piece CIF Montreal
Shipment: October

You are cordially invited to take advantage of this attractive offer. We are anticipating a large order from the United States, and that will cause a sharp rise in price. We look forward to receiving your order.

Yours faithfully,

Reply

Dear Sirs,

"White Rabbit" Brand Woolen Mixed Blanket

Thank you for your quotation of August 24 for 1,000 pieces of the captioned goods.

We immediately contacted our customers and they showed great interest because there is a growing demand for woolen blankets. The prices you quoted, however, are found too much on the high side. ABC Company, one of our customers, told us that they would possibly order 2,000 pieces of the goods, provided that you can reduce your price to US $ 38.00 per piece.

ABC is one of the leading importers in our country, so there is a good chance of finalizing an order with them if the present price can be lowered to meet their requirement. We hope you will take advantage of this chance so that you will benefit from the expanding market.

We are most anxious that you will do your utmost to reduce the price and we await your reply with great interest.

Yours faithfully,

Sample 3

Dear Sir or Madam,

Your company has been introduced to us by one of our business partners as a prospective purchaser of china. As this item comes within our business scope, we shall be pleased to enter into business relations with you at an early date.

To give you a general idea of the various kinds of china now available for export, we are enclosing a brochure and a price list. Quotations and samples will be airmailed to you after receiving your specific inquiry.

We are looking forward to your early reply.

Yours sincerely,

Sample 4

Dear Sir or Madam,

We are enclosing the drawings of two printing machines, requesting you to inform us of the price and the delivery date.

If your quotations are suitable and the machines prove satisfactory, we shall be able to place orders with you, as we need some more machines to complete our factory plant. We shall be pleased if your representatives should call on us as soon as possible.

Yours sincerely,

Sample 5

Dear Sir or Madam,

We have received your circular of May 14, in which a price-list of the Japanese toys was enclosed.

We are interested in this line of the Japanese goods.

We often receive inquiries about them from our clients in various Latin America countries. Therefore, we shall be able to give you considerable orders, if your goods are suitable in quality and reasonable in price.

We would be pleased if you could send us some samples with the best terms at your earliest convenience.

Yours sincerely,

Unit Six　Inquiry and Quotation　询盘与报盘

◆ 本章句式

(1) Heavy enquiries witness the quality of our products.

(2) As soon as the price picks up inquiries will revive.

(3) Inquiries for carpets are getting more numerous.

(4) Inquiries are so large that we can only than allot you 200 cases.

(5) Inquiries are dwindling.

(6) Inquiries are dried up.

(7) They promised to transfer their future inquiries to Chinese Corporations.

(8) Generally speaking inquiries are made by the buyers.

(9) Mr. Baker is sent to Beijing to make an inquiry at China National Textiles Corporation.

(10) We regret that the goods you inquire about are not available.

(11) In the import and export business we often make inquiries at foreign suppliers.

(12) To make an inquiry about our oranges a representative of the Japanese company paid us a visit.

(13) We cannot take care of your inquiry at present.

(14) Your enquiry is too vague to enable us to reply you.

(15) Now that we've already made an inquiry about your articles will you please reply as soon as possible?

(16) China National Silk Corporation received the inquiry sheet sent by a British company.

(17) Thank you for your inquiry.

(18) We have the offer ready for you.

(19) I come to hear about your offer for fertilizers.

(20) Please make us a cable offer.

(21) Please make an offer for the bamboo shoots of the quality as that in the last contract.

(22) We are in a position to offer tea from stock.

(23) We'll try our best to get a bid from the buyers.

(24) We'll let you have the official offer next Monday.

(25) I'm waiting for your offer.

(26) We can offer you a quotation based upon the international market.

(27) We have accepted your firm offer.

(28) We offer firm for reply 11 a.m. tomorrow.

(29) We'll let you have our firm offer next Sunday.

(30) We're willing to make you a firm offer at this price.

(31) Could you offer us FOB prices.

(32) All your prices are on CIF basis.

(33) Can you make an offer, C&F London, at your earliest convenience?

(34) I'd like to have your lowest quotations, CIF Vancouver.

(35) Please make us a cable offer for 5 metric tons of walnut.

(36) Our offer is RMB 300 per set of tape-recorder, FOB Tianjin.

(37) We quote this article at $250 per M/T C&F.

Unit Seven Counter Offer, Firm Offer and Non-Firm Offer
还盘、实盘与虚盘

◆ Learning Objectives

a. Master specific writing requirements of quotations, offers and counter offers.

b. Distinguish and understand the writing differences between the firm offer and non-firm offer.

c. Master specific writing skills and requirements of offer responses.

An offer may either be a firm offer or a non-firm offer. A firm offer is a kind of offer which is made to a specific person or persons to express or imply a definite intention of the offeror to make a contract under a clear, complete and final trade terms. Once it is unconditionally accepted by the offeree within its validity, this firm offer cannot be revoked or amended and is binding on both offeror and offeree. Then the transaction is completed and a contract is concluded right away. A firm offer lapses when it exceeds the term of validity. The lapsed offer is no longer binding on the offeror. At this moment, even if the offeree expresses his acceptance, the offeror is entitled to refuse it.

Contrary to a firm offer, a non-firm offer is an offer without engagement. It is unclear, incomplete and with reservation. It has no binding force upon the offeror. The trade terms are not indicated clearly and definitely. The content is not so completed as that of a firm offer. It has no term of validity. Moreover, the offeror makes the offer with reservation: the offer is subject to his final confirmation. So a non-firm offer often bears such wording "this offer is subject to our final confirmation", or "the prices are subject to change without notice".

Firm offer can encourage offerees to make decision and thus close business. Non-firm offer is more flexible to the offeror as he can make decision of closing business according to the market situation. However, offerees often regard it as ordinary business dealings and pay little attention to it, which does no good to the conclusion of business.

Section 1　Introduction

1. Counter-Offer

An offeree needs to make response to the offer he has received. Sometimes an offeree partly or totally disagrees with the offer but puts forward his own proposals and this is called a counter offer. If the offeree finds any terms or conditions in the offer unacceptable, he can negotiate with the seller and make a counter offer to show his disagreement to the terms of payment, packing, shipment time, quantity or the date of delivery and state his own terms and conditions. In this case, the original offer is invalid, and the counter offer actually becomes a new offer from the original offeree. The original offerer or the seller now becomes the offeree and has the full right of acceptance or refusal. He may make a reply to the buyer's counter offer. This is called a counter-counter-offer. This process can go on for several rounds till business is concluded or called off.

In writing a counter offer, one has to state the terms most explicitly and use words carefully to avoid ambiguity or misunderstanding. When a buyer rejects an offer, he should write to thank the seller and explain the reason for rejection. A letter of counter offer is usually composed of three parts. The first paragraph is designed to acknowledge the receipt of the offer and express the buyer's thanks. The explanation of the reasons to make the counter offer and the raised new terms and conditions are presented in the second part which can be divided into separate paragraphs. The buyer may use the last part to express his hope for a prompt reply or put forward his suggestions to do business together.

(1) **Several kinds of counter offers**

1) Counter offer on price.
2) Asks for reduction of minimum quantity.
3) Counter offer on payment terms.
4) Asks for earlier delivery.
5) Asks for changing the package.
6) Counter offer on the discount of the goods.
7) Asks for more commission.

(2) **The key structure**

1) Opening Paragraph: Express your thanks with a courteous sentence.
2) Transitional Paragraph: (Counter offer)

   Express your difficulties to accept the offer and give your reasons.

   Express your conditions (suggestions) to counter offer.
3) Closing paragraph: Express your hope for acceptance of counter offer

2. Firm Offer and Non-Firm Offer

A firm offer is made when a seller promises to sell goods at a stated price within a stated

Unit Seven Counter Offer, Firm offer and Non-Firm Offer 还盘、实盘与虚盘

period of time. When making a firm offer, the time of shipment and the made of payment desired should be mentioned; in addition, an exact description of the goods should be given and if possible, pattern of sample.

Non-firm offer are usually made by means of sending catalogues, price list, proforma invoices and quotations, they are not legally binding on the offers and cannot be "accepted", however, it can be considered as an inducement to business.

Non-firm offer also means offer without engagement, it has no binding force upon the offeror and the offeree. The offeror is free from any obligations because the offer can be changed, revised and withdrawn at anytime. The non-firm offer are often sent in a variety of ways, sometimes in a form of letter, fax, price list, catalogue or even proforma invoice. Exporters usually make offers in reply to inquiries from importers.

Step 1, the opening part. The letter begins with a thank you expression and refers to a previous letter.

Step 2, the following part. Use the table or list to make the non-firm offer (including commodity, color, size, quantity, price, shipment, payment).

Step 3, the third part promotes the product in order to generate future business. The offeror encourages offeree to act and show confidence in future business.

Step 4, the closing part. To look forward to prompt reply.

Section 2 Examples of Counter Offer

Sample 1 Counter Offer on Price of Refrigerator

Dear Sirs,

Your Offer No.146 for QINDAO-LIEBHERR Refrigerators

We have received your offer No. 146 offering us 2,500 sets for three designs of the subject goods.

In reply, we regret to inform you that our clients find your price much too high. Information indicates that some kinds of the said articles made in other countries have been sold here at a level about 5% lower than that of yours.

We do not deny that the quality of your products is slightly better, but the difference in price should, in no case, be so big. To step up the trade, we counter offer as follows, subject to your reply here by 5 p.m. our time, February 18:

US$ 400.00 for BYD 212

US $ 365.00 for BYD 157
US $ 375.00 for BYD 219

As the market is of keen competition, we recommend your immediate acceptance.

Yours faithfully,

大意

敬启者:
事由:贵方第 146 号关于琴岛-利勃海尔电冰箱的报盘
我方已收到贵方第 146 号提供的 2 500 台三种规格电冰箱的报盘。
很抱歉通知贵方,我方用户发现贵方价格偏高。有信息显示,此地销售的其他国家生产的电冰箱价格要比贵方的低 5% 左右。
我方不否认贵方产品的质量较好,然而,不论怎样,价格也不能差异太大。为促进贸易,我方还盘如下,以贵方于我方时间 2 月 18 日下午五点前回复有效。
由于市场竞争激烈,建议贵方立即接受。
谨上

Sample 2   Counter Offer on Price of Hand-Embroidered Silk Scarf

Dear Sirs,

We thank you for your offer by telex of September 9 for 5,000 pieces of the captioned goods at Stg. 9.50 per piece CIF Hamburg.

We immediately contacted our customers and they showed great interest in the quality and designs of your products. However they said your price is too much on the high side, i.e., 10% higher than the average. They told us if you can reduce your price to Stg. 8.55 per piece, they will increase 1,000 pieces to the quantity. So there is a good chance of concluding a bigger transaction with them if you can meet their requirement.

We hope you will take advantage of this opportunity so that you will benefit from the expanding market.

We await your favorable reply with great interest.

Yours faithfully,

Unit Seven Counter Offer, Firm offer and Non-Firm Offer 还盘、实盘与虚盘

大意

敬启者：

感谢贵方9月3日电传所发标题下货物5 000件的报盘，每件价格为汉堡成本、保费运费在内价9.50英镑。

我方立即与客户取得了联系，他们对贵方产品的质量和设计表现出了极大的兴趣。然而，他们认为贵方价格偏高，也就是说，比平均价高出10％。他们表示，若贵方每件价格降到8.55英镑，将再增加1 000件的订货。因此，如果能满足他们的要求，这将是一大笔交易。我方希望能利用此次机会并从不断扩大的市场中获益。

期盼贵方有利的答复。

谨上

Sample 3 Buyer Asks for Reduction of Minimum Quantity

Dear Sirs,

Your Offer No. 123

We thank you for your fax of April 4 offering us six designs of Ornamental Cloth. However we regret to inform you that the minimum of 10,000 yards per design is too big for this market.

In case you can reduce the minimum to 7,000 yards per design, there is a possibility of placing orders with you, because a considerable quantity of this material is required on this market for manufacturing curtains, bed sheets, etc.

Your early reply will be highly appreciated.

Yours faithfully,

大意

敬启者：

事由：贵方第123号报价

感谢贵方4月4日传真发来的6种图样的装饰布的报盘，然而，很遗憾地告诉贵方10 000码的最低订购量对于该市场来说太多了。

如果贵方把每种花色的最低订购量降到7 000码，可能向贵方订货，因为该市场需要一定

数量的这种布料来做窗帘、床单等。

如蒙早日回复将不胜感激。

谨上

Sample 4 Counter Offer on Payment Terms

Dear Sirs,

We thank you for your quotation of February 3 for 1,000 sets of Panasonic 3188 Color TV. We find your price as well as delivery date satisfactory, however we would give our suggestion of an alteration of your payment terms.

Our past purchase of other household electrical appliances from you has been paid as a rule by confirmed, irrevocable letter of credit at sight. On this basis, it has indeed cost us a great deal. From the moment to open credit till the time our buyers pay us, the tie-up of our funds lasts about four months. Under the present circumstances, this question is particularly taxing owing to the tight money condition and unprecedented high bank interest.

In view of our long business relations and our amicable cooperation prospects, we suggest that you accept either "Cash against Documents on arrival of goods" or "Drawing on us at 60 day's sight".

Your first priority to the consideration of the above request and an early favorable reply will be highly appreciated.

Yours faithfully,

大意

敬启者：

感谢贵方2月3日对1 000台松下3188彩电的报价。我方对贵方的价格及交货期感到满意。但是，我方建议贵方对支付方式作一下改动。

按照惯例，我方以往从贵方购买家用电器的支付方式为保兑的、不可撤销的即期信用证。在此基础上，我方确实花费了很多资金。从开立信用证到用户支付我方货款，占用资金持续4个月左右。在目前情况下，由于银根紧缩及银行空前高的利率，这种支付方式对我方而言特别难以负担。

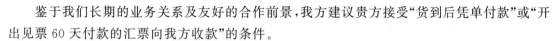

鉴于我们长期的业务关系及友好的合作前景,我方建议贵方接受"货到后凭单付款"或"开出见票60天付款的汇票向我方收款"的条件。

若贵方优先考虑上述要求并早日给予有利回复,我方将十分感谢。

谨上

Section 3　Examples of Firm Offer

Sample 1

Dear Sirs,

Re: Tin Foil Sheets

We have for acknowledgement your letter of May 15, 2021 and confirm having cabled you today in reply, as per confirmation copy enclosed. You will note from our cable that we are able to offer you 50 long tons of Tin Foil Sheets at the attractive price of £135 per long ton CFR Shanghai for delivery within one month after your placing order with us. Payment of the purchase is to be effected by an irrevocable letter of credit in our favor, payable by draft at sight in Pounds Sterling in London.

This offer is firm subject to your immediate reply which should reach us no later than the end of this month. There is little likelihood of the goods remaining unsold once this particular offer has lapsed.

Yours faithfully,

大意

敬启者:

贵方2021年5月15日函接悉。兹证实今日给贵方去电,详见所附电报抄本。从我方电报中,贵方将得悉,我们能以每长吨135英镑CIF上海的便宜价格报给贵方50长吨锡箔,在贵方订货后一个月交货。货款以我方为收益人的不可撤销的、凭即期汇票在伦敦议付的信用证,以英镑支付。

上述报盘,以贵方答复在不迟于本月底到达我方为有效。一旦报盘过期,此货不可能存留不售。

谨上

Sample 2

Dear Sirs,

Re: SWC Sugar

We have received your letter of July 17, 2021 asking us to offer 10,000 tons of the subject sugar for shipment to London and appreciate very much your interest in your product.

To comply with your request, we are quoting you as follows:
    Commodity: Superior White Crystal Sugar
    Packing: To be packed in new gunny bags of 100 kgs each
    Quantity: Ten Thousand tons
    Price: U.S. Dollars One Hundred and Five per ton CIF London
    Payment: 100% by irrevocable and confirmed letter of credit to be opened on our favor and to be drawn at sight
    Shipment: one month after receipt of letter of credit

Your attention is drawn to fact that we have not much ready Stock on hand. Therefore, it is imperative that, in order to enable us to effect early shipment, your letter of credit should be opened in time if our price meets with your approval.

We are awaiting your immediate reply.

Yours faithfully,

大意

敬启者：

    事由：优质白砂糖

    贵方2021年7月17日来函收悉。信中要求我方报标题砂糖10 000吨，发往伦敦。对贵方有意购买我方产品一事，我们表示衷心的感谢。

    兹按贵方要求报价如下：

    商品：优质白砂糖

    包装：新麻袋包装，每包100千克

    数量：10 000吨

    价格：每吨105美元，CIF伦敦

    支付条件：凭即期汇票支付的、保兑的、不可撤销的信用证付款，信用证以我方为受益人

    发货日期：收到信用证后一个月发货

请注意,我们手头的现有存货不多,为使我们尽快装船,你们如同意我方所开价格,务请及时开立信用证。

盼望贵方早日答复。

Section 4 Examples of Non-Firm Offer

Sample 1

Dear Sirs,

We have received your letter of August 7, informing us that you can supply us 15,000 AZ-3467 all-weather compasses at US＄349.00 per set FOB Tokyo.

To be frank with you, we like the design and craftsmanship of your compasses, but I your price is rather too high to be acceptable. As you know. the price of compasses has been declining in the last six months. We have to point out that manufacturers in other countries, including South Korea, are actually lowering their prices according to a market survey made by us recently.

Yours faithfully,

Sample 2

Dear sirs,

We thank you for your letter of July 10, 2023 and have pleasure in offering you the following:

Commodity: embroidered satin mini skirts.
Quantity:10,000 dozens.
Price: ＄50 per dozen CFR New York.
Packing: in see-through plastic bags.
Shipment: in August 2008.
Payment: by irrevocable L/C, payable by draft at sight.

This offer is subject to our confirmation. If you find it acceptable, let us have your reply as soon as possible.

Yours faithfully,

Sample 3

Dear Mr. Green,

We have carefully studied your counter offer of 27 June to our offer of Cotton Underwear but regret to inform you that it is impossible for us to accept it.

The prices we quoted in our letter of 18 May have left us with only a very small margin. In fact, they are much lower than those of other suppliers for products of similar quality. The cotton used in the production of our "Dragon" range undergoes a special patented process that prevents shrinkage and increases durability. Moreover, the fact that we are the largest supplier of Cotton Underwear in this country adequately shows the value of our products.

We will be equally happy whether you accept our present offer or contact us items. We hope to hear from you and will carefully study any proposals likely to lead to future business between us.

Sincerely,

◆ 本章知识提示

还盘(counter offer)是交易的一方在接到一方发盘后,不能完全同意对方的交易条件,为了进一步洽商交易,针对另一方的发盘内容提出不同的建议。这种口头的或书面的表示在国际贸易中称为还盘或还价。实盘(firm offer)是指卖方向买方发出的在一定价格下、一定期限内出售货物的承诺。实盘一经对方接受,就具有法律效力,卖方不得随意撤回。虚盘(non-firm offer)是发盘人所做的不肯定交易的表示,虚盘无须详细的内容和具体条件,也不注明有效期,仅表示交易的意向,不具有法律效力。

还盘不一定是还价格,对支付方式、装运期等主要交易条件提出不同的建议也属于还盘。在拟写还盘的信函时,一定要注意要有礼貌,首先应对对方的报盘表示感谢,然后谈及非常抱歉不能接受对方的某项条件,陈述不能接受的理由,例如价格高出了市场现行价格、装运期太晚等。接着提出自己的建议,最后表示希望对方能够接受,并早日回复等。如果买方不同意某一报价或实盘的某些交易条件,就发还盘。在还盘中,买方可以就某些交易条件提出异议并陈述自己的观点。这样的变更,不管多么微不足道,都意味着交易要在新的基础上重新谈判。原来的发盘人卖方现成了受盘人,完全有权力接受或拒绝还盘。在后一种情况下,也可以发自己的还盘。这个过程可以进行很多回合,直到达成或取消交易。

实盘就是肯定的报盘,即使交易中途价格变动也不能再更改。实盘通常包括以下几项:感谢对方的询盘、商品的名称、质量、数量及规格、价格、支付条件、佣金或折扣、包装及交货日期

Unit Seven Counter Offer, Firm offer and Non-Firm Offer 还盘、实盘与虚盘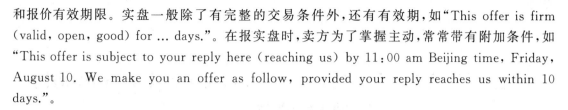

和报价有效期限。实盘一般除了有完整的交易条件外,还有有效期,如"This offer is firm (valid, open, good) for … days."。在报实盘时,卖方为了掌握主动,常常带有附加条件,如 "This offer is subject to your reply here (reaching us) by 11:00 am Beijing time, Friday, August 10. We make you an offer as follow, provided your reply reaches us within 10 days."。

◆ 本章句式

1. Opening

(1) In reply to your letter of offer, we regret to say that our customers here find your price rather high and above the prevailing market level.

(2) We feel regretful for inability to accept your offer.

(3) We are sorry that we cannot take advantage of your firm offer this time.

(4) Unfortunately, we cannot accept your request.

(5) Much to our regret, we are unable to entertain your offer because the … you quoted do not meet our clients' requirement.

(6) We regretfully learn from your letter that your present price is …% higher than …

2. Making Counter Offers

(1) Owing to the heavy commitment of our manufacturer, we are unable to entertain fresh booking for the moment.

(2) According to our investigation, the market is now showing a decline, so we are expecting an adjustment of the price at the end of this month.

(3) We hope this counter offer will meet your approval and we shall place regular orders with you on receipt of your confirmation.

(4) The best we can do is to make a reduction of …% in our previous quotation.

(5) This new model of machine has all the qualities of the one you asked for, and it has added advantage of being lighter, stronger and more durable.

(6) We counter offer as follows:

(7) This is our rock-bottom price; we cannot make any further reduction.

(8) The offer we obtained recently from other sources for the same product is around … below yours.

(9) We have cut price to the limit. We regret, therefore, being unable to comply with your request for further reduction.

(10) Should you be ready to reduce your price by, say, …%, we might conclude terms.

Unit Eight　Orders and Acknowledgements
订单与接受

◆ *Learning Objectives*

a. Master the specific writing requirements of the order;
b. Familiar with the writing format of the order confirmation letter.

The order is a specified term statement of the goods provided by the Supplier and is the order certificate issued to the Supplier. The acknowledgement (acceptance) is in the party trading in the import and export business on the other party's offer or counter offer, and expressed full consent, is an oral or written expression. The acceptance is an essential part of making a deal and making a contract, which is called a commitment in law. It is to refer to the full content of the validity of the contract, willing to conclude a contract.

Section 1　Introduction

The order from a buyer is an offer to buy. Going through inquiry, quotation and several rounds of offer and counter offer, the seller and the buyer come to an agreement and the buyer may place an order with the seller. An order can be sent by a letter, a printed order form, a fax or an E-mail message. Usually well-known customers will probably use a form while a new customer or one placing a single order often writes a letter.

No matter what forms the buyer may choose, the order must be accurate, clear, specific and complete. The buyer must make the seller know clearly the exact goods he/she wants. The language of an order letter should be definite, exact and simple, Experiences show it is important that the buyer should pay special attention to spelling and any decimal point. The writer is strongly recommended to double check all price calculations to avoid making mistakes before sending the letter.

An order may include the descriptions of the following specific items:

a. Name of commodity;

b. Quality requirements and specifications;

c. Quantity;

d. Price;

e. Packing and marking;

f. Terms of delivery;

g. Terms of payment;

h. Documents.

A letter of order is mostly composed of three parts. The buyer prepares the first part to refer to the previous contact, and describes the details of the order in the second part, followed by the last part that states the terms and form of payment, the anticipated date of delivery and the mode of transportation.

Upon receipt of an order, the seller should acknowledge it in good time. If the goods ordered are available, the seller had better lose no time to state the acknowledgement and repeat the terms in the letter of order. The seller, in the acknowledgement, may praise the buyer for his or her wise order, express thanks to longtime customer or deliver a hearty welcome to a new customer. Quite often a letter of acknowledgement includes the following contents:

a. Acknowledgement of the order with expressions of thanks;

b. Restatement of the shipping instructions and the terms of payment;

c. Favorable comments on the goods ordered;

d. Recommendation of other products likely to be of interest;

e. Hope for further orders.

When the seller cannot accept an order because the goods required are out of stock or the price and the specifications have been changed, he or she should write a rejecting letter with utmost care immediately so as to alleviate or eliminate the negative impact on future business with the customer.

Once the order issued by the buyer is accepted by the seller, it cannot be withdrawn at will, and the buyer and the seller will sign the contract to execute the contract in accordance with the conditions on the order. Therefore, when writing an order, people must describe the transaction conditions completely, especially the main transaction conditions clearly, such as the commodity name, specifications, quantity, price, payment terms, delivery date, etc. The order may be accepted by the buyer, or it may be the purchase order sent by the buyer voluntarily. The order should be clearly written with accurate language to indicate all the conditions in the transaction. Many trading companies now use formal printing orders to ensure that no important conditions are omitted.

Section 2　Examples of Orders

Sample 1：Order of Cashmere Sweater

Dear Sirs,

We thank you very much for your quotation of 15 February and the sample sweaters. We find both quality and prices satisfactory and are pleased to place an order with you for the following：

    10 doz. cashmere sweaters, small, US＄120.00 per doz.
    20 doz. cashmere sweaters, medium, US＄150.00 per doz.
    15 doz. cashmere sweaters, large, US＄180.00 per doz.

Packing：Each sweater to be packed in a poly bag, per dozen in a tin-lined carton, with 10 dozen cartons in a wooden case. Other terms as per your quotation.

We expect to find a good market for the above and hope to place further and larger orders with you in the near future.

Yours faithfully,

大意

敬启者：
    感谢贵方2月15日的报价和羊绒毛衣样品。我方对贵方产品的质量和价格均感到满意，兹乐意以贵方所指定的价格订购如下货物：
    10打 羊绒毛衣，小号，每打120.00美元
    20打 羊绒毛衣，中号，每打150.00美元
    15打 羊绒毛衣，大号，每打180.00美元
    包装：每件羊绒毛衣装一塑料袋，每打装一个锡纸箱，每120个锡纸箱装一木箱，其余条款按照贵方报价。
    我方期待着在本区为以上产品开辟一个良好的市场，并希望在未来向贵方下更多、更大的

Unit Eight Orders and Acknowledgements 订单与接受

订单。

谨上

Sample 2: Order of Canned Beef

><><><><><><><><><><><><><><><><><><><><><><><><><

PURCHASE ORDER
No. BD/135
Messrs: China National Cereals, Oils & Foodstuffs
Import & Export Corp, Shaanxi Branch 130 Lianhu Rood, Shaanxi, China

We confirm our agreement on purchase of the following goods:

Description: A-I Grade Canned Pork Luncheon Meat of the following four specifications:
A. 225 GM net weigh
B. 350 GM net weight
C. 425 GM net weight
D. 450 GM net weight

Quantity: (Case)
A. 100
B. 200
C. 300
D. 400

Packing: By standard export case of 120 cans each.

Unit Price: CIF net New York per case in U.S. dollars
A. 30.20
B. 40.50
C. 50.60
D. 60.40

Payment: 100% by irrevocable letter of credit opened immediately through First National City Bank, N.Y. and drawn at sight.

Delivery:
For Item A and B: Prompt shipment;
For Item C and D: One month after receipt of L/C.

Shipping Marks: On each and every case, the following shipping mark should be stenciled.

Remark: In addition to the ordinary shipping documents, please also submit Certificate of Origin for each shipment.

Yours faithfully,

<u>大意</u>

购货确认订单

票号:BD/135

致:中国粮油进出口公司,陕西分公司,莲湖路130号,中国西安

兹确认我方统一订购如下货品:

品名:甲级罐装午餐肉

规格(均为净重装)

A.225克净重装

B.350克净重装

C.425克净重装

D.450克净重装

数量:箱

A.100

B.200

C.300

D.400

包装:每箱装120听的标准出口纸箱

单价:每箱CIF纽约价(单位:美元)

A.30.20美元

B.40.50美元

C.50.60美元

D.60.40美元

支付方式:通过纽约花旗银行开立100%不可撤销的即期信用证

装运:A号和B号货品立即装运

　　　C号和D号货品在收到信用证一个月后装运

装运唛头:每个箱体上都刷上唛头

附记:除了正常的装转单据外,每批货品都应有原产地证明书

谨上

Unit Eight Orders and Acknowledgements 订单与接受

Section 3 Examples of Acknowledgements

Sample 1: Acceptance of Order for Bed Sheets & Pillow Cases

Dear Sirs,

We were very pleased to receive your Order No. 345 for bed sheets and pillow cases. We accordingly accept the order and shall arrange delivery as soon as possible. We have confidence that you will be completely satisfied with our goods when you received them.

As you may not be aware of the wide range of goods we deal in we are enclosing a copy of our catalogue and hope that our handling of your first order with us will lead to further business between us and mark the beginning of a happy working relationship.

Yours faithfully,

大意

敬启者：

非常高兴收到了贵方第345号订购床单和枕套的订单。我方接受订单并将尽早安排装运。我方相信，贵方一定会对我方的货品感到满意。

也许贵方并不了解我方经营的商品范围非常广泛，兹随函附寄产品目录一份。希望我方对贵方首批订单的执行不但能促进我们双方更多的交易，而且将标志着我们愉快合作的开始。

谨上

Sample 2: Acceptance of Order for Canned Beef

Dear Sirs,

We are very pleased to receive your order No. BD/135 Canned Beef. We accept the order and are enclosing you our Sales Confirmation No. 354 in duplicate of which please countersign and return one copy to us for our file. We trust you will open the relative L/C at an early date.

As to the Items A and B, we shall arrange delivery as soon as we get your L/C, and for items C and D we shall ship accordingly.

Hoping the goods will turn out to your entire satisfaction and we may have further orders from you.

Yours faithfully,

大意

敬启者：

我方已获悉贵方第 BD/135 号订购罐装牛肉的订单。我方按相应的条款接受订单并随函附寄我方第 345 号销售确认书，一式两份，请会签后寄回一份供我方存档，我方相信贵方将尽早开立有关信用证。

至于 1 号和 2 号货品，收到贵方信用证后，我方将安排装运。而 3 号和 4 号货品，我方也将按相应的条件装运。

希望货品能令贵方满意，同时也希望继续收到贵方订单。

谨上

Section 4 Different Types of Orders and Replies

1. Offering Substitute

Sample 1: Offering Rayon in Place of Watered Silk

Dear Sirs,

Thank you for your fax of yesterday (April 3) with your order No. 456 for 5,000 meters of 100 cm wide watered silk.

We are sorry we can no longer supply this silk. Fashions constantly change and in recent years the demand for watered silk has fallen to such an extent that we have ceased to produce it.

In its place we can offer you our new "Gossamer" brand of rayon. This is a finely woven, hard wearing, non-creatable material with a most attractive luster. The large number of repeat orders we regularly receive from leading distributors and dress manufacturers is clear evidence of the popularity of this brand. At the low price of only stg. 1.80 a meter this rayon is much cheaper than silk and its appearance is just attractive.

We are sending you by parcel post a sample cutting for your reference hoping you may be interested in our new article. We are awaiting your order with keen interest.

Yours faithfully,

大意

敬启者：

  感谢贵方昨天（4月3号）的第456号传真订单，订购5 000米幅宽100米的水洗丝。

  非常抱歉，这种产品我方现在无货可供。由于时装在不断变化，近年来，水洗丝的需求减少，所以我方已停止生产此类产品。

  我方可以向贵方提供新产品"薄纱"牌人造丝。此产品质地精良，外观漂亮，耐穿且不打皱，因而非常畅销。我方经常收到分销商及服装商的大量复购订单就是例证。此类人造丝售价每米只有1.8英镑，比水洗丝价格低且外观同水洗丝一样漂亮。

  现邮寄一些剪样，以供参考。希望贵方能对我方产品感兴趣。热切盼望贵方的订单。

  谨上

Sample 2: Offering Zinc Oxide 99% in place of Zinc Oxide

Dear Sirs,

We have received your Order No. 246 for a minimum quantity of 100 tons of Zinc Oxide 99.5%.

Had you contacted us earlier we could have complied with your request to the full. But now, with our stock appreciably diminished, the maximum we can supply is 50 tons. The remainder can be replaced by Zinc Oxide 99% which is a new type almost similar to 99.5% but priced lower by 5%. One of our clients purchased some tons a few weeks ago from our stock and he has made a good comment on it.

We are sending you by parcel post some samples of Zinc Oxide 99% for your consideration and appreciate it if you will amend your Order Sheet on or before the 10th of this month.

Yours faithfully,

敬启者：

获悉贵方第246号订单,起定量为100吨氧化锌99.5%。

如果贵方能提早跟我方联系,我方就能完全满足贵方要求。然而,由于我方存货明显减少,最多只能供应50吨,其余部分可用新型产品氧化锌99%替代。此产品不但与氧化锌99.5%性能相近,而且其价格要便宜5%。我方的一个客户几周前购买过此产品,反馈很好。

兹邮寄氧化锌99%样品,以供贵方参考。若贵方能在本月10日(或之前)修正订单,我方将不胜感激。

谨上

2. Letters of Regret

Sample 1: Rejecting Ordered Price

Dear Sirs,

We refer to your Order No. 345 and regret to say that we are not able to accept your bid price for Frozen Rabbit Meat.

As you may be aware that the prices for foodstuffs have gone up sharply owing to the rough weather. So it is impossible to purchase supplies at economic prices. Moreover, we have improved our packing method, as you may have seen from our samples, which cost us a lot. The price, therefore, is 8% higher than your bid.

For the market is firm with an upward tendency, we advise you to accept our price without delay. In view of our long business connection we will definitely keep supplies available for you if you amend the price in your order within 5 days.

Yours faithfully,

大意

敬启者：

回复贵方第345号订单。非常抱歉,我方不能接受贵方对冷冻兔肉的买价。

贵方可能注意到,由于气候原因,食品价格已经急剧上升,所以现在不可能再以较低的价格购买此货。况且贵方从所提供的样品中也可以了解到,我方改进了产品包装。这使我方花费不少,所以产品价比贵方的买价高出8%。

由于市场坚挺且有上涨的趋势,我方建议贵方立即接受我方价格。考虑到我们之间的长期贸易联系,如果贵方能在 5 天内修正订单,我方将保证供货。

谨上

Sample 2: Rejection for the Reason of No Supply

Dear Sir,

Your Order No. 456

Referring to the 50 tons of Silicon Steel Sheet under your Order No. 456, we regret to tell you that we have no stock of the goods you required for the time being and do not expect further deliveries for at least another two months. Before then you may have been able to obtain the goods elsewhere, but if not we will revert to this matter as soon as our new supplies come up.

We are enclosing 2 copies of our catalog coveting all the articles available at present. If you need any of the items please inform us. We assure you that your requirement will receive our prompt attention at all times.

Yours faithfully,

大意

敬启者:
　　回复贵方关于 50 吨硅钢板的第 456 号订单。非常抱歉,贵方订购的货品我方时下无货,而且两个月之内不可能有新的进货。在此之前,也许贵方可以从其他方面获得货源。如果不能,我方愿意在有了新货之后重新考虑此订单。
　　随函附寄两份我方目前可供货品的目录。如果贵方需要某些货品,请告知我方。请相信,贵方的要求随时都会得到我方及时处理。

谨上

Sample 3: Rejecting Buyer's Delivery Terms

Dear Sirs,

Thank you for your Order No. 93120 for 1,000 sets of "SHARP" Brand Color T.V., but since you make delivery before Christmas a firm condition, we deeply regret that we cannot supply you at present.

The manufacturers are finding it impossible to meet current demand for their stock is exhausted but consecutive new orders are pouring in. Though the workers are speeding up the production, the buyers still have to wait. Another client of us placed, through us, an order for 500 sets a month ago, and is informed that his order could not be dealt with until the beginning of February next year.

We are sorry that we can't meet your requirement this time. But if you are interested in other brands, please let us know.

Yours faithfully,

大意

敬启者：

感谢贵方第93120号订单，订购1 000台"夏普"牌彩色电视机，但是贵方坚持要在圣诞节前交货，而我方目前无法供货，对此深表歉意。

生产商认为很难满足目前的市场需求，因为他们的库存几近告急，而新的订单源源不断。尽管工人加紧生产，购货商还是要等货。我方的一个客户在一个月前通过我方订购了500台，最近得到消息说他们的订单等到明年2月初才能执行。

非常抱歉，这次我方无法满足贵方的要求，但贵方如果对其他品牌感兴趣，请告知我们。

谨上

Sample 4: Declining the Order Because of Delayed Loading

Dear Sirs,

We thank you very much for your order No.135 of October 31. We regret having to refuse this, but the delivery date stipulated by you does not give us sufficient time to ship your order.

The minimum period necessary where goods have to be prepared for shipment is five to six weeks. We are anxious to serve you but are sure you will see the need for giving us a little more time to suit your requirement.

Yours faithfully,

敬启者：

非常感谢贵方 10 月 31 日的 135 号订单。很抱歉，我方不得不婉谢此订单，因为贵方指定的交货日期并没有给我方足够的时间装运贵方订购的货品。

准备装运货品最少要 5～6 个星期，虽亟盼能为贵方效劳，但是相信贵方能了解，必须给予我方稍多的时间以达到贵方的要求。

谨上

Sample 5：Refusing to Orders due to Limited Production Equipment

Dear Sirs,

We thank you very much for your order November 3. After careful consideration on your request, however, we have come to the conclusion that it would be better for us to decline your order in this case.

In order to reach the limit you required in your specifications we would have to install a large amount of special equipment at our plant, and this would not be possible before next January next year without interrupting our normal production.

We are really very sorry not to be in a position to accept your order, but hope that you will understand our situation. Please let us have any other inquiries, as we shall be only too pleased to meet your requirements if it is within our power.

Yours faithfully,

大意

敬启者：

多谢贵方 11 月 3 日的订单。在仔细分析贵方要求之后，我方认为这次拒绝贵方的订单对我方较为有利。

为了达到贵方规格说明书所要求的，我方必须在工厂里大规模安装特殊设备。而且在不影响本公司正常生产的情况下，也不可能于明年 1 月之前完成。

无法接受贵方订单，实在感到很遗憾，但是希望贵方体谅我方的处境。如果能力所及，我方必然非常乐于满足贵方的要求，所以请惠赐其他的询价。

谨上

Sample 6: Declining the Order due to the Higher Price

Dear Sirs,

We thank you for your order No.228 asking for the shipment during September. However we regret our inability to book the order at the prices we quoted four months ago.

As you know well, wages and materials have risen considerably in these days in addition to the increase of taxes and we are reluctantly compelled to adjust our prices. The lowest prices we can quote now are as follow:

Model PA-218 $258   Model PB-318 $298   Model PC-428 $328

We do not want to influence you, but we think it is fair to mention that we shall have to increase those prices substantially again when our old stock of the goods is exhausted.

Please inform us by return whether you may book your order at these prices. We should be able to guarantee shipment during September as requested.

Yours faithfully,

大意

敬启者:
　　非常感谢贵方请求于9月装运的228号订单。很抱歉我方无法以4月前的报价确立订购。
　　如贵方所知,最近除了税金增加之外,劳资和材料价格也显著上涨,我方也不得已调整价格。我方现在所能报的最低价如下:
　　PA-218型　258美元
　　PB-318型　298美元
　　PC-428型　328美元
　　我方不想影响贵公司,但我方以为这种产品无存货之后,我方再度大幅度涨价是合理的。
　　请立即通知我方贵方是否能接受此价格确立订购。我方可保证应要求9月装运。
　　谨上

Unit Eight Orders and Acknowledgements 订单与接受

7. Acknowledge Order

Dear Sirs,

We are pleased to place the following order with you if you can guarantee shipment at Hong Kong to Keelung by March 30.

5 units of European furniture No.FA-23
3 pieces of Persian Carpet No. TC-18

Kindly confirm acceptance of our order by return and send advice of shipment with three copies of your invoice with B/L to our office in Beijing. We will send the bank draft upon receipt of them.

Yours faithfully,

大意

敬启者:
　　若贵公司能够保证于3月30日以前由香港驶往基隆的船只装运,兹乐于向贵方订购下列货品。
　　FA-23号欧式家具　5套
　　TC-18号波斯地毯　3件
　　请立即确认接受本公司的订单,并随同提单寄送贵公司发票3张及装运通知到北京公司。收到这些文件后,我方将立刻寄出银行汇票。
　　谨上

8. Orders Based on a Shorter Lead Time

Dear Sirs,

Thank you for your letter of August 23, with which you sent us details of your produce PH-61. We have now seen the samples and are prepared to give them a trial order, provided you can guarantee shipment on or before September 30.

The enclosed order is given strictly on this condition, and we reserve the right of cancellation and refusal of delivery after this date. Upon receipt of our acceptance, we will open a letter of credit immediately.

Yours faithfully,

大意

敬启者：
　　感谢贵方 8 月 23 日内附 PH-61 型产品详情的来信。目前已看过样品，如果贵方能够保证在 9 月 30 日或之前装船，我方准备试订。
　　附寄的订单是以此严格的条件而发的，对于此日期之后的交货，我方保有取消与拒绝的权利。一经收到贵方的承诺，我方会立即开出信用证。
　　谨上

9. Price Order

Dear Sirs,

We enclose a stock order for various merchandise of sundries. This order is not particularly urgent and the shipment within three months would be quite satisfactory, so we would like you to make a careful examination of the quality before shipment.

From the note on our order sheet you will see our approximate price limits and while we leave it to your discretion, we do not want to exceed these limits in any case. Please advice us when our order is completed and forward the shipping documents immediately.

Yours faithfully,

大意

敬启者：
　　兹附寄各种杂货用品的库存订单。这份订单并不特别紧急，于 3 个月内装船即可。因此，希望贵公司于装运前仔细检查货品的质量。
　　从本公司订单的注意要点来看，您会明白我方大概的限价。在留待贵方自行斟酌之际，我方希望在任何情况下都不要超过这些限价。订购的货品完成时，请通知我方，并请立即寄送装船文件。
　　谨上

10. Recommend Excellent Alternatives

Dear Sirs,

Thank you for your order of April 27. Unfortunately the goods ordered Model No. PC-618 are now out of stock and will not be available again before the end of June.

However we can offer the slightly superior and very similar quality model No. PH-628 instead, which is in stock and is perhaps more suitable for your purpose.

Please let us know whether you can accept it and receive the shipment of the goods which we have reserved for you. If you would care to cable us as soon as you receive our offer we would ship the goods at once.

Yours faithfully,

大意

敬启者：

感谢贵方4月27日的订单。非常不巧，贵公司订购的PC-618型货品目前已无存货，而且在6月下旬前也无法供应。

然而，我方可提供质量类似且更高级的PH-628型货品替代。该型目前有存货，而且可能更适合贵方。

请告知贵方是否能够接受及领取本公司为贵方保留的船货。若能收到本公司报价即刻拍发电报给本公司，我方可以立刻装运此货品。

谨上

11. Trial Order

Dear Sirs,

We thank you for your letter of March 23. We have studied your catalog and price list and have chosen five models for which we enclose our order.

We would like to stress that this is a trial order and if we are satisfied with your shipment, you can expect our regular repeat orders. To avoid any difficulties with the customs authorities here, please make sure that our shipping instructions are carefully observed.

For our credit standing we refer you to The XX Bank, Ltd, XX and International Trading Co., Ltd., XX.

Yours faithfully,

大意

敬启者：

　　感谢贵方 3 月 23 日的来信,兹已研讨过贵公司的目录与价目表,并已选定 5 型,随函附寄其订单。

　　我方要强调,这次是实验性订购,若贵公司的装运令人满意,贵方可以预期我方将定期重复订购。为避免与本地海关当局有所争执,请务必仔细审视本公司的装运指示。

　　至于我方的信用状况,请向 XX 银行 XX 分行及国际贸易公司 XX 分公司洽询。

　　谨上

12. Order of Required Documents

Dear Sirs,

We thank you for your letter of May 1 enclosing catalog and details of your terms. We have decided to place the following order with you and instructed the First Commercial Bank, Ltd., Beijing to open L/C in your favor, valid until August 1.

Please attach the following documents to your draft when executing the order: two bills of lading, three commercial invoices and insurance policy. Your invoice should be made on C.I.F. Keelung.

Please inform us by airmail at once when the goods have been dispatched.

Yours faithfully,

敬启者：

感谢贵方5月1日附有目录与交易条件详情的来信。决定向贵方下如下订单，并指示第一商业银行北京分行，以贵方为抬头开立截至8月1日的有效信用证。

履行订单时，将下列文件附列于贵方汇票中：2份提单、3份商业发票及保单。贵方发票应以到基隆到岸价为准。

货品发送后，请立即以航空邮件通知我方。

谨上

13. Quality, Weight, and Color are Required as for Sample Ordering

Dear Sirs,

Many thanks for your offer of October 15 in response to our inquiry for your product LA-115. We enclose our official order for 1,000 units which we understand you can supply from stock.

As indicated in our first inquiry, the quality must be up to the sample you sent to us, and the weight and color of the goods identical to that of the sample. Our order is placed on this condition.

Yours faithfully,

敬启者：

感谢贵方10月15日的报价，以答复我方对贵公司LA-115号产品的询价。随函附寄1 000件的正式订单，本公司知道贵方可由存货供应。

一如本公司在最初的询价函中指出的，质量必须达到贵方致送我方样品的水准。货品的重量与颜色也要与样品一致，本订单依此条件签发。

谨上

14. Confirm Order, Shipping Shipment

Dear Sirs,

We are very glad to receive your order for 50 units of classic furniture to be supplied to your own specifications. As we mentioned in our previous letter, shipment for the furniture made to the supplied specifications is not usually possible in less than five months, but we would like to help you and to give your order special priority.

You may rest assured that your furniture will be ready for shipment by September 30. We will inform you when your order is ready for dispatch and shall be pleased to assist you to the best of our ability at all times.

Yours faithfully,

大意

敬启者：
　　很高兴收到贵方自己提供设计书的50套古典家具订单。一如本公司上封信所提及的，按照所提供之设计书制作的家具，通常装运不能少于5个月。但是，愿优先处理贵方订单。
　　贵公司的家具保证在9月30日前完成装运准备。当贵方的订货发送时，我方会通知贵公司，乐于随时尽力协助贵公司。
　　谨上

15. Request for Delayed Shipment

Dear Sirs,

Thank you for your order No. 263 received today. Although in our letter of the 25th we promised delivery in not more than three weeks from receipt of your order, we now find that the components needed for these products have been held up in Hong Kong and may not arrive in time for us to have your order delivered within three weeks.

We shall, of course, do our utmost to complete your shipment by the date stipulated. However a delay of two weeks seems to be unavoidable, which please note. In the meantime we will keep you informed as to development.

Unit Eight Orders and Acknowledgements 订单与接受

Yours faithfully,

大意

敬启者：

今收到贵方263号订单。虽然25日的信函答应在收到贵方订单后不超过三周交货，但我方现在发现，这些产品所需要的零部件被卡在香港，可能无法及时送达，无法于三周内交出贵方订购货品。

我方自当尽力在约定日期之前完成贵方货品的装运，然而，请了解似乎难以避免会有两周的延误。同时，我会将而后的发展告知贵公司。

谨上

16. Acceptance of Order Requires General Order

Dear Sirs,

We thank you for your order No.225 of May 10 which we have accepted on the terms you proposed. As you know well, we always try to meet the reasonable wishes of our customers.

However we have to ask you to realize that this concession is exceptional and the future orders can be executed only on our normal trade terms.

We have enclosed our trade confirmation and look forward to receiving your repeat orders.

Yours faithfully,

大意

敬启者：

感谢贵方5月10日的225号订单，兹已经接受贵方所提出的条件。如贵方知悉，我方一直试图配合客户的合理要求。

务必请贵方了解，这次让步是例外，将来的订单只能按我方一般的交易条件执行。

附上本公司的交易确认书，并期待贵方再次订购。

谨上

18. Accept Orders and Request a Three-month Notice

Dear Sirs,

We are pleased to confirm your letter of march 15 with an order for 100 units model HP-108. We thank you for your decision to stock our goods regularly, and we are confident that the sales will satisfy you in every respect.

As we pointed out in our previous letter, orders are rushing and our stock has been nearly exhausted. In this order we will ship the goods you demand as requested in your letter. But please note that we need at least three months' advance notice to supply them in time.

In your next order, we would request you to give us more time. We look forward to receiving your further orders.

Yours faithfully,

大意

敬启者：
　　确认贵方3月15日附有100台HP-108型货品订单的信函。感谢贵方决定定期购入本公司产品，我方深信其销售在各方面都能令贵方满意。
　　如同我方前一封信所指出的，订单纷至，故库存几近空虚。在此订购中，将按贵方来函的请求装运贵方所需要的货品。但请贵方了解，要如期供应，我方需要至少3个月的预先通知。
　　下次订购时，请求贵方给我方较为充裕的时间。期待收到贵方再次的订购。
　　谨上

19. Avoid Inventory Shortages

Dear Sirs,

With reference to your letter of March 13, we note that you are not in a position to accept our request for a special discount.

We have decided, however, to give you a standing order for your article No. 28 and enclose our order No. 812. In order to avoid being out of stock of this line, we must ask you to make shipment by the end of May.

As this is very important to you as well as to us, we wish you to try your best in this matter and send your acceptance by return.

Yours faithfully,

大意

敬启者:
　　根据贵方3月13日的来信,注意到贵方不能接受本公司特别折扣的请求。
　　我方决定,继续订购贵方第28号商品,并附上第812号订单。为避免此商品告急,请贵方必须于5月底前装运。
　　由于此事对双方都很重要,希望贵方尽力而为,并立即回复承诺。
　　谨上

20. Confirm that the Order Quantity is Inconsistent

Dear Sirs,

We thank you for your order of August 28. On checking it, we notice a discrepancy between the figure in your letter and the quantities you specified in your order sheet, and therefore cabled you asking the real quantities you required.

Today we received your reply confirming that the figure is 1,500 pieces. We have pleasure in confirming that we have booked your order for 1,500 pieces. Shipment requested will be made as soon as we receive information that a letter of credit has been opened for the amount mentioned above.

Yours faithfully,

大意

敬启者:
　　感谢贵方8月28日的订单。经审核,发现贵方信上的数量与贵方订单所载之数量不符。因此,拍发电报向贵方询问所需要的确切数量。
　　今天收到贵方确认数量为1 500件的回函。兹乐于确认已登记贵方1 500件订单。一收到上述总额开立的信用证通知,将立即执行贵方要求的装运。
　　谨上

21. Notice of Delayed Shipment due to the Typhoon

Dear Sirs,

Your order for 500 units of electronic calculators is acknowledged with thanks.

In our letter of May 30, we stated estimated delivery would be two weeks from receipt of order; however, with the present dockworker's shortage, we doubt if we can keep on this. We assure you that we are doing everything we can do to get the electronic calculators away, and will cable you immediately we arrange shipment.

It is possible that you might prefer us to arrange for air-freight there be an appreciable delay. Please advise if you approve of this.

Yours faithfully,

大意

敬启者:
　　我方确认收到贵方500台电子计算机的订单。
　　在5月30日的信函,兹提到估计的交货日期为接到订单两周后。然而,由于目前码头工人短缺,我方不一定可遵守此日期。兹向贵方保证当尽力发送电子计算器,且在安排装运时立刻打电报通知贵方。
　　万一察觉将延误,可能贵方宁可要本公司安排空运,若您赞成这么做,请惠予通知。
　　谨上

◆ 本章知识提示

　　1.订单是供货方依照买方的要求提供一个指定数量的货物条款声明,是买方向供货方发出的订货凭据。
　　接受是在进出口业务中交易的一方在接到另一方的发盘或还盘,并表示完全同意,是一种口头或书面的表示。接受是达成交易和订立合同必不可少的环节,在法律上叫作承诺。它是指受盘人在发盘有效期内完全同意发盘的全部内容,愿意订立合同的一种表示。
　　2.接受应由受盘人采用声明或做出其他行为的方式表示,并且这种表示传达给发盘人才开始有效。缄默或不行动本身不是接受。所谓声明是指书面文字表达相关意思;所谓行为是根据相关发盘的意思或依照当事人之间已确立的习惯做法所做出的行为,例如,卖方用发运货物或买方用支付货款等行为来表示同意。因此,采用某种行为的方式来表示接受并不是任意的行为,而是必须符合书面文字内容的行为。

一项有效的接受一般具备以下几个条件:第一,一项有效的接受必须是受盘人对一项实盘的完全接受。就是说,接受的内容必须同对方的实盘的各项条件严格一致,若接受中含有对原发盘内容的增加、限制或其他修改,接受均不能成立,应作为拒绝或还盘。第二,一项有效的接受必须是发盘所规定的受盘人表示才有效。任何第三者针对该项发盘表示接受,均无法律效力,发盘人不受约束。公开发盘除外,任何人都可以按规定办法表示接受。第三,一项有效的接受必须是受盘人在发盘的有效期内或合理的时间内表示接受才有效。假如一项实盘规定了明确的、具体的有效期限,发盘人只有在此期限内表示接受才有效。假如一项实盘未规定具体的有效期,应在合理时间内表示接受才有效。

接受可以简单地表示,如"接受贵方×月×日的实盘"。也可以较详细地表示,在接受函中重述主要的交易条件。在表示接受时常用 accept 一词,在使用这个词时要注意其时态。例如:

"We accept your firm offer. / We have accepted your firm offer."表明买方明确接受了卖方的报盘,即交易已宣告成立。

"We are accepting your offer."表明买方正在考虑接受,并没有肯定表示接受,因此交易尚未达成。

3.买卖双方必须多次交换报价、还价,直到双方达成协议。但是,有时买方只凭借卖方邮寄的目录、样品、价目表而直接订购。这时,只要卖方确认订购即可成立买卖契约。因此,双方需要以书面确认买卖契约。

4.必须以书面形式确认的,包括买方寄出的订单、合同、购货确认书,以及卖方发出的销售确认书(soles note)、订单确认书(confirmation of order)等。这些文件无固定格式,也可以书信形式写,但是要详细写明货品名称、数量、价格、装运期、运输方式、保险、付款条件、唛头等,以免买方误解。

5.订单及确认书是根据,必须审慎确认无误,并注意其专门用语,有效加以使用。例如:重量单位要用长吨(英)、短吨(美)或吨(法);清点数量时,应以装船重量条件(shipped weight term)或到岸重量条件(landed weight terms)为标准;是否要以样品决定质量,如有需要,该以卖方样品(seller's sample)或买方样品(buyer's sample)为准;价格是采用到岸价(CIF)、还是离岸价(FOB);付款条件是信用证(L/C)、付款交单(D/P)、承兑交单(D/A),或是订购同时付现(C.W.O)。

6.其他诸如保险采用一切险(A.A.R)、全损险(T.L.O)还是特别条款(Special Clause)?船期明确与否?包装方法如何?质量是以装船质量条件(shipped quality term)或卸货质量条件(landed quality term)为准?这些都是问题。

7.订单是开立信用证的基础,必须审慎记载,以免产生误会。千万不要与信用证字面相异,或以为对方了解而省略简化,防止产生买方拒绝付款等严重后果。

8.订货信的写作应注意三点:

(1)行文式订货内容的写法:①开头语②订货内容(商品名称、数量、单价、付款、交货期、保险、包装等)③结束语。

(2)列表式订货内容的写法。

(3)填写订单/确认书时说明信的写法：order 与 indent 可互换，后者比前者更正式，卖方收到后者只要接受即可，可以把它看作订货合同，因此其内容也更详细。

◆ 本章句式

1. Placing Orders

(1) We are pleased to enclose an order we have received from ... for ...

(2) We place this order on the understanding that the consignment is dispatched by ... and that we reserve the right to cancel it and to refuse delivery after the date.

(3) Reference is made to exchange of correspondence between us, and we confirm having placed with you the following order:

(4) In reply, we wish to order from you the items in your quotation and will apply for governmental approval to import them.

(5) We confirm our agreement on purchase of the following goods:

(6) We find both quality and prices satisfactory and we are pleased to give you an order for the following items on the understanding that they will be supplied from stock at the prices mentioned.

(7) Your samples of ... have received favorable reaction from our clients, and we are pleased to enclose our order for ...

(8) We have the pleasure of sending you an order for ... at US$ ...

(9) The particulars are detailed in the enclosed order sheet No. ...

(10) As we are in urgent need of the goods, we find it necessary to stress the importance of making punctual shipment within validity of L/C.

2. Acknowledging Orders

(1) We have duly received your Sales Contract No. ...

(2) Your compliance will be appreciated.

(3) We are very pleased to receive your order and confirm that all the items required are in stock.

(4) We are very much obliged for your trial order of ... for ...

(5) We have pleasure in informing you that we have booked your order No. ... for ... We are sending you our Sales Confirmation No. ... in duplicate, one copy of which please sign and return for our file.

(6) You may rest assured that this order will have our careful attention.

(7) We are sure you will be pleased to collect good comments about our products from your customers, and build up a market for the product in your region.

(8) We appreciate your cooperation and look forward to receiving your further orders.

Unit Nine   Payment Option
支付方式选择

◆ *Learning Objectives*

a. Master writing requirements of the letter of credit;
b. Know how the letter of credit works;
c. Know different types of letters of credit.

The creditor's rights and debt relationship arising from international economic trade, credit and investment, labor cooperation, tourism and foreign exchange shall be settled through monetary receipt and payment, that is, international settlement. International settlement method refers to the method of monetary receipt and payment used by individuals, enterprises and groups of different countries for the liquidation of creditor's rights and debts in certain forms and conditions. At present, the basic methods of international settlement are: letter of credit, collection, remittance.

Section 1   Introduction

Paying for goods supplied in home trade is a fairly simple matter because payment can be made either in advance or within a reasonably short period after delivery. But this problem is much more complicated in foreign trade. Must the seller wait perhaps several months for his/her money or shall the buyer pay several months before he/she not even sees goods? Clearly, the seller runs certain risks of non-payment if he/she surrounds goods before payment has been made. As it is not often possible for the seller personally to collect payment before delivery, the appointment of agents for this purpose in the importers' countries becomes necessary. This function is usually entrusted to the banker, who has branches or correspondent bank in most towns or cities overseas.

The most generally used method of payment in the financing of international trade is the letter of credit (abbreviated to L/C), which is a reliable and safe method of payment, facilitating trade with unknown buyers and giving protection to both sellers and buyers. The process of issuing a letter of credit starts with the buyer. He/She instructs his/her bank to issue an L/C in favor of the seller for the amount of the purchase.

The buyer's bank (the opening bank) sends to its correspondent bank in the seller's country the L/C, giving instructions about the amount of the credit, the beneficiary, the currency, the documents required and other special instructions. On arrival of it, the correspondent bank advise the seller of the receipt of the credit. Sometimes a seller requires a confirmed L/C. In this case, the correspondent bank usually adds its confirmation, becoming the confirming bank and advices the seller of the same; the seller will then dispatch the goods accordingly.

Payment is sometimes made by collection through banks under the terms of Documents against Payment (D/P) or Documents against Acceptance (D/A). In this case, the banks will only do the service of collecting and remitting and will not be liable for non-payment of the importer, while in the case of an L/C the opening bank offers its own credit to finance the transaction.

Documents against payment calls for actual payment against transfer of shipping documents. There are D/P at sight and D/P after sight. The former requires immediate payment by the importer to get hold of the documents. In the latter condition, the importer is given a certain period to make payment as 30, 45, 60, or 90 days after presentation of documents, but he/she is not allowed to get hold of the documents until he/she pays. Documents against Acceptance calls for delivery of documents against acceptance of the draft drawn by the exporter. D/A is always after sight.

As for as the seller's benefit is concerned, L/C is better than D/P. D/P at sight is better than D/P after sight, whereas D/P is better than D/A. In international trade, payment through collection is accepted only when the financial standing of the importer is sound or where a previous course of business has inspired the exporter with confidence that the importer will be good for payment.

Section 2　Examples of Letter of Credit

A letter of credit is a written document of a conditional promise of payment made by a bank. Letter of credit payment method is a major payment method commonly used in international trade today. It is to transfer the payment of the importer to the bank. The bank guarantees that the exporter receives the payment safely and quickly, and the buyer receives the freight receipt on time to withdraw the goods. The advantage of adopting a credit card for payment is that the first payment liability under the credit card is the issuing bank. As long as the documents provided are in consistent with the provisions of the letter of credit, the bank will pay even if the buyer fails and the price falls.

Unit Nine Payment Option 支付方式选择

1. Irrevocable Letter of Credit

>◇◇◇◇◇◇◇◇◇◇◇◇◇◇◇◇◇◇◇◇◇◇◇◇◇◇◇◇◇◇◇<

LETTER OF CREDIT
TRANSMITTED THROUGH
BANK OF CHINA, LONDON
BANK OF CHINA
BEIING, CHINA

Beijing, February 1st, 2016

Dear Sirs,

We open an irrevocable Letter of Credit No.846 in favor of ... Company, London for account of: China National ... Corporation, Beijing to the extent of: £30,000 (Pounds Sterling Thirty Thousand only, 5% more or less is allowed). This credit is available by beneficiary's draft(s), drawn on us, in duplicate, without recourse, at sight, for 100% of the invoice value, and accompanied by the following shipping documents marked with numbers:

(1) Full set of clean "on board" "freight prepaid" Ocean Bill of Lading, made out to order and blank endorsed, marked: "Notify China National Foreign Trade Transportation Corporation, at the port of destination."
(2) Invoice in (quintuplicate) copies, indicating Contract No.
(3) Weight Memo/Packing List in duplicate, indicating gross and net weights of each package.
(4) Certificate of Quality/Weight in ... copies issued by the manufacturers.
(5) Beneficiary's letter attesting that 4 extra copies each of the above-mentioned documents have been distributed as follows: 1 set ship mailed along with the goods to China National Foreign Trade Transportation corporation at the port of destination.

1 set and 2 sets airmailed to account and China National Foreign Trade Transportation Corporation at the port of destination respectively within 5 days after the departure of the carrying vessel.

EVIDENCING SHIPMENT OF: 20 metric tons (5% more or less is allowed) of 1,000 kilos net each of GAMMA PLCOLINE, Purity 98-99%, £3.60 per kilo net CFR Xin Gang, including packing charges.

Shipment from U.K. port to Xin Gang. Partial Shipment is not allowed. Transshipment is allowed, through B/L required. Shipment to be made on or before March 15, 1993, per SS

"Peace".

This Credit is valid in London on or before March 30, 1993, for negotiation and all drafts drawn hereunder must be marked Drawn under Bank of China Head Office, Banking Department, Beijing, Credit No. 846.

We hereby engage with the drawers, endorsers and bona fide holders of draft(s) drawn under and in accordance with the terms of this credit that the same shall be honored by T.T. on presentation of the documents at this office. Amount(s) of draft(s) negotiated under this credit must be endorsed on the back hereof.

大意

敬启者：

兹开立第846号不可撤销信用证

受益人：伦敦……公司

开证人：北京中国……进出口公司

最高金额：三万英镑，溢短装货物金额以5％为限。本信用证凭受益人开具以我行为付款人按发票金额100％计算的无追索权的即期汇票用款。该汇票一式两份，并附有下列标有数字的装运单据：

(1)全套清洁无瑕疵，"货已装船""运费已付"、空白抬头、空白背书的海洋提单，并须注明"通知目的港中国对外贸易运输公司"。

(2)发票(一式五份)，注明合同号。

(3)重量单/装箱单，一式三份，载明每箱毛重和净重。

(4)制造商出具的品质、数量/重量证明书……份。

(5)受益人出具的证明书证明上述各单据的另外四分已分发如下：

一套已与货物一起随船代交目的港中国对外贸易运输公司，一套已航邮给开证人，另外两套已航空邮寄目的港中国对外贸易运输公司。此单据均已在载货船只启航后5天内付邮。

装运证明：20吨(允许溢短装以5％为限)，每吨净重为1 000公斤的四基吡啶，纯度98％～99％，净重每公斤3英镑60便士CFR新港，包装费在内。

生产国别：英国

制造厂商：ABC有限公司

包装：货物用适宜海运的新铁桶装。自英国口岸运往新港。不得分批装运。准许转船，但须交联运提单，装运日期不得晚于1993年3月30日，并须由"和平"号货轮装运。

本信用证在伦敦议付，有效期至1993年3月30日截止。所有根据本信用证开具的汇票须注明"根据北京中国银行总管理处营业部第846号信用证出具"。

本行向根据本信用证并按照本证内条款开出汇票的出票人、背书人和合法持有人保证，在单据提交本行办公室时，本行即应以电汇方式承兑该汇票。所有根据本信用证议付的汇票金额必须在本证背面批注。

2. Confirmed Irrevocable Letter of Credit

LETTER OF CREDIT
BANK OF BOSTON
THE FIRST NATIONAL BANK OF BOSTON
POST OFFICE BOX 1763
BOSTON, MASSACHUSETTS 02105 U.S.A.
CONFIRMED IRREVOCABLE LETTIR OF
CREDIT No. 9753 Holcroft /Loftus
12068 Market St. Livonia, MI 48150 U.S.A.

Gentlemen:

We hereby authorize you to draw at sight on BANK OF BOSTON, MASSACHUSETTS, U.S.A. up to aggregate amount of $ ... (Say ... DOLLARS ONLY IN U.S.A. CURRENCY), for the account of Asia-American Oil Tools and Services, Ltd. Chiwan, Shenzhen, P.R. China.

Drafts under this Confirmed Irrevocable Letter of Credit must bear on their face the words "Drawn Under Bank of Boston, Massachusetts, Letter of Credit number 9753, dated August 15, 2023".

The sight draft is to be for a maximum amount of ... or 85% of the total amount of Contract Price ... under Contract No. OTl179 dated July 27, 2023, accompanied by the following:

   Three (3) copies of seller's Invoice
   Clean on Board Ocean Bill of Lading
   Packing List
   Certificate of Quality and Quantity
   Copy of fax to Buyers notifying shipment

Except so far as otherwise expressly stated herein, this Letter of Credit is subject to the Uniform Customs and Practice for Documentary Credits (1993 Revision and Amendments thereto) International Chamber of Commerce Publication No. 500.

This Confirmed Letter of Credit shall be irrevocable and binding until the close of business on December 31, 2023, at which time this Letter of Credit will automatically expire. We hereby agree that each draft drawn under and in compliance with the terms of this Letter of Credit will be duly honored at sight if presented at our office in Boston with all above required documents, on or before the close of business on said expiration date.

Very truly yours,

大意

信用证
波士顿银行
波士顿第一国家银行
邮政信箱 1763
美国,马萨诸塞,波士顿 02105
9753 号保兑的、不可撤销的信用证
美国密歇根州利沃尼亚 48150
市场街 12068
霍尔克罗夫特公司

敬启者:

我方在此允许贵方从美国马萨诸塞州波士顿银行,中华人民共和国深圳赤湾亚美石油工具有限公司的账户上提取总计……美元(即……元整美国货币),见票即付。

依据该保兑的、不可撤销的信用证开立的汇票,必须注明"在马萨诸塞州波士顿银行支取,信用证号 9753,日期 2023 年 8 月 15 日"。

即期汇票限额……美元或相当于合同总价的 85%,合同号 OT1179,日期 2023 年 7 月 27 号,并随附下列单据:

三份卖方发票副本
清洁已装船海运提单
装箱单
数量和质量检验证明书
通知买方启运传真副本

除非另有特殊规定,本信用证根据国际商会第 500 号出版物《跟单信用证统一惯例》(1983 年修订本)办理。

在 2023 年 12 月 31 日交易结束之前,本保兑信用证不可撤销,并具有约束力;自交易结束之日起(即自 1992 年 12 月 31 日起),本信用证自动失效。我方在此同意,凡根据此信用证并按照此信用证条款开立的汇票,于上述失效日期即交易结束之日或在此之前提交到我方在波士顿的办事处,并附有以上要求的所有单据,我方将见票即付。

谨上

3. The Buyer Notifies the Seller of a Letter of Credit to Open It

Dear Sirs,

We are glad to inform you that we have now opened an irrevocable letter of credit through

Unit Nine Payment Option 支付方式选择

the Bank of Boston, Massachusetts, U.S.A. for U.S. $... in your favor.

Please make sure that the shipment is effected within September, since punctual delivery is one of the important considerations in dealing with our market.

We are awaiting your Shipping Advice.

Yours faithfully,

大意

敬启者：
　　非常高兴地告知贵方,我们已通过美国马萨诸塞州的波士顿银行开立以贵方为受益人、金额为……美元的不可撤销信用证。
　　请务必于9月份装船,因为在与客户的交易中,按时发货是我方恪守的原则之一。
　　期盼贵方的装船通知。
　　谨上

4. Urging Establishment of L/C

Dear Sirs,

Re: Your Order No. 465 for Ammonium Sulphate

With reference to our faxes dated the 20th of April and the 8th of May, requesting you to establish the L/C covering the above mentioned order, we regret having received no news from you up till now.

We wish to remind you that it was agreed, when placing the order, that you would establish the required L/C upon receipt of our Confirmation. Needless to say, we are placed in a very embarrassing situation now that one month has elapsed and nothing whatsoever has been heard from you. As the goods have been ready for shipment for quite some time, it behooves you to take immediate action, particularly since we cannot think of any valid reason for further delaying the opening of the credit.

Yours truly,

大意

敬启者：
  事由：贵方第 456 号关于硫酸铵的订单
  关于我方 4 月 20 日和 5 月 8 日的传真，要求贵方开立有关标题订单的信用证。非常遗憾，直到目前我方仍没有收到任何消息。
  我方要提醒贵方的是，当下订单时，已经达成了协议，即一收到我方的售货确认书，贵方则应开立必要的信用证。如今一个月时间已经过去了，还没有收到来自贵方的任何消息。这无疑使我方陷入了窘迫的境地。由于货物早已备妥待装，所以贵方应立即采取措施。我方尤其难以想象贵方还有何正当的理由推迟开立信用证。
  谨上

Reply：

Dear Sirs,

Re：Our Order No. 465 for Ammonium Sulphate

We have received your faxes dated 20th of April and 8th of May, urging us to establish the L/C for the captioned order.

We are very sorry for the delay in opening the L/C, which was due to an oversight of our staff. However, upon receipt of your fax of May 8, we immediately opened the covering credit with the Bank of China, and trust the same is now in your hand.

Please allow us to express again our regret for the inconvenience that has been caused to you.

Yours faithfully,

大意

敬启者：
  事由：我方第 456 号关于硫酸铵的订单
  获悉贵方 4 月 20 日和 5 月 8 日催促我方开立有关标题项下货物的信用证的传真。
  因我方职员的疏忽而迟开了信用证，对此深表歉意。然而，一收到贵方 5 月 8 日的传真我方立即通过中国银行开立了此货物的信用证，想必贵方现在已经收到。
  对于给贵方造成的不便之处，再次表示歉意。
  谨上

Unit Nine Payment Option 支付方式选择

5. Amendment to Letter of Credit

Sample 1

Dear Sirs,

Letter of Credit No. 3524 issued by the Bank of New South Wales has duly arrived. On perusal, we find that transshipment and partial shipment are not allowed.

As direct steamers to your port are few and far between, we have to ship via Hong Kong more often than not. As to partial shipment, it would be to our mutual benefit if we could ship immediately whatever is ready instead of waiting for the whole shipment to be completed. Therefore, we are asking you to amend your L/C to read "Part shipments and transshipment allowed".

We shall appreciate it if you will modify promptly the L/C as requested.

Yours faithfully,

大意

敬启者：

　　由新南威尔士银行签发的第 3524 号信用证已如期到达。审证之后，我方发现，贵方不允许转船和分批装运。

　　由于直达贵方港口的货轮稀少，我方经常不得不通过香港转运；至于分批装运，我方认为如果能对备妥的货物立即装运，而不是等到整批货物备齐才装运，将对你我双方都有利。所以请贵方将信用证改成"允许分批装运和转船"。

　　如蒙贵方按要求及时修改信用证，不胜感激。

　　谨上

Sample 2

Dear Sirs,

Re: Your Letter of Credit No. 6477

We have received your captioned Letter of Credit. Among the clauses specified in your Credit we find that the following two points do not conform to the relative contract:

　　1) Your Credit calls for Manufacturer's Certificates, which is not included in the

Contract. In fact, the contracted commodity is a kind of agricultural produce. It is impossible to obtain a manufacturer's certificate.

2) The contract number is 935/1534 instead of 932/1245.

As the goods are now ready for shipment, you are requested to amend your credit as soon as possible.

Yours faithfully,

大意

敬启者：

事由：贵方第 6477 号信用证

我方已收到贵方标题项下信用证。我方发现在贵方的信用证条款中，有如下两点与有关合同不一致：

1) 贵方信用证要求有生产厂家证明书，而合同条款中并无此规定。事实上，合同中所订产品是一种农产品，因此要取得生产厂家证明书则是不可能的。

2) 合同号码 932/1245 应改为 935/1534。

由于货物备妥待运，希望贵方尽早修改信用证。

谨上

Sample 3

Dear Sirs,

Re: L/C No. 345 Issued by First National City Bank

We have received the above L/C established by you in payment for your Order No. 678 covering 200 cases of ...

When we checked the L/C with the relevant contract, we found that the amount in your L/C is insufficient. The correct total CIF New York value of your order comes to US＄2,750.00 instead of US＄2,550.00, the difference being US＄200.00.

Your L/C allows us only half a month to effect delivery. But when we signed the contract we have agreed that the delivery should be made within one month upon receipt of the Letter of Credit.

As to packing, the contract stipulates that the goods should be packed in cartons and reinforced with nylon straps outside, but your L/C required metal straps instead. We think we should arrange the packing according to the contract.

In view of the above, you are kindly requested to increase the amount of your L/C by US＄200.00, extend the shipment and validity to September 15 and 30 respectively, as well as amend the term of packing. Meanwhile please advise us by fax.

Yours faithfully,

大意

敬启者：

　　事由：花旗银行开立的第 345 号信用证

　　我方已收到贵方所开立的支付贵方第 678 号订单项下 200 项……货物的信用证。

　　同有关合同核对之后，我方发现信用证金额不足，贵方订单中纽约到岸价总额是 2 750 美元，而不是 2 550 美元，两者相差 200 美元。

　　贵方信用证中只给我方半个月时间交货。但在签订合同时，我们已经达成协议，在收到信用证后的一个月交货。

　　关于包装，合同规定使用纸箱包装，外用尼龙绳加固。而贵方信用证中要求用金属带加固。我方认为应按合同规定进行包装。

　　基于以上所述，特请贵方增加信用证金额 200 美元，将装船期和有效期分别延至 9 月 15 日和 30 日，修改包装条款。同时希望以传真通知我方。

　　谨上

6. Extention of Letter of Credit

Sample 1

Dear Sirs,

Re: Your L/C No. AG4582

We have received your L/C No. AG4582 for the amount of £2,960 to cover your Order No. 860 for 20 metric tons of ...

The said credit calls for shipment on or before the 31st of December. As the earliest steamer sailing for your port is s.s. "PEACE" scheduled to leave Shanghai on or about January 3, it is, therefore, impossible for us to effect shipment at the time you named.

This being the case, we have to ask you to extend the date of shipment to the 15th of

January, under advice to us by fax.

Yours faithfully,

大意

敬启者:

事由:贵方第 AG4852 号信用证

我方已收到贵方开立的总金额为 2 960 英镑、支付贵方第 860 号订单项下 20 吨……的第 AG4582 号信用证。

该信用证要求在 12 月 31 日之前装运。由于驶往贵方港口的最早货轮"和平号"计划在 1 月 3 日左右从上海启航,所以无法按贵方所指示的时间装运。

既然如此,我方只好请贵方将装运日期延至 1 月 15 日,并用传真通知我方。

谨上

Sample 2

Dear Sirs,

Re: L/C No. 244 5M/T Frozen Rabbit Meat

We thank you for your L/C No. 244 for the captioned goods. We are sorry that owing to some delay on the part of our suppliers, we are unable to get the goods ready before the end of this month. So we write to you asking for an extention.

It is expected that the consignment will be ready for shipment in the early part of May and we are arranging to ship it on s. s. "Red Star" sailing from Shanghai on May 10.

We are looking forward to receiving your extension of the above L/C, thus enabling us to effect shipment of the goods in question.

Yours faithfully,

大意

敬启者:

事由:第 244 号信用证——订购 5 吨冷冻兔肉

感谢贵方为标题货物开立的第 244 号信用证。非常抱歉,由于我方供货商的拖延,我方无法在本月底之前将货备好,所以先写信请求延期。

预计货物将在 5 月上旬备妥装运。现在我方正在安排由"红星号"货轮装运,该货轮将于 5 月 10 日启航离开上海。

我方期盼着贵方展延信用证,以便安排装运。

谨上

◆ 词语知识点

1. extension *n*. 延长,展期

As the steamer is delayed by storm, an extension of 15 days is required. 由于船被风暴耽搁,需要延期 15 天。

We have contacted our customer today asking for a two-week extension of the L/C covering Order No. 8982. 关于第 8982 号订单,我们已与客户联系要求将信用证有效期延长两周。

extend *vt*. 延长,使展期;扩展;给予

Please have your letter of credit extended to July 21. 请将你信用证展期到七月二十一日。

They intend to extend their business to neighboring countries. 他们打算将业务扩展到邻近国家。

We would extend our invitation to you to attend the Miniature Garments Fair to be held in Hong Kong early next month. 兹邀请贵方参加下月初在香港举行的服装小交会。

2. stipulate *v*. 规定,约定

He stipulated payment in advance. 他规定要预付货款。

The commission granted for this transaction is 3% as stipulated in our S/C. 按照合同规定这笔交易的佣金是 3%。

stipulation *n*. 规定的条件,约定的条件;条款

According to the stipulations of our S/C the commission for this transaction is 3%. 按照合同规定这笔交易的佣金是 3%。

3. make up 配齐,弥补,拼凑成

make up an order 备齐订货

We need one more to make up a dozen. 还要一个才够一打。

You're requested to make up the shortage. 请你方补齐所缺部分。

We will do whatever we can to make up the economic losses. 我们将尽全力弥补经济损失。

4. unexpected *adj*. 未料到的;意外的

It is our unexpected result to settle the problem through friendly negotiation. 通过友好协商解决这个问题是我们始料未及的。

We were compelled to suspend our negotiation owing to unexpected incident. 这次意外的事件迫使我们中止了谈判。

5. negotiation *n*. 谈判，磋商；议付

The contract is still under negotiation. 这项合同仍在商谈之中。

Please amend the credit accordingly to enable negotiation of the draft. 请对此信用证做相应修改以使我方能议付汇票。

negotiate *v*. 谈判，磋商；议付

We are negotiating with the council to have this road closed to traffic. 我们正在与市政局交涉封闭这条道路。

negotiating bank 议付银行

negotiable *adj*. 可谈判的；(票据等)可议付的，可转让的，可流通的

Since this dispute is not negotiable, it is necessary to resort to arbitration. 这项争议无法通过谈判解决，需要诉诸仲裁。

Unsigned copies of documents are not negotiable. 未经签署的单据不能转让。

6. respectively *adv*. 分别地

We shall discuss the two questions respectively. 这两个问题我们将分别讨论。

7. provide *vt*. 提供；规定

We can provide a wide range of exports for you to select. 我们可以提供品种繁多的出口商品供你选择。

Can the city provide good postal and telecommunication services? 这座城市能提供良好的邮电通信服务吗？

The contract provides that the goods be supplied within one month after receiving the relative L/C. 合同规定在收到有关信用证后一个月内交货。

◆ 本章知识提示

进出口货物的收付主要涉及支付工具(主要是货币和汇票)、支付时间、支付地点和信用问题。这些收付必须通过一定的支付方式来实现。对外贸易的支付方式很多，用得比较多的基本上有三种：信用证、托收、汇付。

1. 信用证 (Letter of credit)

信用证是银行根据进口人的请求，开给出口人的一种保证支付货款的书面凭证。在信用证内开证行授权出口人在符合信用证规定的条款和条件下，以该行或其他指定银行为付款人，开具不得超过信用证规定金额的汇票，并随附信用证的各种单据(如提单、发票等)，按信用证规定的议付时间和指定地点收取货款。

在国际贸易中，不可撤销信用证的使用最为广泛。所谓"不可撤销"，是指信用证一经开出，有效期内未经受益人及有关当事人同意，开证行不得撤销信用证或修改信用证的内容。只要受益人提供的单证符合信用证，开证行必须履行付款义务。

信用证是一种由银行开立的有条件的承诺付款的书面文件。信用证支付方式是当今国际

贸易中普遍采用的一种主要支付方式。它把由进口人履行付款的责任转为由银行来履行。银行保证出口人安全迅速收到货款，买方按时收到货运单据，从而提取货物。采用信用证支付的好处是信用证项下首先付款责任的是开证行。只要所提供的单据与信用证的规定完全相符，即使是买方倒闭、货价下跌，银行都必须付款。

（1）信用证的主要内容

1）对信用证本身的说明。例如信用证的种类、性质、金额及其有效期和到期地点等。

2）对货物的要求。货物的名称、品种规格、数量、包装、价格等。

3）对运输的要求。装运的最迟期限、起运地和目的地、运输方式，可否分批装运和可否中途转运等。

4）对单据的要求。单据主要可以分为三类：A.货物单据（以发票为中心，包括装箱单、重量单、产地证、商检证明书等）；B.运输单据（如提单，是代表货物所有权的证据）；C.保险单据（保险单）。除上述3种单据外，还有可能提出其他单证，如寄样证明、装船通知副本等。

5）特殊要求。根据进口国政治经济贸易情况的变化或每一笔具体业务的需要，可以做出不同规定。

6）开证行对受益人及汇票持有人保证付款的责任文句。各项要求都要在受益人（出口人）所提供的单据中表示出来，并做到与信用证条款完全一致。

（2）信用证的种类

按付款时间来分：L/C draft at sight/after sight term L/C— time L/C—usance（习惯支付期限，票据期限）L/C

按是否能撤销来分：revocable L/C 和 irrevocable L/C

依照有无另一家银行保兑来分：confirmed L/C 和 unconfirmed L/C

依照受益人对信用证的权利能否转让来分：transferable L/C 和 non-transferable L/C

依照可否循环来分：revolving L/C 和 non-revolving L/C

依照可否分割来分：divisible L/C 和 indivisible L/C

依照可否有单据来分：clean L/C 和 documentary L/C

依照可否有追索权来分：L/C without recourse 和 L/C with recourse

是否可自动循环：automatic revolving L/C 和 non-automatic revolving L/C

是否可积累：cumulative revolving L/C 和 non-cumulative revolving L/C

（3）催证

在以信用证方式付款的合同中，一般都明确规定买方应在什么时间开来信用证，并规定信用证的有效期。比如说在装船前30天开来信用证，有效期为装船后15天在中国到期。但是实际业务中，买方在市场发生变化或自己资金短缺时，往往迟迟不开证。因此，卖方催买方开立信用证常常是出口成交后一项十分重要的工作。

（4）信用证审核

信用证应该严格按照合同条款的规定开立。然而在实践中，由于种种原因，如工作上的疏忽、电文传递中的错误、贸易习惯的不同、市场行情的变化或进出口商故意加列对其有利的条款等，所开出的信用证往往与合同的规定不符。如果卖方没有严格审核对方开来的信用证，没有将信用证中出现的问题（尤其是影响合同执行或卖方安全收汇的问题）及时要求对方修改，那么将会给卖方造成重大的经济损失，带来严重的后果。

对信用证的审核包括审核信用证的性质,审核信用证的金额及货币,审核信用证的有效期和到期地点,审核信用证中规定的装船日期。

另外,还应对信用证里所规定的每个环节,如品名、规格、数量、单价、包装、装运港、目的港等各项内容均进行仔细审核,看看是否与合同规定相符,所要求的单据是否都能提供。除此之外,还应注意信用证中有没有提出特殊要求。

(5)对信用证的要求

对信用证进行全面细致的审核以后,如果发现问题,首先应分析问题的性质,凡是属于不符合我国对外贸易方针政策、影响合同执行和安全收汇的情况,必须要求国外客户通过开证行进行修改,并坚持在收到银行修改信用证通知书后才能对外发货。

2. 托收(Collection)

托收就是一国出口方主动向另一国进口方索款时,开具以进口方为付款人的汇票,委托第三方(银行)向进口方代收货款。作为第三方的银行接收出口商的委托后,还要转托国外分行或代理行才能向国外进口商收款。因此,国际托收业务通常涉及四个当事人,即委托人、托收银行、代收银行、付款人。

在国际贸易中,多使用的是跟单托收。根据交单条件的不同,跟单托收可分为付款交单和承兑交单,即付款交单(D/P, Documents against payment)和承兑交单(D/A, Documents against acceptance)。托收属商业信用,在采用托收方式时,要具体说明使用即期付款交单、远期付款交单或承兑交单。由出口人开具汇票,向出口地银行通过它在进口地的分行或代理行代为向进口人收款,可分为光票托收和跟单托收。

光票托收,是指出口人(或出票人)进开具汇票,不附随任何货运单据托收。这种方式通常用于收取货款尾数和样品费、佣金、代垫费用等贸易从属费用。

跟单托收,根据交单条件的不同分为付款交单、承兑交单两种。付款交单按付款时间又分为即期付款交单和远期付款交单。承兑交单只有远期的。承兑交单支付方式对出口收汇风险很大,使用时要十分慎重。

3. 汇付(Remittance)

汇付是由付款人(通常是买方)通过银行把款项汇给收款人(通常是卖方)的支付方式。汇付方式一般在预付货款、支付佣金、支付样品费、代垫费用、履约保证金及赔款等方面用得较多。汇付就是一国的进口商或其他付款人委托出口商或其他收款人所在国的第三者(一般为银行),对收款人支付一定金额,而不靠输送现金来结算彼此间债权债务关系的一种方式。最通常的汇款方式有信汇(Mail transfer,简称 M/T)、电汇(Telegraphic transfer,简称 T/T)、票汇(Remittance by banker's demand draft,简称 D/D)。在我国对外贸易中,汇付方式通常用于货到付款、赊销和预付货款等业务。

国际结算的主要工具是票据。它是具有一定格式的书面债据,上面载明一定的金额与日期,持票人可据此向发票人或指定付款人支取款项。票据有汇票、本票与支票。

汇票是国际结算中心以汇款方式进行结算的一种票据。它可分为银行汇票与商业汇票;同时按到期日的不同,又可分为即期汇票与远期汇票。

本票是一人向另一人签发的保证即期或定期可以确定的将来时间,对某人或其指定人或持票人付一定金额的无条件书面承诺。

支票是活期存款的存户对银行发出的一种支付通知。在国际贸易结算中,支票是进口商对其存款银行发出的一种支付通知,另一国的出口商凭票可向该行或其国外分行或代理机构提款。

◆ 本章句式

1. Terms of Payment

(1) Considering the small amount involved, we are prepared, as an exception, to accept payment by D/P at sight for the value of your first trial order.

(2) As a special accommodation, we agree to your proposal and accept payment by D/P at sight, but this should not be considered as a precedent.

(3) We understand that you are having some difficulty in opening L/C. Such being the case, we suggest D/P payment.

(4) With regard to terms of payment, we regret being unable to accept documents against payment.

(5) For a few special import items we can adopt "payment by installments".

(6) We will draw on you by our documentary draft at sight, on collection basis, without L/C.

(7) We are willing to draw on you, at 30 days' sight, documents against acceptance (D/A).

(8) In view of the small amount of this transaction, we agree to draw on you documentary sight draft.

(9) It will interest you to know that as a special sign of encouragement, we shall consider accepting payment by D/P during this sales-pushing stage.

(10) In order to facilitate your efforts in introducing our products to your market, we are now giving you a special accommodation by granting D/P.

(11) At your repeated request, we would grant you such favorable terms of payment as D/A 40 days after sight.

(12) For your shipment, we agree to draw on you at 60 days' sight, but this cannot be taken as a precedent.

(13) We regret to inform you that we have to decline your request for D/P terms as we only accept payment by L/C at sight.

(14) Since the amount involved is small, we are prepared, as an exception, to accept payment by D/A.

(15) In compliance with your request, we exceptionally accept delivery against D/P at sight, but this should not be regarded as a precedent.

(16) The usual 3% discount may be deducted if payment is made within 30 days on receipt of this statement.

(17) We were pleased to receive your bank check for US $ ... It has been credited to

— 173 —

your account, which is now completely clear.

(18) We enclose our bank check for US＄1,520 in settlement of your invoice No. 193.

(19) Under this installment plan, 15% of me contract value is to be paid with order.

2. Request for Payment

(1) It has been our usual practice to do business with payment by D/P at sight instead of by L/C. We should, therefore, like you to accept D/P terms for this transaction and future ones.

(2) Please remit the 10% down payment to us by T/T. Payment of balance is to be made in three installments.

(3) It is expensive to open an L/C and tie up the capital of a small company like ours, so it is better for us to adopt D/P or D/A.

(4) It should be pointed out that the contract value in Malaysian dollars will be converted into Hong Kong dollars in payment at the conversion rate then prevailing.

(5) Please surrender these documents to the drawee against their accepting the draft and collect and remit the net proceeds to us.

3. Reminder

(1) Perhaps you have forgotten to send us your last order payment of US＄... which is past due now. It would be appreciated if you could have it remitted to us by July 16.

(2) May we remind you that die payment of this invoice is now past due? A cheque of US＄... by return of post would be appreciated.

(3) We would appreciate payment immediately so that your account can be brought up to date.

(4) Our records show that your January account for US＄... is still unpaid. Would you please send us your check or make payment as soon as you can?

(5) Have you forgotten to send us your last order payment, which was past due now. If you have not mailed it to us, please do so right away after you receive this letter.

4. Inquiries for Overdue Payments

(1) Since you have always paid promptly, we assume that some unusual circumstance has prevented a reply. We would appreciate your remittance by the end of this month so explanation.

(2) Have you overlooked the unpaid balance from your recent purchase? We shall be greatly obliged if you will remit us a cheque of US＄...

(3) We would ask again that you promptly pay your outstanding account or, if you are unable to do so for any reason, you can contact us so that we may discuss the matter.

(4) Please accept this letter as a friendly request for payment without further delay so that we can continue to give you our full service.

5. Urgency for Overdue Payments

(1) For regular customers such as you, our terms of payment are most favorable. If you

are good enough to settle this account promptly, there will be no necessity for us to alter the terms to your disadvantage.

(2) Our patience is exhausted. Unless we receive the overdue payment by July 30, we will have to take necessary steps. The choice you are going to make right now is extremely important to your business.

(3) I certainly would not like to reduce your credit limit for future purchases, not to contact a collection agency, which I shall be forced to do if we do not receive payment in the very near future.

(4) Unless you can settle the balance of US$ ... our business cannot go ahead.

(5) We would like you to contact us immediately so that we may work out a specific arrangement and save your reputation by settling the outstanding account soon.

6. Ultimatum for Overdue Payments

(1) We regret we shall have no alternative but to ...

(2) I greatly regret that I shall be obliged to ...

(3) Unfortunately I shall be compelled to ...

(4) Regrettably I shall have no choice but to ...

(5) If you are unable to settle your account by the end of next week, I am afraid we will be forced to pass the matter over to our legal department.

(6) If we do not receive the total overdue account of US$ ... by October 22, we will have to ask our attorneys to collect it through court proceedings.

(7) We would prefer not to take any legal action against you, but we all have no choice unless you do what we request you to do above.

(8) Like you we prefer to avoid any legal embarrassment, but you would leave us with no choice unless you send your remittance of US$ ... by December 30.

(9) Would you please settle this account within the next 10 days? Otherwise we shall have to hand this matter to our solicitors/refer this matter to our collection agency to seek legal action.

Unit Ten Insurance
保险

◆ Learning Objectives

    a. Know the importance and benefits of insurance;
    b. Master writing requirements of insurance.

Traditionally, export goods should be insured during transportation. In international trade, the goods from the seller to the buyer have to go through the transportation by air, road and sea, and they have to go through multiple loading and unloading and storage processes. In the process, the goods may encounter various dangers or even be lost. In order to protect the goods from these accidents, the seller or the buyer usually applies to the insurance company for insurance on the transportation of the goods. The types of international cargo transportation insurance mainly include maritime cargo transportation insurance, land cargo transportation insurance, air cargo transportation insurance and postal parcel transportation insurance, among which maritime transportation insurance has the longest history, and several other types of transportation insurance are developed on the basis of maritime cargo transportation insurance.

Section 1 Introduction

Insurance is very closely related to foreign trade. In international trade, the transportation of goods from the seller to the buyer is generally over a long distance by air, by land or by sea and has to go through the procedures of loading, unloading and storing. During this process it is quite possible that the goods will encounter various kinds of perils and sometimes suffer losses. In order to protect the goods against possible losses in case of such perils, the buyer or the seller before the transportation of the goods usually applies to an insurance company for insurance covering the goods in transit.

The purpose of insurance is to provide compensation for those who suffer from loss or damage; in other words, it is a contract of indemnity, a contract to restore to someone, either the full amount of the loss that may be incurred, or a specified percentage of the amount of the loss.

A contract of insurance, which is generally made in the form of an insurance policy, is one between a party who agrees to accept the risk (the insurer) and a party seeking protection from the risk (the insured). In return for payment of a premium, the insurer agrees to pay the insured a stated sum (or a proportion of it) should the event insured against occur. The premium, being the name given to the sum of money paid by the insured, is quoted at percentage of the sum insured.

There are mainly two types of insurance coverage, basic coverage and additional coverage. Basic coverage mainly includes FPA (Free from Particular Average), WPA (With Particular Average) and All Risks. Additional coverage includes general additional coverage and special additional coverage. General additional coverage includes coverage of such risks as Theft, Pilferage & Non-Delivery Risks (TPND), Fresh and/or Rain Water Damage Risks, Shortage Risk, Contamination Risks, Leakage Risk, Clash & Breakage Risks, Taint of Odor Risk, Sweating & Heating Risks, Hook Damage Risk, Rust Risk, Breakage of Packing Risk. Special additional coverage covers the risks of War Risk, Strikes Risk, Failure to Delivery Risk, Import Duty Risk, On Deck Risk, Rejection Risk. etc., among which War Risk and Strike Risk are more common.

An insurance claim, if any, should be submitted to the insurance company or its agent as promptly as possible. In order to substantiate an ordinary average claim on cargo, the following documents must be presented: insurance policy or certificate, B/L, original invoice, survey report, master's protest and statement of claim.

When you write a letter of covering insurance, see to it that you should write down clearly the following information: subject matter, duration of coverage, insurance amount and premium, scope of cover, etc.

Section 2 Examples of Insurance Letters

1. Importer Asks Exporter to Cover Insurance

Dear Sirs,

Re: Our Order No. 101. Your S/C No. 013 covering 500 cases Electronic Toys

We wish to refer you to our Order No. 101 for 500 cases Electronic Toys, from which you will see that this order was placed on CFR basis.

As we now desire to have the consignment insured at your end, we shall be much pleased if you will kindly arrange to insure the same on our behalf against All Risks at invoice value plus 10%, i.e. U.S. $2,200.00.

We shall of course refund the premium to you upon receipt of your debit note or, if you like, you may draw on us at sight for the same.

We sincerely hope that our request will meet with your approval.

Yours faithfully,

大意

敬启者：

我方第101号订单，贵方第013号500箱电动玩具

兹谈及我方第101号订单下500箱电动玩具，此笔交易按CFR成交。

我方希望贵方在当地对该批货物投保，如蒙贵方代表按我方发票金额的110%投保一切险，即2 200美元，我方将倍感高兴。

当然，一收到贵方的收款清单，我方将向贵方付清保单费。若贵方愿意，可向我方即期提取相同金额。

衷心希望贵方能满足我方的要求。

谨上

2. Insurance Company Asks to Cancel Breakage Risk

Sample 1

Dear Sirs,

Additional Risk of Breakage

We refer to your L/C No. 157 covering Glazed Wall Tiles, which we have just received.

Please note for this article we do not cover Breakage. You have to, therefore, delete the word "Breakage" from the insurance clause in the credit.

Furthermore, we wish to point out that for such articles as window glass, porcelains, etc., even if additional Risk of Breakage has been insured, the cover is subject to a franchise of 5%. In other words, if the breakage is surveyed to be less than 5%, no claims for damage will be entertained.

Unit Ten   Insurance 保险

We trust that the position is now dear. Please cable the amendment at once.

Yours faithfully,

大意

敬启者：

我方刚刚收到贵方用以支付上釉墙壁瓷砖的第157号信用证。

务请注意，对该批货物我方不投破碎险。因此，贵方必须将"破碎险"从信用证中的保险条款中删除。

此外，我方要指出的是，像窗户玻璃、陶瓷等货物，即使已投保额外的破碎险，保险仍有5%的免赔率。换句话说，如果破碎率低于5%，我方对此损失不作赔偿。

我方相信，贵方已经清楚这些情况，请立即电报修改信用证。

谨上

Sample 2

Dear Sir or Madam,

Thank your letter of 18 December quoting rates for insurance cover of stock already in our warehouse. The value of the stock held varies with the season, but does not normally exceed $60,000 at any time.

Please arrange cover in this sum against all the risks mentioned in your letter and on the terms quoted.

Sincerely yours,

Sample 3

Dear Mr. Manley,

We would like to refer you to our Order No. 6325 for 830 cases of socks, from which you will see that this order was placed on C&F basis.

As we now want to have the shipment insured at your end, we would be much obliged if you could arrange to insure the same on our behalf against All Risks for the 110% of the invoice value.

We shall, of course, refund the premium to you upon receipt of your debit note or, if you like, you may draw on us at sight of the same.

We sincerely hope that our request will meet with your approval.

Yours sincerely,

Sample 4

Dear Mr. Larson,

Thank you for your letter of November 16, requesting us to effect insurance on the DHB shipment for your account.

We are pleased to confirm having covered the above shipment with the People's Insurance Company of China against All Risks for $30,000. The policy is being prepared accordingly and will be forwarded to you by the end of the week together with our debit note for the premium.

For your information, this parcel will be shipped on s.s. "DASHUN" sailing on or about the 11th of next month.

Yours sincerely,

◆ 本章知识提示

国际货物运输保险的种类主要包括海上货物运输保险、陆上货物运输保险、航空货物运输保险和邮包运输保险。其中以海上运输保险历史最悠久,其他几类运输保险都是在海上货物运输保险的基础上发展起来的。

在我国,中国人民保险公司承办各种货运保险,包括海洋运输货物保险(ocean marine cargo insurance)、陆上运输保险(overland transportation insurance)、邮包保险(parcel post insurance)

写作时应该注意将装运的各项条款列明。

保险条款要注意投保的责任人、保险的标的物、保险的险别、选择什么样的保险公司来承保。这些都会影响货物的安全、各方履行合同和订单的责任划分及相应的经济责任等。写这些条款切记认真仔细,审核准确无误。

对外贸易的运输保险是指被保险人(出口人或进口人)对一批或若干批货物向保险人按一定金额投保一定的险别,并交纳保险费;保险人承保后,如果所保货物在运输途中发生约定范围内的损失,应按照其所出具的保险单的规定给予被保险人经济上的补偿。

保险公司接受投保的险别、费率及条款内容往往因客观条件的变更而有所变更或修改。因此,要根据货物的性质、运输条件和理赔范围的情况,选择必要的险别投保。这样既可节省开支,又可避免因风险而引起的损失。

投保时,通常选择三大基本险别中的一种:

(1) FPA (Free From Particular Average) 平安险。

(2) WPA (With Particular Average) 水渍险。

(3) All Risks 综合险,一切险。

附加险是相对于基本险而言的,是指附加在主险合同下的附加合同。不可以单独投保,要购买附加险必须先投保基本险。一般来说,附加险所交的保险费比较少,但它的存在是以基本险的存在为前提的,不能脱离主险,形成一个比较全面的险种。

其他附加险险别:

Theft, Pilferage & Non-Delivery Risks (T.P.N.D) 偷窃提货不着险

Fresh and/or Rain Water Damage Risks 淡水雨淋险

Shortage Risk = Risk of Shortage 短量险

Intermixture & Contamination Risks 混杂、沾污险

Leakage Risk = Risk of Leakage 渗漏险

Clash & Breakage Risks 碰损、破碎险

Taint of Odor Risk 串味险

Sweating & Heating 受潮受热险

Hook Damage Risk 钩损险

Rust Risk = Risk of Rust 锈损险

Breakage of Packing Risk 包装破损险

War Risk 战争险

Strikes, Riots and Civil Commotions (S.R.C.C.) 罢工、暴动、民变险

Partial loss 部分损失

Particular average 单独海损

General average 共同海损

Total loss 全部损失

Actual total loss 实际全损

Constructive total loss 推算全损

本章句式

1. Asking for Insurance

(1) I am looking for insurance from your company, and I want to know what types of cover you usually underwrite.

(2) The goods are ready for shipment and we wish to cover insurance for the consignment.

(3) For the shipment in question, our clients request you to cover insurance against WPA.

(4) We are willing to take out FPA and WPA covers for the shipment. Would you please give us the policy rates for FPA coverage and for WPA coverage?

(5) Will you please arrange to take out all-risks insurance for us on the following consignment of electronic pumps from our warehouse at the above address to Boston.

(6) Please effect insurance for our account of GBP 6,000 on our goods against WPA and War Risk from Shanghai to Liverpool, and at the lowest premium possible, not exceeding 10%.

(7) We would like to know whether you can undertake insurance on wine against All Risks, including breakage and pilferage risks.

(8) We would be obliged if you can hold us covered for the cargo listed on the attached sheet.

(9) We are making regular shipments from ... to ... and should be glad to hear whether you would be prepared to issue an open policy.

(10) According to our usual practice we prefer our export shipment to be insured by the People's Insurance Company of China.

(11) Will you please quote us a rate for the insurance against All Risks of a shipment of ... to ... by S.S. ... ? The invoice value is ...

(12) If you wish to secure protection against TPND, it can be easily done upon the payment of an additional premium.

2. Asking for Extra Insurance

(1) For a shipment of this nature, WPA is too narrow. You are requested to extend coverage to include TPND.

(2) I now wish to increase the amount of cover from its current figure of CAN $25,000 to $30,000 with immediate effect.

(3) Owing to the fact that these bags have occasionally been dropped into the water during loading and unloading, the insurers have raised the premium to ...%. We, therefore, think that it would be to your advantage to have WPA coverage instead of the FPA.

(4) If you desire to cover ... we can provide such coverage at a slightly higher premium.

(5) We should have asked for broader coverage. Please hereafter take out cover on all our purchases of leathers against TPND, Contamination, Fresh and/or Rain Water Damage

in addition to WPA.

3. Replies to The Insurance Request

(1) For transactions concluded on FOB and CFR basis, insurance is to be covered by buyers for CIF sales, insurance is to be covered by sellers for 110% of the invoice value against the risks specified in the contract.

(2) Should you so desire, we shall insure these goods at your cost.

(3) If the business is concluded on CIF basis, we generally insure WPA; other special risks such as TPND, leakage, breakage, freshwater, oil grease, etc., can be covered upon request.

(4) We have pleasure in informing you that we have insured your Order No. SH1606 for the invoice cost plus 20% up to the port of destination.

(5) In the absence of your definite instructions regarding the insurance, we have covered the goods you ordered against WPA for 110% of the invoice value according to our usual practice.

(6) Breakage is a special risk. for which an extra premium will have to be charged. The additional premium is for the buyer's account.

(7) Insurance on the goods shall be covered by us for 110% of the CIF value, and any extra premium for additional coverage, if required, shall be borne by the buyers.

(8) Regarding insurance, the coverage is for 110% of invoice value up to the port of destination only.

(9) We regret being unable to agree to the buyer's request as stated in the L/C stipulations for insurance to be covered up to the island city because our price is based on CIF Hong Kong.

(10) Owing to the risk of war, we cannot accept the insurance at the ordinary rate. At the same time, it would be to your advantage to have particular average cover.

(11) Our terms of insurance is to be effected by the sellers for 110% of invoice value against All Risks and War Risk.

Unit Eleven　Packing and Shipping
包装与装运

Learning Objectives

a. Master the packaging forms, main containers and signs;
b. Master the transportation mode and common terms related to transportation.

Packaging is an important link in foreign trade, it includes transportation packaging (habitually called outer packaging or large packaging) and sales packaging (habitually called small packaging or internal packaging). They are all measures taken to protect the intact quality and complete quantity of the goods. International cargo transport is an important part of international trade, which involves many modes of transport, including road or rail transport, sea or air transport, and multi-modal transport. When the mode of freight is road or railway transportation or air transportation, the transportation contract includes the cabin lease contract. The form of a contract between the shipping company and the shipper is a charter deed or bill of lading.

Section 1　Introduction

Packing is of particular importance in foreign trade because goods have to travel long distance before reaching their destinations—often across oceans or across continents. Accidents, rough weather, unloading and reloading on the way, everything has to be taken into consideration.

As the buyer has the right to expect that the goods will reach in perfect condition, the seller has to get them into a nice, compact shape that will stay that way even during the roughest journey.

Packing must be strictly marked. Conveniently, outer packing marks mainly include transport marks, directive marks and warning marks. The transport marks consist of:

a. consignor's or consignee's code name;
b. number of the contract or the L/C;
c. the port of destination;
d. numbers of the packed goods.

And sometimes weight and dimensions, all of which can greatly facilitate identification and transportation. For example, directive marks are eye-catching figures and concise instructions concerning manner of proper handling, storing, loading and unloading of the packed goods like "USE NO HOOKS.", "THIS SIDE UP.", "KEEP DRY.", etc. Warning marks are obvious symbols or words to warn people against the hidden danger of inflammation, explosives and poisonous products.

Packing usually varies with the nature of the contents. The most commonly used packing containers are cartons, cases, crates, drums, barrels, bales, tins, and carboys.

Details such as manner of packing, kinds of packing materials and the burden of packing cost should be unmistakably stipulated in the contract concerned and strictly observed by both the selling side and the buying side.

Letters about packing issues should be concise and clear. In such letters, the seller can describe in detail to the buyer his/her customary packing of the goods concerned and also indicate clearly that he/she may accept any required packing at the expense of the buyer. The buyer can inform the seller of any formerly unexpected requirements or fears about the packing. Any changes regarding packing stipulated in the contract should be mutually discussed and determined before shipment.

In international trade, the exporter has various means of shipment, for instance, by ship, by truck, by train, or by airline, to ship consignment. The choice will be made according to the nature of product, the distance to be shipped, available means of transportation, time limit as well as freight cost.

One popular method of shipment is to use containers chartered from carriers. These containers vary in size, material and construction, and accommodate most cargoes, but they are best suited for standard package sizes and shapes. Also refrigerated and liquid bulk containers are usually readily available.

In case of an export business covering a large amount of goods, it is necessary to make shipment in several lots by several carriers sailing on different dates. When there are no or few ships sailing direct to the port of destination at the time or the amount of cargo for a certain port of destination is so small that no ships would like to call at the port, transshipment is necessary. Of course, partial shipment and transshipment should be allowed by the buyer in advance.

Usually there are three parties involved in most transportation of goods, the consignor, the carrier and the consignee. Shipment covers rather a wide range of work, such as:

a. buyers sending shipment instructions;
b. sellers sending shipping advice;
c. booking shipping space;
d. chartering ships;
e. appointing shipping agent;
f. arranging shipment;

g. nomination of vessels, etc.

After the shipment is made, the seller should promptly advise the buyer of its effectiveness, no matter whether the transaction is concluded on FOB, CFR, or CIF basis. For FOB and CFR transactions, the buyer will have to effect insurance to shipment upon receipt of shipping advice from the seller. It has been a customary practice that in the case of FOB transactions, the seller, before shipping, should ask the buyer to name the vessel on which the goods are to be shipped unless otherwise specified in the contract of L/C.

Letters regarding shipment are usually written for the following purposes: to urge an early shipment, to amend shipping terms, to give shipping advice, to dispatch shipping documents and so on. Taking advantage of this occasion to advise the buyer of the shipment, the seller may also review the course of the transaction and express the desire for further development of business.

Section 2   Examples of Packing Letters

1. Packing Instruction

Sample 1

Dear Sir or Madam,

We enclose the countersigned copy of contract No. 350 of the 4th May 2022 for 350 bales of printed cottons. The letter of credit is on its way to you.

Please mark the bales with our initials, with the destination and contract number as follows:

KT
LONDON
250

This will apply to all shipments unless otherwise instructed.

Please advise us by fax as soon as shipment is effected.

Yours faithfully,

Unit Eleven Packing and Shipping 包装与装运

Sample 2

Dear Sirs,

Thank you for your quotation of March 23 and the sample sweaters sent to us recently. We find both the price and quality satisfactory and herewith enclose our order form for 300 dozen each of men's and women's woolen sweaters at the prices stated in your quotation.

As this is our first order, we would like to state our detailed packing requirements. We want the sweaters to be packed each in a polybag, 6 dozen to a carton lined with waterproof paper. If the cartons are not strong enough, most of them will be liable to go broken on arrival. So we would require that the carton be bound with double iron straps outside.

We hope these packing requirements can be met and await your early shipment.

Yours faithfully,

Sample 3

Dear Sirs,

Please pack the captioned machines in a strong wooden case and wrap and pad generously all polished parts of the machine to avoid scratches and knocks against the container.

Also please put the machine in a case of about 12 cubic meters covered with waterproof cloth and strapped vertically and horizontally with metal bands in the case to minimize condensation.

Thank you for your sincere cooperation.

Yours faithfully,

Sample 4

Dear Sirs,

We regret to inform you that the 145 cartons of iron nails you shipped to Dubai on May 12, 2022 were badly damaged, which is of course not your fault.

We are now writing to you about the packing of these nails, which we think necessary to clarify for our future dealings.

The packing for Dubai is to be in wooden cases of 112 lbs net, each containing 7 lbs 16 packets. For Malta, we would like to have the goods packed in double gunny bags of 50-60 kilos each. As for the British market, our buyers prefer 25-kilo cartons.

Would you please tell us whether these requirements could be met?

Your faithfully,

2. Negotiation over Shipping Marks

Dear Sirs,

Sales Confirmation NO. 89A/56

We thank you for your letter of October 12, 2006, enclosing the above Sales Contract in duplicate but wish to state that the packing clause in the contract is not clear enough. The relative clause should read:

Packing: Seaworthy export packing, suitable for long distance ocean transportation.

The shirts under the captioned contract should be packed in plastic bags, five dozen to one carton, 20 cartons on a pallet, and 10 pallets in FCL container. On the outer packing please mark our initials: JHCL in a triangle, under which the port of destination and our order number should be stenciled. In addition, directive marks like fat WATERPROOF, etc., should also be indicated.

We have made a footnote on the contract to that effect and are returning herein one copy of the contract, duly countersigned by us. We hope you will find it in order and pay special attention to the packing.

We look forward to receiving your shipping advice soon and thank you in advance.

Faithfully yours,

3. Packing Seller Advising Packing and Shipping Marks

Dear Sirs,

We thank you for your letter dated June 5 inquiring about the packing and the shipping marks of the goods under Contract No. B321, and are pleased to state as follows:

All milk powders are wrapped in plastic bags and packed in tins, the lids of which are sealed with adhesive tape. Ten tins are packed in a wooden case, which is nailed, and secured by overall metal strapping.

As regards shipping marks outside the wooden case, in addition to gross, net and tare weights, the wording "Made in Australia" is also stenciled. Should you have any special preference in this respect, please let us know and we shall meet your requirements to the best of our ability.

We assure you of our close co-operation and await your further comments.

Yours faithfully,

4. Negotiation on Carton Packing

Dear Sirs,

We are pleased to inform you that for your future orders we shall pack our garment in carton instead of in wooden cases, as packing in cartons has the following advantages:

It will prevent skillful pilferage, for the traces of pilferage will be more in evidence.

It is fairly fit for ocean transportation.
  (1) Our cartons are well protected against moisture by plastic lining.

(2) Cartons are comparatively light and compact, so they are more convenient to handle.

(3) Our comments about come from a comparative study of the characteristics of the two modes of packing, i.e. carton packing and wooden case packing, as well as the results of shipments already made.

We hope you will accept our carton packing and assure you of our sincere cooperation.

Yours faithfully,

A Reply to the Above from Buyer

Dear Sirs,

We have received your letter of August 13 with pleasure and immediately approached our clients about the packing. After our repeated explanation, they say they will have no objections to your packing of the garments in cartons if you guarantee that you will pay compensation in all cases wherein they cannot get indemnification from the insurance company for the reason that the cartons used are not seaworthy.

We deem it our duty to inform you of this and consider it a tacit understanding that you would hold yourselves responsible for the losses our clients night sustain on account of your using such cartons if the insurance company refuses compensations.

We think you will understand that our candid statements are made for our mutual benefits as packing is a sensitive subject, which often leads to trade disputes.

We appreciate your cooperation.

Yours faithfully,

5. Packing and Shipping Marks Instructions

Dear Sirs,

We thank you for your packing instruction, but regret our inability to comply with your request for special packing.

In order to finalize this initial trade activity between us, we would like to make the following suggestions for your consideration.

(1) The bed spreads will be packed 6 dozen to a packet, 4 packets to a carton and 8 cartons to a crate.

(2) Your initials will be printed in a diamond instead of the full name.

(3) The name of the country of origin of the goods will be marked on the carton and crate, not on every packet.

(4) Special directions and warnings will be stenciled on the crate, not on every carton.

Please inform us your comments by return fax.

Yours truly,

6. Suggestion for Carton Packing

Dear Sirs,

Please be informed that for your future orders we shall pack our garments in cartons instead of in wooden cases, as packed in cartons has the following advantages.

(1) It will prevent skillful pilferage as the traces of pilferage will be more in evidence.

(2) It is fairly fit for ocean transportation.

(3) Our cartons are well protected against moisture by plastic lining.

(4) Cartons are comparatively light and compact, so they are more convenient to handle.

Our comments above come from a comparative study of the characteristics of the two modes of packing, i.e. carton packing and wooden case packing, as well as the results of shipments already made. We hope you will accept our carton packing and assure you of our sincere cooperation.

Your faithfully,

7. Suggestion for Improvement of Packing

Dear Sir or Madam,

We regret to inform you that of the 160 cartons of machine parts delivered to us last week, 2 were found broken and some of the contents were badly damaged clearly through improper packing.

In view of our long-standing business relations, we would not lodge a claim against you for the loss this time. But we feel it necessary to stress the importance of seaworthy packing for our future dealings.

Usually valves and all delicate machine parts should be wrapped in soft material packed in cardboard boxes. These in turn are to be packed in wooden cases in such a manner that movement inside the cases is impossible. Besides, rope and metal handle should be fixed to the cases to facilitate consignment.

We look forward to your comments on the above.

Yours faithfully,

8. Urging for Prompt Delivery

Sample 1

Dear Sirs,

We are very anxious to know about the shipment of our Order No. 123 for 1,000 cases of Tin Plates.

As the contracted time of delivery is rapidly falling due, it is imperative that you inform us of the delivery time without any further delay. We stated explicitly at the outset the importance of punctual execution of this order and cannot help feeling surprised at your silence about our fax inquiry of the 18th June (6 days ago), a copy of which is enclosed.

We are in urgent need of these goods and have to request you to execute the order within the time stipulated.

Your sincerely,

Sample 2

Dear Sirs,

Re: Contract No. W4433

We refer to the above contract signed between us on July 1, 2018 for 6,000 long tons of wheat, which is stipulated for shipment in October, 1998. However, up till now we have not received from you any information concerning this lot. As our end users are in urgent need of this material, we intend to send our vessel S.S. "Feng Qing" to pick up the goods, which is expected to arrive at Vancouver around the end of November. You are requested to let us have your immediate reply by fax whether you are agreeable to this proposal. If not, please let us know exactly the earliest time when the goods will be ready.

We have been put to great inconvenience by the delay in delivery. In case you should fail to effect delivery in November, we will have to lodge a claim against you for the loss and reserve the right to cancel the contract.

Yours faithfully,

9. Shipping Instructions

Sample 1

Dear Sirs,

Re: Our Order No. 123

We have received your fax of March 2 and noted that you have booked our Order No. 123 for 4 sets of Model 790 Machine. Our confirmation of the order will be forwarded to you in a few days.

It is of great importance to our buyers that the arrival date of this order should be arranged as early as possible to meet their requirements. So you are supposed to ship the goods by a steamer of ... Co., the main reason is that their steamers offer the shortest time for the journey between China and Germany. We shall appreciate it if you will endeavor to ship the consignments as follows:

Order No.123: by s. s." ..." due to sail from Hamburg on 15/4/98 or latest by s.s "..." due to sail from Hamburg on 25/4/98 arriving in Amoy on 30/5/98 and 15/6/98 respectively. Thanking you in advance for your cooperation.

Yours faithfully,

Sample 2

Dear Sirs,

Re: Our Order No. 168

With reference to the shipment of our Order No. 168 for 100 cases of China Wares, we wish to draw your attention to the following: As the goods are susceptible to be broken, the wares must be packed in seaworthy cases capable of withstanding rough handling.

Please mark the cases with our initials in a diamond, under which comes the destination with contract number and stencil conspicuously the words: "FRAGILE, HANDLE WITH CARE" on both sides of the cases.

We trust that the above instructions are clear to you and that the shipment will give the users entire satisfaction.

Yours faithfully,

10. Booking Shipping Containers

Dear Sirs,

We have 50 cases of medicines and chemical reagents at the above address ready for dispatch to any European Main Port, and shall be glad if you will arrange for your shipping container to collect them. Each case weighs 60 kgs.

As our client requires us to ship the goods not later than July 15, please quote us for a shipping container from Hong Kong to the above mentioned port before that deadline.

Your early quotation will be highly appreciated.

Yours faithfully,

Reply:

Dear Sirs,

Thank you for your inquiry of 5 June, asking us to quote shipping container to any EMP for 50 cases of medicines and chemical reagents.

The shipping containers we provide are of two sizes, namely 10 ft. and 20 ft. long and built to take loads up to two to four tons respectively. They can be opened at both ends, thus making it possible to load and unload at the same time. They are both watertight and airtight and can be loaded and locked at the factory, if necessary.

There is also a saving in freight charges when separate consignments intended for the same port of destination are carried in one container and an additional saving on insurance because of the lower premiums charged for container shipped goods.

We enclose a copy of our tariff and look forward to receiving your instructions.

Yours faithfully,

11. Packing and Shipping Explanation

Sample 1

Dear Sir or Madam,

We are very anxious to know about the shipment of our order for 5,000 cases of apples.

As the contracted time of delivery is falling due, it is imperative that you make the shipment without any further delay. We recall that we stated explicitly the importance of punctual execution of this order in our purchase confirmation we sent you. Therefore, we cannot help feeling surprised at your silence about our fax inquiry of the 13th July, a copy of which is enclosed.

We need these goods urgently and have to remind you to process this order within the time stipulated.

Sincerely yours,

Sample 2

Dear Mr. Balkin,

Thank you very much for your letter of 5 January.

First of all, we must apologize for having not given you any news about your present order. We have been urging our manufacturer to give us definite delivery date of your order, and we think it is no use writing to you before any definite information is obtained.

We are now pleased to inform you that our manufacturer has just promised to deliver the goods within two weeks. Arrangements are also being made to ship the goods per s.s. "BEAUTY", which is scheduled to sail for your port early next month. We shall, of course, fax you details of the shipment as soon as the goods are placed on board the steamer.

We sincerely hope that our delay in writing to you has not caused you any inconvenience and that the shipment will turn out to your satisfaction.

Sincerely yours,

Sample 3

Dear Mr. Kato,

We are sending you the goods ordered on March 13, on s.s. "SHUNFENG", which departs today from Kobe. Enclosed are an invoice and a bill of lading.

We have taken great care in packing and handling the goods, so that they will reach you in good condition. In order to assist you in opening and checking the goods, they were divided into three parts. Each case has a number corresponding to that which is on the invoice.

We trust that you will be satisfied with them, and also hope that we shall have more opportunities to fill orders for you.

Yours sincerely,

本章知识提示

包装是对外贸易中一个重要的环节,包括运输包装(习惯称外包装或大包装)和销售包装(习惯称小包装或内包装)。它们都是为了保护商品的品质和数量而采取的措施。在国际贸易中,还有一种中性包装。它是在商品包装上既不注明生产国别、地名和厂名,也不注明原有商标和牌号的包装。中性包装分为无牌中性包装和定牌中性包装,其目的是打破进口国所实施的关税与非关税壁垒,或满足买方的特殊需求而采取的措施。

国际货物运输是国际贸易的一个重要组成部分,涉及的运输方式很多,其中包括公路或铁路运输、海洋或航空运输,以及多式联运。货运方式为公路或铁路运输、航空运输时,运输合同包括舱位租借契约。船公司与托运人之间的合同形式便是租船契约或提单。

运输包装不仅要起到防止货物在运输途中受损的作用,同时也应具备方便装卸、储存和防盗的功能。销售包装形式多样,用料各异,既要便于携带和使用,又要美观、新颖达到促销的目的。在商品的外包装上要刷上包装标志,主要有运输标志(唛头或墨头)、指示性标志和警告性标志,其中运输标志是必不可缺的。按照国际标准组织建议,为了简化单证,便于用打印机一次做成,运输标志不宜用几何图形。

集装箱化运输(containerization)是近年来使用最广泛的一种新型运输方式,包括三部分——集装箱、集装箱船和现代化装卸设施。自从集装箱运输日益发展以来,对外包装的要求有了较大的变化，有时甚至可以完全省去外包装，但对内包装的要求则从结构造型、色彩向更新潮化的方向发展。目前，已有堆叠式、挂式、展开式、开窗式、惯用式、易开式、喷雾式、套式、礼品式或复用式等新颖包装。

装运一般是指将货物装上运输工具，与交货是两个不同的概念。在国际贸易中，由于采用FOB/CIF/CFR三种价格术语时，卖方只要根据合同的有关规定将货物装上船、取得提单就算交货。提单签发日期亦即为交货日。因此，装运一词常被用来代替交货的概念。这种凭单交货被称为象征性交货（symbolic delivery）。凭单交货时，装运期和交货期是一致的。实际交货（physical delivery）是指货物运抵目的地，因而，装运时间与交货时间并不是一致的。在买卖合同中，合理地规定装运期（交货期）是很重要的。装运期（交货期）可分为定期装运、近期装运和不定期装运。装运前，买方通常把他们对所订购货物的包装、装运标志和运输方式等要求以书面形式通知卖方。这被称为装运指示。反之，卖方一经将货物装上指定的运输工具就立即将此情况通知买方。这被称为装运通知，尤其是以FOB和CFR条款成交的交易。装运通知一般包括合同号、信用证号码、商品名称、包装物编号、运输总量、轮船名称及起航日期等。如果交易是按照CIF条件或CFR条件达成的，卖方则应承担租船订舱的责任。出口货物数量较大需要整船载运的，应办理租船手续；对出口货物数量不大，不需要整船装运的，则安排租订班轮和租订部分舱位运输。

货物装船后，卖方应及时向买方发出装船通知，尤其是在按照FOB或CFR条件成交的情况下，买方接到通知后要即刻办理保险手续，如果卖方没有及时通知买方，使买方没能办理投保或误了办理保险的时间，那么由此而产生的经济损失将由卖方承担。如果按照CIF条件成交的，虽说是由卖方办理保险，但货物装船后，也要及时向买方发出装船通知，因为买方需要做好接货、卸货准备、办理进口报关手续等。

运输标志一般包括4行，每行不超过7个字母，其中包括数字和符号：①收货人或发货人的代号名称，②合同号码或信用证号码，③目的港，④件号、序号。这样易于识别货物，方便运输。指示性标志是针对一些易碎、易损、易变质的商品用醒目的图形和简单的文字提醒有关人员在装卸、搬运和存储时应注意的事项。警告性标志是对一些易燃、易爆、有毒等危险品在其包装上清楚而明显地刷制的标志，以示警告。

本章句式

1. Customer's Instruction to Supplier

(1) As is necessary to make transshipment at Singapore for the goods to be shipped to our port, your packing must be seaworthy and strong enough to stand rough handling during transit.

(2) When packing, please take into account that the boxes are likely to receive rough handling at this end and must be able to withstand transport over every bad road.

(3) The packets must be made up in piles of suitable size before being given their airtight tinfoil cover, and then packed in cases. The cases must be cleated and battened so as to eliminate the risk of damage caused by pressure.

(4) We usually pack each piece of men's shirt in a polybag, half dozen to a box and ten

dozen to a wooden case.

(5) Packing in sturdy wooden cases is essential. Cases must be nailed, battened and secured by overall metal strapping.

(6) Our cotton prints should be packed in cases lined with draft paper and water-proof paper, each consisting of 30 pieces in one design with 5 color-ways equally assorted.

(7) In view of the fragile nature of the goods, they should be wrapped in soft material and firmly packed in cardboard boxes so as to reduce damage in transit to a minimum.

2. Supplier's Information to Customer

(1) Our usual packing for dyed poplin is in bales lined with water proof paper, each containing 500 yards in single color.

(2) We packed our shirts in plastic-lined, waterproof cartons, reinforced with metal traps.

(3) All export bicycles are wrapped in strong waterproof material at the port and packed in pairs in lightweight crates.

(4) A special crate with reinforced bottom will be needed for the transport of such a large machine, and both padding and bolting down will be essential.

(5) We will pack the material in bales of approx. 1 meter in length and 3 meters in girth. The protective canvas will be provided with ears to facilitate lifting.

(6) We regret to inform you that the goods delivered by our factory are packed single size of a box instead of assorted size as required.

(7) You will note that our packing has been greatly improved with the result that all our recent shipments have turned out to the satisfaction of our clients.

(8) You may rest assured that the packing is strong enough to withstand rough handling.

3. Instructions on Shipping Marks and Others

(1) We give you on the attached sheet full details regarding packing and marking. These must be strictly observed.

(2) In case your shipping marks are required, your order should clearly indicate such marks and reach us one month before the shipment time.

(3) All boxes are to be marked as usual, but please number mem consecutively from No. 11.

(4) The goods are to be marked with our initials in a diamond, and warning marks are to be clearly marked.

(5) The order mentioned above is completed. We are urgently awaiting your instructions regarding labeling to each package for shipment on board S. S. "Red Star".

(6) We regret being unable to accept your request for indicating the full name and address of the consignee on each package, as shipping marks comprising the initials of buyer's name will suffice for your purpose.

(7) For dangerous and poisonous cargo, the nature and the generally adopted symbol shall be marked conspicuously on each package.

(8) Please stencil our shipping marks in letters 10 cm high, and give gross and net weight on each box.

4. Urging Shipment

(1) We regret up to the time of the writing we have not heard anything from you about the order in question.

(2) We are now referring to the Contract No. AG 6678 signed between us on 23rd April, 2006 for 1,000 cases Tin plates, which is stipulated for shipment in May 5th, 2006. However, up to now we have not received from you any information about this consignment.

(3) We wish to call your attention to the fact that up to the present moment no news comes from you about the shipment under the captioned contract.

(4) We are in urgent need of these goods and would have to request you to execute the order within the time stipulated.

(5) As the contract time of delivery is rapidly falling due, it is imperative that we hear from you without any further delay.

5. Shipping Instructions

(1) We shall be very much appreciative if you effect shipment as soon as possible, thus enabling them to fill the brisk demand at the start of the season.

(2) Please try your utmost to ship our goods by S. S. "Freedom" which is due to arrive at Hamburg on September 12 and confirm by return that the goods will be ready in time.

(3) We should be much obliged if you could effect shipment of these milk power in two equal lots by direct steamer as soon as you receive our L/C.

(4) Please ensure that all the cases are marked clearly with our initials in a triangle, under which comes the destination with the contract number below.

(5) As these goods are apt to break if not handled with care in transportation, we suggest that the parcel should be sent by container vessel, to avoid possible damage in loading and discharge.

(6) The first partial goods will be shipped on the first available steamer in the middle of July. The transshipment may be allowed at Hong Kong. The port of destination is Los Angeles.

(7) It has to be stressed that shipment must be made within the prescribed time limit, as a further extension will not be considered.

(8) It is stipulated that shipment should be made before and, if possible, we should appreciate your arranging to ship the goods at an earlier date.

(9) As the cargo is to be transshipped at Hong Kong, we shall require through Bs/L.

(10) As direct steamers to your port are few and far between, we have to ship via Hong Kong.

6. Shipping advice

(1) We are pleased to inform you that the consignment under your order No. 1129 has now been shipped per S. S. "Luck" which is to leave here on Aug. 1 and due to arrive at your port on Aug. 10, 2006.

(2) We are pleased to advise that your order for shipment per S.S. "Dove" on Aug. 23 was collected yesterday by your forwarding agent.

(3) We thank you for your letter of January 10 and now are pleased to inform you that we have completed the above shipment in accordance with stipulation set forth in the L/C and the goods you ordered will be dispatched to you per S. S. "China Prince" tomorrow morning.

(4) In compliance with the terms of the contract, we forwarded you by airmail a full set of duplicate shipping documents immediately after the goods were shipped. The original documents are being sent to you by the Bank of China.

(5) We have shipped the above goods on board S.S. ... which will sail to your port tomorrow. Enclosed is one set of the shipping documents covering this consignment.

Unit Twelve　Complaints and Claims
申诉与索赔

◆ *Learning Objectives*

a. Understand the basic knowledge of international trade complaints and claims;

b. Master the writing steps of complaint and claim letters according to different trade situations.

Complaints is the incorrect result of a trade transaction and a retransaction. Claims is the two parties who sign the contract. One party violates the provisions of the contract and causes losses to the other party, and the other party who suffers the losses claims for damages to the breaching party according to the contract or the law. Claims has 3 kinds of circumstance commonly, namely: goods sale claim, transport claim, insurance claim. The act of the breaching party to handle the claim filed by the party suffering the loss is called the claim.[①]

Section 1　Introduction

In business activities, no matter how perfect an organization may be, complaints from the customers are certain to arise. Generally speaking, complaints may be of several kinds, and may arise from the delivery of wrong goods, damaged goods, or too many or too few goods or quality may have been found unsatisfactory, and etc.

If a complaint or claim has to be made by the buyer, the matter should be investigated in detail and these details should be laid before the party charged.

People must handle complaints or claims in accordance with the principle of "on the first grounds, to their advantage and with restraint" and settle them amicably to the satisfaction of all parties concerned. Usually a complaint or claim letter should follow the following principles.

a. Begin by regretting the need to complain.

---

① 申诉(投诉)是贸易交易和再交易的不正确结果。索赔是签订合同的双方中,一方违反合同约定给对方造成损失,另一方根据合同或者法律向违约方要求赔偿损失。索赔一般有三种情况,即货物销售索赔、运输索赔、保险索赔。违约方处理遭受损失方提出的索赔的行为被称为索赔。

b. Mention the date of the order, the date of delivery and the goods complained about.

c. State the reasons for being dissatisfied and ask for an explanation.

d. Refer to the inconvenience caused.

e. Suggest how the matter should be put right.

f. Be careful in choosing the wording in the correspondence so as to avoid any misunderstandings.

Sometimes, a reference to the previously satisfactory deliveries and services may help to win more sympathetic consideration of the present complaint or claim.

Having been given a complaint or claim letter by the buyer, the seller should deal with the matter according to the following rules without delay.

a. The first thing that has to be decided is whether the complaint is justified.

b. If so, then the seller has to admit it readily, express his/her regret and promise to make the matter right.

c. If the complaint is not justified, point out politely and in an agreeable manner. It would be a wrong policy to refuse the claim offhand.

d. If the seller cannot deal with a complaint promptly, acknowledge it at once. Explain that he/she is looking into it and that he/she will send a full reply later.

e. All complaints should be treated as serious matters and thoroughly investigated.

Letters concerning disputes should be written tactfully and reasonably. They must be confined to a statement of facts and insist on the absolute truth.

Section 2   Examples of Complaints and Claims

1. Complaint of Wrong Goods Delivered

Dear Sir,

Our Order No. 167

We duly received the documents and took delivery of the goods on arrival of the s/s "Lucky" at Shanghai. We are much obliged to you for the prompt execution of this order. Everything appears to be correct and in good condition except in case No. 1-95.

Unfortunately when we opened this case we found it contained completely different articles, and we can only presume that a mistake was made and the contents of this case were for another order.

As we need the articles we ordered to complete deliveries to our own customers, we must ask you to arrange for the dispatch of replacements at once. We attach a list of the contents of case No. 1-95, and shall be glad if you will check this with our order and the copy of your invoice.

In the meantime, we are holding the above-mentioned case at your disposal. Please let us know what you wish us to do with it.

Yours faithfully,

大意

敬启者：

  我方第167号订单

  我方按期收到了装船单据，并且在"好运"号轮抵达上海港时提到了货物。

  非常感谢贵方对此订单及时执行。除了1—95号箱货物外，全部货物正确无误，安全抵达。

  遗憾的是，当我方打开1—95号货箱时，发现里面装的是完全不同种类的货品。我方猜测，可能是出现了差错。此货属于另外的订单。

  由于我方急需该货以便履行给我方客户交货的职责，请贵方务必尽快更换。兹函附寄第1—95号箱货品清单一份。敬请贵方将此订单与我方订单和贵方发票副本核对。

  同时，我方将保存上述货箱货物，等候贵方处理。请将贵方处理意见告知我方。

  谨上

Reply：

Dear Sirs,

Your Order No. 167 per s/s "Lucky"

Thank you for your letter of ... We were glad to know that the consignment was delivered promptly, but it was with great regret that we heard case No. 1-95 did not contain the goods you ordered.

On going into the matter we find that a mistake was indeed made in packing, through a confusion of number, and we have arranged for the right goods to be dispatched to you at once. Relative documents will be mailed as soon as they are ready.

We will appreciate it if you will keep case No. 1-95 and contents until called for by the local agents of World Transport Ltd., our forwarding agents, whom we have instructed accordingly.

Please accept our many apologies for the trouble caused to you by the error.

Yours faithfully,

大意

敬启者：

贵方第 167 号订单

感谢贵方……的来信，货物能够按时抵达，非常高兴。得知所发 1-95 号箱所装货物并非贵方订购之货，我方感到十分抱歉。

经过调查，我方发现，由于数字混淆，包装中确实出现差错。现在我方已经发出了正确的货物。有关单据也将尽早邮寄给贵方。

如果贵方能暂时保存 1—95 号货箱及货物，我方将不胜感激。我方将把上述情况通知我方的运输代理"环球运输公司"的当地部门前往你处做出恰当的处理。

由于我方的差错，给贵方造成了麻烦，特此致歉。

谨上

2. Complaint for Late Delivery

Dear Sirs,

Our Order No. 764

We are referring to our Order No. 764 for Hand Tools. When we gave you our order on June 1st we stated explicitly that we wanted delivery not later than 15th July and you have confirmed our order accordingly.

Since the date you confirmed our order, one month has passed but we are surprised that we have not yet received the goods or any advice from you when we can expect delivery.

We must point out to you that this delay is very seriously inconveniencing us, and we ask you to give the reason of the non-execution, of our order. As in the event of your being unable to supply us we shall be compelled to cancel the order and get these goods from another firm.

Yours faithfully,

大意

敬启者：

  我方第764号订单

  我方第764号订单订购手工工具。我方7月1日寄发的订单中已经明确指出交货期不得迟于7月15日，贵方也相应地给予了确认。

  自从贵方确认至今，一个月过去了。令我方吃惊的是，至今尚未到货，也未收到有关何时可以交货的消息。

  必须指出的是，此次延误给我方造成了极大的不便，我方要求贵方对没有执行的订单的原因做出解释。若贵方无法供货，我方将转向其他公司购买此货。

  谨上

Reply：

Dear Sirs,

Your Order No. 764

We have received your letter of July 15 and very much regret the delay which has occurred in the execution of your Order No. 764. This was occasioned by a serious breakdown in our supplier's machinery, in consequence of which all their work was brought to a standstill for several days. The damage, however, has been repaired, and we can assure you we will lose no time in the prompt delivery of the goods.

You may expect to receive the goods by the 25th. We regret the inconvenience you have sustained, but trust this unavoidable accident will not influence you unfavorably in future orders.

Yours faithfully,

回复：

敬启者：

  贵方7月15日来信收悉，对于延误执行贵方第764号订单深表歉意。此事的偶然发生是由于我方供货商的机器发生严重的故障造成的。在此期间，他们停产数天。然而故障已经排除，请相信我方将抓紧时间完成交货。

Unit Twelve Complaints and Claims 申诉与索赔

贵方可望在 25 日之前收到货物。对于给贵方造成的不便,在此深表歉意。同时也相信,这种难免的事故不会对今后的订单造成不利影响。

谨上

3. Complaint for Inferior Quality

Gentlemen:

We have received the goods of our Order No. A100 for 200 cases Muslins, which you shipped by the S.S. "Feng Qing", but much to our regret we have to inform you that we have received serious complaints from our buyer. He states that the goods are not only much inferior in quality, but a number of pieces are woven narrowly to the pattern submitted by you. These faults make the goods quite unsalable in this market.

We are, however, making efforts to settle the matter amicably, but in case our buyer persists in making complaint, there is no way for us but put the matter before the Chamber of Commerce of Singapore for arbitration, and any allowance that we may have to make will be debited to you in due course.

We hope the matter will come to your best attention.

Yours truly,

大意

敬启者:
　　贵方由"丰庆号"轮装运的我方第 A100 号订单订购的 200 箱平纹细布已收到。但是非常遗憾地告知贵方,我方客户提出了严厉的申诉,说货物不但质地非常低劣,而且有多块布匹的布幅织得比贵方提供的样品窄。这些缺陷使得产品在该市场很难销售。
　　我方正竭力和解此事,但是如果我方客户坚持申诉,只能将此送交新加坡商会仲裁。我方所要支付的任何费用到时都将计入贵方账户。
　　希望此事引起贵方特别关注。
　　谨上

4. Claim for Inferior Quality

Sample 1

Dear Sirs,

Re: Claim for 10,000 pcs. Of Valves

We are enriching a copy of the Inspection Certificate No. (98)204 issued by the Shanghai Commodity Inspection Bureau. The certificate proved that the above goods we received on May 5 are much inferior in quality to your previous samples.

As these goods are of no use at all to us, we require you refund the invoice amount and inspection fee of the goods amounting to US …

We trust you will promptly settle this claim. As soon as the settlement is accomplished, we will send the goods back to you. All the expenses will be for your account.

Yours faithfully,

End. as stated

大意

敬启者：

事由：关于10 000个阀门

兹随函附寄由上海商品检验局出具的第(98)204号检验单之副本一份。该单证明我方5月5日所收到的上述货物的品质比贵方预先提供的样品差得多。

由于这批货物对我方毫无用处，我方向贵方提出……美元的损失赔偿，包括发票金额和检验费用。

希望贵方能及时理赔。一经贵方理赔，我方将把货物退还贵方。一切费用由贵方负担。

谨上

附件：如文所示

Favorable Replies:

Dear Sirs,

Your Claim on 10,000 pcs of Valves

We have received your fax of May 10, with enclosure, claiming for inferior quality on the consignment of 10,000 pieces of valves.

In order to settle the claim, we will immediately send a representative to investigate this matter. If our party was at fault, the compensation will be made at once.

We apologize for the trouble caused to you and assure you that we will give you a satisfactory answer.

Yours faithfully,

大意

敬启者：
  关于贵方 10 000 个阀门的索赔
  贵方 5 月 10 日的传真及附件已收悉，就 10 000 个阀门的低劣质量提出索赔。
  为解决该项索赔，我方将立刻派人对此事进行调查。如果责任在我方，我方将立即做出赔偿。
  给贵方造成麻烦，深表歉意，并保证会给贵方做出满意的答复。
  谨上

Dear Sirs,

Your Claim for 10,000 pcs of Valves

Further to our fax of May 16, we are writing to tell you that our representative has looked into the matter and found that it was a mistake by our staff at the warehouse. We are, therefore, going to settle the claim.

But our proposal of settlement is that we will immediately send to you replacements of which the quality is guaranteed. As to the valves you received, we will be highly appreciate it if you will try to sell for us in your market at our quoted price, i.e. US $... per piece including your ...% commission. If you agree with our proposal, please inform us by fax.

We feel greatly regretful for the inconvenience you have sustained and would like to assure you that all possible steps will be taken to avoid such mistakes happening again.

Yours faithfully,

大意

敬启者：

关于贵方 10 000 个阀门的索赔

继我方 5 月 16 日传真。通知贵方，我方代表已对此事进行了调查，发现是我方货舱职员的工作失误。因此，我方将进行理赔。

但是，我方建议的解决方法是，我方立即发运保证质量的替代物。至于贵方收到的阀门，如果能代表我方在贵方市场销售，我方将不胜感激。售价按我方报价，即每个……美元，包括贵方……％佣金。若同意上述意见，请以传真告知我方。

此事给贵方带来了麻烦，在此深表歉意，并向贵方保证我方将采取一切措施避免此类差错再次发生。

谨上

Sample 2

Dear Sirs,

Our Order No. A105

We have duly received the goods of our Order No. A105 for Cotton Jacquard Bath Towels. But we are regret to say that the goods we received are not up to our standard and they are quite unsalable in this market.

Needless to say, we have suffered a great loss and the inferior quality of the lot put us into great trouble, for our end users refused to accept these goods and they are going to seek for other resources.

Under these circumstances, we have to make a claim with you as follows:

Claim Number	Claim for	Amount
CM-90113	Quality	US$ 2,152.00

We feel sure that you will give our claim your most favorable consideration and let us have your settlement at an early date.

Yours faithfully,

Unit Twelve　Complaints and Claims 申诉与索赔

[大意]

敬启者：

关于我方第 A105 号订单

我方第 A105 号订单项下提花浴巾已及时收到。但非常遗憾地告知贵方，我方所收到的货物不符合标准，在我方市场很难销售。

毫无疑问，我方已经损失很大。而且这批货物的质量使得我方陷入困境，因为我方客户拒绝购买这批商品而转向其他供货商。

在这种情况下，我方不得不向贵方提出如下的索赔：

索赔号	索赔理由	索赔金额
CW-90113	质量问题	2 152 美元

我方相信，贵方一定会对我方的索赔给予特别关照，并且尽早告诉我方结果。

谨上

An Unfavorable Reply：

Dear Sirs，

Your Claim on Order No. A105

With reference to your claim on Order No. A105 for inferior quality. We have looked into this matter in details and so far as we have found that there is no ground for such a claim to be lodged against us. If you can examine the goods with great care with the sample you will find they are of the exactly same quality. Since the goods are manufactured according to your supplied sample and all your requirements are complied with，we assume no responsibility whatsoever if you now find them unsuitable for sale in your market.

As we are in no way liable for the quality of the goods，we regret being unable to entertain your claim.

We hope our explanation will convince you to withdraw your claim and hope this matter will have no harmful effect on the dealings between us in future.

Yours faithfully，

敬启者:

兹回复贵方对第A105号订单项下货物因质量低劣提出的索赔。我方已对此事进行了详细调查,认为贵方提出的索赔是没有根据的。

如果贵方能将货物与样品进行仔细比较,贵方就会发现两者质量完全相同。因为货物是按贵方提供的样品生产的,并且符合要求,所以如果贵方现在认为此货物不宜在贵方市场销售,我方不应承担任何责任。

由于我方对产品质量不负有责任,所以很抱歉不能接受贵方索赔。

希望我方的解释能使贵方撤回索赔,并且在未来的交易中不会受到不利的影响。

谨上

5. Claim for Improper Packing

Dear Sirs,

Our Order No. C426

We received this morning the 20 cartons of Wool Carpet under our Order No. C426 per s.s. CHANGFU. We found that one side of 8 cartons were worn and torn and 4 cartons were broken and the carpets were in the open. It was obviously attributed to improper packing.

Though the carpets can be used, we have to sell them at a price much lower than usual. In view of the above we suggest you give us 20% of discount on the invoice value or we will return the goods to you and ask for replacements.

Please let us know your decision as soon as possible.

Yours faithfully,

敬启者:

关于我方第C426号订单

今天早上刚刚收到由"长福"轮装运的我方第C426号订单项下的50箱羊毛地毯。我方发现其中8个箱体的一侧磨损破裂、4个箱体破碎,以致地毯暴露。这显然是包装不良所致。

尽管地毯还能使用,但我方售价只能大大低于正常价格。鉴于此,我方建议贵方向我方提供发票金额20%的折扣,否则我方将把货物退还,要求更换。

请尽早将贵方决定告知我方。
谨上

Reply：

Dear Sirs,

Your Claim on Order No. C426

We regret to learn from your letter of September 8 that your Order No. C426 of 20 cartons of Wool Carpet arrived in poor condition.

If we were at fault we would be responsible to agree to your proposal. But in view of the fact that our goods were carefully packed by experienced workman and sent out in perfect condition as shown by a copy of the clean B/L which we enclose herewith. We are certain they were damaged through careless handling while in transit.

We therefore suggest you had better enter a claim immediately against the Shipping Company. If you will send us the papers which show exactly the condition the goods reached you, we will take up the matter for you with the view of recovering damages from the Shipping Company.

We are awaiting your reply.

Yours faithfully,

大意

敬启者：
  关于贵方第 C426 号订单的索赔
  从贵方 9 月 8 日的来信获悉，贵方第 C426 号订单中所订购的 20 箱地毯抵达时货物状况不良，对此深表遗憾。
  如果是我方责任，我方理应同意贵方所提的建议。但是由于货物是经过我方富有经验的工人仔细包装，并且托运时完好无损，随函所附的清洁提单副本即可证明。我方相信破损是由于运输过程中的粗鲁搬运所致。
  因此我方建议贵方立即向装运公司提出索赔。如果贵方能将货物抵达时确切状况的文件寄给我方，我方将替贵方办理此事，以便从装运公司获得补偿。
  盼复
  谨上

6. Claim for Short Weight

Dear Sirs,

Re: Our Order No. 234 for 10 M/T Chemical Fertilizer

We have just received the Survey Report from Shanghai Commodity Inspection Bureau evidencing that the captioned goods unloaded here yesterday was short weight 1,120 kg. A thorough examination showed that the short weight was due to the improper packing, for which the suppliers should be definitely responsible.

On the basis of the SCIB's Survey Report, we hereby register a claim with you for Stg. £270.00 in all.

We are enclosing the Survey Report No.(2023)607 and look forward to settlement at an early date.

Yours faithfully,

大意

敬启者：
  事由：我方订购10吨化肥的第234号订单
  我方刚刚收到上海商品检验局的检验报告，昨天送达的标题所述的货物短重1 120千克。经仔细检验发现，短重是由于包装不良所致，供货方应对此完全负责。
  根据上海商品检验局的检验报告，我方向贵方提出总额为270英镑的索赔。
  随函附寄第(2023)607号检验报告，希望贵方早日处理。
  谨上

Reply:

Dear Sirs,

Your Claim No. 145

With reference to your claim No. 145 for a short weight of 1,120 kg Chemical Fertilizer, we wish to express our much regret over the unfortunate incident.

After a check-up by our staff, it was found that some 28 bags had not been packed in 5-ply strong paper bags as stipulated in the contract, thus resulting in the breakage during transit, for which we tender our apologies.

In view of our long-standing business relations, we will make payment by cheque for stg.£ 270.00, the amount of claim, into your account with the Bank of China, upon receipt of your agreement.

We trust that the arrangement we have made will satisfy you and look forward to receiving your further orders.

Yours faithfully,

大意

敬启者：
　　贵方第 145 号订单
　　兹谈及贵方第 145 号订单索赔函，索赔短重 1 120 千克化肥。对这一事件，我方深感歉意。
　　经过核查，我方发现大约有 28 袋没有按照合同规定使用 5 层耐用纸袋包装，所以在运输途中造成破损。
　　鉴于我们之间长期的贸易关系，一经接到贵方的许可，我方将通过中国银行以支票向贵方支付索赔金额 270 英镑。
　　相信我方的处理会使贵方感到满意，并且期待贵方更多的订单。
　　谨上

◆ 本章知识提示

　　在国际贸易中，索赔虽然不是每一笔交易都涉及，但还是时有发生。一般情况下，索赔是在当购买方受到某种较大损失时未获得赔偿向买方提出来的。此损失有可能是货物没有送达、推迟交货、短装短量、质量低劣、不良包装、违约等造成的。当然，卖方也可以因为买方为开信用证或者违约而向买方提出索赔。

　　提出索赔时要有理有据，首先要表明提出索赔的原因、陈述清楚所遭受损失的程度，然后提出要求对方赔偿损失的方法，如重新发货、补发货物、赔偿金额。在索赔时还应附上货到目的港后由当地商检机构出具的商品检验证明书作为索赔的依据。另外，索赔一定要在合同规定的期限内提出。

索赔或理赔都要严肃、谨慎,力争友好解决,尽可能避免提交仲裁或诉诸国际法庭。

在写这类有关申诉或索赔的信函时应注意:

(1)评估损失的大小,并根据双方的合作状态决定是申诉或索赔。

(2)查找申诉或索赔的理由或原因,并就此问题引起对方的注意。

(3)提出解决问题的方案,并寻求谅解。

(4)在解决问题时要分清问题的责任人是谁,并就此问题和对方进行商榷。信文写作要有礼貌,有理有据。

◆ 本章句式

1. Complaints about Quality and Replies

(1) Upon examination, we found that many of the goods were severely damaged, though the cases showed no trace of damage.

(2) Although the quality of these goods is not up to that of our usual lines, we are prepared to accept them if you will reduce the prices, say, by …

(3) We are sorry to inform you that your last shipment is not of your usual standard. The goods seem to be too roughly made and are inclined to be interior and out of shape.

(4) We regret to have to inform you that the computers, which you sold us on … has caused numerous complaints.

(5) Upon examination, we have found that the quality of the products is too inferior to meet the requirement at our local market.

(6) You must clearly understand that unless what you can supply is with the best quality in every case, we shall have to fill our requirements elsewhere.

(7) We were sorry to receive your complaint that the material you received was not of the quality expected.

(8) Needles to say, we are most willing to replace the faulty articles.

2. Complaints about Poor Packing and Replies

(1) We have examined them one by one, and found that each of them was leaking more or less.

(2) In our opinion, the damage was caused by improper packing. A machine of this size and weight should be blocked in position inside the export case.

(3) The packing inside was too loose with result that there was some shifting of the Contents and several cups and plates have been broken. The attached list will give you details.

(4) We have had the case and its contents examined by the insurance surveyor but, as you will see from the enclosed copy of this report, he maintains that the damage was probably due to insecure packing and not to any unduly rough handling of the case.

(5) The cases were found to be badly damaged. This was apparently attributable to faulty packing.

(6) We are sorry that we cannot accept your claim because the cases were damaged in the transit, which should be the responsibility of the shipping forwarder.

(7) We are sorry that we cannot bear the responsibility for the damages incurred to your goods, because we have the documents to prove that the goods were received by the carrier in perfection.

3. Complaints about Shortages and Replies

(1) In checking the contents against your enclosed invoice, it was found that several items were missing.

(2) There is a discrepancy between the packing list of case No. 56 and your invoice; 3 dozen Tea Sets are correctly entered on the invoice but there were only 2 dozen in the case.

(3) The Inspection Certificate shows that there is a shortage of 561 kilos, which in the opinion of the Bureau had occurred before shipment because the packing remained intact when the parcel was landed at our port. Would you please send us a check for US$15,00 to cover this shortage and the Inspection fee of US$250?

(4) The alleged shortage might have occurred in the course of transit, and that is a matter over which we can excise no control.

(5) We would like to compensate you for the shortage in weight mentioned in your letter of ... percent by offering you an allowance of ... percent.

4. Complaints about Delay in Shipment and Replies

(1) This delay has inconvenienced us considerably. We should appreciate it if you would inform us by return mail when we may expect the goods.

(2) For the past weeks we have been urging you for an immediate dispatch of these goods, and unless this order is already on the way, it will arrive too late for the season, and so be of no use to us.

(3) We trust you will now consider this matter seriously and make an effort to prevent the reoccurrence of this annoying delay.

(4) Please inform us soon whether you can deliver the goods by the end of July. If your answer is the negative, we shall have to cancel the order as we cannot possibly wait any longer.

(5) As you know, the demand for these goods is seasonal. We shall, therefore, be forced to cancel this order and buy elsewhere unless we can get immediate shipment.

(6) Due to your excessive delay in delivery, we notify you of our cancellation of contract.

(7) As the time of shipment is now considered overdue, we hope you will inform us by return of the reason for delay.

(8) The delay on your part has already put us in a very serious and awkward position toward our customers, and we must ask you kindly to do your best to help us out of it.

(9) Please take the matter up at once and see to it that the goods are delivered without

delay.

(10) The goods are promised to be delivered within ... and we have been put to considerable inconvenience through the long delay.

5. Complaints about Wrong Goods and Replies

(1) We are sorry to inform you that you have sent us the wrong goods, and this error is inconvenient and annoying to us.

(2) On going into the matter we find a mistake was indeed made in the packing through a confusion in numbers, and we have arranged for the right goods to be dispatched to you at once.

(3) Upon examining your first delivery, we find that it does not contain the assortment which we ordered.

(4) We have found that the goods shipped to us in execution of our Order No. 35/26 do not correspond with the sample, which led to our placing the order. You should explain the reason on the matter.

(5) Unfortunately, we find that the bulk of the goods delivered is not up to sample.

Unit Thirteen　Agency
代理

◆ Learning Objectives

a. Learn about the agent writing content, writing points, common expressions and related examples;

b. Learn to write an agency letter from the perspective of the principal or the agent.

Agency refers to a practice that is habitually adopted in the import and export business of international trade. It means that the principal entrusts an agent as his/her foreign representative and authorizes the agent to engage in various activities related to trade abroad. The relationship between agent and principal is agency. There are many agents in the international market, including procurement, sales, transportation, insurance, advertising and other agents. When signing the agency agreement, to clear agent commodity name, specifications, agent area, granted agent authority and agent obligations, such as the agent must be stipulated within a certain period of time in accordance with the transaction conditions and price to complete the minimum sales quota, and limit the agent shall not operate other suppliers similar products.

Section 1　Introduction

Many transactions in international trade are handled not only by direct negotiations between buyers and sellers but by means of agencies. A foreign agent is well familiar with the local business environment, and knows clearly what goods are needed and what prices are the best in the local market. Therefore, it may be convenient and economical for a company to do business through agencies.

An agency is an organization, especially a company, acting as the representative, agent, or subcontractor of a person or another company. It indicates a legal relationship involving a person or an organization and another who acts for the person or the organization. The person or the organization that empowers another to conduct business performance is called the principal, and the empowered is termed the agency. The most prominent feature of this form of business in international trade is that the principal enters into relations with the customers abroad by the agent who is on behalf of the principal but is not his/her employee.

Generally, there are two main types of agencies: the exclusive agency and the non-exclusive agency. The exclusive agency, also known as the sole agency, is a firm or a person who acts for his/her foreign principal with exclusive rights to sell in a specific area on a commission basis and he/she will not sell products that compete with the products of the principal. The non-exclusive agency, also called the general agent, is a firm or a person who acts under instructions from his/her principal to sell or buy on the best terms obtainable and who may sell or buy the competitors goods. Mostly, a principal has only one agency in a certain area, and cannot empower other people or organizations the same rights in that area.

The principal should make careful investigations about the prospective agencies, and has to make sure the firm or person to be appointed has sufficient means to develop the trade and reliable connections in the designated area. The company should also make inquires into the qualifications, experiences and other necessary information of the agent candidates, such as the reliability and financial soundness, their market connections and sales channels, and whether they are agents of the principal's competitors. Though the terms of agency vary with different circumstances, they should be made clear and definite, particularly for dealings involving large sales. A formal agreement on agency may include the following items: the nature and duration of the agency, the territory he/she covered, the duties of the parties concerned, the method of purchase and sale, and the commission for the agency.

This is an incoming letter from a firm abroad, requesting for a sole agency for household and decorative wares on a commission basis. Besides, they offer the business relations with their counterpart, the China National Handicrafts and Arts Import & Export Corporation, Shanghai Branch.

In international trade, a lot of business has been done through selling or buying agents, and most of large firms in the world have agencies or agents. In order to enlarge business activities, we have to choose some reliable agents for the sale of our products, and make an agreement (better: a time agreement) with them so as to facilitate opening new markets in every part of the world. In choosing competent agents, we have to pay more attention to their qualification, experience, commercial moral, reputation and what is more important, the ability in doing business. As for the rewards to the agency company, they are paid on a commission basis, that is, according to the quantity of the goods sold.

Section 2 Examples of Agent Letters

1. Asking to be Sole Agency

Dear Sirs,

We understand from E/E Corporation of New York City, U.S.A. that you are looking for a reliable firm with good connections in medical equipment trade to represent you in North America.

Having had experience in marketing medical equipments, we are familiar with customers' needs and are confident we could develop a good market for you in North America. We have spacious and well-equipped showrooms and an experienced staff of sales representatives who could push your business effectively.

We should be pleased to learn that you are interested in our proposal and on what terms you are willing to conclude an agency agreement.

For general information concerning our credit standing and integrity in the trade we suggest you refer to E/E Corporation.

Yours faithfully,

大意

敬启者：
　　我公司从美国纽约 E/E 公司获悉贵方正在寻找一家在医疗设备贸易方面具有广泛联系的商号作为贵方在北美地区的代理。
　　我公司在销售医疗设备方面具有经验并熟悉顾客的需要，有信心定能为贵方在北美地区开辟广阔市场。我公司拥有宽敞的、设备良好的展室，以及具有丰富经验的销售人员。他们一定能有效促进贵方的业务。
　　期望贵方对我公司的建议感兴趣，并希望了解到贵方按什么条件愿意达成代理协议。
　　关于我公司的资金状况及商业信誉请向 E/E 公司查询。
　　谨上

Reply：

Dear Sirs,

After a careful consultation with E/E Corporation, New York, and a friendly discussion with Mr. Green, the manager of your corporation, we have decided to entrust you with the sole agency for our Type MD-4 Brand Medical Device in the territory of North America.

The appointment will be for a trial period of twelve months in the first instance. We shall pay you a commission of 5% on the net value of all sales against orders received through you. If you will confirm these terms we will arrange for a formal agreement to be drawn up and, when this is signed, prepare a circular for distribution to our customers in North America, announcing your appointment as our agents.

Yours faithfully,

大意

敬启者：

通过向纽约 E/E 公司查询，并与你公司经理格林先生友好协商之后，我方决定委托贵方为我方 MD-4 型品牌治疗仪在北美地区的独家代理。

委托期限先定为 12 个月的尝试期，我方将根据从贵方获得的订单按所销售额的净值支付贵方 5% 的佣金。

如果贵方确认上述条件，我方将安排拟定正式的协议。协议一经签署，我方立即向北美地区的客户发出通函，宣布委托贵方为我方代理。

谨上

2. Sole Agency Agreement

This Sole Agency Agreement is entered into through friendly negotiations between China National XXX Import and Export Corporation, Xi'an, China (hereinafter called Party A), and XXX Company, New York, U.S.A. (hereinafter called Party B) on the basis of equality and mutual benefit to develop business on the terms and conditions set forth below:

(1) Party A agrees to appoint Party B to act as its Sole Agents in the territory of North America for the sale of Type MD-4 XXX Brand Medical Device.

(2) Price: Party B is under obligation to push sales energetically at the price quoted by Party A. Each transaction is subject to Party A's final confirmation.

(3) Quantity:

During the under-mentioned period, Party B shall place orders with Party A for not less than 6,000 sets of Type MD-4 XXX Brand Medical Device. Party B shall order at least 3,000 sets in the first six months from the date of signing this agreement. Should Party B fail to fulfill the above-mentioned quantity (namely 3,000 sets) in this duration, Party A shall have the right to sell the goods under this agreement to other customers in North America.

In case Party B places orders for less than 1,000 sets in three months from the date on which the agreement is signed, Party A shall have the right to terminate this agreement by giving notice in writing to Party B.

(4) Payment:

Payment is to be made by confirmed, irrevocable letter of credit, without recourse, available by sight draft upon presentation of shipping documents. The Letter of Credit for each order shall reach Party A 30 days before (prior to) the date of shipment. Should Party B fail to establish the Letter of Credit in time, any loss or losses including bank interest, storage, etc., which Party A may sustain shall be borne by Party B.

(5) Commission:

Party A agrees to pay Party B a commission of 5% (five percent) on FOB value of orders. The commission is to be paid only after full payment for each order is received by Party A. As slated in Article (3) of this agreement, no commission shall be paid on orders secured and executed by Party A itself.

(6) Reports on Market Conditions:

Party B shall have the obligation to forward once every three months to Party A detailed reports on current market conditions and on consumers' comments. For Party A's reference, Party B shall, from time to time, forward to Party A samples of similar commodity offered by other suppliers, together with their prices, sales position and advertising material.

(7) Advertising & Publicity Expenses:

Party B shall bear all expenses for advertising and publicity within the above-mentioned territory in the duration of this Agreement and submit to Party A all drafts and/or drawings intended for such purposes for prior approval.

(8) Validity of Agreement:

This Agreement, when duly signed, by the parties concerned, shall remain in force for one year to be effective as from January 1, 1998 to December 31, 1998. If a renewal of this Agreement is desired, notice in writing should be given by either party within one month prior to its expiry. Should one of the parties fail to comply with the terms and conditions of this Agreement, the other party is entitled to terminate this Agreement.

(9) Arbitration:

All disputes arising from the execution of this Agreement shall be settled through negotiation between both parties. In the event that no settlement can be reached, the case in dispute shall then be submitted for arbitration to the Foreign Trade Arbitration Commission of the China Council for the Promotion of International Trade, Beijing, in accordance with the Provisional Rules of Procedure of the Foreign Trade Arbitration Commission of the China Council for the Promotion of International Trade. The decision made by this

Commission shall be regarded as final and is binding on both parties.

(10) Other Terms & Conditions:

a. Party A shall not supply the contracted commodity to other buyers in the above-mentioned territory. Direct inquiries, if any, will be referred to Party B. However, should any other buyers insist on dealing direct with Party A, Party A shall have the right to do so. In the latter case, Party A shall send to Party B a copy of relevant S/C and reserve ... per cent (...%) commission for Party B on the net invoice value of the transactions concluded.

b. Should Party B fail to send their orders to Party A for a minimum of ... for a period of ... months, Party A shall not be bound to this Agreement.

c. For any business transacted between governments of both parties, Party A shall have full right to handle such direct dealings as authorized by Party A's government without binding themselves to this Agreement. Party B shall not interfere with such direct dealings, nor shall Party B bring forward any demand for compensations or commission there of.

d. Other terms and conditions shall be subject to those specified in the formal S/C signed by both parties.

This agreement is made out in quadruplicate, each party holding two copies.

Party A (Supplier)　　　　　　　　　Party B (Agent)

大意

本独家代理协议书由中国国家XXX进出口公司(以下简称A方)和美国纽约XXX公司(以下简称B方)在平等互利发展贸易的基础上,通过友好协商根据下列条款签署。

(1)A方同意委托B方为在北美地区销售MD-4型XX品牌治疗仪的独家代理。

(2)价格:B方应尽力按照A方所报的价格推销。每一笔交易都应以A方最后确认为准。

(3)数量:在下述期限内,B方向A方下的订单不得少于6 000台MD-4型XX品牌治疗仪。从本协议签署后的前6个月内,B方订货不得少于3 000台。如果B方在此期间内没能完成上述数量(即3 000台),A方将有权在此协议下向北美地区的其他客户销售该商品。如果B方的订货在协议签署后的前三个月少于1 000台,A方将有权以书面形式通知B方终止本协议。

(4)支付:以保兑的、不可撤销的、无追索权的信用证支付,在提交单据时凭即期汇票支付为有效。每批订货的信用证均需与装船日期前30天到达A方。如果B方没能及时开立信用证,A方所遭受的所有损失包括银行利息、存贮费用等均由B方承担。

(5)佣金:A方同意按订单的FOB价向B方支付5%的佣金。佣金必须在A方收到了每份订单的全部货款后再予以支付。如属本协议中条款(3)中所述情况,由A方自己获得且执行的订单不支付佣金。

(6)市场情况报告:B方每三个月应向A方呈交一份有关当前市场情况和客户评价的详细报告。B方还不时地向A方提供其他供货商的类似商品样品,并随附这些商品的价格、销售情况及广告资料供 A 方参考。

(7)广告及宣传费用：在本协议期限内，B 方应承担上述地区的所有广告及宣传费用，并向 A 方呈交为上述广告宣传所拟定的所有草案及方案，以便获得事先批准。

(8)协议有效期：本协议一经双方签署便开始生效，有效期为一年，即从 1998 年 1 月 1 日起到 1998 年 12 月 31 日止。如要展延本协议，任何一方都必须于协议到期日前 1 个月内书面通知另一方。如果一方没有履行本协议条款，另一方有权终止本协议。

(9)仲裁：由执行本协议所引起的所有争议都应由双方协商解决。如果不能解决，争议应提交北京中国国际贸易促进委员会对外贸易仲裁委员会，依据中国国际贸易促进委员会对外贸易仲裁委员会的仲裁程序暂行条例进行仲裁。该委员会做出的裁决将被作为最终裁决，对双方均具有约束力。

(10)其他条款：

a. A 方不得将合同所规定的商品提供给上述地区的其他买主。如有直接询价应介绍给 B 方。然而，如果任何其他买主坚持要与 A 方直接交易的话，A 方有权与其做交易。在后者的情况下，A 方应向 B 方发送一份有关合同的副本，并按照所达成的交易的净发票价值为 B 方留出……%的佣金。

b.如果 B 方在……个月内没能向 A 方发送至少……的订单，A 方将不再受本协议的约束。

c.对于双方政府间的交易，A 方由其政府授权有充分权利直接做上述交易而不受本协议的约束。B 方不得干预上述直接交易，也不得要求赔偿或佣金。

d.其他条款以双方签署的正式销售合同中所规定的条款为准。

本协议制作一式四份，双方各持两份。

A 方(供方)   B 方(代理)

3. Compensation Trade and Processing with Supplied Materials

Sample 1

Dear Mr. Stuart,

Thank you for your letter of July 15. We agree with your proposal that you will provide component parts and the technical information for us to assemble them into finished products.

As you may know, we are one of the leading manufacturers and exporters of Phoenix Bicycle in China with over 20 years' experience in this line of business. We can assure you we can process the supplied materials to your complete satisfaction.

We are looking forward to hearing from you about the details of this processing trade and signing the contract with you.

Sincerely,

Sample 2

Dear Sir or Madam,

Last month, your delegation visited our company and at the same time we discussed the possibilities of compensation trade with you.

During the previous two years, our two sides have conducted sincere and smooth co-operation. Now, we would like to provide you with the equipment of high quality in the form of compensation trade. If the equipment fails to operate properly, we will repair them at our cost.

Our overseas director will be in Shanghai early next month to further discuss the matter with officials from your head office. We hope that our detailed negotiations in Shanghai will result in the signing of a contract.

We look forward to your reply.

Yours sincerely,

Sample 3

Dear Mr. Wang,

Thank you for the hospitality extended to us during our stay in Shanghai. We think this was very productive.

As was explained to you in Shanghai, our idea is to work with the main producer of tyre-making equipment, who can provide you with the best possible technology and equipment for the manufacture of tyres.

On our return from China, we approached a well-known firm of long standing in this city, who are interested in Chinese tyres for trucks and automobiles. They have now expressed their willingness to cooperate with us in the distribution of your products through their worldwide channels.

We hope that you will give this matter your further consideration and let us have your comments as soon as possible. We can, therefore, put forward concrete proposals before the parties concerned. As this is an important matter, we think representatives from both sides would have to hold another meeting to discuss it in detail.

We are looking forward to your reply.

Sincerely yours,

本章知识提示

代理是指在国际贸易进出口业务中被习惯采用的一种做法。它是指委托人委托代理人作为其国外代表,并授权代理人为其在国外从事与贸易有关的各项活动。代理人和委托人的关系是委托代理关系。国际市场上的代理名目繁多,其中有采购、销售、运输、保险、广告等多方面的代理。在签订代理协议时,要明确代理商品的品名、规格、代理的地区、授予代理人的权限和代理的义务,比如要求代理人必须在一定期限内按照协议所规定的交易条件和价格完成最低销售定额,并限制代理人不得经营其他供应商类似的产品。

销售代理。在进出口业务中,委托人委托国外的代理在一定地区、一定时期内按照委托人的交易条件,借助代理人的经营能力、业务关系和对当地市场的了解来推销委托人的产品。销售代理有三种:总代理(general agent)、独家代理(exclusive agent)、普通代理(agent)。代理商积极推销代理商品的义务,并享有收取佣金的权利。

总代理是指代理商在指定地区内不仅有权代销指定商品,而且还有权代表委托人办理一些其他非商品性的事务。

独家代理。在指定的地区,由他单独代表委托人行为的代理人,委托人不得在该地区再委托他人作为代理。委托人在一定时期、特定地区给予代理人推销指定商品的专营权,委托人向代理人支付佣金,负担经营风险,一般不再向该地区其他商人销售该种商品;即使直接销售,也要按协议规定给独家代理应得的佣金。这种佣金叫作隐佣(sleeping commission)。独家代理则代表委托人与买主洽谈交易,并以委托人的名义或由委托人自己同买主签订合同。

委托代理。在委托代理之前,要对对方的资金状况、商业信誉的可靠性,以及推销的业务能力等有详细的了解。

一般代理是指不享有对某种商品的专营权,但其他权利、义务和独家代理一样。在同一地区同一时期内,委托人可以选定一家或几家客户作为一般代理商。根据销售商品的金额付给佣金。委托人可以直接与其他买主成交,无须另给代理商佣金。

包销（exclusive sales）是国际贸易中习惯采用的方式之一，指出口人通过协议把某一种商品或某一类商品在某一个地区和期限内的经营权单独给予某个客户的贸易做法。

区别：在包销协议中，包销商与出口商之间的关系是买卖关系，包销商自负盈亏，承担风险。独家代理双方是委托关系，独家代理不自负盈亏，不承担风险，有固定的佣金收入。

本章句式

1. Ask to Be an Agent

（1）This is to inform that we are acting as agents on commission basis. We shall be pleased if you could accord us exclusive selling rights for your ... in ...

（2）We have already represented several other manufacturers and trust you wilt allow us to give you similar services.

（3）We would like to ask to be the exclusive agent to handle your ... in the territory of ...

（4）We have good knowledge of the local market and are confident that we can expand your business here.

（5）I wonder whether your company is presented in our country.

（6）Considering we have a bright prospect for the sales of your new products, we should like to act as your agent in the market here in this line of business.

（7）We wish to handle as an agent the goods you are exporting now, because we are commanding an extensive domestic market in this line.

（8）We have been dealing with you in this line for many years and have offices or representatives in all major cities and towns in this country, therefore, we are confident that our capability will justify your appointing us as your exclusive agent.

（9）In case you are interested in a representative in the territory of ..., we believe we can do a substantial job for you.

2. Reply to a Request for an Agency

（1）We thank you for you letter offering your services and would like to discuss the possibility of an agency with you.

（2）Please let us be notified whether you now represent any manufacturers in the same line.

（3）As our sole agent, you should undertake neither to sell any products of any other manufacturers in the same line nor re-export our products to any other areas outside ...

（4）We inform you with great regret that our agency representation has been taken over by someone else in ...

（5）As regards the matter of exclusive agency, we are not yet prepared to consider it now. We shall revert to it when business has developed to our mutual satisfaction.

（6）We appreciate your offer to help market our products in .... but I have to point out that we have never conducted any agency agreement with your company.

(7) Our agency in your district has been vacant and we can appoint you for this position.

(8) After careful consideration, we have decided to appoint you as our agent for the territory of ... on the terms and conditions agreed with you.

(9) In view of your past efforts in pushing the sales of our products, we have decided to accept your proposal and appoint you as our sole agent.

(10) We appreciate your suggestion that you sell our goods on an exclusive basis, but we would like to know the approximate quantity you may sell in the year to come.

(11) We are prepared to appoint you as our agent for your district on a ...% commission basis, which will be remitted to you every three months after our receipt of the payments. We will pay against the relative invoices, the advertising expenses incurred to you for the promotion of sales of our products.

3. Reply to Being Offered an Agency

(1) Thank you for your offering us the agency in ... for your products and appreciate the confidence you have placed in us.

(2) We are pleased that you are prepared to appoint us as your sole agent for your products.

(3) We hope that we will double our efforts to build a large turnover so as to justify a close arrangement like sole agency.

(4) As your agency, we will make great efforts to push the sales of your products.

(5) I am willing to accept your offer to act as your sales agency.

4. Terminate an Agency

(1) With considerable regret, we must inform you that effective ... (specific date) our exclusive agent agreement with you will be terminated.

(2) I am afraid we cannot agree to appoint you as our sole agent because the annual turnover you promise is too low.

(3) We have noticed that in canvassing for orders, you have more than once exceeded the limit of your district.

(4) We regret to inform you that our agency representation has taken over by someone else.

(5) After careful consideration of our operation, we think that it would be in our best interest to change our marketing approach in ...

Unit Fourteen　Contracts and Agreements
合同与协议

Learning Objectives

a. Learn the writing content and related examples of relevant agency contracts and agreements;

b. Know the structure of the contract and agreement: the first contract, the text and the end of the contract;

c. Master the ways to clearly explain the subject matter or matters of the relevant transaction, as well as the basis of the agreement between the buyer and the seller, the rights and obligations of both parties, the distribution of interests, the settlement of disputes, and the acceptance of the contract.

Section 1　Introduction

A contract is founded on agreement, and agreement arises from offer and acceptance. One person makes an offer, another person accepts that offer. When that has happened, there is a contract.

The contract is an agreement reached by the two parties after the transaction negotiation, which is used as the basis to restrain the rights and obligations of the parties to the contract. In international trade, once a sales contract is effectively established in accordance with the law, the parties concerned shall honor the contract, keep their faith, and each assume the agreed obligations and enjoy the rights stipulated in the contract. The performance of the contract is the process of realizing the transfer of goods and funds in the agreed way. There are many links in the performance process, and the procedures are complex, mainly including price, payment method, packaging, transportation, insurance, and complaints and claims, claims and arbitration arising in the performance.

A contract sets forth binding obligations of the parties concerned. It should be detailed and specific, giving all the terms and conditions agreed upon. Once entered into, a contract is enforceable by law. Any party who fails to fulfill contract obligations may be sued and ordered to make a compensation. In other words, contract has lawful effects which bind the relevant parties to perform their duties.

1. Basic Knowledge

It is more difficult to write a contract or an agreement than writing a letter or a fax message, but if you know the essentials and basic knowledge of the writing, you are surely to be able to write contracts and agreements well. Generally speaking, if you can write a contract in Chinese, and have a good grasp in English, then you can write English contract and agreement versions according to forms and stipulation. Also you can write a contract or an agreement in Chinese first then translate it into English. When write, please pay attention to the following principles: writing complete, clearly, grammatically, and arranging properly and logically.

2. The Form of a Contract or an Agreement

Contracts or agreements don't have unified or fixed forms. In practice, complete and valid contracts or agreements usually consist of three parts: head, body and end.

(1) Head

The head covers the following contents:

a. The title of the contract or agreement. e.g. Purchase Contract, Agency Agreement, Exclusive Sales Agreement, Contract for Export of Labor Service, etc. The title indicates the character of the contract or agreement.

b. The number of the contract or agreement.

c. The date and the place of signing the contract or agreement (some contracts or agreements put the date and the place in the End).

In the preface of the contract or agreement, there are the parties' names, state clearly the Sellers and the Buyers or Party A and Party B, explain the principles and the purposes of signing the contract or agreement. e.g. XX Company, XX Country (hereinafter called Party A) and XX Company, PRC (hereinafter called Party B) through friendly negotiation reached the following agreement on the basis of equality and mutual benefit.

(2) Body

The body is the most important part in the contract or agreement. You may use the style of stipulations or the style of forms or you may combine the two styles together to state clearly the contents negotiated by the parties concerned.

For instance, the stipulations in an Import or Export Contract are the name and the specification of the commodity, quantity, unit price and total value, package, the time of shipment, the port of shipment, the port of destination, payment, insurance, inspection, claim and arbitration, etc.

The contents of other contracts or agreements (e.g. Agency Agreement, Joint Venture Contract, Investment Agreement, the Contract for Export of Labor Service, the Agreement for Technology Transfer) are complicated. The terms and conditions are different. But they have certain forms and formulas. When you write them you can consult example versions.

(3) End

The contents in this part are usually the following: the copies and the conserves of the contract or agreement, the language(s) used, the full names of the parties, and the seals affixed by the parties, etc. If the contract or agreement is companied by some enclosure(s), you should state clearly the name(s) of the enclosure(s) as well as the number of the copies as the integral parts of the contract.

3. The Requirement of Writing a Contract or an Agreement

1) The contents of contracts or agreements should conform to the principle of equality and mutual benefit and through common negotiations.

The versions of the contract or agreement are legal documents. The parties concerned are equal in legal status. Neither party has privilege to force the other party to accept its own will(s), so both parties should respect the other side's interests. The stipulations should be discussed by the parties concerned and reach an agreement.

2) The stipulations of contracts or agreements should be complete, concrete, definite and without careless omissions, in order to avoid unnecessary economic losses.

For example, in an Import and Export Contract, the stipulation of shipping marks seems to be an unimportant term, but if it is indefinitely and unclearly stated, that would cause trouble when deliver the goods.

Another example, the arbitration clause is the most important term in all the contracts. Though it is not used in the execution of every contract, but if you neglect it, it will be a great problem when a dispute occurs and no agreement can be reached. Such things happened to some companies in the past. When disputes occurred the foreign party directly sued to a court of their own country that thrown the other party into passivity—if the other party responded to the action, the foreign laws might not be beneficial to the other party; if the other party did not response, the foreign court would make a judgment by default.

3) Using words and expressions accurately, arrange the contents properly, logically and without mistakes.

The words and expressions used in the contract should not be ambiguous and no different meanings. For example, for the term of package you should state clearly and definitely the packing materials and methods, i.e. pack in cartons, wooden cases, casks, gunny bags, etc., and mark clearly the volume, weight (net weight and gross weight) and quantity, avoid using "seaworthy packing" or "packing as usual", for these expressions are too ambiguous. The expression of "Ship the goods in two lots." is not complete and unclear, you'd better add "50% for each lot", or "60% for the first lot and the rest for the second" to the clause. These expressions are rigorous.

A contract or an agreement set forth bonding obligations of the parties concerned. Once entered into, a contract or an agreement is enforceable by law. Neither of the parties has the right to amend or cancel it as their pleases. If some terms should be amended or supplemented, or if a contract (an agreement) should be ended for some special reason, the parties need to consult and agree upon the matter first. Then they should sign an agreement for the amendment or cancellation. Any party who fails to fulfill its contract obligations (except caused by force majeure) should bear the economic losses of the other party (or parties).

Section 2　Example of a Contract

1. Scope

This contract (including Appendices I through V) defines total scope of work to be performed by the three parties. Seller recognizes that over the course of contract execution, End-User may wish to amend the scope of work. Should such amendments be necessary, Seller shall promptly submit additional proposals for End-User's review. Seller will not, make any amendments unless they have been agreed to in writing by the contracting parties. However, Seller reserves the fight to change the details of construction to Seller fabricated equipment, as specified in the Seller's proposal if, in its judgment, such changes of substitutions shall be to the best interest of both End-User and Seller.

2. Contract Effective Date

This contract will go into effect on the latest date at which all approvals required by the contracting parties have been obtained. Such approvals will be obtained within sixty (60) days of the signing of the contract. Seller reserves the right to revise the contract price if Buyer fails to obtain approvals within the sixty (60) days period. Buyer and Seller shall notify each other by fax immediately upon receipt of approvals. With respect to the Seller, the contract must be ratified by an officer of Seller's Parent Company.

3. Contract Equipment

This contract is made by and between the Buyers, the End-Users, and the Sellers, whereby the Buyers and End-Users agree to buy and the Sellers agree to sell the under-mentioned commodity (here-in-after referred as the Contract Equipment) according to the terms and conditions stipulated here in:

Base Prices	Accessories	Spare Parts
(Omitted)	(Omitted)	(Omitted)
Subtotal	Less Discount	Final Sales Price

4. Payment

A: Terms of Payment:

①15% down payment within thirty (30) days of the contract date.

②20% upon receipt of Floor Plan.

③65% immediately upon shipment.

B: Conditions of Payment :

①Payment No. 1

By Telegraphic Transfer to Seller's account number 551-17-001 at First National Bank of Boston when Buyer receives the following documents:

—Three (3) copies of Seller's Invoice

—Two (2) copies of Sight Draft

—Seller's standby Letter of Credit (sample attached as Exhibit 1)

②Payment No. 2

By Telegraphic Transfer to Seller's account number 551-17-001 at First National Bank of Boston when Buyer receives the following documents:

—Three (3) copies of Seller's Invoice

—Two (2) copies of Sight Draft

—Floor Plan drawing

③Payment No. 3

Against a Confirmed Irrevocable Letter of Credit (sample attached as Exhibit 2) at sight when following documents are submitted:

—Three (3) copies of Seller's Invoice

—Clean on Board Ocean Bill of Lading

—Packing List

—Certificate of Quality and Quantity

—Seller's standby Letter of Credit (sample attached as Exhibit 3)

Copy of fax to Buyer notifying shipment Buyer shall establish this Letter of Credit in favor of the Seller at the China Bank, XX Branch within thirty (30) days after contract effective date.

5. Late Payments

All late payments will carry an interest at a rate of Prime rate plus 3% per annum pro-rated to the actual delay with a grace period of fifteen (15) days.

6. Export License

Requirements regarding United States Export License change periodically. Seller will make a determination whether a license is required. Buyer will cooperate with Seller in signing the certificates which may be necessary to complete the application for the license. Seller assures the Buyer that this requirement has never in the past impeded execution of such types of contracts.

7. Shipment

Date of shipment is to be in October, 2014. Port of shipment will be an East Coast Port, U.S.A. Port of Destination will be Guangzhou, P. R. China. All equipment is to be shipped C.I.F.

8. Terms of Shipment

(1) The Sellers shall, 40 days before the date of shipment stipulated in the contract, advise the End-Users by telex of the Contract No., commodity, quantity, value, number of

packages, gross weight, and measurements.

(2) The Sellers shall, no later than 10 days before the estimated date of arrival of the vessel from the port of shipment, notify the End-Users of the name of vessel and estimated date of loading. If the schedule of the vessel is changed, Seller's shipping agents shall promptly notify the End-User.

(3) The Sellers shall bear all expenses and risks of the commodity until it arrives at the port of destination. Once the goods arrive at the port, any and all charges shall be borne by the End-User.

(4) If goods need to be stored at the docks, the responsibility for safekeeping of same shall rest with the End-User.

(5) Bills of Lading shall constitute Proof of Delivery.

9. Storage at End-User's Plant

All material must be stored by the End-User indoors in a warm and dry place. Damage to material due to improper storage (regardless of how packaged) will not be Seller's responsibility. If End-User unpacks the goods in the absence of Seller's representative, Seller will not be responsible for missing parts and shortages.

10. Delays and Escalation

In the event the End-User delays shipment of material and; equipment, directly or indirectly, the seller shall have a right to impose escalation and/or storage charges for the term of the delay.

11. Cancellation & Default

End-User may cancel only upon written notice to seller and upon payment to seller of reasonable and proper cancellation charges, including direct and indirect costs with proportionate profit.

12. Documentation

Seller shall provide documentation as outlined in Appendix II.

13. Training

Seller shall provide training to End-User's personnel as outlined in Appendix III. End-User must recognize that the Seller can accommodate only a limited number of trainees at any given time. End-User shall be responsible for the conduct of its personnel while in the U. S. All expenses relating to trainees will be borne by the End-User; however, Seller will arrange for the daily transportation on working days from the hotel to Seller's plant and provide a working lunch. The training shall, under no circumstances, include information which Seller deems proprietary.

14. Field Supervision and Start-Up

Seller shall provide supervision and start-up services as outlined in Appendix IV.

15. Force Majeure

Seller shall not be responsible for any loss, damage, delay in shipment or non-delivery of the goods due to Force Majeure (causes such as fires, theft, acts of war, insurrection or riot, strikes and lockouts or any other cause beyond Seller's control) which might occur during the process of manufacturing or in the course of loading or transit. The Sellers shall advise the End-Users immediately of the occurrence mentioned above. As soon as possible thereafter, the Sellers shall send by airmail to the End-Users for their acceptance a certificate of the accident.

Under such circumstances, the Seller however, is still under the obligation to take all necessary measures to hasten the delivery of the goods. In no event shall the Seller be liable for any special, indirect or consequential damages or loss of profits for causes attributed to Force Majeure.

16. Taxes and Duties

End-User will be liable for all taxes and import or export duties outside the Seller's country. In addition, End-User shall be responsible for all port charges, demurrage, etc., at the port of destination. End-User further agrees to indemnify Seller against all liabilities for such taxes or duties and legal fees or costs incurred by Seller in connection herewith.

17. Arbitration

All disputes in connection with the execution shall be settled through friendly negotiations. Where no settlement can be reached, the disputes shall be submitted for arbitration. Arbitration shall take place in Stockholm. Each party shall appoint an arbitrator within thirty (30) days after receipt of notification from the opposite party and the two Arbitrators thus appointed shall jointly nominate a third person as umpire to form an Arbitration Committee.

The said umpire shall be confined to the citizens of Swedish nationality. The decision of the Arbitration Committee shall be accepted as final and binding upon both parties; neither party shall seek recourse to a law court or other authorities to appeal for revision of the decision. Arbitration expenses shall be borne by the losing party.

18. Warranty

Seller guarantees the quality of the workmanship and materials of its supply that will be used in this installation for a period of one year from the date of Final Acceptance Certificate of the Contract Equipment signing, but not to exceed twenty (20) months from date on which goods arrive at the port of Destination. Should any defects develop within said period, Seller shall supply replacement/repair parts, F.O.B. its shop in Livonia, Michigan, without charge, except for expendable items like recuperates, radiant tubes, etc., which will be replaced on a pro-rated basis.

This guarantee, however, does not cover:

(1) Normal wear and tear;

(2) Improper or negligent use and operation of the equipment.

Equipment not manufactured by the Seller will be guaranteed on the same terms as Seller's vendor's guarantee. In such case, Seller will provide full assistance to End-User's manufacturing process or the quality of End-User's product. Losses or damage resulting from equipment failure or from the time consumed in delivering, installing, or testing the equipment are not covered by the guarantee.

In no event shall the Seller be liable for any special indirect or consequential damages or loss of profits for causes covered under this guarantee. Seller will make no guarantee for repairs of alterations to the product made by the End-User, unless made with the advance written consent of Seller. Seller will not assume liability for costs of disassembly, reassembly, or re-machining of defective product. Seller makes no guarantee, express or implied, other than the above.

Section 3 Examples of Agreements

1. **Exclusive Sales Agreement**

Through friendly negotiations, this Agreement is entered into between China National XXX Import and Export Corporation, Jiangxi, China (hereinafter called Party A), and XXX Company, Russia (hereinafter called Party B) on the following terms and conditions:

(1) Party A entrust Party B with the exclusive sales in the territory of Russia for "YAYA" Brand Down Coat. This Agreement is valid from 1st September, 2008 to 31st August, 2010.

(2) Quantity: During the above-mentioned period, Party B shall endeavor to push sales of not less than ... of "YAYA" Brand Down Coat, the quantity of which should be spread over quarterly periods in approximately equal proportions.

(3) During the validity of this Agreement, Party A refrain from offering the above-mentioned goods to other merchants with any place of Russia as place of destination, while Party B undertake to refrain from purchasing, pushing sales of or acting as agents for the commodity of other suppliers same as or similar to that stated in Article 1 and guarantee not to transship in any way the said goods supplied by Party A to any area, where exclusivity or sales agency has been granted by Party A. If any violation of the above is found, Party A have the right to cancel this Agreement.

(4) Should other buyers in the territory under exclusivity approach party A for the purchase of the above-mentioned goods, Party A should refer them to Party B. If such buyers insist on concluding business direct with Party A, Party A may do so. Party A may likewise conclude business with Russian buyers who come to visit China or attend the

Chinese Export Commodity Fair at prices not lower than those quoted to Party B. In the above event, Party A agree to reserve for Party B a commission of 1% on basis of FOB value of the business thus concluded and send a copy of the relative contract to Party B.

(5) During the period of this agreement, both parties should strictly abide by the terms and condition of this Agreement. In the event of any breach of them by one party, the other party are entitled, when necessary, to claim the termination of this Agreement.

(6) Party B should be responsible for the sending of reports every month to Party A for their reference, setting forth local market conditions of the said goods (including details of price level and demand for variety in articles).

(7) This Agreement is not binding on inter-government (authorized state enterprises and cooperatives in the nature of a state-owned enterprise) tenders and barter transactions of any nature.

(8) At its expiration, the termination or renewal of this Agreement will be decided by both parties through negotiation.

(9) This Agreement is made out in Chinese and Russian languages, both texts being equally binding. One copy each is kept by either party.

2. Consignment Agreement

December 6, 1998

China National Light Industrial Products Imp.&Exp.Corp., Beijing Branch (hereinafter called Party A) held talks with U.S. Max Factor&Co., (hereinafter called Party B) about the consignment of Max Factor Cosmetics. Through friendly negotiation both parties confirm the principal points as stipulated hereunder:

(1) Item for Consignment

It mainly covers four product categories, i.e. Treatment, Fragrance, Cosmetics, and Toiletries. The detailed specification, unit price and quantity of the above goods shall be provided in a list to Party A by Party B. After confirmation by Party A, a concrete contract signed by both parties will then be effective.

(2) Terms of Consignment

1) Period of Time. Both parties agree that sales of Max Factor Cosmetics will commence on or about January 15, 1999 and continue through December 31, 1999.

Party A agrees to sell exclusively Max Factor Cosmetics during this one year time in Beijing and agrees that no other cosmetics lines including perfumes, beauty cosmetics, cosmetics for protecting skin, hair lotions and nail enamels will be sold in Beijing Hotel, Beijing Friendship Store or any other location in Beijing.

In order to facilitate Party A's work of starting the consignment sales on time, Party B should ship the first lot of consignment goods to Party A before Dec. 31, 1998. On or about March 15, 1999, Party A and Party B shall meet to mutually determine on acceptable sales level for the remainder of the consignment period.

2) Port of Destination. Xingang, Tianjin (by sea) and Beijing (by air). Party B agrees to sell CIF named Chinese Port.

In assurance certificate will be ALL RISKS with a warehouse to warehouse clause. While the goods are in the warehouse and during the course of selling Party A shall take the responsibility of insurance on behalf of Party B.

3) Party B will submit to Party A the actual retail prices of aforesaid articles in Hong Kong and Japanese Markets for Party A's reference. Party B has no right to interfere with Part A's selling price, spot and method, but it has the right to make positive proposals. Party A is responsible to submit Party B regular reports to selling situation (covering retail prim), problem arising in the course of selling and making proposals to improve sales. Party B should provide Party A with various arrangement are conductive to sales (including samples free of charge, articles for trial sales, data for promoting cosmetic goods, technical exchange and conditions for storage, etc.).

4) All expenses for advertisement of these items should be paid by Party B. The contents of advertisement are subject to the approval of Party A.

5) In the case of problems occurring due to quality, damage or any other matter of Party B's responsibility, Party B should compensate such a loss to Party A by the replacement of goods or the deduction of the sum in question from Party A's remittance to Party B against Party A's certificate. One percent of the sum from Party A's remittance to Party B should be dedicated by Party B as a damage allowance during the course of selling.

6) During the consignment period if Party A wishes to increase the quantity of salable items, Party B should cooperate on this matter through best efforts. For those articles which can not be sold Party B should make readjustment, replacement or withdrawal of the goods in question.

(3) Terms of Payment

1) Within one month after expiration of the consignment period, Party A shall remit Party B the total sum in U.S. Dollars based on the contracted unit price for those items which have been sold.

If at any time the total value of goods sold exceeds the amount of U.S. Dollars 150,000, Party A shall remit the total sum in U.S. Dollars to Party B within one month's period of time.

2) For those items which cannot be sold, Party A should send a list of these items to Party B in order to make an appropriate settlement by sending these items back or any other method.

(4) All disputes arising in the course of the consignment period shall be settled amicably through friendly negotiation. In the case that no settlement can be reached through

negotiation, both parties agree the case should be submitted for arbitration to a third country which can be accepted by both parties.

(5) At the beginning of December, 1999, both parties shall meet and discuss the future business possibility in Beijing in 2000.

本章知识提示

合同是买卖双方经过交易磋商后达成的协议,是作为约束合同各当事人权利和义务的依据。在国际贸易中,买卖合同一经依法有效成立,有关当事人就应重合同、守信用,各自承担约定的义务并享受合同规定的权利。合同的履行是实现货物和资金按约定方式转移的过程。履行过程中环节很多,程序复杂,主要涉及包括价格、支付方式、包装、运输、保险以及抱怨和索赔、理赔及仲裁等。

协议是针对已经做或准备做的相关事宜,经过谈判、协商后取得一致意见,以口头或书面形式做出的约定。根据协议拟制,当一方发出报盘另一方表示接受时便产生协议。

根据协议拟制,当一方发出报盘另一方表示接受时便产生协议。一旦有协议产生,便会产生合同。合同中任何一方如没能履行合同职责将被另一方起诉并要求赔偿。合同具有法律效力,该效力约束合同各方履行其职责。书面合同的内容一般由以下三部分组成:

约首:合同的序言部分,包括合同的名称、订约双方当事人的名称和地址(要求写明全称)。除此之外,还常常须写明双方签订合同的意愿和执行合同的保证。序言对双方均具有约束力,因此在写序言时应慎重考虑。

正文:这部分是合同的主体,包括交易的各项条款,如品名、品质规格、数量、价格、支付方式、包装、交货时间和地点、运输及保险条款,以及检验、索赔、不可抗力和仲裁条款等。上述各条款明确了双方当事人的权利和义务。

约尾:一般列明合同的份数、使用的文字及效力、订约的时间和地点,以及合同生效的时间,最后是双方的签字。订约合同的地点往往要涉及和合同准据法的问题,因此不能随便填写。我国出口合同的订约地点一般都写我国进出口公司的所在地或者写中国。有的合同将"订约时间和地点"在约首订明。

寄售(consignment sales)是一种委托代收的贸易方式。它是指委托人(货主)先将货物运往寄售地,委托国外某个代销人(委托人),按照寄售协议规定的条件,由代销人代替货主进行销售。在货物出售后,由代销人向货主结算货款的一种贸易做法。在寄售方式中,寄售人与代销人之间是委托代售关系,而非买卖关系。代销人按其销售额收取佣金。这是扩大外销,尤其是打开新产品新市场的有效方法之一。这种不属于成交(conclusion of business)。寄售者将货物发运给海外的受托者(consignee)。受托者只是代寄售者出手货物,从中收取佣金,不承担任何价格涨落的风险,盈亏由寄售者自负。寄售的优点是货物在国外展销,购货人可以到现场去看货、试样、论价、成交、提货。这种做法受买主欢迎,有助于推销货物。缺点是收款迟、风险大,若销售不出去,就得将货物运回或是削价蚀本处理。因此,必须谨慎行使。

Unit Fifteen Invitation for Bids and Advertisements
招标和广告

◆ *Learning Objectives*

a. Know the procedures of international bidding;

b. Know the basic contents of the international bidding documents and tender documents;

c. Master professional terms, common expressions and basic contents of commercial letters related to international bidding and advertising.

Invitation for bids (Bidding) refers to the act of the tenderer (the buyer) in issuing a bidding announcement at the prescribed time and place, proposing the name, quantity and relevant transaction conditions of the goods to be purchased, and inviting the seller to bid. Bidding and tendering is a common way in international trade. It is often used in the state government agencies, state-owned enterprises or public institutions to purchase equipment, materials, equipment and other transactions, and is more used for international contracted projects.

Advertisements (Advertising) generally consists of three parts: title, text and sign-off. The title is the title of an advertisement. New words in advertisements identified in ideas can often be used as titles. The main task of the text part is to illustrate the characteristics and advantages of a commodity or service with persuasive facts or examples. Commodity advertising should inform consumers of the use, performance, specifications and characteristics of the goods; service advertising should explain the types and characteristics of the service provided; public advertising should introduce the quality, ability and contribution of the enterprise, publicize the spirit of the enterprise, has achieved the purpose of establishing their own image and improving their popularity. In the signature part usually specify the name and address of the advertising unit, as well as telephone, telephone, fax number, etc.

Section 1　Introduction

At present, invitation for bids and bidding are widely used in the world economic activates. When enterprises, utilities as well as governments are in need of certain materials, products or planning to build a project they often invite people to bid. With the development of international trade, more and more kinds of business are involved in this type of trade, more and more kinds of business are involved in this type of trading, ranging from contracting a big project to importing a kind of commodities.

Commercial advertising is one of the key means to expand trade. It is essential when seeking markets and promoting sales.

Bidding is another form of trading in international business. When enterprises, utilities as well as governments are in need of certain materials, products or planning to build a project they often invite people to bid. With the development of international trade, more and more kinds of business are involved in this type of trading, ranging from contracting a big project to importing a kind of commodities.

Section 2　Examples of Invitation for Bids

Sample 1

CHINA PETRO-CHEMICAL INTERNATIONAL COMPANY (SINOPEC INT'L)
INVITATION FOR BIDS

FOR ANQING ACRYLIC FIBRE EQUIPMENT
BID NO. SINOPEC 93305
LOAN NO. PRC-1116

In accordance with the Loan Agreement between Chinese Government and the Asian Development Bank (ADB) for ANQING Acrylic Fibre Project, Sinopec Int'L now invites bids from eligible suppliers from member countries of ADB for the supply of the following Goods to be financed with the proceeds of ADB:

　DCS Systems for Acrylonitrile and Acrylic Fibre Units (Package No. 11)
　Refrigeration Equipment (Package No. 20)
　Stretch-Breaking Machines (Package No. 21)
　Primary Gill Box, Bailing Gill Box (Package No. 22)
　(For Package No. 11, only the eligible bidders who have signed the secrecy agreement

with BP Chemicals America, Inc., can obtain the bidding documents and are entitled to bid.)

Interested eligible bidders who are willing to participate in the bidding may obtain detailed information from the address below and inspect the bidding documents. A set of bidding documents may be purchased in the 4th floor at the address below between 9:00 am and 11:00 am (Sundays and holidays excepted) from February 16, 2015 or be promptly dispatched by express mail upon receipt of non-refundable payment of FEC (RMB) 1,200 Yuan (or US$ 200) plus US$ 50 postage fee.

The bids should reach the address below before 16:00 on March 22, 1998 and will be opened publicly by Sinopec Int'L at 9:00 am on March 23, 2015. Each bid package must be submitted in separate sealed envelopes and be accompanied by a bid bond. Those bids which are not accompanied by a bid bond will not be accepted.

Bids will be opened in Rm. A0401 at the address below.

The 3rd Petro-Chemical Department
China Petro-Chemical International Company
Hui Bin Office Building, No. 8 Beichendong St.,
Chaoyang District, Beijing, China
P.O. Box: 9802
Post code: 100101
Telex: 22655 CPCCI CN
Tel.: 4916649, 4916650
Fax: 4216612

Sample 2

INVITATION TO TENDER-TENDER

Far East Oil Tools & Services Ltd.
Chiwan Petroleum Supply Base.
Shekou, Shenzhen, P.R.C.
Atm: Felix Jiang

Dear Sirs,

No. HB-403 TENDER TITLE-SUPPLY OF DRILLING-TOOLS

You, are hereby invited by GALL Petroleum Development (Purchaser) to submit a Tender for the above Goods and services, in accordance with this Letter of Invitation and the Invitation to Tender Document transmitted herewith. It is understood that if your Tender is accepted; Purchaser will issue a Purchase Order on the Terms and Conditions contained in this Invitation to Tender and your offer, for the provision of DRILLING TOOLS and associated equipment and services. One copy of the Invitation to Tender Documents is enclosed herewith and comprises:

  Section A   — Instructions to Tendered
  Section B   — Form of Tender
  Section C   — Conditions d Purchase

Summary of Work

The Goods and services, described in this Invitation to Tender agreement is to provide drilling tools and ancillary equipment/services in support of Purchasers drilling activities in contract area 15/23 off-shore People's Republic of China in the South China Sea. The firm Scope of Supply will be for the provision of drilling tools and ancillary equipment/services with an option for standby tools at a later date. The intended date for spudding the firm well is early November 2023.

  provisions are briefly:
  —provision of fishing tools
  —provision of back up fishing tools
  —provision of standby tools running tools
  —provision of service engineer (optionally)

If you cannot or do not wish to submit a Tender for the services described in this Invitation to Tender then please return the documentation to us in accordance with the requirements of the Instructions to Tenderer stating that you do not wish to submit an offer.

Tendering Details

You are requested to check the contents of the Invitation to Tender package for completeness when you receive it and then return the enclosed Tender Acknowledgment.

Tenders shall be submitted in accordance with the Instructions to Tenderers and Form of Tender. Any deviation from the requirements of these Instructions may render your Tender invalid.

Your Tender must be received no later than 12.00 hours on Friday, 3rd July, 2023 (closing date) at the office of the Purchaser in Shenzhen, People's Republic of China.

Tenders shall be forwarded by courier service or delivered safe-hand, sealed and clearly addressed and marked on the outside in accordance with the Instructions to Tenderers.

Please note that uninvited visits to our offices to discuss the Invitation to Tender are not acceptable and that all contact shall be in writing (by letter or fax) asset out in the Instructions to Tenderer.

The Tenderer shall consider this Letter of Invitation and the enclosed Invitation to Tender documents to be confidential, and the contents shall not be divulged to any person or persons not directly concerned with the preparation of the Tender.

This Invitation to Tender is subject to your signing and returning to the Purchaser the Tender Acknowledgment contained within Section A.

Section 3   Examples of Advertisements

Sample 1

SHANGHAI TOYS IMPORT AND EXPORT CORPORATION

Shanghai Toys Imp.&Exp. Corp, the first "combination of industry and trade" in China approved by the State Council of the People's Republic of China, is an enterprising Corp. professionally handling toys import and export business.

Toys handled: metal and plastic flexible toys (friction-type & clock-work toys, battery-operated toys, radio-control, voice-control and light-control electronic toys), push toys, dolls, wooden toys, musical toys, inflatable toys, children's vehicles, toy cores and motors, etc.

The category is complete and products sell well both at home and aboard. Shanghai Toys Imp.&Exp. Corp. has always been faithful in carrying out its contracts. Reasonable in price, superior in quality, timely in delivery, flexible in trade, the Corp. serves clients whole-heatedly. Foreign friends are warmly welfare to establish trade ties, including expanding business of process on supplied materials, samples and mould, compensation trade, joint-venture factories and cooperative production.

Add:165 Puan Road, Shanghai, China
Post code: 200021
Cable: CHINSTOYS Shanghai 33037 CN
Tel: 32626401
Fax: 31127612, 32033534

Sample 2

Hainan Provincial Nationality Foreign Trade General Corporation

A foreign trade company with the special entitlement to declare the Customs on written export declaration anywhere in China.

The Hainan Nationality Foreign Trade General Corporation, entitled by the Ministry of Foreign Economic Relations and Trade to declare Customs anywhere in China, is one of the first local foreign-trade companies in the province. It has played an active role in the past 12 years in economic and cultural development for the province's minority nationalities.

The corporation handles import and export business, and real estate development, as well as establishing joint venture and con-management enterprises.

Since the founding of the Hainan Province, the corporation has made many export achievements and has been appraised as the mast advanced local company by the provincial government for five years running.

The corporation wishes to join hands with business people from home and abroad for economic development.

Address: 298, Baipoli, Nanhang Road, Haikou City, Hainan Province, China
Tel: 7785933, 772692
Fax: 7734479
Post code: 570006

Unit Fifteen　Invitation for Bids and Advertisements 招标和广告

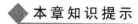 本章知识提示

招标投标是国际贸易中常见的方式,常用在国家政府机构、国有企业或公共事业单位采购设备、物资、器材等的交易中,更多地用于国际承包工程。

招标(invitation for bid):招标人(买方)在规定时间、地点发出招标公告,提出准备买进的商品名称、数量和有关的交易条件,邀请卖方投标的行为。

投标(submission of bid):投标人(卖方)应招标人的邀请,根据招标公告的规定条件,在规定投标的时间内向招标人递盘的行为。投标是国际贸易中的一种形式。当企业、公共事业公司及政府需要某种材料、产品或计划建设一个项目时,他们通常邀请人们投标。随着国际贸易的发展,越来越多的业务涉及该贸易形式,其范围从签署一项宏大项目的合同到进口一种商品的交易。

广告(advertisements)一般由标题、正文、落款三个部分组成。标题是广告的眉目。在构思立意中确定的广告新词语往往可作为标题。正文部分的主要任务是用有说服力的事实或例证说明商品或服务的特点和优势。商品广告应告诉消费者商品的用途、性能、规格、特点;服务广告要说明提供服务的种类、特色等;公共广告要介绍企业的素质、能力和贡献,宣传企业精神,已达到树立自身形象、提高知名度的目的。在落款部分通常写明发广告单位的名称、地址,以及电话、电话、传真号码等。

招标公告:招标公告有邀请投标人参加投标的作用,要求文字简洁、易懂,因此不可不将招标的各详细细节叙述完备,具体的条件需用招标文件逐一说明,然后将招标文件发送(或出售)给投标人。

招标公告一般由标题、正文和结尾三个部分组成。标题要写明招标单位的名称和文件的种类。如果招标单位是招标公司,还应在标的下写出编号,以便归档和查对。在正文的开头首先写明招标的目的、依据和项目名称。在正文的主体部分要提出招标的具体内容及有关事项。该部分因是招标书的核心,因此要求用准确、简洁的文字将招标的项目与要求写清楚。如果是购买大宗商品的招标,要写明商品的品名、数量、规格;属工程建设项目的招标,要写明招标工程概况、工程质量、工程日期等。另外,要写明招标的程序、起止时间、报名地点等。在结尾部分应写明招标单位的名称、地址电话、传真号码等,以便投标者参加投标。

附 表

附表1 外贸函电常用词汇

英文	中文	英文	中文
inquiry n.	询盘,询购	offer n./v.	报价,报盘
order n./v.	订购,订单	complicate v.	使复杂化
to ask for	请求;要价	to be liable to	易于……的
to put aside	放在一边	facsimile (fax) n./v.	传真,发传真
on the web	在互联网上	ecommerce	电子商务
pompous adj.	浮夸的	acknowledge receipt of	承认收到
inst. (=this month)	本月	clear one's account	结账
as a result	所以	trace v.	跟踪,查询
in connection with	与……有关	indebtedness n.	负债
balance n.	收付差额,余额	illustrated catalog	附有插图的目录
if possible	如有可能	time of delivery	交货期
delivery n.	交货	firm n.	公司,商号
standing n.	声望	reliability n.	可靠
approach vt.	与……联系	enter into business relations with	与……建立业务关系
catalog n.	目录	pamphlet n.	小册子
for your reference	供你方参考	in the meantime	与此同时
transaction n.	交易	embassy n.	大使馆
hand-made adj.	手工制作	hide n.	皮革
steady adj.	稳定的	fashionable adj.	流行的,时髦的
detail(s) n.	详情	terms of payment	支付条款
a range of	一系列	elegance n.	优美,雅致
couple together	使联结,使成对	superb adj.	极好的,一流的
workmanship n.	工艺	appeal (to) v.	吸引

英文	中文	英文	中文
discriminating adj.	有识别力的,敏锐的	representative n.	代表,代理
authorize v.	授权	negotiate v.	洽谈
in reply	兹答复	inform v.	通知,告知
be connected with	与……有联系	appreciate v.	感激,感谢
rush v.	赶紧(做),抓紧(做)	place an order with	向……订购
C&F (cost & freight)	成本加运费价	T/T (telegraphic transfer)	电汇
D/P (document against payment)	付款交单	D/A (document against acceptance)	承兑交单
CO (certificate of origin)	原产地证书	GSP (generalized system of preferences)	普惠制
CTN/CTNS (carton/cartons)	纸箱	PCE/PCS (piece/pieces)	只,个,支
DL/DLS (dollar/dollars)	美元	DOZ/DZ (dozen)	一打
PKG (package)	一包,一捆,一扎,一件	WT (weight)	重量
GW (gross weight)	毛重	NW (net weight)	净重
C/D (customs declaration)	报关单	EA (each)	每个,各
W (with)	具有	W/O (without)	没有
IMP (import)	进口	EXP (export)	出口
MAX (maximum)	最大的,最大限度的	MIN (minimum)	最小的,最低限度
M or MED (medium)	中等,中级的	M/V (merchant vessel)	商船
S.S. (steamship)	船运	MT or M/T	公吨
DOC (document)	文件,单据	INT (international)	国际的
P/L (packing list)	装箱单,明细表	INV (invoice)	发票
PCT (percent)	百分比	REF (reference)	参考,查价
STL (style)	式样,款式,类型	EMS (express mail special)	特快专递
RMB (renminbi)	人民币	T or LTX or TX (telex)	电传
S/M (shipping marks)	装船标记	PR or PRC (price)	价格
PUR (purchase)	购买,购货	S/C (sales contract)	销售确认书
L/C (letter of credit)	信用证	B/L (bill of lading)	提单
FOB (free on board)	离岸价	CIF (cost, insurance & freight)	成本、保险加运费价

附表2　外贸函电常见词组搭配

英文	中文	英文	中文
Letter			
ESP: English for Specific/Special Purposes	专门用途英语	BE: Business English	商务英语
Correspondence for Import & Export	进出口函电	good quality stationery	优质信纸
neat typing	版式整洁	even spacing	间隔匀称
short paragraphs	段落精短	correct grammar, spelling and punctuation	语法、拼写、标点正确
Inquiries			
potential business	潜在业务	prospective customer	潜在顾客
customers of long standing	长期顾客	potential supplier	潜在供应商
trade fair	贸易博览会	the latest issue of	最新一期的
integrated software package	完整软件包	substantial order	大宗订单
quantity discount	数量折扣	cash discount	现金折扣
list price	标价，目录价格	export terms	出口条件
pictured/illustrated catalog	带插图的目录	article number/Art. No.	货号
bulk buyer	大买主	business concern	商行
business relations/relationship	业务关系	business status	业务状况
commercial counselor	商务参赞	commercial counselor's office	商务参赞处
means of packing	包装方法	parent company	母公司
sales literature	促销资料	trading association	贸易关系
trade journal	行业刊物	firm offer	实盘
non-firm offer, offer without engagement	虚盘	trade discount	同业/批发折扣
bill of exchange (bill/draft; B/E)	汇票	shipping documents	装运单据
line of business	业务/经营范围	specific inquiry	具体询价
Replies and quotations			
regular customer	老顾客	be in a position to do	能够做

续表

英文	中文	英文	中文
for your consideration	供你方考虑	promotional novelties	促销小礼品
profit margin	利润率	by separate post/mail/cover	另邮/函
bathroom fittings	浴室设备	building contractor	建筑承包商，营造商
net price	净价	Cash With Order, CWO	订货付款，随订单付现
sample cutting	剪样	ceiling price	限价
consumer goods	消费品	counter offer	还盘
counter-bid	还价	current/prevailing price	现价
durable goods; durables	耐用品	fancy goods	花俏商品
gross price	毛价,总价	lead time	从订货到交货的间隔时间
offer sheet	报盘单	quotation sheet	报价单
retail price	零售价	rock-bottom price	最低价
make an offer/a quotation	报盘/价	offer firm	报实盘
quote a price	报价	credit status	资信状况
correspondent bank	往来行	publicity brochure	宣传小册子
down payment	预订金	find a ready sale/market for	畅销
end-user	最终用户	Ex Works, EXW	工厂交货(价)
Carriage & Insurance Paid to, CIP	运费保险费付至	Carriage Paid to, CPT	运费付至
Delivered At Frontier, DAF	边境交货	Delivered Duty Paid, DDP	完税后交货
Delivered Duty Unpaid, DDU	未完税交货	Delivered Ex Quay, DEQ	目的港码头交货
Delivered Ex Ship, DES	目的港船上交货	Free Alongside Ship, FAS	船边交货
Free Carrier, FCA	货交承运人	Free On Board, FOB	装运港船上交货
Cost, Insurance and Freight, CIF	成本加保险费加运费,到岸价格		
Orders and acknowledgement			
captioned order	标题所述订单	by courier	由快递公司传递
make out a contract	缮制合同	make up the order	备货
sign and return one copy for our file	请签退一份供我方存档	bulk delivery	大宗货物的交付
replenish stocks	补充库存/进货	maximum discount	最大折扣

续表

英文	中文	英文	中文
contractual obligation	合同义务	counter-sign	副署,会签
counter-signature	连署签名	general terms and conditions	一般交易条件
Import License,I/L	进口许可证	mode of payment	付款方式
Proforma Invoice,P/I	形式发票	prompt shipment	即期装运
provisional order	临时订单	Purchase Confirmation,P/C	购货确认书
purchase contract	购货合同	Purchase Order,P/O	订单
regular order	经常订单,定期订单	regular purchase	定期购货
repeat order	重复订单,续订	Sales Contract,S/C	销售合同
trial order	试销订单	accept an order	接受订单/订货
acknowledge an order	(卖方)确认订单	arrive at/come to an agreement	达成协议
book an order	接受订单/货	cancel an order	撤销订单/货
complete an order	处理订单,备货	confirm an order	(买方)确认订单
decline an order	谢绝订单	deliver an order	交付订货
draft a contract	起草合同	enter into a contract	订立合同
fill/fulfill/make up an order	处理订单,备货	meet an order	备货
place an order	下/放订单,订货	process an order	处理订单,备货
refuse/reject an order	拒受订单	supply an order	(根据订单)供货
unit price	单价		

Insurance

英文	中文	英文	中文
obtain indemnity	获得赔偿	a cover note	承保单
a marine policy	海洋运输保单	a floating policy	全额保单
an open policy	预约保单	a valued policy	定值保单
declaration form	启运通知书	a claims form	索赔申请书/表
be for the buyers' account	由买方付款	assessor's report	估损报告
survey report	货物检验报告	insurance certificate	保险凭证
insurance claim	保险索赔	insurance surveyor	(保险公司)货物检查员
write-off	销帐	at your end	在贵方所在地
the People's Insurance Company of China,PICC	中国人民财产保险股份有限公司	the state-owned company/enterprise	国有公司/企业

续表

英文	中文	英文	中文
Packing			
bar code	条形码	bulk cargo	散装货,统装货
bulky cargo	（体大质轻的）轻泡货	bulky parcel	大宗包裹
color assortment	颜色搭配	country of origin	原产地,原产国
customary packing	习惯包装	equal assortment	平均搭配
flexible container	集装包/袋	gunny bag	麻袋
iron drum	铁桶	lot number	批号
trade mark	商标	open-top container	开顶式集装箱
state-of-the-art	最先进的	indicative marks	指示性标志
shipping marks	装运标志,唛头	warning marks	警告性标志
neutral packing	中性包装	nude cargo	裸装货
packing list	装箱单	paper bag	纸袋
long ton	长吨	short ton	短吨
seller's usual packing	卖方习惯包装	size assortment	尺寸搭配
Transportation			
Estimated Time of Arrival, ETA	估计到达时间	Estimated Time of Departure, ETD	估计离开时间
secure the vessel	弄到船只	cargo capacity	载货能力
charter party	租船合同	airway bill	空运提单
carrying vessel	运货船	direct steamer	直达船
dock receipt	码头收据	document of title	产权单证
freight prepaid	运费已付	freight to collect	运费到付
general cargo vessel	杂货船	negotiable instrument	可流通/转让票据
sailing schedule	船期表	sailing date	启航日期
shorthanded memo	短卸单	take delivery of	取货
make delivery of	发货	dispatch money	速遣费,快装费
freight ton	运费吨	measurement ton	尺码吨
weight ton	重量吨	weight memo	重量单
ocean transportation	海洋运输	Full Container Load, FCL	整箱货
Less than Container Load, LCL	拼箱货	Bill of Lading, B/L	海运提单

续表

英文	中文	英文	中文
partial/part shipment	分批装运	port of destination	目的港
port of shipment	装货港	shipping advice	装船通知
shipping order	装船通知单，装货单	shipping space	（水运）舱位，订舱
storage cost/charges	仓储费	time charter	定期租船
voyage charter	定程租船	time of shipment	装运/船期
Payment			
aggregate amount	总价/金额	L/C amendment advice	信用证修改通知书
accepting bank	承兑行	days of grace	宽限期
expiry date	失效期	extension of the L/C	信用证展期
operative instrument	有效票据	waiver of legal rights	放弃合法权利
banking/bank charges	银行手续费	cash against documents	凭单付款
cash against documents on arrival of goods	货到后凭单付款	conversion rate	兑换率
exchange rate	外汇率	financing of projects	项目融资
fine bank bill	有信用的银行汇票	first class bill	信誉好的汇票
foreign exchange	外汇	protest for non-payment	拒付证书
protest note	拒付通知书	finance a project	为项目提供资金
honor a draft	承兑汇票	dishonor a draft	拒付汇票
protect a draft	备妥货款以支付汇票	on board bill of lading	装船提单
opening/issuing bank	信用证开证行	correspondent bank	往来行
advising/notifying bank	通知行	blank endorsement	空白背书
more or less clause	溢短装条款	bona fide holder	善意持票人
accompanying documents	随附单据	time/usance letter of credit	远期信用证
without recourse	无追索权	Mail Transfer, M/T	信汇
Telegraphic Transfer, T/T	电汇	Demand Draft, D/D	票汇
debit note	索款通知书	D/P after sight	远期付款交单
financial standing	财务状况	status inquiry	资信调查
Complaints			
short-open	（信用证）少开	arbitration body	仲裁机构

续表

英文	中文	英文	中文
arbitration clause	仲裁条款	breach of the contract	违反合同,违约
color deviation	色差	compulsory arbitration	强制性仲裁
faulty goods/packing	劣等货物/包装	force majeure	不可抗力
legal action	法律诉讼	non-conformity of quality	质量不符
non-performance of the contract	不履行合同	settlement of claims	理赔
shoddy goods	次货	voluntary arbitration	自愿仲裁
slip up	出错	wear and tear	磨损;损耗
customs examination	海关检查	Fair Average Quality, FAQ	中等品,大路货
commodity inspection bureau	商品检验局		

Agencies

英文	中文	英文	中文
confirming house	保付商行	opportune moment	恰当时机
sales room	拍卖场,售货处	authorized agent	指定代理人
channel of distribution	销售渠道	del credere agency	信用担保代理人
exclusive distribution	总经销	exclusive/sole agency	独家代理
exclusive sales	包销	exclusive sales agreement	包销协议,独家经销协议
general agency	总代理,一般代理	forwarding agent, forwarder	货运代理,运输代理商
Procurement Authorization, P/A	采购授权书	salesmen's traveling and entertainment expenses	销售员旅费及招待费
volume discount	总购量折扣	trade volume	贸易额,交易额
volume of business	营业/交易额	advertising agency	广告公司
advertising agent	广告代理商/人	agency commission	代理佣金
annual turnover	年营业额,年成交量	buying agent	采购代理商/人
commission house	佣金商行	insurance agent	保险代理商/人

Document

英文	中文	英文	中文
certificate of conformity	一致性证书	certificate of quality	质量证书
test report	测试报告	product performance report	产品性能报告
product specification report	产品规格型号报告	process data report	工艺数据报告
first sample test report	首样测试报告	price/sales catalogue	价格/销售目录

续表

英文	中文	英文	中文
party information	参与方信息	mill certificate	农产品加工厂证书
post receipt	邮政收据	weight certificate	重量证书
weight list	重量单	valid certificate	有效证书
combined certificate of value and origin	价值与原产地综合证书	movement certificate	移动声明
certificate of quantity	数量证书	quality data message	质量数据报文
query form	查询单	response to query	查询回复
purchase order	订购单	manufacturing instructions	制造说明
stores requisition	领料单	invoicing data sheet	产品售价单
packing instruction	包装说明	internal transport order	内部运输单
statistical and other administrative internal documents	统计及其他管理用内部单证	direct payment valuation request	直接支付估价申请
direct payment valuation	直接支付估价单	povisional payment valuation	临时支付估价单
payment valuation	支付估价单	quantity valuation	数量估价单
quantity valuation request	数量估价申请	contract bill	承包标书
unpriced tender BOQ	不计价投标数量单	priced tender BOQ	标价投标数量单
inquiry list	询价单	interim application for payment	临时支付申请
agreement to pay	支付协议	letter of intent	意向书
order number	订单号	blanket order	总订单
sport order	现货订单	lease order	租赁单
rush order	紧急订单	repair order	修理单
call off order	分订单	consignment order	寄售单
sample order	样品订单	swap order	换货单
purchase order change request	订购单变更请求	purchase order response	订购单回复
hire order	租用单	spare parts order	备件订单
delivery instructions	交货说明	delivery schedule	交货计划表
delivery just-in-time	按时交货	delivery release	发货通知
delivery note	交货通知	packing list	装箱单
price quotation	报价	request for quote	报价申请
contract number	合同号	acknowledgement of order	订单确认

续表

英文	中文	英文	中文
final invoice	终结发票	partial invoice	部分发票
operating instructions	操作说明	name/product plate	铭牌
request for delivery instructions	交货说明请求	booking request	订舱申请
shipping instructions	装运说明	shipper's letter of instructions (air)	托运人说明书(空运)
cartage order (local transport)	短途货运单	ready for despatch advice	待运通知
despatch order	发运单	certificate of analysis	分析证书
despatch advice	发运通知	advice of distrbution of document	单证分发通知
commercial invoice	商业发票	credit note	贷记单
commission note	佣金单	debit note	借记单
corrected invoice	更正发票	consolidated invoice	合并发票
prepayment invoice	预付发票	hire invoice	租用发票
tax invoice	税务发票	self-billed invoice	自用发票
delcredere invoice	保兑发票	factored invoice	代理发票
lease invoice	租赁发票	consignment invoice	寄售发票
factored credit note	代理贷记单	instructions for bank transfer	银行转账指示
application for banker's draft	银行汇票申请书	collection payment advice	托收支付通知书
documentary credit payment advice	跟单信用证支付通知书	documentary credit acceptance advice	跟单信用证承兑通知书
documentary credit negotiation advice	跟单信用证议付通知书	application for banker's guarantee	银行担保申请书
banker's guarantee	银行担保	documentary credit letter of indemnity	跟单信用证赔偿单
pre-advice of a credit	信用证预先通知书	collection order	托收单
document presentation form	单证提交单	payment order	付款单
extended payment order	扩展付款单	multiple payment order	多重付款单
credit advice	贷记通知书	extended credit advice	扩展贷记通知书
debit advice	借记通知书	reversal of debit	借记撤销
reversal of credit	贷记撤销	documentary credit application	跟单信用证申请书
documentary credit	跟单信用证	documentary credit notification	跟单信用证通知书

续表

英文	中文	英文	中文
documentary credit transfer advice	跟单信用证转让通知	documentary credit amendment notification	跟单信用证更改通知书
documentary credit amendment	跟单信用证更改单	remittance advice	汇款通知
banker's draft	银行汇票	bill of exchange	汇票
promissory note	本票	financial statement of account	账户财务报表
statement of account message	账户报表报文	insurance certificate	保险凭证
insurance policy	保险单	insurance declaration sheet (bordereau)	保险申报单（明细表）
insurer's invoice	保险人发票	cover note	承保单
forwarding instructions	货运说明	forwarder's advice to import agent	货运代理给进口代理的通知
forwarder's advice to exporter	货运代理给出口商的通知	forwarder's invoice	货运代理发票
forwarder's certificate of receipt	货运代理收据证明	shipping note	托运单
forwarder's warehouse receipt	货运代理人仓库收据	goods receipt	货物收据
port charges document	港口费用单	warehouse warrant	入库单
delivery order	提货单	handling order	装卸单
gate pass	通行证	waybill number	运单号
universal (multipurpose) transport document	通用（多用）运输单证	goods receipt of carriage	承运人货物收据
house waybill	全程运单	master bill of lading	主提单
bill of lading	提单	bill of lading original	正本提单
bill of lading copy	副本提单	empty container bill	空集装箱提单
tanker bill of lading	油轮提单	sea waybill	海运单
inland waterway bill of lading	内河提单	non-negotiable maritime transport document (generic)	不可转让的海运单证（通用）
mate's receipt	大副收据	house bill of lading	全程提单
letter of indemnity for non-surrender of bill of lading	无提单提货保函	forwarder's bill of lading	货运代理人提单
rail consignment note (generic term)	铁路托运单（通用条款）	land freight	陆运费

续表

英文	中文	英文	中文
escort official recognition	押运正式确认	recharging document	分段计费单证
road consignment note	公路托运单	air waybill	空运单
master air waybill	主空运单	substitute air waybill	分空运单
effects declaration	物品申报	passenger list	乘客名单
delivery notice (rail transport)	铁路运输交货通知	despatch note (post parcels)	邮递包裹投递单
combined transport document (generic)	联合运输单证(通用)	through bill of lading	直达提单
forwarder's certificate of transport	货运代理人运输证书	clean transport document	清洁运输单据
multimodal transport document (generic)	多式联运单证(通用)	combined transport bill of lading/multimodal bill of lading	多式联运提单
booking confirmation	订舱确认	calling forward notice	要求交货通知
freight invoice	运费发票	arrival notice (goods)	货物到达通知
notice of circumstances preventing delivery (goods)	无法交货的通知	notice of circumstances preventing transport (goods)	无法运货通知
delivery notice (goods)	交货通知	cargo manifest	载货清单
freight manifest	载货运费清单	road transportation	公路运输
container manifest (unit packing list)	集装箱载货清单	charges note	铁路费用单
advice of collection	托收通知	safety of ship certificate	船舶安全证书
safety of radio certificate	无线电台安全证书	safety of equipment certificate	设备安全证书
civil liability for oil certificate	油污民事责任书	loadline document	载重线证书
derat document	免于除鼠证书	maritime declaration of health	航海健康证书
certificate of registry	船舶登记证书	ship's stores declaration	船用物品申报单
export licence application	出口许可证申请表	export licence	出口许可证
exchange control declaration	出口结汇核销单	despatch note moder T	T出口单证(海关转运报关单)(欧盟用)

续表

英文	中文	英文	中文
despatch note model T1	T1出口单证（内部转运报关单）（欧盟用）	despatch note model T2	T2出口单证（原产地证明书）
control document T5	T5管理单证（欧盟用）	resending consignment note	铁路运输退运单
despatch note model T2L	T2L出口单证（原产地证明书）（欧盟用）	goods declaration for exportation	出口货物报关单
cargo declaration (departure)	离港货物报关单	application for goods control certificate	货物监管证书申请表
goods control certificate	货物监管证书	application for phytosanitary certificate	植物检疫申请表
phytosanitary certificate	植物检疫证书	sanitary certificate	卫生检疫证书
veterinary certificate	动物检疫证书	application for inspection certificate	商品检验申请表
inspection certificate	商品检验证书	certificate of incorporation	公司注册证书
certificate of weight	质量证书	declaration of origin	原产地申明
regional appellation certificate	地区名称证书	preference certificate of origin	优惠原产地证书
certificate of origin form GSP	普惠制原产地证书	consular invoice	领事发票
dangerous goods declaration	危险货物申报单	statistical document	统计报表
international trade statistics	国际贸易统计申报单	delivery verification certificate	交货核对证明
import licence	进口许可证	import surcharge	进口附加税
customs declaration without commercial detail	无商业细节的报关单	customs declaration with commercial and item detail	有商业和项目细节的报关单
customs declaration without item detail	无项目细节的报关单	related document	有关单证
document operator	单证部门	application for exchange allocation	调汇申请
foreign exchange permit	调汇许可	exchange control declaration (import)	进口外汇管理申报
goods declaration for importation	进口货物报关单	goods declaration for home use	内销货物报关单

续表

英文	中文	英文	中文
customs immediate release declaration	海关即刻放行报关单	customs delivery note	海关放行通知
cargo declaration (arrival)	到港货物报关单	value declaration	货物价值申报清单
customs invoice	海关发票	customs declaration (post parcels)	邮包报关单
tax declaration (value added tax)	增值税申报单	tax declaration (general)	普通税申报单
tax demand	催税单	embargo permit	禁运货物许可证
goods declaration for customs transit	海关转运货物报关单	TIF form	TIF 国际铁路运输报关单
TIR carnet	TIR 国际公路运输报关单	EC carnet	欧盟海关转运报关单
EUR1 certificate of origin	EUR1 欧盟原产地证书	ATA carnt	暂准进口海关文件
single administrative document	欧盟统一单证	general response (Customs)	海关一般回复
document response (Customs)	海关公文回复	error response (Customs)	海关误差回复
package response (Customs)	海关一揽子回复	tax calculation/confirmation response (Customs)	海关计税/确认回复
quota prior allocation certificate	配额预分配证书	end use authorization	最终使用授权书
government contract	政府合同	statistical document import	进口统计报表
application for documentary credit	跟单信用证开证申请书	previous Customs document message	先前海关文件/报文
ordinary trade	一般贸易		

附表3　商务贸易类型词汇及其解释

英文	中文	解释
barter trade	易货贸易	国家之间不通过货币媒介直接交换货物
compensation trade	补偿贸易	利用外资进口国外技术或设备,用产品偿还
agreement trade	协定贸易	根据各国政府间签订的贸易协定和清算协定进行的贸易
processing with imported materials	进料加工	进口原材料、零部件加工成品后再出口
processing with customer's materials	来料加工	由国外厂商提供原材料、零部件,由国内厂商按外商要求加工装配,成品交外商销售,加工方收取工缴费
outward processing	出料加工	由国内厂商提供原材料、零部件,国外厂商按要求加工装配,成品返销,加工方收取工缴费
consignment trade	寄售贸易	寄售人将货物运到国外,委托代销人销售
international lease	国际租赁	根据国际租赁契约,出租人将设备租赁给他国承租人使用
frontier trade	边境贸易	边境城镇与接壤国家边境城镇之间及边民互市贸易
entrepot trade	转口贸易	经过转口国进行的进出口贸易
license trade	许可贸易	商标、专利技术、专有技术以许可协议形式进行的贸易
forward trade	期货贸易	通过国际期货市场进行远期商品买卖
contract project	承包工程	承包国外工程技术项目或劳务项目的进出口设备和货物
international bid	国际招标	通过国际招标形式进行的一种进出口贸易
international exhibition	国际展览	通过国际展览会和国际博览会等形式进出口货物
international exhibition	国际拍卖	通过国际拍卖进行的一种贸易
international loan	国际贷款进口	国际金融机构或外国政府提供贷款项目的进口
reimburse loan	归还贷款出口	国家批准的国际贷款项目通过出口产品来归还贷款
imports by foreign-invested enterprises	外商投资企业进口	根据国家有关规定,外商投资企业进口货物
exports by foreign-invested enterprises	外商投资企业出口	根据国家有关规定,外商投资企业出口货物
international aid	国际援助	国际组织或外国政府提供无偿援助的进出口货物
donation	捐赠	民间团体和个人捐赠给我国的物资
present	赠送	外国组织或个人赠送给我国组织或个人的物资
other trade	其他贸易	国际贸易中使用的上述贸易方式之外的贸易方式

附表4 进出口业务常见流程及词汇

Processes(流程)
Establishing business relations(建立业务联系——流程1)
Inquiries(询问/询价——流程2)
Replies and offers(回函与报盘——流程3)
Acceptance and orders(接受与订购——流程4)
Standing inquiries(资信调查——流程5)
Packing(包装——流程6)
Insurance(保险——流程7)
Shipment(装运——流程8)
Payment by L/C(信用证支付——流程9)
Other modes of payment(其他支付方式——流程10)
Collection(催款——流程11)
Complaints and claims(抱怨与索赔——流程12)
Claim settlement(理赔——流程13)
Agency(代理——流程14)
Compensation trade and processing with supplied materials(补偿贸易与来料加工——流程15)

Establishing business relations key vocabulary			
brochure *n.*	小册子	general terms and conditions	一般交易条件
business negotiation	商务磋商	handle *v.*	经营
business scope	业务范围	leaflet *n.*	单页/活页(说明书)
certificate	证书	offer *n.*	报盘
chemical *n.*	化学品	packing *n.*	包装
commercial counselor	商务参赞	pharmaceutical *adj.*	制药的
commission *n.*	佣金	pottery *n.*	陶器
commodity *n.*	商品	price list *n.*	价格单
consulate *n.*	领事馆	prospective *adj.*	预期的,未来的
customs duty	关税	purchaser *n.*	买主
customs *n.*	海关	quotation *n.*	报价
detailed specification	详细规格	rebate *n.*	回扣
discount *n.*	折扣	sample *n.*	样品
embassy *n.*	大使馆	sister corporation	姐妹公司
enclose *v.*	附寄	specialize in	专门经营
business relations	业务联系	transaction *n.*	交易
export control	出口管制		

续表

Inquiries key vocabulary

advertisement n.	广告	lines of business	业务范围, 经营范围
associate n.	合伙人	manufacturer n.	生产商
at one's earliest convenience	请尽早地	merchandise n.	商品（总称）
booklet n.	小册子	model n.	型号, 款式
bulk buyer	大买家	order n./v.	订购
business concern	商行, 企业	pamphlet n.	小册子
businessperson n.	商人	pattern n.	模式, 样式
catalogue/catalog n.	产品目录	representative n.	代表
chamber of commerce	商会	retailer n.	零售商
circular n.	通函	sales literature	销售资料
client n.	客户	showroom n.	陈列室
considerable adj.	大批量的	specification n.	规格
deal n.	生意, 交易	subsidiary n.	子公司
deliver v.	交货	supply v.	供应
discount n.	折扣	terms n.	条件
enquire/inquire v./n.	询问/询价	trade fair	交易会
inspection n.	检验	wholesaler n.	批发商

Replies and offers key vocabulary

a selection of	一系列	high grade	高档
accept v.	接受	illustrated catalogue	带有插图的目录
assortment n.	花色品种	low grade	低档
attend to	执行	margin n.	利润
ceiling price	最高价	net price	净价
commission n.	佣金	offerer n.	报盘人
competitive price	竞争性价格	patent n.	专利
concerning prep.	关于	proposal n.	建议
counter offer	还盘	purchase n./v.	购买
current price	现价	quote v.	报价
durability n.	耐用	sales representative	销售代表
examine v.	检验	shrinkage	缩水
fashion n.	款式	sliding price	滑动价格
gross n.	一罗, 毛收入	trade discount	商业折扣
hand-made adj.	手工制的	under separate cover	另寄
unit price	单价	undergo v.	经过
CFR (Cost and Freight)	成本加运费	DES (Delivered Ex Ship)	目的港船上交货
CIF (Cost, Insurance and Freight)	成本加保险加运费	DDU (Delivered Duty Unpaid)	未完税交货
		DEQ (Delivered Ex Quay)	目的港码头交货
CIP (Carriage and Insurance Paid to)	运费、保费付至	EXW (Ex Works)	工厂交货
CPT (Carriage Paid to)	运费付至	FAS (Free Along Side)	装运港船边交货
DDP (Delivered Duty Paid)	完税后交货	FCA (Free Carrier)	货交承运人
DAF (Delivered at Frontier)	边境交货	FOB (Free on Board)	装运港船上交货

Acceptance and orders key vocabulary

a letter of credit	信用证	glove n.	手套
assorted cotton socks	花色各异的袜子	handkerchief n.	手帕
cancel an order	取消订购	in duplicate	一式两份
captioned adj.	标题下的	in good time	及时
carry out the order	执行订单	negotiation n.	磋商,谈判
conclude a transaction	达成交易	place an order	订购
confirm an order	确认订购	promptly adv.	及时
dispatch v.	发货	reach an agreement	达成协议
effect v.	实现	regular customer	老客户
enter into a contract	签订合同	sales confirmation	销售确认书
file n.	存档	shipment n.	装运

Standing inquiries key vocabulary

accord v.	给予	obliged adj.	感激的
amendment of contract	合同修改书	open an account with	建立业务联系
article/clause n.	条款	original adj./n.	正本的;原件
attachment n.	附件	partnership n.	合作关系
bankruptcy n.	破产	punctual adj.	守时的
commercial position	资信状况	purchase contract	购买合同
confidential adj.	绝密的	reference n.	证明人
copy n.	副本	renewal of a contract	重订合同
countersign v.	会签	respecting adj.	关于
credit standing	资信状况	sales contract	销售合同
detriment n.	危害	straightforward adj.	直截了当的
expiration of contract	合同到期	cancel a contract	取消合同
financial position	财政状况	draft a contract	起草合同
in confidence	秘密地	perform a contract	履行合同
in quadruplicate	一式四份	sign a contract	签订合同
in triplicate	一式三份	unfavorable adj.	不利的
obligation n.	义务	unquestionable adj.	毫无疑问的

Packing key vocabulary

bar code	条形码	containerization n.	集装箱化
batch number	批号	corrugated cardboard	瓦楞纸板
bind v.	捆绑	customary packing	习惯包装
bundle n./v.	捆;绑	deliver goods	交货
carton n.	纸板箱	drum n.	桶
cloth bag	布袋	faulty packing	包装欠佳
comprise v.	包括	freight charge	运费
consignee n.	收货人	gross weight	毛重
consigner n.	交货人	inadequate packing	包装不当
contain v.	含有	inner packing	内包装
container n.	集装箱	label n.	标签

续表

measurement *n.*	体积	shortly *adv.*	不久
moldy *adj.*	发霉的	staff *n.*	员工
net weight	净重	stain *n.*	污迹
neutral packing	中性包装	stuffing material	塞物料
outer packing	外包装	trademark *n.*	商标
packaging *n.*	包装材料	waterproof *adj.*	防水的
plywood case	胶合板箱	wooden case	木箱
replacement *n.*	代替	wooden peg	木栓
rough handling	粗率的处理	wrap *v.*	包装
seaworthy packing	海运包装		

Insurance key vocabulary

actual total loss	实际全损	parcel *n.*	货物
All Risks	全险	partial loss	部分损失
breakage of packing risk	包装破裂险	particular average	单独损失
Insurance Clause	保险条款	policy *n.*	保险单
cover *n.*	保险	premium *n.*	保险费
debit note	索款通知单	rate *n.*	费用，价格
draw *v.*	开汇票	refund *v./n.*	退款
exceed *v.*	超过	rust risk	锈损险
F.P.A. (free from particular average) 平安险		shortage risk	短量险
		taint of odor risk	串味险
for your account	记入你方账户	time of validity	有效期
forward *v.*	递送	theft, pilferage and non-delivery risks 偷窃及提货不着险	
general average	共同海损		
Institute Cargo Clause	协会货物条款	total loss	全损
insurance cover	保险范围	underwriter *n.*	保险商
insurance rate	保险费率	vary *v.*	变化
insurance value	保险值	W.P.A. (with particular average) 水渍险	
insure *v.*	投保		
insurer *n.*	保险商	war risk	战争险
invoice value	发票金额	warehouse *n.*	仓库
leakage risk	渗漏险	warehouse to warehouse clause	仓至仓条款
obliged *adj.*	感激的		

Shipment key vocabulary

assist *v.*	帮助	corresponding *adj.*	相符的
bill of lading	提单	delivery *n.*	交货
carrier *n.*	承运人	demurrage *n.*	滞期费
clean bill	光票	direct B/L	直达提单
consignee *n.*	收货人	dispatch money	速遣费
consigner *n.*	交货人	due *adj.*	到期

续表

execution *n.*	执行	process this order	执行订单
explicitly *adv.*	明确地	prompt shipment	迅速装运
forwarding agent	货运代理	purchase confirmation	购买确认书
imperative *adj.*	紧急的	sail for	驶往
inconvenience *n.*	不便	schedule *v./n.*	安排
invoice *n.*	发票	shipping advice	装船通知
manufacturer *n.*	制造商	shipping documents	运输单据
on board	在船上	shipping instructions	装船指示
optional port	选择港口	shipping marks	唛头,运输标志
order B/L	指示提单	stipulate *v.*	规定
partial shipment	分批装运	through B/L	直达提单
port of destination	目的港	time charter	期租
port of discharge	卸货港	load *v.*	装（货）
port of shipment	装运港	unload *v.*	卸（货）
port charge	港口费用	voyage charter	程租船
Payment by L/C key vocabulary			
manufacturer's certificate	厂方证明	drawer *n.*	出票人
acceptor *n.*	承兑人	effect shipment	装运
advice *n.*	通知	establish *v.*	开立
advise *v.*	通知	holder/bearer	持票人
agricultural produce	农产品	in line with	与……相符
amendments to a credit	信用证修改书	in one's favor	以……为受益人
as regards	关于	irrevocable L/C	不可撤销信用证
at ... days sight	出票后……天付款	open *v.*	开立
back to back L/C	背对背信用证	payee *n.*	收款人
beneficiary *n.*	受益人	payer *n.*	付款人
bill of exchange	汇票	presentation *n.*	提交
call for	要求	reciprocal L/C	对开信用证
clean L/C	不跟单信用证	revolving L/C	循环信用证
commodity *n.*	商品	sight bill/draft	即期汇票
concerned *adj.*	有关的	sight L/C	即期信用证
confirmed L/C	保兑信用证	specify *v.*	规定
divisible L/C	可分割信用证	standby L/C	备用信用证
documentary L/C	跟单信用证	time draft	远期汇票
draft *n.*	汇票	transferable L/C	可转让信用证
draw *v.*	出票	valid *adj.*	有效的
drawee *n.*	受票人		

续表

Other modes of payment key vocabulary

account number	账户号码	facilitate v.	促进
advising bank	通知行	invoice n.	发票
collecting bank	托收银行	M/T (mail transfer)	信汇
collection n.	托收	misplace v.	误放
collection on clean bill	光票托收	negotiating bank	议付行
collection on documents	跟单托收	opening/issuing bank	开证行
confirming bank	保兑行	paying bank	支付行
considerable adj.	大量的	precedent n.	先例
D/P at sight	即期付款交单	preferential adj.	优惠的
D/P (documents against payment)	付款交单	premises n.	办公楼
D/D (demand draft)	票汇	principal n.	委托人
dishonor n.	拒付	push the sales	推销
D/A (documents against acceptance)	承兑交单	reimbursing bank	偿付行
		remit v.	汇付
endorsee n.	被背书人	remittance n.	汇付
endorsement n.	背书	remitting bank	汇款银行
endorsement in blank	空白背书	shipping documents	运输单据
endorser n.	背书人	trust receipt	信托收据
		TT (Telegraphic Transfer)	电汇

Collection key vocabulary

account n.	账户	negotiation n.	议付
applicant n.	申请人	outstanding adj.	未结清的
balance n.	余额	overdue adj.	过期的
C.W.O (cash with order)	随订单付现	pay in cash	现金付款
circumstances n.	情况	pay in full	全部付清
clear one's account	结账	payment by/on installments	分期付款
clearance account	结算账户	payment in part	部分付款
clearing agreement	清算协定	payment of interest	付息
credit n.	信用	payment on arrival	货到付款
deferred payment	延期付款	prepared adj.	愿意的
deficit n.	赤字	recover v.	收取
document of settlement	结汇单据	reputation n.	名誉
due adj.	到期的	settlement n.	结算
foreign exchange broker	外汇经纪人	soft currency n.	软货币
foreign exchange control	外汇管制	solicitor n.	律师
hard currency n.	硬货币	statement n.	账单
international settlement	国际结算	unsettled adj.	未结算的

Complaints and claims key vocabulary

breach *n./v.*	违反	material breach	重大违约
claim clause	索赔条款	minor breach	轻微违约
compensation *n.*	补偿	order *n.*	订购的货物
consequence *n.*	后果	penalty *n.*	惩罚
consignment *n.*	货物	press *v.*	催促
default *n.*	违约	promptness *n.*	迅速
deprive *v.*	剥夺	purchase price	购买价
discrepancy *n.*	不一致	refund *n./v.*	退款
dispatch *n./v.*	发货	remedial *adj.*	补救的
dispute *n.*	争议	replace *v.*	替换
duly *adv.*	按期地	rough handling	粗暴装卸
eyesore *n.*	碍眼	scratch *v.*	刮擦
fade *v.*	褪色	shade *n.*	颜色,色度
indemnification *n.*	赔偿	spot *v.*	玷污
injured party	受损方	warranty *n.*	保证书
install *v.*	安装	withstand *v.*	抵住
live up to	达到		

Claim settlement key vocabulary

impartial judgment	公正判决	in view of	考虑到
arbitration *n.*	仲裁	inferior *adj.*	劣等的
attest *v.*	证明	investigation *n.*	调查
award *n.*	裁决	liable *adj.*	有义务的
case *n.*	案例	litigation *n.*	诉讼
compulsory *adj.*	强制性的	lodge a claim	索赔
conciliation *n.*	和解调停	long-standing *adj.*	长期的
consultation *n.*	磋商	mediation *n.*	调停
contradict *v.*	相矛盾	quality control	质量控制
dealing *n.*	交易	registered *adj.*	已注册的
decree *n.*	法令	remainder *n.*	剩余部分
deliberate *adj.*	蓄意的	respray *v.*	重新喷漆
exempt *adj./v.*	免除的;豁免	second to none	一流的
final *adj.*	终局性的	settle the case amicably	友好解决
force majeure	不可抗力	short delivery	交货短量
hook *n.*	钩子	slip up	失误
in part	部分地	unload *v.*	卸货
in transit	在运输中	warehouse *n.*	仓库

续表

Agency key vocabulary

advise v.	通知	garment n.	服装
agency agreement	代理协议	general agent	总代理
at one's earliest convenience	请尽早	line n.	行业
bank reference	银行证明信	moderate adj.	中等的,适度的
broker n.	经纪人	turnover n.	营业额
commission agent	佣金代理	overhead expenses	营业开支
connection n.	业务联系	proposal n.	建议
considering prep.	考虑到	purchasing agent	购买代理
consignment agent	寄售代理	push the sale	推销
draw up	草拟	renew an agreement	续约
duration n.	期限	showroom n.	陈列室
entrust v.	委托	subagent	副代理人
exclusive/sole agent	独家代理	terminate an agreement	终止协议
expiration n.	到期		

Compensation trade and processing with supplied materials key vocabulary

approach v.	接近	line of production	生产线
assemble line	装配线	manufacturer n.	生产商
assemble v.	装配	official report	正式报告
assembly work	装配业务	packing material	包装材料
auxiliary material	辅助材料	processing fee	加工费
blue print	蓝图	productive adj.	有成效的
channel n.	渠道	profit sharing	利润分配
compensation trade	补偿贸易	raw materials	原材料
component n.	配件,部件	semi-finished product	半成品
counter trade	对销贸易	technical data	技术材料
exempt from customs duty	免征关税	technological innovation	技术革新
finished product	成品	technology-intensive product	技术密集型产品
head office	总部	tyre n.	轮胎
hospitality n.	好客,热情款待	well-established adj.	确立已久的
in detail	详细地	manufacturer n.	制造厂
introduction of technology	技术引进		
labor-intensive product	劳动密集型产品		

外贸函电写作
实训习题册

段 婕 编

西北工业大学出版社

西 安

目　录

Exercise 1	Basic Knowledge of Business Letters Writing	1
Exercise 2	Structures and Styles of Business Letters	5
Exercise 3	Establishing Business Relations	8
Exercise 4	Inquiries and Replies	12
Exercise 5	Quotations, Offers and Counter Offers	17
Exercise 6	Orders and Acknowledgements	23
Exercise 7	Payment by Letter of Credit	28
Exercise 8	Other Methods of Payment	32
Exercise 9	Collection Letters	35
Exercise 10	Packing	38
Exercise 11	Shipping	40
Exercise 12	Insurance	44
Exercise 13	Complaints and Claims	47
Exercise 14	Agency	50
Exercise 15	Contracts and Agreements	54
Exercise 16	Invitation for Bids and Advertisements	58
Exercise 17	Memorandums	59
Exercise 18	E-mails	61
Exercise 19	Notices and Instructions	66
Exercise 20	Agendas and Minutes	67
Exercise 21	Business Reports	68
Exercise 22	Resume (CV), Application Letters, and Follow-Up Thank-You Letters	72
Exercise 23	Letters for Social Purpose	73
Exercise 24	Letters for Other Purposes	83

Exercise 1 Basic Knowledge of Business Letters Writing

1. Rewrite the following sentences to make them concise and clear.

(1) We ask you to send your product catalogue for all kinds of goods being handled by your corporation for reference with your buyers.

(2) We are famous computers importers and there are branches in three neighboring cities.

(3) American business has a goal which is to try to raise the standard of living.

(4) It is true that often great affluence is accompanied by another problem, unrest socially.

(5) Adam Smith as a matter of fact arrived at the conclusion that the division of labor makes it possible to increase the amount of goods we produce; this was in 1776.

(6) In socialist economies as well as in capitalist economies, increasing numbers of workers who are highly qualified are unable to find jobs required by their skills and by their training.

(7) The salesperson told us that we should write to the main office directly for whatever information we were in need of.

(8) The convention, which was scheduled for the month of January was cancelled due to the fact that there are restriction placed on travel.

(9) It goes without saying that we are acquainted with your policy on filing tax returns, and we have every intention of complying with the regulation, which you have stated.

(10) In the event that you cannot accept our invitation to come to the meeting, we would appreciate your informing us of this fact as soon as possible.

2. Revise the following sentences to make them positive rather than negative in tone.

(1) Your misunderstanding of our February 9th letter caused you to make this mistake.

(2) Unfortunately your shipment cannot be delivered until next week.

(3) Your carelessness in this matter caused the damage to the computer system.

(4) To avoid the damages to your image of company, please remit your payment within

ten days.

(5) We regret to inform you that we cannot accept the method of payment you suggested for this shipment.

(6) You cannot visit our assembly line except on Saturday.

(7) We have received your complaint about the late arrival of the consignment. We close at …‰ p.m.

(8) We do not believe that you will have cause for dissatisfaction.

(9) Your order will be delayed for two weeks.

3. Change the following wordy phrases into concise ones.

(1) are desirous of   (2) as a general rule

(3) as per your suggestion   (4) consider favorably

(5) due in large measure to   (6) in all probability

(7) in the process of preparation   (8) in the event that

(9) in the normal course of   (10) in view of the fact that

(11) during the time of   (12) enclosed herewith

(13) for the reason that   (14) fullest possible extent

(15) give consideration to   (16) make inquiry regarding

(17) on the grounds that   (18) not in a position to

(19) pertaining to   (20) pursuant to our agreement

4. Correct the mistakes in the following letter.

Dear Sirs,

We thank you for your letter of Oct. 12 regarded iron scraps, for which you have received inquiries from your customers in Attica.

We wish we had received your inquiry a little earlier. On the very day it reached us, a contract was placed with Mexico for a total of 360,000 tons. Because of this, our government has decided not to grant export licenses for the commodity for areas other than Mexico until December 31, 2006, expected the shortage, which may be caused in the domestic market.

Therefore, we shall be pleased to inform you with detail as soon as the circumstances becomes favor for us to do business on this line.

Yours sincerely,

Exercise 1 Basic Knowledge of Business Letters Writing

5. Compare the following letters and tell which one is better and why.

Letter A

Dear Sirs,

We wish to acknowledge receipt of your credit application dated February 17 giving trade and bank references, and we thank you for the same. Please be advised that credit accommodations are herewith extended as per your request and your order has been shipped.

Hoping you will give us the opportunity of serving you again in the near future, we remain ready for it.

Very truly yours,

Letter B

Dear Sirs,

Thank you for sending so promptly the trade and bank references we have asked for. I am glad to say that your order has already been shipped on the terms you requested.

We hope you will give us the chance to serve you again.

Very truly yours,

6. Answer these questions.

(1) What is a business letter?

(2) State the forms and structures of business letters.

(3) State some rules of good writing.

(4) State some writing principles of business letters.

7. Translate the following sentences into Chinese.

(1) This is the main part of the letter. It expresses the writer's idea, opinion, purpose and wishes, etc. so it should be carefully planned. When writing, pay attention to the following:

    a. Write simply, dearly, courteously, grammatically, and to the point.

    b. Paragraph correctly, confining each paragraph to one topic.

c. See that your typing is accurate and the display artistic.

(2) Subject line is actually the general idea of a letter. It is inserted between the salutation and the body of the letter either at the left-hand margin for fully-blocked letter form or centrally over the body for other forms. It calls the receiver's attention to the topic of the letter.

(3) Letterhead includes the sender's name, postal address, telephone number, telex number, fax number, and E-mail address, etc. Usually letterhead is printed in the up-center or at the left margin of a letter writing paper.

(4) The name and address of the receiver is typed at the left-hand margin about two to four spaces below the date. It appears exactly the same way as on the envelope.

(5) It is common to type the name of the writer's firm or company immediately below complimentary close. Then the person who dictating the letter should sign his/her name by hand and in ink, below it. Since hand-written signatures are illegible, the name of signer is usually typed below the signature, and followed by his/her job title or position. Never sign a letter with a rubber stamp.

(6) Business envelopes ordinarily have the return address printed in the upper left corner. The receiver's name and address should be typed about half way down the envelope. The postmark or stamps should be placed in the up right-hand corner, while the bottom left-hand corner is for post notations such as "Confidential", "Secret", "Printed Matter", etc.

Exercise 2　Structures and Styles of Business Letters

1. Arrange the following information in a proper form as they should be set out in a business letter.

(1) Sender's name: China National Textiles Import & Export Corporation, Shanghai Branch

(2) Sender's address: 18th Floor, Sunshine Mansion, 567 Siping Rd., Hongkou District, Shanghai, 200000, P.R.C.

(3) Sender's fax number: 86-21-63209767

(4) Sender's E-mail address: shanghaitexdles@shtextiles.com.cn

(5) Date: March 2nd, 2007

(6) Receiver's name: W. G. Wilkinson Co., Ltd.

(7) Receiver's address: 789 Maple Street, Lagos, Nigeria

(8) Salutation: Dear Sirs

(9) Subject: Embroidered Table-Cloths

(10) The Message: We thank you for your letter of Feb. 24th inquiring for the captioned goods. The enclosed booklet contains details of all our embroidered table-cloths and will enable you to make a suitable selection. We look forward to receiving your specific inquiry with keen interest.

(11) Complimentary close: Yours faithfully

2. Read the following letter and try to point out the problems in this letter.

DATATECH

International, Inc. 4038 Candlewood Drive

Lakewood, California 90711 Tel. (213) 92659023

2006/7/6

Clara J. Smith

Office Occupations Department

North Seattle Co., Ltd.

9600 College Way North
Seattle, WA 98103-3599

Dear Sirs,

Ref: Request for urgent shipment

Attention: Office Occupation Department

We enclose our figures of sales in your product during the past three months. You will see that our sales of the special line are quite disappointing. We requested your urgent shipment of this product, which you accepted. However, five weeks went by before the goods arrived instead of three weeks and we lost a wonderful opportunity of sales.

When inquiring about this matter we found that the goods were not shipped until four weeks after the date of dispatch. If they had been delivered straight to Qingdao. Much valuable time would have been saved. It will be necessary for you to give us your very best attention if you wish to maintain a certain level of sales in this market.

Best wishes.

Yours faithfully,

Elizabeth R. St. James,
Manager, Customer Relations Dept.

3. Fill in each of the blanks in the following letter with an appropriate word given in the box.

but, comparable, attention, to, set, appreciate, dependable, fresh

Dear Mr. Smith,

Your recent experience with a __(1)__ of Monday flashlight batteries is given proper __(2)__. Under separate cover, please find a new flashlight of __(3)__ value with the one you submitted us under guarantee. Fresh Monday batteries are included.

Exercise 2 Structures and Styles of Business Letters

For more than 99.5 percent of our entire Monday battery production is satisfying. It would be nice if this record was 100 percent, __(4)__ in the absence of a perfect record, we do __(5)__ it when a customer brings an unsatisfactory experience to our attention.

We are sure that the __(6)__ Monday batteries we are sending you will give you the same __(7)__ service that has made Monday batteries so famous all over the world.

Very truly yours,

4. Writing practice.

Write a business letter to one of your friends in the format you prefer, in which you give a brief account of ways to keep your letter a neat appearance.

Exercise 3　Establishing Business Relations

1. Translate the following terms or phrases from English into Chinese or vice versa.

(1) workmanship　　　　　　　　　(2) catalogue

(3) consular　　　　　　　　　　　(4) price list

(5) specialize in　　　　　　　　　(6) push the sales of

(7) 另封邮寄　　　　　　　　　　　(8) 开始(某种关系)

(9) 按照他们的要求　　　　　　　　(10) 为了打开中国市场

(11) 稳定的财政状况　　　　　　　 (12) 享有极佳的声誉

2. Fill in the blanks of the following letters with the words given below, and change the form when necessary.

> inform, establish, reputation, proposal, specialize,
> opportunity, purpose, interest, owe

Dear Sirs,

　　We ___(1)___ your name and address to L&R Company, who has ___(2)___ us that you are ___(3)___ in entering the market in China. We hope to ___(4)___ business relations with you for the ___(5)___ of marketing your products here.

　　We like to take this ___(6)___ to introduce ourselves as one of the leading company in China mainly ___(7)___ in electronic products, with high ___(8)___ and reliable outlets.

　　To give you a general idea of our company, we are sending you separately a copy of our brochure. Any ___(9)___ concerning cooperation will be given our immediate consideration.

　　We are looking forward to your early reply.

　　Yours faithfully,

Exercise 3　Establishing Business Relations

3. Complete the following sentences with the Chinese hints given in the brackets.

（1）We ＿＿＿＿＿＿＿＿＿（愿与贵公司建立贸易关系）on the basis of equality and mutual benefit.

（2）It will be highly appreciated if you ＿＿＿＿＿＿＿（立即着手此事）.

（3）If your price is reasonable, we trust we can ＿＿＿＿＿＿＿＿（长期大量订货）.

（4）Our products are ＿＿＿＿＿＿＿＿＿＿（以质量上乘、工艺精湛而闻名）, and have enjoyed great popularity both ＿＿＿＿＿＿＿＿（在国内外）.

（5）We ＿＿＿＿＿＿＿＿＿＿（借此机会）to introduce ourselves as a stated-owned corporation ＿＿＿＿＿＿＿＿（专营电子设备）.

（6）We would like to write to you and see if we can establish business relations ＿＿＿＿＿ ＿＿＿＿＿＿＿＿（通过开始几宗实际交易）.

（7）＿＿＿＿＿＿＿＿（承蒙驻贵国的中华人民共和国大使馆商务处告知贵公司的名称和地址）who informed us that your are in the market for men's apparel.

（8）＿＿＿＿＿＿＿＿＿（兹介绍本公司为领先的丝绸出口商之一）, having relations with more than 100 countries and regions in the world.

（9）We are ＿＿＿＿＿＿＿＿（同这里的所有经销商关系密切）and feel sure we can sell large quantities of your goods if we get your offers at competitive prices.

4. Translate the following letters into English.

（1）

敬启者：

承蒙我国驻巴黎商务参赞处告知贵公司名称和地址,我们得知贵公司有意在中国开展业务。

今借此机会特向贵公司介绍,本公司多年来一直经营通信设备,是中国主要经销商之一。如能收到你方产品目录和报价,将不胜感激。同时我方很愿意研究贵公司产品在我方市场的销售前景。

盼早日回复。

谨上

（2）

敬启者：

我们得知贵公司的地址,要感谢英国驻北京大使馆商赞处。该处已告知我们贵公司要购买化工产品。为此,今特与贵公司联系,希望与贵公司建立互利的贸易关系。

我公司是国有公司,独家经营化工产品进出口业务,现随函附寄我公司目前可以供应的主要出口商品表一份。如贵公司需要该表所列项目以外的任何商品,我公司一经接到贵方详细货单,将尽力为贵方提供所需商品。

我们在同欧洲国家的客户进行贸易时,一贯坚持平等互利、互通有无的原则,以便通过共同努力,促进业务和友谊,共同受益。

盼早日收到贵方的询盘。

(3)

敬启者:

我们从贵国驻伦敦使馆商赞处得知贵公司的地址,现特去函与贵公司建立业务关系。

我公司专门出口中国化工产品和药品。这些产品在世界上久享盛誉。随函附上目录表一份,以供参考。如有兴趣,请立即与我公司联系。

盼早日回复。

5. Writing practice.

Write a letter with the following hints:

- 经北京商会介绍,我方得知贵公司的名称和地址
- 我公司专门经营电机产品出口业务
- 我方另寄去一本目录册
- 如对目录中的产品感兴趣,请询价

6. Answer these questions.

(1) How to establish business relations with a new customer?

(2) How to write a letter to establish a business relationship?

7. Fill in the blanks with the best choice.

(1) We are sending you the samples _____ requested.

    a. be   b. are   c. as   d. for

(2) We trust that you will find our goods _____.

    a. attracting   b. to be attractive   c. attract your attention   d. attractive

(3) The brochure covers _____ wide range of products we deal in.

    a. the   b. a   c. of   d. about

(4) We would _____ very much if you send us some samples immediately.

    a. appreciation   b. appreciate it   c. appreciate   d. appreciatively

(5) If any of the items is _____ to you, please let us know.

    a. interest   b. interesting   c. interested   d. interests

(6) Our products enjoy _____ in world market.

    a. most popular   b. great popularity   c. good seller   d. selling fast

(7) We are _____ a copy of our catalog for your reference.

    a. send   b. covering   c. closed   d. enclosing

Exercise 3 Establishing Business Relations

(8) We are anxious to _____ the market for our Antimony Trioxide, which at present enjoys a limited sale in Europe.

    a. increase   b. enlarge   c. expand   d. extend

(9) We are sure that both of our companies will _____ from the joint venture.

    a. make benefit   b. benefit   c. be benefited   d. mutual benefit

(10) We would like to take this _____ to establish business relations with you.

    a. opening   b. opportunity   c. popularity   d. advantage

8. Choose the appropriate word or words in the parentheses.

(1) As (regard, regards) machine tools, we regret to (say, inform) that we are not able to supply for the time being.

(2) Being (specialized, handled) in the import and export of Art and Crafts, we express our desire to trade (with, to) in this line.

(3) To acquaint you (of, with) our products, we are sending you (by, under) separate airmail a copy of catalog and several sample books for your reference.

(4) (In case, Provided, If) you find our products (interested, interesting) to you, please let us have your specific (order, inquiry).

(5) Please telex us the detailed information of your products (available, provide) at present.

(6) As you may aware that our goods enjoy great (sales, popularity) in many countries.

(7) As to our business and (finances, financing), please refer (with, to) the Bank of Barclay, London.

(8) In (comply, compliance) with your request, we sent you this morning 3 samples of our computer disk.

9. Translate the following sentences into English.

(1)我公司是该地区电子产品的主要进口商之一。我们借此机会与贵方接洽,希望与贵方建立贸易关系。

(2)我公司经营机械设备的进出口业务已多年,我们的产品在许多国家享有盛誉。

(3)承蒙我国驻北京大使馆商务参赞处介绍,我们得知贵公司的名称、地址。

(4)我们了解到你们是日用化学品制造商。我们有一个客户想要购买贵国化妆品,如能立即航寄目前所能供之货的目录及价格表我们将不胜感激。

(5)有关我们的资信情况,请向中国银行上海分行查询。

Exercise 4　Inquiries and Replies

1. Translate the following terms or phrases from English into Chinese or vice versa.

(1) special price discount　　　　(2) latest price list

(3) cash payment　　　　　　　　(4) proforma invoice

(5) in response to　　　　　　　　(6) pamphlet

(7) 现货供应　　　　　　　　　　(8) 随函

(9) 大宗交易　　　　　　　　　　(10) 经营范围

(11) 货物已售　　　　　　　　　　(12) 操作指南

2. Fill in the blanks of the following letters with the words given below, and change the form when necessary.

> oblige, inform, prefer, convince, discount, quantity,
> purchase, quotation, interest

Dear Sirs,

　　We are ___(1)___ to buy large quantity of corn and should be ___(2)___ if you would give us a ___(3)___ per metric ton FOB Los Angels, USA and ___(4)___ the earliest date you can ship.

　　We used to ___(5)___ corn from other sources, but we now ___(6)___ to buy from your corporation because we are given to the understanding that you are able to supply larger ___(7)___ with a special ___(8)___. Besides, we are ___(9)___ that your corn is of better quality.

　　We look forward to hearing from you by return.

　　Yours faithfully,

3. Complete the following sentences with the Chinese hints given in the brackets.

(1) The Showner Co., Ltd. informs us that you are _____ (知名的男女针织套衫

生产厂商).

（2）We are _____（随函附寄我方最新的图解目录和价格单）giving the details you asked for.

（3）We would like to point out that we usually _____（用即期信用证付款）which will be agreeable to you.

（4）The illustrations will also give you _____（我们其他产品的信息）in which you will be interested.

（5）Our products are enjoying a high reputation in your area because of _____（质优价廉）. You can be sure they will _____（帮你开拓市场）.

（6）If you _____（提供现货）please tell us the quantity and _____（最低的 FOB 上海报价）.

（7）Some of our clients _____（对贵方产品很感兴趣）and wish to _____（得到贵方对以下产品的报价）.

（8）Shipment will be made within 3 weeks _____（自接受订单日起）.

（9）As requested in your letter of February 27, 2007, we are now _____（寄上新式发票一式四份）for our BCL Receiver T-34.

（10）However, we have to point out that all the contents you fill in are _____（对我方不具有任何约束性）.

4. Translate the following letters into English.

（1）

×××先生：

微波炉 SU472

兹确认贵方 6 月 17 日要求我方报微波炉 SU472 产品实盘来电。今晨我方电告,以每台××美元 FOB 上海价报给你方 3 000 台 SU472 微波炉,2007 年 8 月至 9 月装运。此报盘为实盘,以我方 7 月 20 前收到回复为准。

请注意,我方所报价格为最优惠价格,不再接收任何形式的还盘。

关于微波炉 SU472,兹告知,我方现有的存货已向其他地方发盘。不过,倘若贵方能给我们一个可接受的价格,你们有可能获得该货。

贵方熟知,近期原材料上涨幅度较大,而这定会引起微波炉价格上涨。因此,若贵方能立即给予答复,你们会得到目前微波炉价格看涨的好处。

谨上

（2）

敬启者：

第 5 号询购单

贵方和我方之间不久前签订了贸易协定。这对双边贸易的发展具有十分重要的意义。

我方现拟采购负担所开各项货物,希望贵方能尽早航寄最优惠的 CFR/CIF 汉堡价格,详尽列明规格及交货日期,并随函附寄英文说明书三份。

如果贵方不能完全按我方要求供货,则能否报来最近似的规格,或将本询盘转接给能确切报盘的有关商号?

贵方复函、报价或邮寄有关商品目录或样品时,请注明本询单的编号,以方便查找。

谨上

(3)

敬启者:

我方2017年3月8日第60号函,曾请贵方报来FOB价格。如果你方尚未发出此项报价单,则请速航寄。事实上,我方现已收到其他供货人的报价单数份。

你方当能知晓,我们正在大规模发展生产。如贵方能利用这一时机,为双方的合作铺平道路,则我们之间的贸易前景将是十分广阔的。

谨上

5. Writing practice.

Situational writing 1

Suppose you were now working at Beijing Hardware Import and Export Co., Ltd. and your company is going to import some hardware products from a Rome-based foreign company.

You are now requested to write an inquiry to the sales department of the foreign company, asking for data about quotation, discount, range of hardware products, and if necessary, the enclosure of the price list and catalogue.

Situational writing 2

Please read the following letter of inquiry, and write a reply to that letter.

Dear Sir or Madam,

We are interested in purchasing large quantities of steal cleats in all sizes. We would appreciate it if you would give us a quotation per kilogram CFR Liverpool, England. We would also be grateful if you could forward samples and your price list to us.

We used to purchase these products from other suppliers. We may prefer to buy from your company because we understand that you are able to supply larger quantities at more attractive prices. In addition, we are confident about the quality of your products.

We look forward to hearing from you by return.

Your faithfully,

Robert Smith
Purchasing Manager

Situational writing 3

Write a letter with the following hints:
- Learn your name and address in a magazine.
- We are one of the largest importers of digital products.
- Please quote us your best CIF C5% Tokyo prices.
- Send samples and catalogue.

6. Fill in the blanks with the best choice.

(1) We thank you for your letter of May 17 and the _____ catalogue.
  a. sent   b. enclosed   c. given   d. presented

(2) The letter we sent last week is an inquiry _____ color TV sets.
  a. in   b. for   c. to   d. as

(3) We produce decorative fabrics _____ different kinds.
  a. in   b. of   c. for   d. with

(4) This chemical is made _____ a special formula.
  a. from   b. according to   c. of   d. in

(5) We should be pleased to send you some samples of our new typewriters on approval, _____ our own expense.
  a. at   b. on   c. for   d. in

(6) If you are interested, we will send you a sample lot _____ charge.
  a. within   b. with   c. for   d. free of

(7) Your full cooperation _____.
  a. will be thanked very much   b. is to be appreciated
  c. is to appreciate   d. will be highly appreciated

(8) This price is _____ of your 5% commission.
  a. includes   b. coveting   c. inclusive   d. including

(9) _____ your inquiry No.123, we are sending you a catalog and a sample book for your reference.
  a. According   b. As per   c. As   d. About

(10) While _____ an inquiry, you ought to inquire into quality, specification and price, etc.

    a. making   b. offering   c. sending   d. giving

7. Translate the following sentences into English.

(1) 请报你方最优惠的上海到岸价,包括我方3%佣金。

(2) 如果你方价格有竞争力的话,我们打算订购30万码棉布。

(3) 我方有一家客户对贵国××电冰箱感兴趣,请电开400台伦敦到岸价4月船期的报盘。

(4) 为了便于你方了解我方的产品,我们立即航寄目录5份、样品书2本。

(5) 为答复你方4月28日询价,随函寄去我方最新价目单以供参考。

8. Draw a letter of a general inquiry asking for all the information you need.

9. Write a specific inquiry according to the following information.

(1) The name of the commodity you want:

    a certain kind of Household Electrical Appliance

(2) You ask for:

    a. specification

    b. catalogue

    c. price list

    d. payment terms

    e. delivery date

    f. other information

10. Write a replay to a specific inquiry.

Exercise 5   Quotations, Offers and Counter Offers

1. Translate the following terms or phrases from English into Chinese or vice versa.

(1) market survey   (2) make a concession

(3) validity   (4) margin of profits

(5) binding on   (6) firm offer

(7) 减价 7%   (8) 副本

(9) 及时装运   (10) 试订

(11) 达成协议   (12) 提出建议

2. Fill in the blanks of the following letters with the words given below, and change the form when necessary.

> follow, arrive, pay, commodity, discount, ship, minimum,
> expand, acknowledge, please

Dear Sirs,

We are very ___(1)___ to receive your inquiry of November 24 and ___(2)___ your interest in our products. We confirm our fax of this morning as ___(3)___:

___(4)___: handmade cotton embroidered gloves

___(5)___: by L/C at sight

___(6)___: within 5-6 weeks after the ___(7)___ of the L/C

We feel sure you will realize that our quoted price is very reasonable. However, in order to help you to ___(8)___ your new business, we are prepared to allow you a special ___(9)___ of 5% if your ___(10)___ quantity order is not less than 10,000 pairs.

Yours faithfully,

3. Rearrange the following sentences in logic order to make them a perfect letter.

(1) It is known that our products are superior in quality and moderate in price, and are very popular in the international market. We hope you will agree to our offer.

(2) As Christmas is approaching, please send us your orders without any delay.

(3) Thank you for your inquiry of November 23 for Christmas trees.

(4) Your prompt reply will be highly appreciated.

(5) As requested, we are offering Model 325 plastic trees you require at US＄478 per dozen CDPC 1.5％ Copenhagen subject to our final confirmation.

4. Translate the following letters into English.

(1)

敬启者：

我们非常感谢你方10月29日的询盘,并高兴地获悉你方愿与我们建立贸易关系。按照要求,现向你方报盘如下,你方答复于2006年11月24日前到达我地有效。

规格:"秀奈尔"牌男式睡衣

数量:3万套

价格:CIF米兰价,每套40美元

支付:保兑的、不可撤销的凭即期汇票支付的信用证

装运:2007年1月起

我方相信上述条件能为你方同意。市价很可能会上涨,尽早订购对你方有利。

希望早日收到你方订单。

谨上

(2)

敬启者：

5月15日来信收到,得悉你方对我方的化肥很感兴趣,但认为我方4月25日的价格偏高,无法成交。

我们要告诉你方的是,我方的报价已经为你地其他客户所接受,而且已有大量成交。数月来,许许多多的询价单源源而来。在这种情况下,我们无法考虑你方的报价。事实上,鉴于你我双方公司之间长期的贸易关系,我们才给你方报这样优惠的价格。

希望你们重新考虑这一优惠报价,早日来电订货,以便使我们确认。

谨上

(3)

敬启者：

事由:优质白砂糖

Exercise 5 Quotations, Offers and Counter Offers

贵方2007年7月17日来函收悉。信中要求我方报标题砂糖10 000吨,发往伦敦。对贵方有意购买我方产品一事,我们愿表示衷心的感谢。

兹按贵方要求报价如下:

商品:优质白砂糖

包装:新麻袋包装,每包100千克

数量:10 000吨

价格:每吨105美元,CIF伦敦

支付条件:凭即期汇票支付的、保兑的、不可撤销的信用证付款,信用证以我方为受益人

发货日期:收到信用证后一个月发货

请注意,我们手头的现有存货不多,为使我们尽快装船,你们如同意我方所开价格,务请及时开立信用证。

盼望贵方早日答复。

(4)

敬启者:

事由:锡箔

贵方2010年5月15日函接悉。兹证实今日给你方去电,详见所附电报抄本。从我方电报中,你方将得悉我们能以每长吨135英镑CIF上海的便宜价格报给你方50长吨锡箔,在你方订货后一个月交货。货款以我方为收益人的不可撤销的、凭即期汇票在伦敦议付的信用证,以英镑支付。

上述报盘以你方答复在不迟于本月底到达我方为有效。一旦报盘过期,此货不可能存留不售。

谨上

5. Translate the following letter into Chinese.

Dear Mr. Smith,

Thank you for your letter of October 6th, 2006 in which you requested about our product Electric Saws BNT-3.

While the specifications of the product are enclosed, our commercial terms such as price and shipping and payment terms are indicated as follows:

Quantity: 100 units

Price: US＄100.00 per unit, CIF New York

Payment Terms: L/C to be established within one week after order

Shipment: within one month after receipt of L/C

We hope the above quotations are of interest to you and we are looking forward to getting your reply soon.

Sincerely yours,

6. Writing practice.

Situational writing 1

Write a firm offer covering the following contents:

毛皮手套

颜色有黑、棕、红 3 种

材料选用优质羊皮

价格:CIF 大连价,13 美元一副

有装船前 30 天开立的保兑的、不可撤销的即期信用证支付

包装由买方决定

10 月船期

Situational writing 2

Write a letter with the following hints:

- Thanks for inquiry
- Making an offer
- Commodity:"Butterfly" brand bed sheet TN7032
- Price: at US＄478 per dozen
- Packing: one dozen per box, 12 boxes per carton
- Payment: by confirmed, irrevocable L/C payable by draft at sight
- Expectation of favorable reply

7. Choose the best choice.

(1) As we are _____ the market for tablecloths, we should be glad if you would send us your best quotation.

  a. in   b. on   c. entering   d. at

(2) We _____ a copy of our price list.

  a. put   b. enclose   c. envelop   d. wrap

Exercise 5 Quotations, Offers and Counter Offers

(3) We shall appreciate samples _____ your offer.
    a. concerned   b. covered   c. including   d. covering

(4) _____ receipt of your instructions we will send the goods.
    a. In   b. Having   c. Upon   d. To

(5) We always adhere _____ our commitments.
    a. to   b. for   c. towards   d. in

(6) By joint efforts, we can _____ both friendship and business.
    a. promote   b. cover   c. improve   d. develop

(7) We are interested _____ a specimen of the new type.
    a. to receiving   b. to receive   c. in receiving   d. in receipt

(8) Your letter has been passed on to us for _____.
    a. attendance   b. care   c. attention   d. cooperation

(9) We regret _____ to offer you this article at present.
    a. to be able   b. being able   c. being unable   d. unable

(10) Should your price be found competitive and delivery date _____, we intend to place a large order with you.
    a. accepted   b. acceptable   c. accepting   d. accept

(11) You will receive _____ on the sale.
    a. two commissions   b. two terms of commissions
    c. two items of commissions   d. two commission

(12) The buyer demands that the seller _____ the goods within a week.
    a. ship   b. to ship   c. shipped   d. be shipping

(13) We trust this new product of ours will appeal _____ your market.
    a. for   b. to   c. by   d. with

(14) The offer is _____ to confirmation.
    a. subjected   b. subject   c. subjective   d. subjection

(15) It has _____ us that Type 32 might suit your purpose as well.
    a. happened to   b. occurred to   c. been happening to   d. occur

8. Translate the following sentences into English.

(1) 我们正在仔细研究你方报盘,希望将此盘保留到月底有效。

(2) 我方的产品质量好、价格合理,因此相信贵方能大量订货。

(3) 如果你方能订购 5 000 打或 5 000 打以上,我们将给予 10%的折扣。

(4) 关于支付条件,我们通常要求保兑的、不可撤销的、凭即期汇票支付的信用证。

(5) 请接受此难得再有的报盘。最近可望有大笔订单自美国方面来,届时将导致价格猛涨。

(6) 如果 3 月 10 日之前收到你方订单,我方将报 5 月上旬船期的实盘。

(7) 由于此货需求量甚大,所以该盘有效期不能超过 5 天。

(8) 兹报实盘,以我方时间 7 月 10 日星期二下午 5 时以前回复为有效。

9. Write a quotation or a firm offer covering the following contents.

- 女士皮靴
- 式样新颖,有 20 余种,颜色有黑棕及大红色(详见目录)
- 材料选用高级牛皮
- 价格:CIF 价,按照不同式样,每双价格为 95 美元至 300 美元不等
- 有装船前 30 天开立保兑的、不可撤销的即期信用证支付
- 包装由买方决定
- 9 月船期

Exercise 6   Orders and Acknowledgements

1. Translate the following terms or phrases from English into Chinese or vice versa.

(1) double check   (2) shipping advice

(3) sales contract   (4) form order

(5) cardboard carton   (6) process the order

(7) 付款交单   (8) 推荐合适的替代产品

(9) 首笔订单   (10) 一式两份

(11) 需求增长   (12) 延迟装运

2. Fill in the blanks of the following letters with the words given below, and change the form when necessary.

inform, full, comment, lead, through, sure, for, receive, arrange, work

Dear Sirs.

We have ___(1)___ with thanks your order ___(2)___ 1 M/Ts of tea. We are ___(3)___ on your order and will keep you ___(4)___ in time of the progress.

We are expecting to ___(5)___ the establishment of the related Confirmed Irrevocable Letter of Credit ___(6)___ the bankers.

Since it is the best season for tea, we hope you make ___(7)___ use of the opportunity. I am ___(8)___ you will be pleased to collect good ___(9)___ about our tea from your consumers.

We hope this will ___(10)___ to more considerable orders.

Yours faithfully,

3. Compare the following two letters and point out why the revision is made so.

(1) The Original Letter

Dear Lucy,

We would like to change our order of the plastic Christmas trees which I sent you November 23 due to the increasing demand for them here. Although the order of 7,000 plastic Christmas trees is very large, more people want to purchase. So please send 3,000 more CT732 Christmas plastic tress. We are sorry to confuse you.

As the Christmas is coming, please give careful attention to our change.

Awaiting your prompt reply.

Yours faithfully,

Louis

(2) The Revised Letter

Dear Lucy,

We would like to make a change in our order of November 23.

Would you please send 3,000 more CT732 Christmas plastic trees? The reason is that your products enjoy great popularity here, and there is an increasing demand for them.

Since the Christmas is coming, could you please make the shipment by the end of this month?

Looking forward to your reply.

Yours sincerely,

Louis

4. Translate the following letter into Chinese.

Dear Sirs,

Exercise 6 Orders and Acknowledgements

We thank you for your letter of November 8 with which you enclosed your price list and catalogue.

We agree that the quality is up to the standard and the prices you quoted are satisfactory. We also note that you will allow us a discount of 3％ on an order worth US ＄30,000 or more. We, therefore, have airmailed you our Order No. 879 on November 6.

Please note that as these goods are urgently required here, we should be most grateful if you could dispatch the goods as soon as possible.

Yours faithfully,

5. Translate the following letter into English.

敬启者：

兹高兴地确认按照下列条款买进你方德声(TECSUN)9波段收音机4 000台。

4 000台德声9波段收音机,上海成本、保险及运费价格,每台53美元。收到信用证14天内从上海运至孟买。

请特别注意货物的包装,以免货物在运输途中受损。

我们现在正在申请办理信用证,在接到你方确认书后,即可开出以你方为受益人的信用证。

谨上

2006年12月5日

6. Writing practice.

Write a letter with the following given particulars：

• 确认收到卖方寄来的样品,表示感谢。

• 订购2 000台尼康D80数码相机。

• 要求迅速发货。

• 随信附上678号购买确认书,一式两份。

7. Translate the following sentences into Chinese.

(1) We have heard from China Council for the Promotion of International Trade that you are in the market for Electric Appliances.

(2) We would also like to know the minimum export quantities per color and per designs.

(3) All quotations are subject to our final confirmation. Unless otherwise stated or

agreed upon, all prices are net without commission.

(4) Under separate cover we are sending you several copies of our catalogue, enabling you to make suitable selection.

(5) The price we quoted is accurately calculated, but in order to encourage business, we are prepared to allow you a discount of 5%.

8. Choose the best choice.

(1) Following your order _____ 400 pieces of electronic toys last year, we are pleased to receive your order No. 456 _____ the some quantity.

  a. for, of   b. of, of   c. of, for   d. with, for

(2) We _____ your terms satisfactory and now send you our order for 2 sets of the generator.

  a. find   b. believe   c. think   d. trust

(3) We place an order provided your goods can be supplied _____ stock.

  a. out   b. after   c. on   d. in

(4) The goods are urgently needed. We _____ hope you will deliver them at once.

  a. therefore   b. so   c. that   d. should

(5) We place this order _____ the understanding that the discount is 10%.

  a. based on   b. with   c. through   d. on

(6) In this case, the buyer _____ cancel the contract.

  a. reserve to   b. may have   c. has the right to   d. reserve the right to

(7) As agreed upon in our negotiations, payment _____ L/C.

  a. by   b. will   c. is to be made by   d. is by

(8) We regret to report that a consignment of silk piece goods _____ Order No. 567 has not been delivered.

  a. with   b. for   c. on   d. under

(9) We feel sorry to say that the rugs supplied _____ Order No. 456 have not yet reached us.

  a. by   b. for   c. with   d. to

(10) _____ the present market trend, we have to say that our price is really the best we can quote.

  a. With   b. On   c. Because   d. For

9. Translate the following sentences into English.

(1) 如果你方能给我方5%的佣金,我方将试购500台。

(2) 我们正在执行你方678号订单。请相信我们定将在你方所规定的期限内安排装运。

(3)由于大量承约,许多客户的订货都未发出,因此我们目前只能接受10月船期的订单。

(4)因为存货售罄,我们不能接受新订单。但是一旦新货源到来,我们即去电与你方联系。

(5)该货须分三批装出,每月100吨。

10. Write an order covering the following contents.

- 有意订购对方公司的某品牌录像机、录像带、微型收录两用机
- 数量:

  录像机　　1 000 台

  录像带　　1 000 盒

  微型收录两用机　　5 000 台

- 价格:FOB 新港,包括我方 5% 佣金

  录像机　　每台××美元

  录像带　　每盒××美元

  微型收录机　　每台××美元

- 付款方式:90 天期信用证装船前开立
- 包装:适合于海运的出口包装
- 交货日期:一批或分二批 8 月底前交完

11. Translate the following messages into English.

你方3月10日订购500台绒线编织机的传真收悉,谢谢。

我们已即刻与厂家取得了联系,但由于该货销路甚佳,已接的订货太多,况且原料紧缺,他们婉言拒绝。经过我方再三努力磋商,厂方答应接受订货,从明年1月起每月交100台。

我们知道你方急需此货。不知上述交货时间你们是否同意?目前我们正在和其他地方的制造厂联系,若有好消息,当即告知。

与此同时,我们附上我方目前可供货物的目录及价格表供你方参考,如有兴趣请立即告知,我们自当迅速办理。

Exercise 7 Payment by Letter of Credit

1. Translate the following terms or phrases form English into Chinese or vice versa.

(1) beneficiary (2) an irrevocable L/C
(3) documentary L/C (4) sales confirmation
(5) bill of lading (6) delivery date
(7) 商业发票 (8) 汇票
(9) 保险单 (10) 议付行
(11) 催开信用证 (12) 信用证延期

2. Fill in the blanks of the following letters with the words given below, and change the form when necessary.

> speed, complete, via, on, stock, issue, read, delay

Dear Mr. Gray,

Your letter of credit No. 8965 __(1)__ by the Bank of Cyprus has arrived. __(2)__ examination, we find that transshipment and partial shipment are not allowed.

As direct sailings to Limassol are infrequent, we have to ship __(3)__ Rotterdam more often than not. As a result, transshipment may be necessary. With regard to partial shipment, it would __(4)__ matters up if we could ship immediately the goods. We have in __(5)__ instead of waiting for the whole shipment to be __(6)__ .

With this in mind, I faxed you today, asking for the letter of credit to be amended to __(7)__ : "Partial shipment and transshipment allowed".

I trust this amendment will meet with your approval and you will fax us to that effect without __(8)__ .

Yours sincerely,

Exercise 7 Payment by Letter of Credit

3. Translate the following sentences into English.

(1) 我们的惯例是接受保兑的、不可撤销的、有效期为装船后3周的即期信用证。

(2) 请注意第267号合同项下的600辆自行车备妥待运已久,但至今我们尚未收到你方的有关信用证。请尽早开来,以便装运。

(3) 我们很高兴地告知,以你方为受益人的金额为35 000美元的MI1926号信用证已由商业银行开出。

(4) 根据328号合同的规定,有关信用证应不迟于3月2号到达我处,我们希望你能及时开出信用证,以免延误装运。

(5) 请把985SD86号信用证修改为"允许转运"。另因此笔交易是以CFR条款达成,请删除保险条款。

(6) 由于供应商的延误,我们不能按信用证规定在8月20号之前发货,故请将信用证的船期和有效期分别延展一个月。

(7) 非常遗憾,我们不得不拒绝贵方付款交单支付方式的请求,因为我们只接受即期信用证的支付方式。

(8) 因此,在与国外客户的所有交易中暂时难以接受D/A条款。

4. Write a letter in English asking for amendment to the following letter of credit by checking it with the given contract terms.

COMMERCIAL BANK OF THATTOWN

Date: Oct. 5, 2006

To: Shanghai Cereals & Oils Foodstuffs Imp. & Exp. Corporation
    Shanghai, China

Advised through Bank of China, Shanghai

No. BOC 06/10/05

DOCUMENTARY LETTER OF CREDIT IRREVOCABLE

Dear Sirs,

You are authorized to draw on Hong Kong Food Company, Vancouver for a sum not exceeding CAN $120,000 (SAY CANADIAN DOLLARS ONE HUNDRED AND TWENTY THOUSAND ONLY) available by draft drawn on them at sight accompanied by the following documents:

(1) Full set of Clean on Board Bill of Lading made out to order and blank endorsed, marked "freight to collect" dated not later than November 30, 2006 and notify accountee.

(2) Signed Commercial Invoice in quintuplicate.

(3) Canadian Customs Invoice in quintuplicate.

(4) Insurance Policies (or Certificates) in duplicate covering Marine and War Rides.

Evidencing shipment from China port to Montreal, Canada of the following goods: 50,000 tins of 430 grams of Maling Brand Strawberry Jam, at CAN $2.50 per tin CFR C3% Vancouver, details as per your S/C No. 06/8712.

Partial shipments are allowed.
This credit expires on November 30, 2006 for negotiation in China.
合同主要条款如下：
卖方：上海粮油食品进出口公司
买方：温哥华香港食品公司
商品名称："梅林"牌草莓酱
规格：340 克听装
数量：50 000 听
单价：CFR 温哥华每听 2.5 加元，含佣金 3%
总值：125,000 加元
装运期：2006 年 11 月自中国港口运往温哥华，允许转船和分批装运。
付款条件：凭不可撤销的即期信用证付款。信用证议付有效期应为最后转运期后第 15 天在中国到期。
合同号码：06/8712

5. Writing practice.

Situational writing 1

You have received an order of 200 computers amounting to US$12,000, and you are preparing to make shipment by the end of this month. But you have not received your L/C. So you will request your buyer to open an irrevocable L/C in your favor soon.

Please write a letter to ask for establishment of L/C so that you can ship the goods earlier and accordingly.

Situational writing 2

You are an importer and are writing to your exporter, informing the company that you have just received an import license and you can increase your total amount of L/C No. NBB879 to USD 160,000. You will send an L/C amendment advice to your exporter, telling him/her that you will make an amendment to the original letter to extend the shipment and validity dates of the L/C to November 16 and 30 respectively.

You are requested to write a letter in which you inform the exporter of the above-mentioned particulars.

6. Translate the following L/C stipulation into Chinese.

（1）Provided such drafts are drawn and presented in accordance with the terms of this credit, we hereby engage with the drawers, endorsers and bona-fide holders that the said drafts shall be honored on presentation.

（2）Transshipment are permitted at any port against through bill of lading.

（3）Draft(s) drawn under this credit must be negotiated in China on or before XXX after which date this credit expires.

（4）Documents must be presented for negotiation within XXX days after the on board date of bills of lading.

（5）"Shipped on Board" Bills of Lading are essential and the statement "Freight paid" must appear thereon. The Bills of Lading must cover shipment as detailed below. Short form Bills of Lading are not acceptable.

（6）Special conditions：Documents have to be presented within 14 days after the date of issue of the bills of lading or other shipping documents.

7. Translate the following Chinese into English.

(1)信用证345号,请修改：
- 长吨改为吨;
- 目的港伦敦改为汉堡;
- 展装运期到8月底并允许分运转船。

(2)你方信用证3350号,数量与合同不符,总金额相差75.60英镑,请速改。

(3)信用证2345号,请来电取消"银行费用由受益人负担"的条款。

(4)信用证3346号,金额不足,请按合同增加520英镑(请按合同增至3 125英镑)。

(5)请将你方信用证6789号的船期及有效期分别延展至10月15日及10月30日。

Exercise 8 Other Methods of Payment

1. Translate the following terms or phrases from English into Chinese or vice versa.

(1) D/A   (2) remittance

(3) time draft   (4) D/P after sight

(5) documentary collection   (6) balance

(7) 电汇   (8) 预付现金

(9) 承兑交单   (10) 分期付款

(11) 不可撤销信用证   (12) 汇票

2. Fill in the blanks of the following letters with the words given below, and change the form when necessary.

> on, standing, inquiry, place, trial, therefore, prospect

Dear Sirs,

We are the largest wholesaler in Kuwait and have recently received a number of ___(1)___ for your stainless steal cutlery. We think there are good ___(2)___ for the sale of this cutlery, but at present it is little known here and as we cannot count ___(3)___ regular sales we do not feel able to make purchases on our own account. We are, ___(4)___, writing to suggest that you send us a ___(5)___ delivery for sale on D/A terms. We make the proposal hoping to ___(6)___ firm orders when the market is established.

We believe our proposal offers good prospects and hope you will be willing to give it a trial. As to our ___(7)___, you may check it with our bankers, the National Bank of Kuwait.

Yours faithfully,

3. Compare the following two letters and point out why the revision is made so.

(1) The original letter

Exercise 8 Other Methods of Payment

Dear Sir or Madam:

With reference to your due commission, our records show that a money order in the amount of US$166.83 was indeed sent to the following address:

Mid-West Travel Service, Inc.
Evanston Illinois Branch
225 Church Street
Evanston, Illinois 60201
USA

Faithfully yours,

(2) The revised letter

Dear Sirs,

Thank you for your message of April 30 inquiring about the commission due.

Our records show that a money order for US$166.83 was sent to the following office:

Mid-West Travel Service, Inc.
Evanston Illinois Branch
225 Church Street
Evanston, Illinois 60201
USA

Enclosed are copies of the statements and money order.

To avoid future problems, would you please let us know if we should send our commission check(s) directly to the branch office that makes the reservation, or to your home office?

Faithfully yours,

John Mak
Manager

4. Translate the following letter into English.

敬启者：

你方3月10号的来信收悉。我方已认真考虑过你方以 D/A 的方式试销我方餐刀之建议。兹奉告，以试销方式促进交易，我方能够破例做到的只能按即期 D/P 条件办理。

因我方餐刀以质量上乘、设计新颖、价格合理而著称，所以接受我方建议后你们不会承担任何风险。此种餐刀正畅销许多国家。我们相信，在你方店里也一定会畅销。

如对我方建议感兴趣，请复函，我方将再次同你方联系。

谨上

5. Writing practice.

Situational writing 1

Write an English letter by making use of the ideas given below：

- 我方一直以保兑的、不可撤销的信用证支付从贵处购买的产品。
- 但是，此种支付方式对我方来说费用高，资金占用时间长，银行利息高。
- 建议采用"即期付款交单"或"见票后30天付款"。

Situational writing 2

You have already shipped the goods and passed on your shipping documents including bill of lading, invoice, and insurance, etc, as well as a draft to the remitting bank for collection. You are now requested to write a letter to inform the importer of the above mentioned particulars and ask the company to pay the draft 30 days after sight.

Exercise 9　Collection Letters

1. Translate the following terms or phrases from English into Chinese or vice versa.

（1）invoice

（2）overdue payment

（3）outstanding balance

（4）bill

（5）repayment

（6）legal collection

（7）信用度

（8）结账

（9）支票

（10）诉诸法律

（11）公司形象

（12）履约

2. Fill in the blanks of the following letters with the words given below, and change the form when necessary.

Letter A

clear, reminder, stand, agree, on, receipt

Dear Mr. Smith,

Thank you for your order No. 7342 of 29 January for 20 dozen ladies' skirts.

We would like to continue to serve you ___(1)___ open account terms, but to do this, your bills must be paid within 30 days as ___(2)___. Your balance on account No. 6784 is long overdue and ___(3)___ at US＄3,000. This is a second ___(4)___ so please send payment on ___(5)___ of this letter.

Immediately, the overdue sum is ___(6)___, we will fulfill your current order.

Thank you for your cooperation.

Yours faithfully,

Letter B

> overlook, miss, whatsoever, outstanding, extend, repossession, relate, meet

Dear Mr. Chen,

You recently received a statement of account showing credit repayment __(1)__ to your purchase of YOYTA from Anglo Motors in October. According to our records you have failed to make any repayments __(2)__ and the sum of £7,200 is now overdue.

We understand that it is sometimes difficult to __(3)__ debts, especially at this very expensive time of year. So we are prepared to __(4)__ the fact that you have __(5)__ the first two repayments if you undertake to meet the repayment schedule from now on.

Also, if you would like to __(6)__ the period of credit so that repayments are made easier, we should be happy to discuss the matter with you.

However, if we do not hear from you within the next seven days, I am afraid we shall be forced to consider passing the matter over to our legal department for __(7)__ of the car and collection of the __(8)__ sum.

I look forward to hearing from you within the next week.

Yours sincerely,

3. The following sentences are not appropriately written in the letters of collections. Please revise them in the way that can well suit the tone and style in collections.

(1) After the telephone conversation we conducted this afternoon, I checked our records ...

(2) You still owed us US$ ...

(3) We look forward to the honor of receiving a remittance from your esteemed selves at your earliest convenience.

(4) Should you not pay up soon, we would like to get our lawyers onto you.

Exercise 9 Collection Letters

4. Translate the following letter of collection into English.

敬启者：

我方已多次催促你方尽快处理欠款一事，但是到目前为止我们没有收到你方任何关于这一问题的消息，我们不得不再一次提醒你方尽早处理这笔款项。

我们不清楚你方不能按商定时间结清帐款的原因，但是请你们严格按合同的约定履行付款义务。

除非我们能在一周内收到你方的答复，否则我们将提起诉讼。我们相信大家都不愿意看到你方信用受损，我们也无须走到这一步。

如你方已付款，敬请忘记这封信。静候你方早日回复。

谨上

5. Writing practice.

You are now a manager of a Beijing-based company, and you have not received the payment for one consignment of cotton shirts, which was exported to a company in Singapore about 5 months ago. During the lime of which, you wrote 3 reminders and 2 letters, requesting the company to settle the account immediately, but you only got one letter from the importer in which some excuses were given to refuse to honor the payment. This time you are going to write a letter of ultimatum to ask for payment this week.

Exercise 10 Packing

1. Translate the following terms or phrases from English into Chinese or vice versa.

(1) shipping mark   (2) packing list

(3) seaworthy packing   (4) directive marks

(5) consignment   (6) outer packing

(7) 运费   (8) 中性包装

(9) 发货人   (10) 尺寸

(11) 防水的   (12) 密封的

2. Fill in the blanks of the following letters with the words given below, and change the form when necessary.

> grade, transit, inform, grade, notify, place, promise, per

Dear Sirs,

Thank you for your Quotation No. 239 about Round Steel Bars.

We regret to ___(1)___ you that among the five lots of Round Steel Bars arrived here ___(2)___ S. S. "Mary" on May 11, 2006 were six bundles of different ___(3)___, which were in scattered and mixed condition because their packing was not ___(4)___ strong and their iron hoops were broken in ___(5)___. Since it was very difficult to assort them, inconvenience and losses occurred. Although we had in time ___(6)___ you of such unfortunate things occurred before, the present case has showed that our comments were ignored, for no improvement in packing has been made.

Therefore, we must have your ___(7)___ to take effective measures to improve your packing before we could ___(8)___ this new order with you.

We await your early reply.

Exercise 10 Packing

Yours faithfully,

3. Translate the following sentences into English.

(1) 玻璃制品是易碎的货物,需要特别采取防止颠簸的包装措施。

(2) 我方男士衬衫的包装为每件套一塑料袋,5 打装一纸箱,内衬防潮纸,外打铁箍 2 道。

(3) 我方第 125 号清洁剂用盒装,不用袋装。每盒内散装 5 千克,然后再装入纸板箱。这样做更适合洗衣店、医院及餐厅使用。

(4) 遵照贵方要求,我们按你方来样在装袋一侧印一种颜色,但来样至少须在装运前 30 天抵达我方。

(5) 所有的粉末都要用塑料袋包装,并装在罐子里,罐子盖要用胶袋封紧。

(6) 阀门及所有精密部件应以软材料裹住,稳固地装于硬纸盒中,纸盒放入木箱时应妥善放置,使其在箱内不可移动。

4. Writing practice.

Situational writing 1

Write a letter to your customer informing him that you have improved your packing according to his instructions and that from today on all shirts and footwear are to be packed in cartons instead of wooden cases.

Situational writing 2

Write a letter by making use of the following ideas:

• 本函附寄已会签的销售合同 No. CJ120

• 请对方注意以下事项:

• 目的港:"上海"字样须印刷在每个箱子上;由于该批货物为精密仪器,还应该在箱子上印刷"DO NOT DROP"字样。

• 希望尽早得到答复。

Exercise 11　　Shipping

1. Translate the following terms or phrases from English into Chinese or vice versa.

（1）sailing date　　　　　　　　　　（2）port of destination

（3）order B/L　　　　　　　　　　　（4）port of discharge

（5）dock receipt　　　　　　　　　　（6）shipping advice

（7）运输代理　　　　　　　　　　　（8）舱位

（9）清洁提单　　　　　　　　　　　（10）船期表

（11）运输标志　　　　　　　　　　　（12）仓储费

2. Fill in the blanks of the following letters with the words given below, and change the form when necessary.

> capable, basis, part, transit, book, designate, liquefy, hitherto

Dear Sirs,

We have received your fax of March 3rd, 2006 from which we understand that you have our order for three Model 686 precision grinding machines.

Our Confirmation of Order will be sent to you in a few days. The Transaction of Order will be sent to you in a few days.

Since the transaction is made on FOB ___(1)___, you are to ship the goods from London on a steamer we ___(2)___. As soon as the shipping space is ___(3)___, we shall inform you of the name of the steamer, on which the goods are to go forward. For further instructions, please contact our forwarding agents, Messers, Brown Company, London, who have ___(4)___ been in charge of shipments from you. As some parts of the machines may be damaged easily by shock, the machines must be packed in seaworthy cases ___(5)___ of withstanding rough handling. The bright metal ___(6)___ should be protected from dampness in ___(7)___ by a coating of slashing compound that will keep out dampness, but will not

（8）_____ and run off under changing weather conditions.

We believe that above instructions are very clear to you and hope that the users will be entirely satisfied with the shipment.

Yours faithfully,

3. Translate the following letter into English.

敬启者：

你方 4 月 30 日询盘已收悉，谢谢。我公司的集装箱有两种尺寸，分别为 20 英尺和 30 英尺。

集装箱两面门开，可同时进行装卸。由于装运的货物易被湿气和水损坏，故这种集装箱具有不漏水、不透气之优点。如有必要，集装箱还可在工厂装货后封闭。这样可避免偷窃事件发生。

该集装箱有气温调控，可装需要特别照顾的任何货物。人们在装运时可充分利用其优点。如在同一集装箱内装有发往同一港口的几批货可节省运费，同时还可以节省保险费，因为集装箱运输保险费率较低。

现随函附寄我公司费率表一份，请指示。

谨上

4. Writing practice.

Situational writing 1

Write an English letter with the following information given below:

Passage 1

Order No. 832，S/C No. 669703

stipulated two equal lots，Sept，and Oct.，2006-11-18

your letter of May 3rd requesting 80% June, balance July, 2006

Passage 2

Although quantity in stock too late for June shipment

especially few direct sailings

no relevant L/C yet

Passage 3

Suggesting 80% July, balance Aug., 2006

L/C June 20 latest

Prompt reply

Situational writing 2

Read the following letter and write a reply to it.

Dear Sir or Madam,

We refer to Contract No. 6789 signed between us on Nov. 10th, 2006 for 4,500 cases Tin Plates, which is stipulated for shipment in February, 2006. However, up to the time of writing we have not received from you any information about the order in question. As you know, the contracted time of delivery is rapidly falling due and we should have received your shipping advice by the end of last month.

No doubt there must have been some reason for the delay in shipping and to cover this contingency we advised you that we were extending the Letter of Credit to the end of March. We feel sure we shall soon be hearing from you about this business.

We are awaiting your reply.

Yours truly,

5. Choose the right answer to complete the sentences.

(1) We will do our best to _____ shipment to meet your requirements in time.

  a. comply   b. make   c. expedite   d. arrange

(2) Passenger liners often take a certain amount of _____.

  a. cargoes   b. cargo   c. shipments   d. quantities

(3) We have the pleasure to inform you that the shipment has gone _____ per s.s. "East Wind" and hope that it will arrive at the destination in _____ condition.

  a. on, good   b. for, complete

  c. forward, perfect   d. onto, perfect

(4) The shipment time is June or July at our _____ and the goods will be shipped in one _____.

  a. choice, shipment   b. option, lot

  c. decision, cargo   d. option, consignment

(5) We regret our inability to _____ with your request for Shipping the goods in early November.

  a. compliance   b. comply   c. manage   d. arrange

(6) Before deciding which form of transport to use, a _____ will take into account

Exercise 11 Shipping

the factors of cost, speed and salty.

    a. consignor   b. consignee   c. shipper   d. ship owner

(7) Any loss or damage noticed when the goods are delivered must be reported to the _____ at the time, otherwise he will not be liable for it.

    a. carrier   b. shipper   c. consignee   d. consignor

(8) They intended to lower the cost of the products. _____ they did not succeed in reducing the package costs.

    a. Therefore   b. And   c. However   d. Furthermore

(9) As the _____ of the goods was not strong enough to with-stand the rough sea voyage, shipment was withhold at the last minute in order to give time for _____ improvement.

    a. pack, packet   b. package, packing

    c. package, packaging   d. packing, packaging

(10) Since three/fifths of the voyage is in tropical weather and the goods are liable to go moldy, we think it advisable to have the shipment _____ the risk of mould.

    a. covered insurance   b. taken out insured

    c. covered against   d. insured for

6. Translate the following messages into English.

1992年12月1日签订的CT345号合同规定,5 000长吨棉花应于1993年3月交货,可是迄今为止未听到你方任何有关发货的消息。

我方客户急需此货,务请你方在合同规定的期限内交货。否则,我方只好向你方提出索赔并保留取消合同的权利。

Exercise 12   Insurance

1. Translate the following terms or phrases from English into Chinese or vice versa.

(1) insurance rate   (2) FPA
(3) TPND   (4) open policy
(5) general average   (6) insurance claim
(7) 保险费   (8) 保险条款
(9) 相对免赔额   (10) 特殊附加险
(11) 仓对仓条款   (12) 保险索赔

2. Fill in the blanks of the following letter with the words and expressions given, and change the form when necessary.

> conclude, as per, comply, so, should, make, accordingly, account, in, bear

Dear Sirs,

In reply to your letter of the 3rd November inquiring about the insurance on our CIF offer for cosmetics __(1)__ to you on 12th November, we wish to give you the following information.

For transactions __(2)__ on CIF basis, we usually effect insurance with the People's Insurance Company of China against All Risks, __(3)__ Ocean Marine Cargo Clause of the People's Insurance Company of China, dated the 1st January, 1981. __(4)__ you require the insurance to be covered as per Institute Cargo Clauses, we would be glad to __(5)__. But if there is any difference in premium between the two it will be charged to your __(6)__.

We are also __(7)__ a position to insure the shipment against any additional risks if you __(8)__ desire, and the extra premium is to be __(9)__ by you. In this case, we shall send you the premium receipt issued by the relative underwriter.

Exercise 12 Insurance

Usually, the amount insured is 110% of the total invoice value. However, if a higher percentage is required, we may do ___(10)___ but you have to bear the extra premium as well. We hope our above information will provide you with all that you wish to know and we are now looking forward to receiving your order.

Yours faithfully,

3. Put the following sentences into the right order to make a complete letter.

(1) As discussed in our E-mail, we now desire to have the order insured at your side.

(2) We sincerely hope our request will meet your approval.

(3) Referring to our Purchase Contract No. BT-67 for 300 Shandong Groundnuts, you will see the transaction is concluded on CFR basis.

(4) We will refund the premium to you upon receipt of your draft at sight on us or a debit note.

(5) We shall very much appreciate it if you could have the goods covered for our account against FPA and Aflatoxin Risk for 110% of the invoice value, totally GBP 55,000.

(6) Looking forward to your early reply.

4. Translate the following sentences into English.

(1) 我们要为这批货投保平安险和水渍险,请告知上述两种险别的保险费率。

(2) 破碎险是一种特殊险,需要为此支付额外保险费,其增加的保险费由卖方负担。

(3) 我方将在此按照我方的预约保单办理保险。

(4) 保险费随着承保范围的不同而不同,如需投保附加险,额外保险费将由买方承担。

(5) 我们很遗憾地得知你方货物在途中严重受损,保险公司将按照投保险别赔偿损失。

(6) 在 CIF 的基础上售出的货物,我们通常按发票金额加成 10%投保一切险和战争险。

(7) 我们将保险事宜留给你方安排,希望这些货物投保一切险和战争险。

(8) 我们企业是一家国有企业,享有理赔迅速、公正的声誉,并在世界上主要港口和地区都设有代理处。

5. Writing practice.

Write an English letter based on the following particulars:

• 通知对方所订 30 箱摄像机将由"东风号"货轮于本月底或下月初运出。

• 告诉对方将根据此批货物的性质代对方投保一切险。

• 如对方有异议,请赶紧告知。

6. Translate the following messages into English.

关于我们购货确认书 345 号项下的 5 000 条白兔牌毛毯,现通知你方,我们已由××银行开立了保兑的、不可撤销的信用证789号,总金额计……美元,有效期至8月31日。

请注意上述货物必须在8月底前装运,保险须按发票金额的130%投保一切险。我们知道,按照你们的一般惯例,你们只按发票金额另加10%投保,因此额外保险费由我方负担。

请按我方要求洽办保险,我方等候你方的装船通知。

Exercise 13　　Complaints and Claims

1. Translate the following terms or phrases from English into Chinese or vice versa.

(1) faulty packing　　　　　　　(2) force majeure
(3) breach of the contract　　　(4) short weight
(5) inspection report　　　　　　(6) shoddy goods
(7) 理赔　　　　　　　　　　　　(8) 仲裁条款
(9) 不履行合同　　　　　　　　　(10) 取消订单
(11) 做工低劣　　　　　　　　　 (12) 诉讼

2. Fill in the blanks of the following letter with the words and expressions given, and change the form when necessary.

> make, in, instant, far, forward, due, amply, with, inconvenience, late

Dear Mr. Xia,

We have received your fax of 2nd March, and very much regret the delay ___(1)___ delivering the above. We are now ___(2)___ the necessary arrangements for immediate delivery, which means you will have both excavators by 20th March at the latest.

The HERCULES JBM is the most successful excavator we have so ___(3)___ produced. It was an ___(4)___ success at its first appearance last year at the Hong Kong Building Exhibition and we were soon inundated ___(5)___ orders. Your own order was received in November and according to the waiting list we had then was not ___(6)___ to delivery until April. Nevertheless, we put the delivery date ___(7)___ so that you would have the machines in March. In February production was slightly set back by the ___(8)___ arrival of some special parts and this has been responsible for the delay in the present case.

We trust that you will not be unduly ___(9)___ by having to wait a few more days. The performance of the HERCULES JBM excavators will ___(10)___ compensate you.

Yours sincerely,

3. Rearrange the following paragraphs in logic order to make them a perfect letter.

(1) We are looking forward to receiving your remittance we are due to get.

(2) You are perfectly correct in saying that packing and insurance are normally less for air cargo. However, we remind you that your request to send the goods by air was made at very short notice. It was impossible for us to use the lighter airfreight packing materials. Furthermore, our insurance is on open policy, and depends on the value of the goods, not on the method of transportation.

(3) We have read carefully your letter of complaint on the discrepancy of the goods with the original sample. This was apparently caused by the oversight of our production department. Please allow us to offer an apology for your inconvenience. We are sending you a new lot by air at once, and would ask you to return the faulty goods at your convenience with freight forward or you may keep them for sale at a reduced price of 34% discount.

4. Translate the following letter into English.

敬启者：

你方7月16日关于本公司服务质量问题之来函已收悉，十分感谢你方提出的注意事项。我能够理解延迟交货给你方造成的巨大损失。

我们已向运输公司核实，近几次交货确有延误，让你方久等，我们对此也难以接受。对于此事给你方带来的不便，本人深感歉意。我向你方保证我们正在考虑更换运输公司，以免此类错误再次发生。

我们素来重视客户的意见。本着这一原则，我们非常乐意对贵公司此次订货做出特别安排，在三天之内发货。

给贵公司所添加的麻烦，谨再次由衷致歉。

谨上

5. Writing practice.

Situational writing 1

Your company ordered from New Century Company 60 sets of air conditioners. They included 30 sets of Model A and 30 sets of Model B. But when the goods arrived, you found that there were 25 sets of Model A and 35 sets of Model B. You are now requested to write to Mr. Peter, sales manager of New Century Company, and complain about the wrong delivery of the goods.

Situational writing 2

Suppose your company had just received 40 sets of machines, 4 of which had been found inferior in quality. You are requested to write a letter of claim against the supplier, ABR

Machine Company, on the poor quality of the machines.

Situational writing 3

Your company got a letter of complaint in which your client stated that you had delivered one wrong case of goods. Now you are requested to write a reply to inform that you are going to deliver the correct goods to substitute the wrong case and the relevant documents will be soon prepared. The costs of the shipment will be borne by your company.

6. Translate the following sentences into English.

(1) 检验报告证明,箱子及货物受损系运输途中粗鲁搬运而不是你们所说的因包装不善引起的。

(2) 损坏是由于包装不良所致,这样又大又重的机器应在出口木箱内定位填塞。

(3) 经检查,未发现有任何质量低劣或工艺不佳的迹象,所用料是最优质的。

(4) 你方愿接受错发货物,致谢。我们可按发票价降8%,希望你方同意。

(5) 请速传真告知9月15日以前你方能否发货,倘若不能,我方不得不撤销订单。

7. Write a letter of complaint of late delivery of a certain kind of goods.

8. Write a letter of claim to a supplier covering the following contents.

- 123号订单50箱家用器皿货物收到;
- 其中7个箱子破裂,内装器皿损坏;
- 检验报告证明损坏系不良包装所致;
- 要求赔偿损失费及检验费计……元。

Exercise 14   Agency

1. Translate the following terms or phrases from English into Chinese or vice versa.

(1) turnover

(2) principal

(3) sole agent

(4) business integrity

(5) advertising and publicity expenses

(6) entrust ... with exclusive agency

(7) 终止代理协议

(8) 交易记录

(9) 代理协议草案

(10) 书面通知

(11) 互利贸易

(12) 代理区域

2. Fill in the blanks of the following letter with the words given below, and change the form when necessary.

> approve, entrust, message, duration, territory, notice, enclose, review, careful, renew

Dear Sirs,

Thank you for your ___(1)___ of February 3 asking to be our sole agent. After ___(2)___ consideration, we decided to ___(3)___ you with the sole agency for our products in the ___(4)___ of Portugal.

The agency agreement has been drawn up for the ___(5)___ of one year, automatically ___(6)___ on expiration for a similar period unless ___(7)___ is given to the contrary. ___(8)___ is a copy of the draft. Please ___(9)___ the provisions and advise us whether they meet with your ___(10)___ .

We are looking forward to your reply.

Yours faithfully,

Alfred Liu

Exercise 14 Agency

3. Complete the following sentences with the Chinese given in the brackets.

（1）The question of agency is _____（正在考虑之中），and we hope that _____（贵方将继续努力提高我方产品的销售）.

（2）Commission rate will be increased _____（与贵方的销售数量成正比）.

（3）Once an agency agreement is concluded，_____（委托方与代理方都将承担一定的义务）.

（4）The agency must not divulge confidential material or information to a third party _____（在代理期间和之后）.

（5）If the present trend continues，Showner will have _____（将把市场份额提高到 30%）by the end of the year.

（6）As an exclusive agent of yours，I have every reason to _____（使受托人知晓我最近做的调查）.

（7）This agency agreement is entered into between the parties concerned _____（在平等互利的基础上按照以下双方同意的条款进行贸易）.

4. Translate the following letter into English.

敬启者：

谢谢贵方 2 月 4 日的来函，自荐担任我方在摩洛哥的代理。

鉴于目前交易金额不大，我们认为考虑代理事宜为时尚早，双方有必要再试行合作一段时间，看交易情况如何。这对你我双方更为有益。贵公司应该进一步增加营业额，以便证明可以签订代理协议。

相信你方能够理解我方看法，共同努力以促进彼此之间愉快的合作关系。

谨上

5. Writing practice.

Situational writing 1

Write a letter with the following given particulars：

• 自荐担任独家代理
• 对本地市场了如指掌
• 拥有良好的分销和零售渠道
• 当地市场对所代理产品的需求持续增长

Situational writing 2

Suppose you are working for a US medical equipment company. You received a claim from your agent complaining that your agent in Canada exceeded the limit of their district to canvass for orders in Ottawa. You made an investigation and found that it was true. You are requested to write a letter to the agent in Canada to terminate the agency agreement.

6. Choose the best answer.

(1) We need an agent in that district to help us to _____ our products.

    a. market   b. send   c. sell   d. buy

(2) It is our hope that, after proving our ability to dispose of large quantities, you will appoint us as an _____.

    a. sell agent   b. selling agent   c. sale agent   d. exclusive agent

(3) We are not _____ in your country now and would very much like to work an arrangement with you. We can provide our references from leading banks.

    a. buying   b. represented   c. selling   d. exporting

(4) After careful consideration, we have decided to entrust you _____ the sole agency for our products in the territory of South Asia.

    a. of   b. for   c. with   d. about

(5) Both of the parties hope that after the trim period is over, the agreement _____.

    a. is made   b. is continued   c. expands   d. extends

(6) Please send us an indication of the conditions under which we can _____ your company in Brazil.

    a. represent   b. work as an agent   c. handle   d. be on behalf of

(7) The general agent has to take care of the advertising and publicity _____.

    a. entitled   b. authorized   c. been entitled   d. entrusted

(8) We would like to know on what terms you are willing to _____ an agency agreement.

    a. come   b. conclude   c. agree   d. arrange

7. Translate the following stipulations in agency agreements.

(1) Transactions with Governmental Bodies: Transactions concluded between governmental bodies of Party A and Party B are not restricted by the terms and conditions of this agreement, nor shall they be considered as the target fulfilled by Party B under this agreement.

(2) Party B shall undertake to supply Party A once every three months with a market report in writing on prevailing market conditions as well as customers' comments on quality,

packing, and price, etc. of the bicycles under this agreement. If there is any particular change of local import regulations, Party B shall notify Party A at once.

(3) In case of a breach of any of the provisions of this agreement by one party, the other party shall have the right to terminate this agreement forthwith by giving notice in writing to its opposite party.

Exercise 15 Contracts and Agreements

1. Translate the following contract stipulations into Chinese.

(1) Packing:

To be packed in strong new wooden case(s), suitable for long distance ocean/parcel post/air freight transportation and to change of climate, well protected against moisture and shocks. The Sellers shall be liable for any damage of the commodity and expenses incurred on account of improper packing and for any rust attributable to inadequate or improper protective measures taken by the Sellers in regard to the packing. One full set of service and operation instructions concerned shall be enclosed in the case(s).

(2) Terms of Shipment:

1) In case of FOB terms:

(a) Booking of shipping space shall be attended to by the Buyer. The Sellers shall, 45 days before the date of shipment stipulated in this contract, advise the Buyer by fax or telex of the contract number, commodity, quantity, value, number of packages, gross weight and measurement and date of readiness at the port of shipment.

(b) The Buyer or his/her shipping agent shall, 12 days before the estimated date of arrival of the vessel at the port of shipment, advise the Sellers the name of the vessel, contract number, the name of the shipping agent. The Sellers shall come into contact with the shipping agent and arrange for the goods to be ready for loading. When it becomes necessary to change the carrying vessel or in the event of the arrival having to be advanced or delayed, the Buyer or the shipping agent shall advise the Sellers in time.

(c) The Sellers shall be liable for any dead freight or demurrage, should it happen that they have failed to have the commodity ready for loading after the carrying vessel has arrived at the port of shipment on time.

(d) The sellers bear all costs and risks before it passes over the vessel's rail and is released from the tackle.

2) In case of CFR terms:

The Sellers shall ship the goods within delivery time as per this contract from the port of shipment to the port of destination and advise shipment as stipulated in clause 12 of this contract for the Buyer to arrange insurance in time.

(3) Inspection and Claim:

The Buyer shall have the right to apply to the Guangdong Commodity Inspection Bureau (GCIB) for re-inspection after discharge of the goods at the port of destination. Should the quality, specification and/or quantity/weight be found not in conformity with the Contract, Letter of Credit or Invoice, the Buyer shall be entitled to lodge claims (including re-inspection fee) with the Sellers on the basis of GCIB's Inspection Certificate, within 90 days after discharge of the goods at the port of destination, with the exception, however, of those claims for which the shipping company and/or the insurance company are to be held responsible.

2. Translate the following sentences into English.

(1) 建议你方以后以寄售方式发运不锈钢餐具。

(2) 若接受我方寄售货物的报盘,你方将不承担任何风险,因为我方将支付未售出商品退货的所有费用。

(3) 请你方在行情下跌前将寄售货物售出。

(4) 我们对你方出售这笔寄售货物的拖延甚感失望,希望尽快得到有关消息。

(5) 希望你方对我方目前经营寄售的情况满意,并在以后给予更多的机会。

3. Translate the following terms of a consignment contract.

(1) Terms and Conditions:

A. Term Of Consignment: Six months (180 days) starting from the goods' arrival at the destination.

B. The locations, methods and prices for selling shall be decided by Party A according to the situation, and Party B will not intervene. However, Party B may make proposals in this respect. Both Parties should exchange information in a timely way, study together, and settle any problems that may arise during the consignment period while Party B shall facilitate sales in every possible way.

C. If any adverting or promotion should be undertaken in any sales location, Party A will make proposals, and Party B shall bear the expenses.

D. If any breakage of containers is found at the goods' arrival for which Party B is responsible, or any deterioration of quality occur during the period of consignment, Party B shall make compensation at the contracted prices or replace the substandard goods with fresh goods against Party A's certificate.

E. During the period of this consignment if Party A requires an increased quantity of said commodity, Party B shall, cooperate with Party A in order to expand sales.

(2) Terms of Payment:

A. Party A shall, within 15 days after the expiration of the period of consignment (180 days), remit the total amount to Party B at the contract unit prices according to the varieties and quantities actually sold.

B. For unsold goods, Party A shall make a list to Party B. The two Parties shall decide through mutual consultations, whether to return the unsold goods to Party B or to automatically transfer them to the next consignment contract.

C. The price of the portion of the shipment suffering quality deterioration or breakage shall be deducted from the total amount to be remitted, with the exception of those already disposed of or settled. However, Party A must furnish Party B with detailed invoice of deductions.

4. Translate the following terms into English.

(1) 品质、数量和重量的异议与索赔：货到目的口岸后，买方如发现货物品质及数量与合同规定不符，除属于保险公司及船运公司的责任外，买方可以凭双方认可的检验机构出具的检验证明向卖方提出异议。品质异议须于货到目的口岸之日起30天内提出，数量异议须于货物到目的口岸之日起15天内提出。

(2) 仲裁：凡因执行本合同或与本合同有关事项所发生的一切争执，应由双方通过友好方式协商解决。如果不能取得协议时则在被告国家（地区）根据被告国（地区）仲裁机构的仲裁程序规则进行仲裁。仲裁决定是终局的，对双方具有同等约束力。仲裁费用除非仲裁机构另有决定外，均由败诉一方负担。

5. Translate the following passage into Chinese.

(1)

1) Unless otherwise agreed to by the Sellers, payment is to be made against sight draft drawn under a Confirmed, Irrevocable, Divisible and Assignable Letter of Credit without Recourse for the full amount, established through a first class bank acceptable to the Sellers. The Letter of Credit in due form must reach the Sellers at least 15 days before the month of shipment stipulated in this Sales Contract, failing which the Sellers shall not be responsible for shipment as stipulated; in case the Buyers' credit still fails to reach the Sellers after the expiry of the shipping period, the Sellers shall have the right to cancel this Sales Contract and claim for damage against the Buyers.

2) The Sellers are to cover insurance at invoice value plus 10% thereof the goods sold on CIF basis. If the Letter of Credit stipulates that the goods after arrival at the port of destination are to be transported to an inland city or some other ports, the Sellers will cover

Exercise 15 Contracts and Agreements

insurance up to that city or ports, and the Buyers are to be responsible for payment of this additional premium.

3) Claims for damage should be filed by the Buyers with the Sellers within 30 days after arrival of the goods at destination and supported by sufficient evidence for Sellers' reference so that claims can be settled through friendly negotiation.

4) The Buyers are requested to sign and return one original copy to the Sellers for file immediately upon receipt of this Sales Contract. Should the Buyers fail to do so within 10 days after the arrival of this Sales Contract at the Buyers' end, it shall be considered that the Buyers have accepted all the terms and conditions set forth in this Sales Contract.

(2)

1) We hereby engage with the drawers, endorsers and bona fide holders of draft(s) drawn under and in accordance with the terms of this credit that the same shall be honored by T.T. on presentation of the documents at this office. Amount(s) of draft(s) negotiated under this credit must be endorsed on the back hereof.

2) Disposal of Documents: It is a condition of this credit that the documents should be forwarded to us by two consecutive airmails, the first mail consisting of all documents except one of each item, if more than one, to be sent by second mail.

3) REIMBURSEMENT of this credit is available by T.T. as soon as the documents called for by the credit have been received by us and found correct. Please advise this credit to the beneficiary.

Exercise 16　Invitation for Bids and Advertisements

Translate the following passage into Chinese.

1. (1) Interested eligible bidders who are willing to participate in the bidding may obtain detailed information from the address below and inspect the bidding documents. A set of bidding documents may be purchased in the 4th floor at the address below between 9:00 am and 11:00 am (Sundays and holidays excepted) from February 16, 1998 or be promptly dispatched by express mail upon receipt of non-refundable payment of US$200 plus US$50 postage fee.

(2) The bids should reach the address below before 16:00 on March 22, 1998 and will be opened publicly by Sinopec Int'L at 9:00 am on March 23, 1998. Each bid package must be submitted in separate sealed envelopes and be accompanied by a bid bond. Those bids which are not accompanied by a bid bond will not be accepted.

(3) Bids will be opened in Rm. A0401 at the address below.

2. Shanghai Toys Imp. & Exp. Corp, the first "combination of industry and trade" in China approved by the State Council of the People's Republic of China, is an enterprising Corp. professionally handling toys import and export business. Toys handled: metal and plastic flexible toys (friction-type & clock-work toys, battery-operated toys, radio-control, voice-control and light-control electronic toys), push toys, dolls, wooden toys, musical toys, inflatable toys, children's vehicles, toy cores and motors, etc.

3. A foreign trade company with the special entitlement to declare the Customs on written export declaration anywhere in China. The Hainan Nationality Foreign Trade General Corporation, entitled by the Ministry of Foreign Economic Relations and Trade to declare Customs anywhere in China, is one of the first local foreign-trade companies in the province. It has played an active role in the past 12 years in economic and cultural development for the province's minority nationalities. The corporation handles import and export business, and real estate development, as well as establishing joint venture and con-management enterprises.

Exercise 17　Memorandums

1. Work in pairs. Look at the following subjects of a memo and find out which one is good, if no one is good, you need to write one for the memo.

　(1) Subject:"Important! Read Immediately!"
　(2) Subject: "Meeting"
　(3) Subject: "Questions about Meeting"
　(4) Subject: "Monthly Meetings"

2. Work in pairs to improve the following parts of a memo.

To	Department managers
From	Training manger
Subject	Training program
Date	11/12/2022

3. Medicine International is sending a delegation of executives to Japan for the first time to negotiate an important contract, so the executives are going to attend a series of seminars given by Tomomi Yamohama, a Japanese consultant. Read the memo from the Managing Director to the Human Resources Manager and provide a subject for it.

Date	8th June, 2022
To	Robert Burton, Human Resources Manager
From	Peter Jackson, Managing Director
Subject	_____

Robert,

The trip to Japan has been confirmed for the 15th of next month. I've decided to go ahead with the seminars as we discussed.

Please contact the consultant you mentioned and get back to me about the following:

• The topics she covers
• Short description of each topic
• Whether you think we should use her services or look for someone else

We haven't much time, so please do this ASAP and also check the availability of the executives who will be involved in this training.

PJ

4. You work for Dunn's Wholesale Confectionery. The office manager is Miss Helen Black. You arrive at work one morning and find the following note from her on your desk. Carry out her instructions.

> Write a memo under my name to all the company's representatives, informing them that the new supply of company-headed writing paper, and ball-pens embossed with the company's name and address, which are to be given to customers, have arrived and will be available to the company reps from next Tuesday from the office. I need to know in writing by next Monday the quantities of these items each rep requires.

5. Write a memo using a suitable format for the situation given below. Remember that your memo should be clear and concise, and contain only relevant information.

> Your section moved to a new office on Thursday morning. However, the Maintenance Department within your organization has failed to carry out certain work. Computers have not been wired to the laser printer; a metal bookshelf hasn't been built properly; the fire door sticks and the bottom drawer of the filing cabinet which holds standard forms, was damaged in the move and now doesn't open. Write a memo complaining about the situation and asking for action.

6. Please write an English memo according to the following information.

> 2022年5月23日人事部告知全体员工,任命李晨先生为本公司人力资源部经理。李先生已在本公司工作5年。之前,他曾就职于长城工业公司,任人力资源开发部经理,负责组织规划、人才选拔、管理开发等工作。

7. There are many grammar and spelling mistakes in the following memo. Work in pairs to correct them:

> Memo
> From: The Manager
> To: All grade B stuff and lower
> Date: June 6, 2022
> Subject: Safe at Work
>
> Last Thursday, when 'B' shift were clocking off, one of the men beat his head against a safety leader where someone had carelessly left out. He has to have stiches in his head because this.
> I am fed up with telling you about this kind of things. One of these days, we'll have a serious accident, and then it will be late. Until I see a great improvement in your attitude towards keeping the place tidy and safe, I'm afraid I'll have to punish you offenders.

8. What do you think of the content and layout of the following memo? Does it have a clear purpose? Work in pairs to rewrite it.

> Memo
> From: The Managing Director
> To: Divisional HR Managers
> Date: March 3, 2022
> Subject: Coffee-Making Facilities
>
> There have been a number of comments about the amount of coffee consumed in our company. I do not want sound as though I am against coffee-drinking; indeed our personnel consultants have emphasized how important coffee can be if you want an efficient and motivated office staff. But timesaving machines for making tea and coffee do exist.
> We can expect a little opposition to the idea if we are not careful. You can never be sure how the office staff will react. They might take it badly. In any case, we're thinking of putting in tea and coffee machines. Please send me a report.

Exercise 18   E-mails

1. Work in pairs to improve the following sentences according to the E-mail writing tips you have studied. You may change the passive voice, noun phrases or old-fashioned phrases in them.

(1) We are in receipt of your payment.

_____

(2) Your early reply would be appreciated.

_____

(3) Thank you for the inquiry.

_____

(4) Your response to this questionnaire should be submitted by April 30.

_____

(5) Kindly send me a price list for your M-series.

_____

(6) I would be much obliged if you could sign both copies of the contract and return.

_____

2. Work in pairs. Improve the following E-mail according to the E-mail writing tips you have studied. You may delete the old-fashioned expressions in it.

Subject: Billing Error, Invoice NO. A-28250

Dear Mr. Jones,

This is to acknowledge your message dated April 10 concerning the above referenced billing error. Upon checking our records, we found that the invoice should indeed read as US $ 300 instead of US $ 350. We apologize for this oversight and attach herewith the correct invoice.
Thank you in advance for your kind consideration.

Yours faithfully,

3. Write an E-mail to Denman Sons, telling them that you wish to enter into business relations with them, with the following particulars:

Introduced by Mr. A.G. Topworth of Swanson Bros., of Hamburg.

The main line of your business is exporting air-conditioners.

Ask Denman Sons to give you the name of their bank.

Illustrated catalogue and price-list will be airmailed against their specific inquiries.

4. Work in pairs. Delete the unnecessary phrases and sentences from the following bodies of E-mail.

I am writing to inform you of a serious problem in our company. The other day, I happened to find many heavy boxes near fire doors. Later I was told that because of shortage of space, employees have put heavy boxes near fire doors. This is against our company's policy. There should be access to fire doors, as workers must leave the building quickly if there is a fire. Fire doors should be unblocked and obstructions should be removed. Otherwise, there will be really dangerous for our employees in case of a fire.

According to a report submitted by our Mr. Burton, sales manager, sales have fallen recently. The reason is that our packaging is unattractive although it is functional. We must do something before our competitors have achieved a great increase in their sales. I think we should develop new and appealing designs. We should have a meeting to discuss this. Could you please attend a meeting in the boardroom at 10:00 am tomorrow to discuss this matter?

We are providing courses for our staff during next two months. There are twenty vacancies on training courses being given in May and June. The courses provide useful training for junior staff in computers, time management and other aspects of modem office work. These are very important for our or junior staff. Could you kindly recommend suitable staff before the end of the week? Please remember there is a limit of twenty for the training.

5. Exercises.

Task One

Yesterday Mr. Wang, the General Manager of your company, received the following E-mail from a company in your district. He has now handed the E-mail to you, together with his comments (which he has handwritten on the E-mail). Write a reply according to the E-mail and the GM's comments.

Thank Mr. Ho for his E-mail, we're very happy, too.

Dear Mr. Wang,

We are happy to report good sales of the new Language Translator (Model ZS 508). Our customers find these pocket machines very useful for translating words and phrases for a variety of purposes. The machines, however, are most popular of all among business people, and we are writing to inform you of numerous requests which they have made for the translators to include a number of common business terms.

An excellent idea!

A few customers from business and various other fields also ask if it is possible for Japanese,
Arabic and Indonesian to be added to the 4 languages in the translator. A special card can be fitted into next model to provide more languages.

Unfortunately, however, the translator is too heavy and large to put in a pocket and too small to put in a briefcase. A small leather case is now urgently required for the machine. The casing is very strong a leather case would only add to price.

Finally, we are also happy to inform you that the electronic dictionaries have sold well, and I now wish to order a further 200 of these machines in addition to 300 language translators. Certainly!

I very much look forward to hearing form you.

Yours sincerely,

Ho Tse Teng
General manager

Task Two

There is also a reply below. Compare yours with this one. Do you think it's rather wordy? If it's true, delete the unnecessary phrases and sentences in it.

A reply to the above E-mail:

Dear Mr. Ho,

We would like to inform you that we have received your E-mail dated 23 November. Please forgive us for replying to your E-mail so late. After reading the E-mail, we are delighted to know the fact that your customers find our machines to be really useful.

In your E-mail, your have mentioned the inclusion of business terms in the new machines. Actually, the inclusion of business terms is an excellent idea, and we shall develop this idea. Thank you for telling us this wonderful idea, which is so important to the development of our products.

Other languages are also mentioned in your E-mail. Thank you for reminding us of that. We shall produce special cards, which can be fitted into the translators to provide more languages in the next model. However, the inclusion of a leather case would add considerably to the price of our machines and might not be necessary as the casing is very robust. So we are very sorry that we cannot meet your needs in this regard. Sorry again.

Last thing required in your E-mail is the new order of 200 electronic dictionaries and 300 language translators. We will of course provide the best service for you. We are taking steps and measures to supply you immediately with 200 electronic dictionaries and 300 language translators.

We are looking forward to your new orders.

Yours sincerely,

Wang Luen Fung
General Manager

6. It is always necessary to write an E-mail to confirm information after an important telephone conversation. Write a reply to the following E-mail written after a telephone call. You should write according to this structure: opening (acknowledging the E-mail)—purpose (confirming plans)—polite expressions (offering more help and being positive).

Dear Mr. Bush,

In our telephone conversation yesterday, we discussed plans for our meeting at your conference center—the Arrowhead Conference Center. I would like to confirm these plans. The meeting will be from March 15th to the 17th. We will need two rooms. Eighty people attend the meeting.

I have additional requests:
Could you provide ten tables for each room?
Is it possible to have a TV and DVD in one room?
Would you be able to serve lunch on the 16th?

I would appreciate your answers by next Friday. If you need any more information, please call me.
I would like to thank you for your help in planning our meeting.

Sincerely yours,

Robert White
Special Projects Office

7. Write a reply to the following E-mail, which is for requesting information. You reply should follow this structure: opening (acknowledging the E-mail)—purpose (providing the information requested)—action (asking the reader to contact your local dealers)—polite expressions (offering additional help and thanking the reader).

Dear Sir or Madam,

In the April 4 *Boston Daily News* I read about your new camera, the XL-Lite. Since I am a photographer with *Bay State Magazine*, it is important that I know about new cameras.

Would you please send me information on the camera? I would like to know when the camera will be available and how much it will cost.

Thank you for your attention. I look forward to your reply.

Sincerely yours,

Jane Wilson
Photo Department

8. What do you think of the style of the following E-mail? Rewrite it using a modern style.

19 January, 2022

Dear Sir,

Your request for our catalogue and price list

As requested, we enclose for your attention our price list and catalogue. I should like to take this opportunity of drawing your attention to the fact that all our products are manufactured from completely natural ingredients and that we do not utilize any artificial additives whatsoever. There are 234 different items in the catalogue and our prices are reasonable and our quality is outstanding. This is the first time that we have included BHJ samples of our ten most popular aromas.

Should you require further information, please do not hesitate to contact us. If the undersigned is unavailable, the Sales Manager's personal assistant will be more than delighted to assist you. We look forward to receiving your esteemed order in due course.

Yours faithfully,

Jack Williams
Sales Manager

Exercise 19   Notices and Instructions

Exercise.

You work at the Hospitality Hotel, Bath Road, Harrogate, Yorkshire HG23NF. The manager is Mr. David Lloyd. The telephone number is 01423-505861 and the fax number is 01423-568534. You suggest to Mr. Lloyd that it would be a good idea to stress some aspects of security in a notice to be put in all bedrooms. He looks at your notes and asks you to write a notice under your own name.

Here are your notes:

We cannot accept responsibility for thefts or for items lost/damaged. (Lock your rooms when you go out.) If guests have anything valuable or important, hand it in at reception/locked away in our safe. (Only if staff members of Hospitality Hotel are negligent are we responsible.) Outside doors are locked at 11 o'clock at night. If they forget their key (guests are given a key when they register) they should ring the bell which is to the right of the front door. (Some guests have even left valuables and important documents in their cars!)

Exercise 20   Agendas and Minutes

Please write the minutes of the following business meeting.

Different people in North Travel Agency are offering different opinions on whether or not to open new travel agencies. (Informal meeting at 3:00 p.m. on 26 April, 2022)
Chairperson: Richard   Marketing Manager: Lily   Other members: Mark, Peter, Tom

> **Richard:** Well, everyone is here. Shall we start? As you know, we are having this meeting to discuss whether or not this is the right time to expand our business, particularly whether we should open more agencies next year. Lily, you are the manager of the Marketing Department, perhaps you can briefly introduce the situation first.
>
> **Lily:** Yes. I've been looking at our sales figures from the past few years, and it seems to me that we should set up agencies in new areas where there is a great deal demand for our sort of travel services.
>
> **Mark:** Sorry to interrupt, I think you're a bit quick with your conclusion there. I have a rather different interpretation of the situation. Personally speaking, I'm in favor of expanding our present agencies rather than setting up new ones. Please think of the cost of risking new ventures in new places with new overheads.
>
> **Tom:** Excuse me, Mark I would like to break in here. I think you're over-pessimistic. I agree with you that we have to spend on facilities, staff training, advertising and so on. But Lily is right because the demand is there. Maybe Peter can tell you something about the Youth Tourism Corporation.
>
> **Peter:** Yes. I was going to mention that. The day before yesterday, I overheard from a friend that the Youth Tourism Corporation is planning to expand their business in the southwest of the country. I mean, if we don't grasp the opportunity, our competitors will. Don't you think so?
>
> **Mark:** Well, I still stick to my point. I think it is more advisable to upgrade our present facilities and postpone opening new agencies to next year instead of this year.
>
> **Lily:** Well, everybody knows the saying: "Time is money." If we miss the opportunity, our rivals will take over the market. And I do think it is necessary to open new agencies.
>
> **Richard:** All right, I feel we've discussed this matter fully. You have made some valuable points and suggestions. To sum up, there are strong reasons for opening new agencies this year. I will present your ideas to the board of directors. Is there any other business? No? Okay, that's all for today. I'd just like to conclude by thanking you all for your time and contributions. I'll get back to you as soon as I get a response from the board.

Exercise 21　Business Reports

1. The following data is a summary of the questionnaires that were filled in by staff at ABC Company. The questionnaires asked staff what they thought about the layout of their offices, the most important features of furniture, and the type of image the company should project. Skim quickly through the data and try to write down the general idea about what the staff think. You may write three sentences.

Present layout:	
very good	0%
good	7%
adequate	13%
poor	62%
very poor	18%
Furniture should:	
be comfortable	20%
be durable	36%
be attractive	25%
function efficiently	19%
Company image should be:	
very modern	42%
traditional	26%
simple and functional	18%
extravagant	14%

2. Write the terms of reference (or introduction) for your report based on the following excerpts of telephone messages. There is an example for you.

Example:

John, can you get that report ready for me by next Thursday? I want you to come up with an overview of the Human Resources Department; you know, structure and organization—you get the idea. (The purpose of this report is to give an overview of the structure and organization of the Human Resources Department.)

(1) Jane, don't forget the weekly sales report is due on Friday—usual sort of thing—product progress update, survey of week's events in the market. Look forward to seeing it on my desk on Friday then.

(2) Jack, I read your report last night—very interesting. I particularly liked the part

where you presented the results of your interviews. I'd never have guessed that the man in the street would prefer to see less rather than more television. Also, your findings as regards favorite program type were quite eye-opening.

(3) Linda, about the report you sent me yesterday. Are you sure you can conclude from your limited evidence that this company should expand into the European market? I mean, surely we need to look at our potential competitors' activities very closely before we can do that with any confidence.

3. The following sentences are chosen from different kinds of business reports. Decide which part of a report they belong to: findings, conclusions or recommendations.

(1) The surface of the internal flooring is still smooth, while the external floor covering appears to have been badly scratched.

(2) We should strongly recommend that policing of the compound be stepped up.

(3) We feel that the most likely cause of this incident was electrical failure.

(4) The market is extremely sensitive to price fluctuations.

(5) In terms of personnel, we feel that additional staff should be recruited before the end of the financial year.

(6) In line with our findings, we believe that the future looks hopeful for the company if the following recommendations are taken up.

4. Read the following report and match the headings to the paragraphs.

Stockholder information	Financial statements and notes
Report of management	Selected financial data
Corporate message	Financial highlights
Letter to stockholders	Auditor's report
Management discussion	Board of directors and management

The main structure of an annual report

While most annual reports contain optional elements, all reports contain information required by the Securities Exchange Commission or SEC, the commission that controls and administers the activities of US stock exchanges.

SEC-required elements include:

➢ Auditor's report. This summary by independent public accountants shows whether the financial statements are complete, reliable, and prepared consistent with generally accepted accounting principles (GAAP).

➢ Report of management. This letter, usually from the board chairperson and the chief financial officer, takes responsibility for the validity of the financial information in the annual report, and states that the report complies with SEC and other legal requirements.

➢ _____(1)_____ These provide the complete numbers for the company's financial performance and recent financial history. The SEC requires:

• Statement of earnings: The statement of earnings shows how much revenue a company brings into the business, and the costs and expenses associated with earning that revenue during that time.

• Statement of cash flows: The statement of cash flows reports the flow of cash into and out of a company in a given year. Cash is a company's lifeblood. Cash includes currency and deposits in banks. Cash equivalents are short-term, temporary investments that can be quickly and easily converted to cash.

• Statement of financial position: The statement of financial position reports a company's financial status at a set date. The statement is like a snapshot because it shows what the company is worth at that set date. That statement shows what the company owns (assets), what the company owes (liabilities) and what belongs to the owners (stockholders' equity).

➢ _____(2)_____ This information summarizes a company's financial condition and performance over five years or longer, including gross profit and net earnings.

➢ _____(3)_____ This series of short, detailed reports discusses and analyzes the company's performances. It covers results of operations, and the adequacy of resources to fund operation.

Optional elements include:

➢ _____(4)_____ This list gives the names and position titles of the company's board of directors and top management team. Sometimes companies include photographs.

➢ _____(5)_____ This information covers the basics—the company's headquarters, the exchanges on which the company trades its stock, the next annual stockholders' meeting, and other general stockholder service information. It is usually in the back of the annual report.

➢ _____(6)_____ This may be from the chairperson of the board of directors, the chief executive officer, or both. It can provide an analysis and a review of the year's events, including any problems, issues, and successes the company had. It usually reflects the business philosophy and management style of the company's executives and it often lays out the company's direction for the next year.

➢ _____(7)_____ Some consider this an advertisement for the company. However, it almost always reflects how a company sees itself, or how it would like others to see it. Here, the company can explain itself to the stockholders, using photographs, illustrations, and text. It may cover the company's lines of business, markets, mission, management philosophy, corporate culture, and strategic direction.

➢ _____(8)_____ Probably the most often-read section of any annual report, these give a quick summary of a company's performance. The figures appear in short table, usually accompanied by supporting graphs.

5. You are the General Manager of HGC Tractors. You are looking for ways in which you can increase your business and you have asked two senior members of your staff to conduct a survey of opinions of your tractors as well as those of BBF Tractors, your chief competitor.

Exercise 21 Business Reports

Read the following table showing the results of the survey. Use the information in the chart to write a short report (about 120 to 140 words) about the manufacture and sales of your company's tractors in comparison to BBF Tractors. Suggest ways in which improvements can be made.

Items	HGC	BBF
Pricing	Good (=Cheap)	Average
Quality	Average	Excellent
Reliability	Good	Very Good
Ease of Servicing	Very Good	Average
Appearance	Poor	Good
Availability	Good	Excellent

(Grades=Poor, Average, Good, Very Good, Excellent)

6. Use the information in the table to write a short report (**120-140 words**), recommending the best company to supply the paint and do the work.

Items	ASP Paints	SDF Paints	HIJ Paints
Price (RMB) per 10 liters including painting	450	400	380
Colors available	dark red, light red, green, deep yellow, dark blue	green, cream, white	red, cream, pale yellow, dark blue
Quality	very good	good	good
Speed of drying	fast	slow	average
Wash resistance	fair	very good	good
Length of time before completion	10 days	12 days	3 weeks

7. Your manager is keen to introduce new practices into your company. He has asked you to write a report that includes details of two practices from another company which you would suggest adopting in your own company. Your report should include the following information. You should write about 200 to 250 words.

➢ What you admire about the other company?
➢ Which two of its practices you would adopt?
➢ Why your company would benefit from them?

Exercise 22 Resume (CV), Application Letters, and Follow-Up Thank-You Letters

1. There are some mistakes and ambiguous expressions in the following letter. Rewrite it after making the corrections or amendment to it.

Application for a Job as a Salesperson

July 3, 2022

Dear Sir or Madam:

Noticing the enclosed advertisement in today's *Yangcheng Evening Newspaper*, I wish to apply a part-time job as a salesgirl for the direct selling of your beauty products.

I am a junior student at Guangdong College of Commerce. My major is Marketing. I studied Marketing, Marketing Techniques, Psychology of Consumption, Psychology of Women, Business Law, Labor Law, Business Ethics, Communications, Public Relations, etc.

I have some experiences in marketing in the last two years. During the summer vacation and winter vacation of 2021, I once stayed at the Beauty Products Counter the Taibai Department Store as a salesgirl. Last year I worked as a part-time salesgirl on Sundays for Procter and Gamble (Guangzhou) Ltd. I come from house to house to sell Rejoice 2-in-1, and Head and Shoulders shampoos.

I think my education and some experience in marketing will let me to offer services for your sales promotion. If you give me a trial, I would do my best to give you every satisfaction. I will await for your answer.

Sincerely yours,

Kay Jin

2. You have seen the following recruiting advertisement in the local press and would like to apply for the position. Read the advertisement carefully and write a letter of application within 100 to 120 words, giving details of previous experiences, salary, etc.

Welcome to Our Team-Top Salary

ASSISTANT SALES MANAGER wanted by an international company manufacturing textile piece goods. The applicant must have had adequate experience in the sales division of a large company and be willing to accept responsibility.

Exercise 23　Letters for Social Purpose

Letters of introductions, recommendations and references

1. Guess the word with the help of the first letter and the hints in the brackets.

(1) I am pleased to r_____ Miss Lin as a competent secretary. (Meaning: speak favorably of somebody or something)

(2) His records i_____ that he is good at both English and French. (Meaning: show)

(3) She is a c_____ and energetic person. (Meaning: able)

(4) He once had an o_____ to work as an assistant to a manager. (Meaning: chance)

(5) Mr. Tarter is always c_____ and hard-working. (Meaning: guided by one's sense of duty)

(6) I am sure he will be a great a_____ to your company. (Meaning: a valuable or useful person)

(7) If you need any further information, please do not h_____ to contact me. (Meaning: be slow to speak or act because one feels uncertain or unwilling)

(8) I would appreciate it if you could f_____ his smooth enrollment. (Meaning: making something easy or less difficult)

(9) Anything you could do for her would be very much a_____. (Meaning: recognize an action gratefully)

(10) I can therefore recommend him without r_____. (Meaning: reserve)

2. Complete each sentence with a suitable preposition.

(1) Since her graduation in 1998, she has been working _____ a secretary at our company for three years.

(2) She is very popular _____ our customers.

(3) I am glad _____ this opportunity to give Mr. Lee an introduction.

(4) His teachers thought highly _____ him.

(5) She takes rapid dictation _____ ease and transcribes her notes _____ speed and accuracy.

(6) I therefore recommend him _____ anyone who is looking for a young man

willing and able to prove his worth.

(7) Mr. Tam frequently travels to the States and could meet _____ your representatives there to discuss items of mutual interest.

(8) I am _____ a position to offer some concrete information on his qualifications.

(9) He is serious _____ his work and demonstrates a high degree of competence in engineering.

(10) He would be good for the position he applies _____.

3. Complete the sentences with an appropriate word or phrase below.

| at the New York office   helpful and conscientious   As her immediate superior |
| with her family   fulfilled   without reservation   my pleasure   shorthand |
| obliging   her graduation |

To Whom It May Concern:

It is ____(1)____ to recommend Mrs. Jane Jones as a competent secretary.

Since ____(2)____ from the New York Public Administration School in July of 2001, she has been working as a secretary ____(3)____ of the Rome Company. ____(4)____ for the last three years, I can state that she is a very outstanding secretary. She is very good at typing and ____(5)____.

She also writes excellent business letters and ____(6)____ her other duties well.

I found Mrs. Jones a most ____(7)____ young woman. She was hard-working and popular at work. We often turned to her for help. Frankly, I was certainly sorry to lose her when she moved to Chicago ____(8)____.

I recommend her ____(9)____, as I know you find her a most ____(10)____ secretary.

4. Correct one wrong word or cross out an unnecessary word in each line in the following letter body.

(1) A friend of mine, Mr. Zhong, would very much likes to meet you. He is a student of Economics
(2) at the Jiaotong University, Shanghai, and plans to enter on the insurance business in a few
(3) months' time. Meanwhile, he is making a study trip to Japan in order for contribute towards a
(4) book which is prepared entitled "Social Insurance Abroad".
(5) You were kind enough, when you were here, to offer with me your assistance. I would very much
(6) appreciate for it if you could find time to see Mr. Zhong, or to give him an introduction to someone on your staff.

Exercise 23 Letters for Social Purpose

5. Work with your partner to improve the following letter.

Hints for Improvement:

➢ Spelling ➢ Wording

➢ Grammar ➢ Sentence combining

➢ Prepositions and articles ➢ Language style and layout

Dear Mr. John,

I want to study in a America university. Can you tell me what university is good? And also can you introduce a professor for me? I plan to learn the major of business administrate. I thank you if you do that for me? I will come America in the next month. So I need the information very quickly. Can you write the letter for me? I need it in the end of the mouth. I'm look forward to receive your letter.

Yours sincerely,

Jack Lee

Letters of invitations and their reply

1. Guess the word with the help of the first letter and the hints in the brackets.

(1) I am pleased to know that you will bring a d_____ to the United States next month. (Meaning: group of delegates)

(2) We are pleased to invite r_____ of China National Textile import and Export Corporation, Shanghai Branch to visit Britain in July. (Meaning: delegate)

(3) It will be a great pleasure for our company to act as a s_____ for your delegation. (Meaning: person or firm that pays for a program or a sporting event in order to use them for advertising)

(4) We will a_____ them throughout their entire stay. (Meaning: walk or travel with somebody as a helper or companion)

(5) When your travel s_____ is settled, please let us know the time of your arrival. (Meaning: timetable)

(6) We hope you will be able to s_____ the time to come. (Meaning: be able to afford to give time or money)

(7) Mr. White will host a r_____ after the game. (Meaning: formal social occasion to welcome someone)

(8) It is a great pleasure to e_____ this invitation to the meeting. (Meaning: offer or give something)

(9) If you would like to p_____, please confirm your flight with us by the end of

this month. (Meaning: take part or become involved in an activity)

(10) Please accept my h_____ congratulations on this remarkable success. (Meaning: enthusiastic)

2. Complete each sentence with a suitable preposition.

(1) We are planning a dinner party _____ our home from 6:00 to about 9:00 on May 7.

(2) Our idea is to share the special occasion _____ a few of our closest friends.

(3) The conference will consist _____ a series of discussions about our current sales.

(4) The tour is scheduled _____ April 16.

(5) Please confirm your schedule _____ us by the end of this month.

(6) We are looking forward to seeing you _____ the conference in New York.

(7) Thank you for your kind invitation _____ the dinner party on May 19.

(8) I greatly appreciate your concern _____ my attendance at this conference.

(9) I am afraid that my schedule will have to force me to withdraw _____ the conference.

(10) This would call _____ someone qualified to speak for me.

3. Correct one wrong word or cross out an unnecessary word in each line in the following letter body.

(1) Mr. Alexander, Chairperson of the Nell Group, thank very much for the invitation to a dinner
(2) party at the Ambassador Hotel on September 14, in the honor of the senior management of the
(3) American Car Company. Mr. Alexander unfortunately will not be able to attend to the dinner
(4) party. He would be pleased to accept, but as he has already made arrangements to attend
(5) another important meeting that cannot be cancelled. Mr. Alexander has asked me to expand his warm greetings to you and Mr. Scanlon.

4. Complete the sentences with an appropriate word or phrase below.

| your conference | projector | delighted | on May 7 | available |
| members | confirm | inviting | me | look forward to |

Dear Ms Lee,

Thank you for your letter __(1)__ to speak at your conference __(2)__ on the subject of "Smooth Communication". I am __(3)__ to accept your invitation, and __(4)__ I will require overnight accommodation. For my presentation, I will require use of a __(5)__ and hope this can be made __(6)__. I __(7)__ renewing my acquaintance with __(8)__ of your Association at __(9)__ and wish you every

Exercise 23 Letters for Social Purpose

success.

Yours sincerely,

5. Work with your partner to improve the following letter.

Hints for Improvement:

➢ Grammar/Collocation   ➢ Sentence combining

➢ Wording   ➢ Language style and layout

Dear Mrs. Ellis,

I take the liberty to thank your kind invitation for dinner party on Sunday, June 16. Unluckily, I can't go. Because I am very busy that day. I meet a important customer in airport and give him a reception. I must do it myself. I understand you can know it. I want to thank your invitation once again. Thank you!

Sincerely yours,

Paul Morris

Letters of thanks

1. Guess the word with the help of the first letter and the hints in the brackets.

(1) The lecture is very i_____. (Meaning: giving much information; instructive)

(2) I am writing to thank you for your kind h_____. (Meaning: friendly and generous reception and entertainment of guests or strangers)

(3) I look forward to developing the relationship to the m_____ benefit of our organizations. (Meaning: having the same relationship to each other)

(4) Thank you for the beautiful vase you gave me at the c_____ party last month. (Meaning: alcoholic drink consisting of a spirit or spirits mixed with fruit juice, etc.)

(5) It was indeed a r_____ and enjoyable meeting. (Meaning: worth doing; satisfying)

(6) We hope you will continue to favor us with your g_____ support. (Meaning: giving or ready to give freely)

(7) Thank you for the lovely b_____ which you had delivered to my room during my stay in Cambridge University. (Meaning: bunch of flowers for carrying in the hand)

(8) It is displayed in our sitting room as a r_____ of our dear friends in

Britain. (Meaning: thing which reminds somebody of a fact or person)

(9) I am pleased to e_____ the pictures taken with my very simple camera. (Meaning: putting something in an envelope, letter or parcel)

(10) Thank you for making our trip so m_____. (Meaning: easily remembered)

2. Complete each sentence with a suitable preposition.

(1) Thank you _____ the hospitality you extended on my recent visit to your country.

(2) I hope that our business relationship will also expand _____ our mutual benefit.

(3) It was very kind _____ you to invite us to see you again after such a long time.

(4) I hope our cooperation will bring _____ the rewarding results.

(5) Participating _____ the conference has made me aware of the changing economic patterns of your country and the huge potential there.

(6) She was pleased _____ the beautiful Chinese knot you presented to her.

(7) I regret the delay in writing to you _____ behalf of Mr. Lin and myself to thank your warm hospitality on January 8.

(8) I look forward to the chance to repay your kindness _____ the occasion of your next visit to Hong Kong.

(9) The design is _____ excellent taste and reflects your personal interest.

(10) We would now like to look _____ the possibility of cooperating with you.

3. Correct one wrong word or cross out an unnecessary word in each line in the following letter body.

(1) I thoroughly enjoyed your hospitality during my three-day staying in Tokyo. Your new house is
(2) wonderful and your wife's cooking is excellent. Please thank her for the wonderful meal and for
(3) making us feeling so welcome.
(4) The trip was a success. We landed the contract and it should provide a great number of
(5) business for us. In the future, I think we will have more than opportunities to continue the growth
(6) of our relationship. It was great in getting together with you once again. Thank you again for your hospitality.

4. Complete the sentences with an appropriate word or phrase below.

| take the time to | your fine staff | subsequent | our discussions |
| my sincere appreciation | informative | repay | enclosing | convey | took |

Dear Mr. Reilly,

Please accept ____(1)____ for all the trouble you and your staff ____(2)____ during my

Exercise 23 Letters for Social Purpose

visit to your research institute. The tour and ___(3)___ discussions with you and your staff were very ___(4)___. I find that I am now more confident and courageous than before.

It was especially kind of you to ___(5)___ have dinner with me. I only hope to ___(6)___ your kindness some time soon.

I am ___(7)___ some written material relevant to ___(8)___ and I hope you will find it informative.

In closing, I would like to ask you to ___(9)___ my appreciation to every member of ___(10)___.

Sincerely yours,

5. Work with your partner to improve the following letter.

Hints for Improvement:

➢ Salutation   ➢ Wording
➢ Prepositions   ➢ Sentence combining
➢ Grammar   ➢ Language style and layout

Dear Mr. Peter,

It was very nice for you to company me in my visit to Huston. Thank you very much. You done all the things to me in my visit times. The visit was very useful and enjoyable. I learn a lot from the visit. I think we will have a lot chances to cooperate in future. I take this time and chance to thank you again. And look forward to see you soon.

Yours faithfully,

Jeff Nicholson

Letters of goodwill

1. Guess the word with the help of the first letter and the hints in the brackets.

(1) I am sure that you will a_____ to the new environment soon. (Meaning: become adjusted to new condition)

(2) I have just heard that you have been elected p_____ of your company. (Meaning: head of a bank, business firm, etc.)

(3) Your p_____ to vice-president was great news to us. (Meaning: rising to a higher rank or position)

(4) Please convey our h_____ condolence and deepest sympathy to his family. (Meaning: sincere)

(5) We were most g_____ to hear of Miss Joan Harvey's death. (Meaning: cause sorrow to somebody)

(6) News of the tragic loss of your b_____ wife has just reached me. (Meaning: much loved)

(7) I wish you and your c_____ every success in the New Year. (Meaning: person with whom one works)

(8) Your great a_____ did not come as a surprise. (Meaning: gaining or reaching sth.)

(9) It was a great honor to have made you're a_____ during my visit to London. (Meaning: get to know somebody)

(10) I was surprised to learn that you will r_____ the post of vice-president after April 18. (Meaning: give up one's job, position, etc.)

2. Complete each sentence with a suitable preposition.

(1) I am delighted to hear _____ your promotion to senior manager of your company.

(2) I will be getting _____ touch with you in the near future.

(3) I am sure that you are equal _____ this difficult task.

(4) I personally wish you and your colleagues great success _____ the years to come.

(5) Please accept our heartiest congratulations _____ your promotion to CEO of your company.

(6) We learned _____ your success in your new market.

(7) Over the years I have always been impressed _____ your outstanding leadership in your organization.

(8) I am surprised to learn of your retirement _____ day-to-day management.

(9) I sincerely admire you _____ the inspiring way in which you handled this crisis.

(10) It is _____ great sorrow that we have received the sad news of the sudden death of your husband.

Exercise 23 Letters for Social Purpose

3. Correct one wrong word or cross out an unnecessary word in each line in the following letter body.

(1) I have just learned of that you have been appointed Regional Manager for the Middle East.
(2) Looking back at your activities so far, I know that your enthusiasm and experience are the very
(3) qualities that are need for this position.
(4) I wish you ever success in managing the affairs of this branch, and my colleagues join me in sending you our warmest congratulations.

4. Complete the sentences with an appropriate word or phrase below.

Served	our sincere sympathy	deeply distressed	knew him
unreservedly	a great loss	grateful	firm	passing away	his associates

Dear Mr. Stein,

I am ___(1)___ to hear of the sudden death of Mr. Gerald Skinner who ___(2)___ in your consultancy ___(3)___ for so long.

His ___(4)___ must mean ___(5)___ to your company and ___(6)___ We, who ___(7)___ have good cause to be ___(8)___ to him for his sound judgment and advice that he gave us ___(9)___.

Our staff members join me in conveying ___(10)___ to members of his family.

Yours sincerely,

Brent Voss

5. Arrange the following words and phrases into proper order.

(1) our/convey/would like to/best wishes and congratulations/We/on your promotion/to you

_____

(2) he is/your achievement/very proud/of/I/that/hear

_____

(3) of vice-president/I/to learn/that/will resign/you/the post/after April 1/was surprised

_____

(4) let me know/If/I can do/please/to help you/hesitate to/there is anything/do not

_____

(5) your Christmas/May/good times and good cheer/be filled with/and/may/bring/the New Year/you every joy

_____

(6) is/the fruit/obviously/of/your hard work/and intelligence/Your success

(7) will/We/that many business people/be/by your success/are sure/inspired

(8) valuable/that/your experience here/I am confident/will be/in your future career/to you

(9) know/how much/I/meant/he/to you/and/your family

(10) the pain and grief/Your tragedy/when/I experienced/I lost my father/several years ago/brings back to mind

6. **Work with your partner to improve the following letter.**

Hints for Improvement:
- Grammar
- Sentence combining
- Collocation
- Wording and language style
- Spelling

Dear Mrs. Roberts,

I congratulates your promotion to be the market manager of your company. You service your company for many years. Now you are rewarded. I and my colleague are very happy to your result. All of us send our best wishes to you for your bright and sunny future.

Yours truly,

Benjamin Stevenson

Exercise 24 Letters for Other Purposes

1. Please rearrange the sentences in the following letter.

Dear Mr. Jackson,
(1) If so, could you book a room for me?
(2) I look forward to hearing from you.
(3) Could we postpone the lecture to Friday, 21st May, from 10.00 to 11:00 a.m.?
(4) I should be most grateful if you could supply me with details about the fee and expenses.
(5) I regret that I shall not be free on 14th May to lecture on your company's training program.

2. Here is a message from a secretary.

Mr. Todd,

Mr. Asano of Sabron Electronics phoned today, complained that the batteries on 2 new HTW machines caught fire. Didn't we recall them all to fit new types of batteries when this fault was first discovered? Could you write to him?

Jane

Please write a letter to Mr. Asano, which should include the following points:
➢ Apologizing for this fault,
➢ Telling him what action you took,
➢ Asking (if you can) why he was not contacted earlier,
➢ Advising him what to do and telling him how long the repairs will take.

3. Rearrange the following sentences in the letter.

Dear Mr. Johnson,
(1) I would appreciate any help you can give me in this matter.
(2) I look forward to seeing you again on this occasion, and to meeting other members of your staff.
(3) I wonder if you could give me some recommendations on coach and train trips.
(4) This will be my first visit to Denmark, and I should also like to travel privately during the weekend following the meeting.
(5) As you know, I shall be attending the business meeting you are having on Thursday, 26th September.
Yours sincerely,

外贸函电写作实训习题册

(教师使用答案)

段 婕 编

西北工业大学出版社

西安

目 录

Exercise 1 Basic Knowledge of Business Letters Writing 1
Exercise 2 Structures and Styles of Business Letters 5
Exercise 3 Establishing Business Relations 7
Exercise 4 Inquiries and Replies 11
Exercise 5 Quotations, Offers and Counter Offers 17
Exercise 6 Orders and Acknowledgements 23
Exercise 7 Payment by Letter of Credit 27
Exercise 8 Other Methods of Payment 30
Exercise 9 Collection Letters 32
Exercise 10 Packing 34
Exercise 11 Shipping 36
Exercise 12 Insurance 39
Exercise 13 Complaints and Claims 42
Exercise 14 Agency 46
Exercise 15 Contracts and Agreements 49
Exercise 16 Invitation for Bids and Advertisements 52
Exercise 17 Memorandums 53
Exercise 18 E-mails 56
Exercise 19 Notices and Instructions 59
Exercise 20 Agendas and Minutes 60
Exercise 21 Business Reports 61
Exercise 22 Resume (CV), Application Letters, and Follow-Up Thank-You Letters 63
Exercise 23 Letters for Social Purpose 65
Exercise 24 Letters for Other Purposes 69

Exercise 1 Basic Knowledge of Business Letters Writing

1.

(1) Please send us a catalogue for all your products for one buyer's reference.

(2) We are famous importers of computers with branches in three neighboring cities.

(3) The goal of American business is to try to raise the standard of living.

(4) Great affluence is often accompanied by social unrest.

(5) In 1776, Adam Smith concluded that division of labor makes it possible to increase the amount of goods produced.

(6) In socialist economies and capitalist economies alike, increasing number of highly qualified workers cannot find jobs that require their skills and their training.

(7) The salesperson told us to write to the main office directly for information.

(8) The convention scheduled for the month of January was cancelled owing to travel restriction.

(9) We certainly know that your policy on filing tax returns, and intend to comply with the stated regulations.

(10) If you cannot attend the meeting, please let us know as soon as possible.

2.

(1) If you had understood our February 9th letter, you have done it correctly.

(2) Your shipment can only be delivered next week.

(3) If you had taken proper care of the computer system, it would have been in a good condition.

(4) Pleas remit payment so that you can maintain your image of company.

(5) For the time being, we can serve you only on the method of payment basis.

(6) You can visit our assembly line only on Sunday.

(7) Thank you for calling our attention to the late arrival of ...

(8) We feel sure that you will entirely be satisfied.

(9) Your order will be shipped in two weeks.

3.

(1) want to   (2) generally

(3) as you suggested   (4) approve

(5) because, since (6) probably
(7) being prepared (8) if
(9) normally (10) because, since
(11) when (12) enclosed is/are
(13) because, since (14) most
(15) consider (16) inquiry
(17) because (18) cannot, not able to
(19) about, of (20) as we agreed

4.

Dear Sirs,

We thank you for your letter of Oct. 12 <u>regarded</u> (regarding) iron scraps, for which you have received inquiries from your customers in Africa.

We wish we <u>had</u> (could have) received your inquiry a little earlier. On the very day it reached us, a contract was <u>placed</u> (signed) with Mexico for a total of 360,000 tons. Because of this, our government has decided not to grant export licenses for the commodity for areas other than Mexico until December 31, 2006, <u>expected</u> (expecting) the shortage, which may be caused in the domestic market.

Therefore, we shall be pleased to inform you <u>with detail</u> (in detail) as soon as the circumstances <u>becomes favor</u> (become favorable) for us to do business <u>on</u> (in) this line.

Yours sincerely,

5.

The first letter reads unnatural, for some chunks of words are outdated or archaic, such as "acknowledge receipt of your credit application", "Please be advised", "Hoping ... we remain", etc. They sound distant and cool, which cannot arouse friendly feelings in the audience.

The second letter has an oral style, and is easy to understand, more effectively conveying the messages that the author intends to get across.

6.

(1) The business letter is the principal means used by a business firm to keep in touch with its customers; often enough it is the only one and the customers from their impression of the firm form the tone and quality of the letters.

Exercise 1 Basic Knowledge of Business Letters Writing

(2)

A. There are mainly four forms of business letters:

a. full block form

b. modified block form with indented style

c. modified block form

d. simplified form

B. Structures of business letters:

a. letterhead

b. reference and date

c. inside name and address

d. attention line

e. salutation

f. subject line

g. body

h. complimentary close

i. signature

j. enclosure

k. carbon copy notation

l. postscript

(3)

a. study your reader's interests

b. adopt the right tone

c. write naturally and sincerely

d. avoid wordiness

e. write clearly and to the point

f. be courteous and consideration

g. avoid commercial jargon

h. write effectively

i. avoid monotony

j. plan your letter

k. pay attention to first and last impressions

l. check your letter

(4) Letter writing does not differ from any other form of creative writing. Good English is one of the important bases of good business letters. What you write should be free from grammatical blemishes, and also free from the slightest possibility qualities of business letters, which can be summed up in the seven Cs, i. e. courtesy, consideration, completeness, clarity, concreteness, correctness, conciseness.

7.

(1) 这是信的主要部分,表达写信人的观点、意见、目的和期望等内容,所以应认真对待,并注意:

  a. 简明扼要,真诚礼貌,合乎语法。

  b. 分段正确,每段都有一个主题。

  c. 打印无误,布局美观。

(2) 信的主题行展示信的主旨,位于称呼和信文之间。在齐头式信中,主题行多位于左边空格处,其他格式的信中多位于信文的中上部。它能引起收信人对信文主题的注意。

(3) 信头应包括发信方名称、邮政编码、电话号码、电传号、传真号及电子邮件地址等。一般情况下,信头印在信笺中上方或左上方。

(4) 收件人姓名和地址多位于信笺左边,在写信日期下方2~4行位置,其形式与其在信封上的形式完全相同。

(5) 写信人公司的名称紧接在结尾敬语下面,用钢笔在公司名称之下签署自己的姓名。由于辨认上的需要,大多数商务书信也将写信人的姓名及职务打印在签名下方。绝不能使用图章发信函。

(6) 商务信封的左上角一般有提前打印好的写信人地址。收信人的姓名和地址则在信封的中部,邮票贴在信封的右上角,左下角可加印诸如"绝密""秘密""印刷品"等字样。

Exercise 2 Structures and Styles of Business Letters

1.
China National Textiles Import & Export Corporation, Shanghai Branch
18th Floor, Sunshine Mansion, 567 Siping Rd.,
Hongkou District, Shanghai, 200000, P.R.C.
Fax number: 86-21-63209767
E-mail address: shanghaitexdles@shtextiles.com.cn

Date: March 2nd, 2007

W. G. Wilkinson Co., Ltd.
789 Maple Street,
Lagos, Nigeria

Dear Sirs,

   Re: Embroidered Table-Cloths

We thank you for your letter of Feb. 24th inquiring for the captioned goods. The enclosed booklet contains details of all our embroidered table-cloths and will enable you to make a suitable selection. We look forward to receiving your specific inquiry with keen interest.

   Yours faithfully,

2.
   1) The writing and position of the date are wrong. The date should be written like "June 7th, 2006".
   2) The position of "attention" is not correct. The attention line should be placed above the salutation line in a letter. But in this letter, there is no need to write attention line, for

the inside address indicates that this letter is only addressed to that Department.

3) Dear Sirs should be changed into "Dear Clara J. Smith".

4) Delete the "Best wishes." line.

3.

(1) set (2) attention (3) comparable (4) but (5) appreciate (6) fresh (7) dependable

4.

Dear Tom,

Thank you for your letter in which you ask me to tell you about ways to keep your letter a neat appearance.

There are some ways to help us to keep letters a clear and neat appearance, and they usually vary to a great extent, but the following are some well-accepted guidelines:

- Leave a good margin on both sides (2 – 5 cm) and on top and bottom (3 – 5 cm);
- Use quality paper for both your letter and envelope;
- Use a good printer, preferably a laser printer, to achieve the best position effect;
- Eliminate spelling mistakes and use good English.

Hope that these can help you a lot.

If you have any questions, please let me know.

Yours sincerely,

John

Exercise 3 Establishing Business Relations

1.
(1) 工艺　　　　　　　　　　　　(2) 目录
(3) 领事　　　　　　　　　　　　(4) 价格单
(5) 专营　　　　　　　　　　　　(6) 促进……销售
(7) by separate mail　　　　　　　(8) to enter into ... relations with ...
(9) in compliance with their requirements　　(10) to open up a market in China
(11) stable financial status　　　　(12) to enjoy high reputation

2.
(1) owe　　　　　　　　　　　　(2) informed
(3) interested　　　　　　　　　　(4) establish
(5) purpose　　　　　　　　　　　(6) opportunity
(7) specializing　　　　　　　　　(8) reputation
(9) proposal

3.
(1) would like to establish business relations with your company
(2) take immediate measures
(3) place large and regular orders
(4) known for their superior quality and fine workmanship; at home and abroad
(5) take this opportunity; specializing in electronic equipment
(6) by the commencement of some practical transactions
(7) We owe your name and address to the Commercial Counselor's Office of the Chinese Embassy in your country
(8) We would like to introduce our company as one of the leading exporters of silk products
(9) in close contact with all the distributors here

4.
(1)
Dear Sirs,

We owe your name and address to the Commercial Counselor's office of the Chinese

Embassy in Paris, through whom we understand that you are interested in doing business in China.

We take this opportunity to introduce ourselves as one of the important dealers in the line of communication equipment in China for many years. We should appreciate your catalogues and quotations of your products, and we shall gladly study the sales prospects in our market.

We will appreciate your early reply.

Yours faithfully,

(2)
Dear Sirs,

We have obtained your address from the Commercial Counselor of your Embassy in Beijing, who informed us that you are in the market for chemical products. We approach you today in the hope of establishing mutually beneficial business relations with your corporation.

We are a specialized state-operated corporation handling with the export and import of Chinese chemical products. We enclose a copy of our catalogue covering the main items suppliable at present. If you want to buy any other goods shown out of our catalog, please inform us of your detail requirements. We'll try our best to supply the products that you need when we are in receipt of your letter.

As you know, it is our policy to trade with the people of European countries on the basis of equality and mutual benefit and exchanging what one has for what one needs. We believe we shall be able, by joint efforts to promote friendship as well as business, and to share profits.

We look forward to receiving your early inquires.

Your faithfully,

(3)
Dear Sirs,

We have obtained your address from the Commercial Counselor of your Embassy in

London. Now, we are writing you for the establishment of business relations.

We specialize in the exportation of Chinese Chemical and Pharmaceuticals, which have enjoyed great popularity in world market. We enclose a copy of our catalogue for your reference and hope that you would contact us if any item is interesting to you.

We hope you will give us an early reply.

Your faithfully,

5.
Dear Sirs,

From the Chamber of Commerce of Beijing, we have come to know the name and address of your firm and we shall be pleased to enter into business relations with you.

We specialize in the exportation of various electric machines which have enjoyed great popularity in the world market. At present, we mainly supply machines made in China at competitive prices.

We send you separately by airmail a copy of the latest catalog. Please let us know if there are any items which are of interest to you, and we look forward to receiving from you.

Yours faithfully,

6.
(1)
Well, he/she may do so through the following channels or with the help of:
a. advertisements in newspapers
b. introduction from business connections
c. introduction from subsidiaries or branches, agents abroad
d. market investigations
e. attendance at the export commodities fairs
f. visit abroad by trade delegations and groups
g. self-introductions or inquiries received from the merchants abroad
h. banks
i. the Commercial Counselor's Office

j. chambers of commerce both at home and abroad

k. company's web

l. yellow page of telephone

(2)

He/She may write the following things:

a. the source of information

b. intention

c. business scope of the firm

d. the reference as to the firm's financial position and integrity

e. expectations

7.

(1) c (2) d (3) b (4)b (5)b (6)b (7)d (8)c (9)b (10)b

8.

(1) regards, say   (2) specialized, with   (3) with, by

(4) If, interesting, inquiry   (5) available   (6) popularity

(7) finances, to   (8) compliance

9.

(1) We are one of the leading importers dealing in electronic products in this area, and take this opportunity to approach you in the hope of establishing business relations.

(2) We have been engaged in handing importing and exporting of machinery and equipment for many years, and our products have enjoyed great popularity in many countries.

(3) We owe your name and address to the Commercial Counselor's Office of our Embassy in Beijing.

(4) We are given to understand that you are a manufacturer of daily chemicals. One of our clients intends to buy cosmetics from your country. We will appreciate it highly if you airmail the catalogue and price list of the goods available at present.

(5) For our credit standing, please refer to the bank of China, Shanghai Branch.

Exercise 4 Inquiries and Replies

1.
(1) 特别折扣
(2) 最新价格单
(3) 现金支付
(4) 形式发票
(5) 回应
(6) 宣传册
(7) supply from stock
(8) enclosed
(9) bulk transactions
(10) business scope
(11) sold items
(12) operating instructions

2.
(1) interested
(2) obliged
(3) quotation
(4) inform
(5) purchase
(6) prefer
(7) quantities
(8) discount
(9) convinced

3.
(1) a well-known producer of sweaters for ladies and men
(2) enclosing our latest illustrated catalogue and price list
(3) pay by irrevocable L/C at sight
(4) information on our other products
(5) their superior quality and competitive prices; help you enlarge your market shares
(6) can supply from stock; the lowest quotation FOB Shanghai
(7) are interested in your products; have your quotations for the following items
(8) since the date of receiving the order
(9) sending you the proform invoice in quadruplicate
(10) not binding on our party

4.
(1)
Dear Sirs,

Microwave oven SU472

Thank you for your fax of June 17 requesting us to offer firmly our Microwave oven

SU472. This morning we faxed to offer you 3,000 sets of SU472 Microwave Oven at XX US dollars per set FOB Shanghai, shipped in August and September, 2007. This offer is firm, subject to acceptance by July 20.

Please note we offered you the most favorable price and are unable to entertain any counter offer.

As regards SU472 Microwave oven, we would like to inform you that we have made other offers for the current stock. However, if you give us an acceptable price, you are likely to get them.

You know well that recently the raw material prices have been increasing sharply and this will definitely cause the prices of microwave oven to rise. Therefore, you will benefit from this increase if you make a prompt reply.

Yours faithfully,

(2)
Dear Sirs,

Re: Inquiry No. 5

We are pleased at the signing of the Trade Agreement between our two parties some time ago, in which, we believe, will be of far-reaching significance in the development of our bilateral trade.

We are now in the market for the goods mentioned in the attached list and shall appreciate it if you will airmail to us at your earliest convenience your best quotation CFR/CIF Hamburg port, showing full particulars as to specifications and time of delivery, along with three copies of descriptive literature in English.

Should you be unable to supply the goods exactly as specified, would you please offer goods of the nearest specifications or pass this inquiry to your associate who is able to make the right offer?

When replay, or sending relevant catalogs or samples, please indicate the number of this inquiry for easy identification.

Faithfully yours,

(3)
Dear Sirs,

This serves to remind you of our letter No. 60 dated March 8, 2017, wherein we requested you to offer FOB price. If you have not yet sent your quotation, will you please airmail it to us as soon as possible. As a matter of fact, we have already had several offers on hand from other suppliers.

You are quite aware that we are now developing production in large scale. The prospects of trade between us will be very broad if you make use of this opportunity to pave the way for cooperation between us.

Faithfully yours,

5.

Situational writing 1

Dear Sirs,

We are a company that imports and exports hardware products and we have enclosed our company's brochure for your reference.

We have learned from one Spanish company of the same trade that you are a producer of hardware items in Italy. We are interested in the hardware products made in Italy, for there is a steady demand in our market for them.

We will be appreciative if you send us a copy of your latest catalogue and price list, with details of your price, terms of payment, discount policies, and range of your products.

We look forward to hearing from you soon.

Yours faithfully,

Situational writing 2

Dear Mr. Smith,

We thank you for your inquiry of June 23 and are pleased to send you our latest illustrated catalogue and price list for our steal cleats. We feel confident you will be satisfied with our goods because they are both excellent in quality and reasonable in price.

As for your requested quotation, we can reassure you that there is no problem in granting you the term on per kilo CFR Liverpool basis.

We also produce a wide range of steel products in which we think you may be interested. They are fully illustrated in the catalogue and are of the same high quality as our cleats.

We look forward to hearing from you.

Yours faithfully,

Situational writing 3

Dear Sirs,

We have learned your name and address from the latest issue of *Digital World* and are interested in your newly designed TF58 digital cameras.

We are one of the largest importers of digital products in China, and have wide connections with the local distributors in most large cities.

In order to acquaint us with functions and workmanship of your cameras, we shall be pleased if you could send us your catalogue, some samples and other necessary information on TF58 digital cameras.

You are kindly requested to quote your best CIF C5% Tokyo prices.

Your immediate attention to the above is appreciated.

Yours faithfully,

6.

(1) b (2) b (3) b (4) b (5) a (6) d (7) d (8) c (9) b (10) a

7.

(1) Please quote us your best price CIF Shanghai, inclusive of our 3% commission.

(2) Should your price be found competitive, we intend to place with you an order for 300,000 yards of Cotton Cloth.

(3) One of our customers is now interested in the XX Refrigerator made in your country. Please offer CIF London for 400 sets to be delivered in April.

(4) To enable you to have a better understanding of our products, we are sending you by air 5 copies of our catalogue and 2 sample books.

(5) In reply to your inquiry dated April 28, we are now sending you our latest price list for your reference.

8.

Dear Sirs,

We learn from a friend in Shenzhen that you are exporting light industrial products, especially electric appliances. There is a steady demand here for the above-mentioned commodities of high quality at moderate prices.

Will you please send us a copy of your catalogue, with details of your prices and terms of payment. We should find it most helpful if you could also supply samples of these goods.

Faithfully yours,

9.

Dear Sirs,

We are in market for a certain kind of Household Electrical Appliance. Please send us your latest catalogue and details of your specifications, informing us of your price CIF Xi'an. Please also state your earliest possible delivery date, your terms of payment, and discounts for regular purchase.

If your price prove reasonable and satisfactory, we shall soon place a large order with you.

Faithfully yours,

10.

Dear Sirs,

We welcome you for your inquiry of Oct. 10 and thank you for your interest in our products. We are enclosing copies of our illustrated catalogue and a price list giving the details you ask for. Also under separate cover, we are sending you some samples.

Please note that payment should be made by irrevocable payable at sight against presentation of shipping documents. We allow a proper discount in view of this first business between us.

We await your acceptance by fax.

Faithfully yours,

Exercise 5 Quotations, Offers and Counter Offers

1.
(1) 市场调查 (2) 做出让步
(3) 有效期 (4) 利润空间
(5) 对……具有约束力 (6) 实盘
(7) a reduction of 7% (8) copy
(9) to ship on time (10) trial order
(11) to reach an agreement (12) to put forward a proposal

2.
(1) pleased (2) acknowledge
(3) follows (4) Commodity
(5) Payment (6) Shipment
(7) arrival (8) expand
(9) discount (10) minimum

3.
The rearranged order:
(3) (5) (1) (2) (4)

4.
(1)
Dear Sirs,

We thank you for your inquiry of October 29 and are pleased to know that you are willing to enter into business relations with us. At your request, we make you an offer, subject to the receipt of your reply before November 24, 2006, as follows:

Commodity: "Showner" brand men's pajama
Quantity: 30,000 pieces
Price: US $ 40.00 per piece, CIF Milan
Payment: By a confirmed, irrevocable L/C payable by draft at sight

Shipment: since January 2007

We are convinced that the above quotation can meet with your request. The market price will be go up, therefore it is beneficial for you to place an order earlier.

Hope that we can receive you order soon.

Yours faithfully,

(2)

Dear Sirs,

We note from your letter of May 15 that you are interested in our chemical fertilizer but find our quotation of April 25 too high to conclude business.

We would inform you that our prize has been accepted by other buyer in your city, at which substantial business has been done, and that inquiries have kept flooding in over the past few months. Such being the case, we cannot see our way clear to cut our price. As a matter of fact, it is only in view of our long-standing trade relations that we offered you such a favorable price.

We hope you will reconsider it and cable us your order for our confirmation at your earliest convenience.

Yours faithfully,

(3)

Dear Sirs,

Subject: SWC Sugar

We have received your letter of July 17, 2007 asking us to offer 10,000 tons of the subject sugar for shipment to London and appreciate very much your interest in our product.

To comply with your request, we are quoting you as follows:

Commodity: Superior White Crystal Sugar

Exercise 5 Quotations, Offers and Counter Offers

Packing: to be packed in new gunny bags of 100 kgs each

Quantity: ten thousand tons

Price: U.S. Dollars One Hundred and Five per ton CIF London

Payment: 100% by irrevocable and confirmed letter of credit to be opened on our favor and to be drawn at sight

Shipment: one month after receipt of letter of credit

Your attention is drawn to the fact that we have not much ready stock on hand. Therefore, it is imperative that, in order to enable us to effect early shipment, your letter of credit should be opened in time if our price meets with your approval.

We are awaiting your immediate reply.

Yours faithfully,

(4)
Dear Sirs,

Subject: Tin Foil Sheets

We have received your letter of May 15, 2010 and confirm having cabled you today in reply, as per confirmation copy enclosed. You will note from our cable that we are able to offer you 50 long tons of Tin Foil Sheets at the attractive price of £135 per long ton CIF Shanghai for delivery within one month after your placing order with us. Payment of the purchase is to be effected by an irrevocable letter of credit in our favor, payable by draft at sight in Pounds Sterling in London.

This offer is firm subject to your immediate reply which should reach us no later than the end of this month. There is little likelihood of the goods remaining unsold once this particular offer has lapsed.

Yours faithfully,

5.
史密斯先生：

感谢您2006年10月6日来函询问我方BNT-3电锯产品。

随函附上产品规格说明,同时将我方价格、装运及支付等商业条款报知如下:

数量:100 台
价格:每台 100 美元,CIF 纽约
支付条款:收到订单后 1 周之内开立信用证
装运:收到信用证后 1 月之内装运

希望上述报价能够引起您的兴趣。盼早日回复。

谨上

6.

Situational writing 1

Dear Sirs,

We have received your letter of Sept. 12th, asking us to make firm offers for our leather gloves and are pleased to make you the following offer:

Commodity: leather gloves made from high quality sheep leathers in black, brown or red color
Price: US $13.00 per piece CIF Dalian
Payment: by confirmed and irrevocable L/C at sight to be established 30 days before shipment
Packing: at buyer's option
Shipment: in October

Please see to it that we quote our most favorable price and are unable to entertain any counter offer.

We are looking forward to hearing from you soon.

Yours faithfully,

Situational writing 2

Dear Sirs,

Thank you for your inquiry of July 21, in which you asked for an offer from us for our "Butterfly" brand bed sheet TN7032.

Exercise 5 Quotations, Offers and Counter Offers

We are now making you the following offer:

Commodity: "Butterfly" brand bed sheet TN7032
Price: at US＄478.00 per dozen
Packing: one dozen per box, 12 boxes per carton
Payment: by confirmed, irrevocable L/C payable by draft at sight

We feel you may be interested in some of our other products and therefore enclose our latest illustrated catalogue and a supply of sales literature for your reference.

We are looking forward to your order.

Yours faithfully,

7.
(1) a (2) b (3) d (4) c (5) a (6) a (7) c (8) c (9) c (10) b
(11) c (12) a (13) b (14) b (15) b

8.
(1) We are studying the offer and hope that it will keep open till the end of the month.
(2) We believe that you will place a large order with us owing to the high quality and reasonable price of our products.
(3) We will allow you 10% discount if you purchase 5,000 dozens or more.
(4) As to terms of payment, we often require a confirmed, irrevocable letter of credit payable by draft at sight.
(5) You are cordially invited to take advantage of this attractive offer. We are anticipating a large order from the United States, and that will cause a sharp rise in price.
(6) We will send you a firm offer with shipment available in the early May if your order reaches us before March, 10.
(7) Because there is a brisk demand for the goods, the offer will be open only for 5 days.
(8) We are giving you a firm offer, subject to your reply here by 5 pm our time, Tuesday, July 10.

9.
Dear Sirs,

In reply to your letter of May 5, we're giving you a firm offer, subject to your reply here by 5 pm our time, Thursday, July 27 as follow:

Commodity: boots for ladies

Specifications: more than 20 assortment with new designs of brown or red colors (detailed in catalogue)

Quality: the leather used is of superior quality

Price: CIF US $ 95 to 300 according to various designs

Payment: confirmed, irrevocable letter of credit payable by draft at sight to be opened 30 days before the time of shipment

Packing: at the buyer's option

Shipment: September, 19

Under separate cover, we have sent you sample books of various brands as per your request.

We expecting your early order.

Your faithfully,

Exercise 6　Orders and Acknowledgements

1.

(1) 双重检查　　　　　　　　(2) 装船通知
(3) 销售合同　　　　　　　　(3) 格式订单
(5) 纸板箱　　　　　　　　　(6) 处理订单
(7) document against payment　(8) recommend suitable substitutes
(9) an initial order　　　　　　(10) duplicate
(11) demand increase　　　　　(12) delay in shipment

2.

(1) received　　　　　　　　　(2) for
(3) working　　　　　　　　　(4) informed
(5) arrange　　　　　　　　　(6) through
(7) full　　　　　　　　　　　(8) sure
(9) comments　　　　　　　　(10) lead

3.

(1) The purpose of the author is to make a change in the original order and want 3,000 more CT732 Christmas plastic trees, but the expression in the original letter is not clear.

(2) The first sentence in the original letter is wordy and may confuse the readers.

(3) Too many "we"s are used in the original letter and the principle of using the "You" attitude is ignored.

(4) The word "prompt" in the last sentence of the original letter may impose pressure on the reader.

4.

敬启者：

感谢贵方11月8日来函,并随信寄来产品价格单和目录。

我方认为贵公司产品符合标准,对贵方报价也比较满意。我们同时注意到贵方对超过3万美元的订单给予3%的折扣。因此,我们于11月6日航空邮寄给贵公司我方的879号订单。

请贵方注意这批货物比较紧急,希望贵方尽早发货。

谨上

5.

December 5, 2006

Dear Sirs,

We are pleased to confirm with you our purchase of 4,000 sets of TECSUN 9-band transistor radios on the terms stated below:

Description of article: TECSUN 9-band transistor radio
Quantity: 4,000 sets
Price: US $ 53.00 per set CIF Shanghai
Delivery: To deliver the goods from Shanghai to Bombai within 14 days after receipt of the L/C

Please give special care to the packing of the goods lest they should be damaged in transit.

We are arranging to apply for an L/C and will open our L/C in your favor the moment we receive your confirmation on the order.

Yours faithfully,

6.

Dear Sirs,

We have received the Nikon D80 samples and thank you for your letter of November 11th in which you enclosed the catalogue and price list. We are satisfied with the quality and specifications of your products after we studied the samples and pamphlets.

We are sending you one copy of our purchase confirmation No.678 in duplicate to place an order with you for 2,000 sets of Nikon D80 digital cameras. As these goods are urgently needed, please make shipment of the goods before the end of November.

We are looking forward to your early reply and confirmation.

Yours faithfully,

Exercise 6 Orders and Acknowledgements

7.

(1) 我们从中国国际贸易促进委员会获悉，你们有意购买电器用品。

(2) 我们还想了解各类商品的每种颜色和式样的最低出口起售量。

(3) 所有报价以我方最后确认为准。除非另有规定或经双方同意，所有价格都是不含佣金的净价。

(4) 另行寄上我方目录若干份，以便贵方作出适当选择。

(5) 我方所报价格是经过紧密计算的。不过为促进业务，我们准备给贵方 5% 的折扣。

8.

(1) c   (2) a   (3) d   (4) a   (5) d   (6) c   (7) c   (8) d   (9) b   (10) a

9.

(1) We shall place a trail order with you for 500 sets provided you will give us a 5% commission.

(2) We are working on your Order No. 678 at present and you can trust we will effect the shipment within your stipulated time.

(3) Owing to heavy commitments, many orders haven't been made, and we can only accept orders for October shipment.

(4) Our stock is exhausted and we are not in a position to accept fresh orders. However, we will contact you by cable as soon as new supplies are available.

(5) Shipment should be made in three lots, with 100 tons each.

10.

Dear Sirs,

We are pleased by your prompt reply to our inquiry of July 10, 2013 and now wish to order from you as per our Order No. 987 enclosed.

Please supply the following items:
Description: A. Video Recorder
     B. Video Tape
     C. Mini Radio Cassette Recorder
Quantity: A. 1,000
    B. 1,000
    C. 5,000
Unit Price: FOB Xingang inclusive of our 5% commission
     A. US$ XXX each
     B. US$ XXX each
     C. US$ XXX each
Payment: L/C at sight to be opened 90 days before shipment
Package: by standard export seaworthy cases

Delivery Date: before the end of August in one/two lots

We are waiting for your reply and confirmation.

Your faithfully,

11.
We are pleased to have received your Fax Order dated March 10 for 500 sets knitting machinery.

We have immediately contacted the manufacturer. But they refused our request since the machine sells well, and there is a great shortage of raw materials and still a large number of orders. After our repeated negotiations, they finally promised to accept the order and to make delivery of 100 sets each month, beginning from next January.

We are aware that you are in urgent need of the products, but uncertain whether you will agree on the above delivery date. We are making contact with manufacturers elsewhere and will let you know as soon as there are any favorable news.

Meanwhile, we are enclosing our catalogue covering all the articles available at present. If you are interested in any of the items, please inform us. We will surely give prompt attention to your requirement.

Exercise 7 Payment by Letter of Credit

1.

(1) 受益人　　　　　　　　　(2) 不可撤销信用证
(3) 跟单信用证　　　　　　　(4) 销售确认书
(5) 提单　　　　　　　　　　(6) 发货日期
(7) commercial invoice　　　　(8) bill of exchange
(9) insurance policy　　　　　(10) negotiating bank
(11) to expedite L/C　　　　　(12) to extend the validity of L/C

2.
(1) issued　(2) On　(3) via　(4) speed　(5) stock　(6) completed　(7) read　(8) delay

3.

(1) Our customary practice is to accept the confirmed, irrevocable sight letter of credit, which is valid until 3 months after shipment.

(2) We wish to draw your attention to the fact that the 600 bicycles under Contract No. 267 are ready for shipment for quite some time, but we have not yet received your covering L/C to date. Please open the L/C as soon as possible so that we may effect shipment.

(3) We have the pleasure in advising you that L/C No. MI1926 for the amount of $35,000 has been established in your favor through the Commercial Bank.

(4) According to the stipulations of Contract No. 328, the relevant L/C should reach us not later than March 2nd. We, therefore, hope that you will open it in time so as to avoid any delay in shipment.

(5) Please amend the L/C No. 985SD86 to read "transshipment allowed" and delete the clause of insurance policy because this transaction is concluded on the basis of CFR terms.

(6) Owing to some delay on the part of our suppliers, we cannot ship the goods before August 20th as stipulated in the L/C. Please extend the shipping date and credit validity for one month respectively.

(7) We are sorry to inform you that we will have to reject your request for payment terms of D/P since we can only accept sight L/C.

(8) Therefore, we regret being unable to accept D/A terms for the time being in all our deals with foreign customers.

4.

Dear Sirs,

Thank you very much for your Letter of Credit No. BOC 06/10/05. However, upon checking, we have found the following discrepancies and would appreciate it very much if you will make the necessary amendments as early as possible so as to facilitate our shipping arrangement:

(1) The amount of the credit should be CAN＄125,000 (SAY CANDIAN Dollars one hundred and twenty-five thousand only) instead of CAN＄120,000.

(2) The Bill of Lading should be marked "freight prepaid" instead of "freight to collect".

(3) Please delete Insurance Policies (or certificates) from the credit.

(4) The port of destination should be Vancouver instead of Montreal.

(5) The goods are to be in tins of 340 grams instead of 430 grams.

(6) The credit should expire on Dec. 15, 2006 for negotiation in China instead of Nov. 30, 2006.

We await your early amendments.

Yours sincerely,

5.

Situational writing 1

Dear Sirs,

We thank you for your order for 200 units of computers amounting to US＄12,000. As requested, we are preparing to make shipments by the end of this month and would request you to open an irrevocable L/C in our favor as soon as possible, valid until October 30.

As soon as we receive your confirmation that the Credit has been established, the goods will be shipped and the documents will be presented for clearance with the bank.

Yours faithfully,

Situational writing 2

Dear Sirs,

We are pleased to inform you that a new import license has been granted and that we are able to increase the total amount of L/C No. NBB879 to USD 160,000. You will soon receive our L/C amendment advice through your advising bank.

Exercise 7 Payment by Letter of Credit

As we understand it is impossible to ship the goods before the originally agreed delivery date, we have extended the shipment and validity dates of the L/C to November 16 and 30 respectively. Please refer to the attached copy of our application for amendment to the relevant L/C.

We wish to thank you again for your close cooperation, which has enabled us to obtain the new import license in such a short time.

Yours sincerely,

6.
(1) 凡根据本信用证的条件开出并出示的汇票,本行保证对出票人、背书人及善意持有人履行付款义务。
(2) 只要附有提单,在任何港口都可以转船。
(3) 此信用证的汇票必须在……日或之前在中国议付,次日之后汇票满期。
(4) 单据必须在提单日期……天之内提示议付。
(5) "已装船"提单应作为基本条件,并在其上注明"运费已付"的字样。提单必须包括下列详述的货物。简式提单书不接受。
(6) 特别条款:单据必须在提单或其他装船单据签发日期之后 14 天出示。

7.
(1) Please amend L/C No. 345 as follows:
 • Adjust Long ton as Ton;
 • The "Port of Destination" should read "Hamburg" instead of "London";
 • Extend the shipment date of your L/C to "the end of August".

(2) Your L/C No. 3350 does not conform to the relative contract in quantity, with a difference of £75.60. Please amend it as soon as possible.

(3) Please amend your Letter of Credit No. 2345 by fax so as to cancel the clause of "The expenses of the Bank are to be for the beneficiary's account".

(4) We have received your L/C No. 3346 and found that the amount is insufficient. Please increase by £520.00 (increase up to £3,125.00) as the contract stipulated.

(5) Please extend the shipment date and validity of your L/C No. 6789 to October 15 and 30 respectively.

Exercise 8   Other Methods of Payment

1.

(1) 承兑交单　　　　　　　(2) 汇付
(3) 远期汇票　　　　　　　(4) 远期付款交单
(5) 跟单托收　　　　　　　(6) 未付余款
(7) T/T　　　　　　　　　 (8) cash in advance
(9) D/A　　　　　　　　　 (10) to pay in instalments
(11) irrevocable L/C　　　　(12) bill of exchange

2.

(1) inquiry (2) prospects (3) on (4) therefore (5) trial (6) place (7) standing

3.

In the original letter, we can see that in the first passage, there are some parts of sentences that are aloof and distant in tone, and are inflated in style. These chunks of words are: "With reference to your due commission", "in the amount of" and "indeed". All of them are inefficient in conveying the message for being lengthy and roundabout and, what is worse, cannot help build up a desirable tone in the letter.

In addition, we find that in the second passage, the author makes the unnecessary suggestion for checking with the bank the address of money order, for the copies of statements and money order can well indicate everything. Therefore, this part can be eliminated from the letter. Otherwise, it would have brought about the negative effect.

4.

Dear Sirs,

Thank you for your letter of March 10th. We have carefully considered your proposal to receive a trial delivery of our cutlery on D/A, but wish to inform you that to promote business the best we can exceptionally do as a trial will be on D/P at sight terms.

In accepting our proposal you assume no risks since out cutlery is well-known for its good quality, attractive design and reasonable price. This cutlery sells well in many other countries and we think it well have a good sale in your store.

If you are interested in our proposal, please write us by return and we will approach you further.

Yours sincerely,

5.

Situational writing 1

Dear Sirs,

We have been purchasing from you Mild Steel Sheet from by confirmed, irrevocable L/C.

But as you know, it has indeed cost us a great deal. From the moment to opening credit till the time our buyers pay us, the tie-up of our funds lasts about four months. Now, it is particularly the case, owing to the tight money condition and unprecedented high bank interest.

If you could grant us easier payment terms, it would be conducive to encouraging business between us. Therefore, we would like to propose for your consideration the terms of payment: either "Cash against Documents" or "payment available by draft after 30 days' sight".

We are looking forward to your favorable reply soon.

Yours faithfully,

Situational writing 2

Dear Mr. Zhang,

Order No. 8876

Thank you for your order, which has been completed and is being sent to you today.

As agreed we have forwarded our bill No. 2762 for DM 1,720.00 with the documents to your bank, Industrial & Commercial Bank of China, Caohejing Branch, Shanghai. The draft has been made out for payment 30 days after sight and documents including bill of lading, invoice, insurance policy will be passed on to you via the bank on acceptance.

Your sincerely,

Exercise 9 Collection Letters

1.

(1) 发票　　　　　　　　　(2) 逾期支付

(3) 未支付余款　　　　　　(4) 账单

(5) 偿付　　　　　　　　　(6) 采用法律手段来收缴欠款

(7) credit rating　　　　　 (8) to settle one's account

(9) cheque　　　　　　　　(10) to take legal action

(11) company image　　　　(12) to fulfill one's obligation

2.

Letter A

(1) on (2) agreed (3) stands (4) reminder (5) receipt (6) cleared

Letter B

(1) relating (2) whatsoever (3) meet (4) overlook (5) missed (6) extend

(7) repossession (8) outstanding

3.

Further to our telephone conversation this morning, I have checked out records …

Your account still has an outstanding balance of US $ …

We expect to receive a cheque from you in the very near future.

We regret that if we do not receive full payment within the next three days, we shall be compelled to pass the matter over to our legal department.

4.

Dear Sirs,

We have tried several times to urge you to solve the problem of your overdue account, but till now we haven't got any news from you. We have to urge you again to settle the account at an early date.

We are not well aware of the reasons why you did not settle the account within the agreed period, but we would like you to strictly fulfill your obligation defined in the contract.

Unless we hear from you within a week, we will take actions. Neither of us wants to see

Exercise 9 Collection Letters

your credit standing jeopardized, so we hope this step will not be necessary.

If payment has been made, please ignore this letter. We are waiting for your early reply with earnest.

Yours faithfully,

5.

Dear Mr. Doyle,

It has been 150 days since you obtained our consignment of cotton shirts under Contract No. 8657. And your payment for the goods has been overdue for 120 days. During this time, we have sent you 3 reminders and 2 letters to request your company to settle the account immediately, but we have only got one letter in which you explained away some difficulties in making immediate payment. As you know, it is your obligation to make payment, although we can appreciate your situation, which you can ride out if you make greater efforts.

If we do not receive the total overdue account of US $ 87,769 by August 19th, we will have to ask our attorneys to collect it through court proceedings.

Such actions will be costly to you not only in terms of legal fees, but also in terms of losing business. We would prefer not to take any legal action against you, but we will have no choice unless you do what we state above.

Yours sincerely,

Exercise 10　　Packing

1.

(1) 运输标志　　　　　　(2) 装箱单

(3) 适航包装　　　　　　(4) 指示性标志

(5) 运输　　　　　　　　(6) 外包装

(7) freight　　　　　　　(8) neutral packing

(9) consignor　　　　　　(10) dimension

(11) water-proof　　　　　(12) air-tight

2.

(1) inform　(2) per　(3) grade　(4) quite　(5) transit　(6) notify

(7) promise　(8) place

3.

(1) Glasswares are fragile goods. They need special packing precautions against jolting.

(2) The packing of Men's Shirts is each in a polybag, 5 dozen to a carton lined with water-proof paper and bound with 2 iron straps outside.

(3) Our detergent Art. No. 125 is in loose packing of 5 kilos per case instead of in bags and then packed in cartons. Thus it is more suitable for use in launderettes, hospitals and restaurants.

(4) In compliance with your request, the bags will be printed on one side in one color as per your design, which must be in our hand at least 30 days before the date of shipment.

(5) All powders are wrapped in plastic bags, and packed in tins, the lids of which are sealed with adhesive tape.

(6) Valves and all delicate parts are to be wrapped in soft material and firmly packed in cardboard boxes. These in turn are to be packed in cases in such a manner that movement inside the cases is impossible.

4.

Situational writing 1

Dear Sirs,

We thank you for your packing instructions, and have packed the goods according to your requirements:

1) The silk cloth will be packed 8 dozen to a packet, 6 packets to a carton but not to a crate.

2) Special directions and warning marks have been stenciled on each carton, as you instructed.

3) Each carton has been iron-strapped outside.

We would like to assure you that we have already changed the packing method from today on—all shirts and footwear are to be packed in cartons instead of wooden cases.

If you have any questions relating to packing of this consignment, please let us know soon.

Yours faithfully,

Situational writing 2

Dear Mr. Roger,

Enclosed we are returning for your file the counter-signed Sales Contract No. CJ102 of October 29.

We would like to call your attention to the marking. Please note that the port of destination, Shanghai, should be clearly stenciled on each case with the case number for easy identification. As these machines are precision instruments, which cannot stand rough handling, the wording "DO NOT DROP" should also be marked on each case. We shall appreciate it very much if you will act accordingly.

Please send us advice as soon as shipment is effected.

Yours faithfully,

Exercise 11   Shipping

1.
(1) 启航日   (2) 目的港
(3) 指示提单   (4) 卸货港
(5) 码头收据   (6) 装船通知
(7) shipping agent/forwarding agent   (8) shipping space
(9) clean B/L   (10) sailing schedule
(11) shipping mark   (12) storage charges

2.
(1) basis   (2) designate   (3) booked   (4) hitherto   (5) capable   (6) parts
(7) transit   (8) liquefy

3.

Dear Sirs,

We thank you for your inquiry of April 30th and are pleased to provide you with our information about the container service by our company. The shipping containers we can provide are of two sizes, namely 20 ft and 30 ft respectively.

They can be opened at both ends, thus making it possible to load and unload at the same time. For carrying goods liable to be spoiled by damp or water, they have great advantages of being both watertight and airtight. Containers can be loaded and locked at the factory, if necessary. So pilferage can be therefore impossible.

Being temperature-controlled, our containers are provided for any cargo that needs a special care. This lends its full benefits in shipping. There is also a saving in freight charges. When separate consignments intended for the same port of destination are carried in one container, they will be charged less and an additional saving on insurance because of lower premium charged for container-shipped goods.

We enclose a copy of our tariff and look forward to receiving your instructions.

Yours faithfully

4.
Situational writing1
Dear Mr. Smith,

Re: Order 832, S/C No.669703

From your letter of May 3rd, concerning the captioned S/C, we understand that instead of the stipulated two equal lots in shipment in September and October, 2006 respectively, you now wish to have 80% of the quantity shipped in June and the balance in July this year.

In reply, we wish to inform you that although we have the required quantity in stock, your request came too late for June shipment, especially because direct sailings for your port are few and far between. Besides, the relevant L/C is yet to be opened. Therefore, we would suggest the 80% of the total quantity be shipped in July, and the balance 20% in August, 2006, provided that your L/C reach us not later than June 20. Please let us know promptly whether this arrangement is convenient to you.

Yours sincerely,

Situational writing 2
Dear Sirs,

We have received your letter of Nov. 23rd, 2006.

We thank you for kind cooperation in providing the necessary amendment to your L/C.

We must apologize for the delay in delivery of your order, which has been caused by the unexpected late arrival of the goods from the place of origin.

Now the shipment has been arranged to go forth on board S/S "Seagull", which is scheduled to sail for your port early next month. We shall inform you of details of the shipment as soon as the goods are placed on board the steamer.

We sincerely hope that our delay in communicating with you on the above order has caused you no trouble and that shipment will entirely meet your satisfaction.

Yours truly,

5.

(1) c (2) a (3) c (4) b (5) b (6) b (7) d (8) c (9) b (10) c

6.

Dear Sirs,

We refer to Contract No. CT345 signed on December 1st, 1992, under which we decided 5,000 L/Ts cotton will be delivered in March, 1993. Up till now we have not heard any news about delivery from you.

Our clients are in urgent need for the goods. Please see to it that you should deliver the goods within the time stipulated in the contract, or we have to lodge a claim and reserve the right to cancel the contract.

Yours faithfully,

Exercise 12　　Insurance

1.

(1) 保险费率　　　　　　　　(2) 平安险

(3) 偷窃提货不着险　　　　　(4) 预约保单

(5) 共同海损　　　　　　　　(6) 保险索赔

(7) premium　　　　　　　　(8) insurance clause

(9) franchise　　　　　　　　(10) special additional risks

(11) warehouse to warehouse　(12) insurance claim

2.

(1) made　(2) concluded　(3) as per　(4) Should　(5) comply　(6) account
(7) in　(8) so　(9) borne　(10) accordingly

3.

Dear Sirs,

Referring to our Purchase Contract No. BT-67 for 300 M/Ts Shandong Groundnuts, you will see the transaction is concluded on CFR basis.

As discussed in our E-mail, we now desire to have the order insured at your side. We shall very much appreciate it if you could have the goods covered for our account against FPA and Aflatoxin Risk for 110% of the invoice value, totally GBP 55,000. We will refund the premium to you upon receipt of your draft at sight on us or a debit note.

We sincerely hope our request will meet your approval.

Looking forward to your early reply.

Yours truly,

4.

(1) We are willing to take out F.P.A. and W.P.A. covers for the shipment. Would you please give us the policy rates for F.P.A. coverage and for W. P. A. coverage?

(2) Breakage is a special risk, for which an extra premium will have to be charged. The additional premium is for the seller's account.

(3) We will take out insurance at this end under our Open Policy.

(4) The premium varies with the extent of insurance. Should additional risks be covered, the extra premium is for the buyer's account.

(5) We are sorry to learn that your goods were badly damaged during transit and the insurance company will compensate you for the losses according to the coverage arranged.

(6) We usually effect insurance against All Risks and War Risks for the invoice value plus 10% for the goods sold on CIF basis.

(7) We leave the insurance arrangement to you but we wish to have the goods covered against All Risks and War Risk.

(8) Our insurance company is a state-owned enterprise enjoying high prestige in settling claims promptly and equitably and has agents in all main ports and regions of the world.

5.

Dear Sirs,

We would like to inform you that we will be shipping your order for 30/cs camcorders per s/s "Dongfeng", due to leave here at the end of this month or the beginning of the next month.

Unless otherwise instructed, we will arrange to take out an All Risks insurance policy on your behalf on the above cargo. This type of coverage is, in our opinion, necessary for a cargo of this nature.

If you have any different opinion, please let us know as soon as possible.

Yours faithfully,

6.

Dear Sirs,

We refer to our Purchase Confirmation No. 345 for 5,000 pieces of "White Rabbit" Blanket. We are notifying that we have opened through XX Bank a confirmed, irrevocable Letter of Credit No. 789, totaling U.S. $..., the L/C shall remain in force till 31st August.

Please see to it that the above mentioned articles should be shipped before the end of August and the goods should be covered insurance for 130% of the invoice value against all risks. We know that according to your usual practice, you insure the goods only at invoice value plus 10%, therefore, the extra premium will be for our account.

Please arrange insurance as per our requirements, and we await your advice of shipment.

Yours faithfully,

Exercise 13　　Complaints and Claims

1.

(1) 有缺陷包装　　　　　　　　(2) 不可抗力

(3) 违背合同　　　　　　　　　(4) 短重

(5) 检验报告　　　　　　　　　(6) 次货

(7) settlement of claims　　　　(8) arbitration clause

(9) non-performance of contract　(10) to cancel an order

(11) inferior workmanship　　　(12) to take legal action

2.

(1) in　(2) making　(3) far　(4) instant　(5) with　(6) due　(7) forward

(8) late　(9) inconvenienced　(10) amply

3.

(3)　(2)　(1)

4.

Dear Mr Lee,

I refer to your letter of July 16 regarding the standard of my company's delivery service. Thank you very much for bringing this to my attention. I agree with you that delays in delivery are very damaging.

Having checked with other transport company, it is clear that you have had to wait a long time for recent deliveries, and we, too, find this unacceptable. I really must apologize for the inconvenience have been caused. I can assure you that you are currently considering switching transport company to avoid this type of error occurring again.

We take all our customers' comments seriously. With this in mind, we are more than happy to make special arrangements to have your order delivered in the next three days.

Please accept my apologies once again for the inconvenience.

Yours sincerely,

5.

Situational writing 1

Dear Mr. Peter,

Subject: Incorrect Delivery of Air Conditioners

We have just received consignment of air conditioners from your company.

However, on examination, we found that you had made a mistake with the order. We ordered 30 sets of Model A and 30 sets of Model B. But we found that there were 25 sets of Model A and 35 sets of Model B in your delivery.

We would appreciate it if you could replace the items we don't require. I am sure you will understand this matter is of urgency with summer approaching.

Sincerely yours,

Situational writing 2

Dear Sirs,

Thank you for your prompt consignment, which arrived this morning.

However, after careful examination, we found that 4 sets of machines are of inferior quality.

As a large store, we have supply chains in our nation, and enjoy a good reputation for providing the best quality of our goods. Therefore, we need to have the inferior machines replaced immediately, and shall return the machines to you by air transport, but the cost incurred so far will be borne by you.

Hope that you can take this matter up as a great urgency.

Yours faithfully,

Situational writing 3

Dear Sirs,

Thank you for your letter of May 30th. We were glad to know that the shipment of the order reached you promptly, but we are sorry to learn that case No.3 did not contain the goods you ordered.

We immediately went into the matter and found that the wrong goods were shipped to you through an error on the part of our packers. Please accept our sincere apologies for the trouble caused to you by the error.

Now we have arranged for the right goods to be dispatched to you at once. The relevant documents will be mailed as soon as they are ready.

The wrong pieces may be returned by next available steamer for our account, but it is preferable if you can dispose of them in you market.

Awaiting your reply.

Yours faithfully,

6.
(1) The survey report indicates that the damage to the carton and goods was due to rough handing in transit, rather than poor packing as you stated.
(2) The damage was caused by improper packing, such a big and heavy machine should have been fixed and stuffed in export wooden case.
(3) Upon examination, we found that there was no sign of poor quality and bad handicraft, and the dye used is excellent.
(4) Thank you for your acceptance of the wrongly delivered goods. We will give you a discount of 8% on invoice price. Please agree.
(5) Please let us know by fax whether you may ship the goods before September 15. If not we shall be compelled to cancel the order.

7.
Dear Sirs,

Our Order No. 678

We regret to have to complain about late delivery of the filing cabinets ordered on March 10. We did not receive them until yesterday though you had guaranteed delivery within a week. It was on this understanding that we placed the order.

Unfortunately, there have been similar delays on several previous occasions and their increasing frequency in recent months compel us to say that business between us cannot be continued under conditions such as these.

We have felt it necessary to make our feelings known since we can not give reliable delivery dates to our customers unless we can count on understandings given by our suppliers. We hope you will understand how we are placed and that from now on we can rely upon punctual completion of our orders.

Yours faithfully,

8.

Dear Sirs,

We have just received the 50 cases of chinaware shipped by M/S "President" under our Order No. 123 but regret to inform you that 7 cases are broken and their contents badly damaged.

As you see our Survey Report stating the damage was attributed to improper packing. We must therefore lodge a claim against you for damage and inspection fee of the goods amounting to US $... We hope the matter will call your best attention.

Yours faithfully,

Exercise 14　Agency

1.

(1) 营业额　　　　　　　　　　(2) 委托人

(3) 独家代理　　　　　　　　　(4) 商誉

(5) 广告宣传费用　　　　　　　(6) 授予……独家代理权

(7) to terminate an agency agreement　(8) record of transaction

(9) agency agreement draft　　(10) written notice

(11) mutual benefit business　(12) territory of the agency

2.

(1) message　　　　　　　　　(2) careful

(3) entrust　　　　　　　　　(4) territory

(5) duration　　　　　　　　(6) renewed

(7) notice　　　　　　　　　(8) enclosed

(9) review　　　　　　　　　(10) approval

3.

(1) under consideration; you will continue to make efforts to push the sales of our products

(2) in proportion to your sales volume

(3) both the principal and the agent shall take certain responsibilities

(4) in and after the duration of the agency

(5) to increase the market share up to 30%

(6) let the principal be informed of the survey I made recently

(7) on the basis of equality and mutual benefit to develop business on terms and conditions agreed upon as follows

4.

Dear Sirs,

Thank you for your letter of February 4, in which you offer your services as our agent in Morocco.

As the present turnover is not large enough, we deem it rather premature to take into consideration the matter of sole agency. It would be necessary for both of us to try out a period of cooperation to see how things prove and this will be beneficial to both parties. Also, it would be necessary for you to build a larger turnover to justify the sole agency agreement.

We believe that you can understand our position and continue to make efforts to promote the pleasant cooperation between us.

Yours faithfully,

5.

Situational writing 1

Dear Sirs,

We are interested in your digital cameras and would be very happy to offer our services as your agent in China.

We are one of the largest and long-standing establishments in various digital products in our country. We have better knowledge of the market here and good and effective distributing channels. If you give us an opportunity to be your agent, we think it will be a mutual-benefit deal.

There is a growing demand for digital cameras in our market. We shall be pleased if you could accord us selling rights for your digital cameras in China.

We are looking forward to your favorable reply.

Yours faithfully,

Situational writing 2

Dear Sirs,

After careful consideration, we think it would be in our best interest to maintain the market order for the sales of our products. We must inform you with great regret that our sole agency agreement with you will be terminated, effective from July 19, 2007.

We received a claim from our agent that you exceeded the limit of your district to canvass for orders in Ottawa. We made a thorough investigation and collected many evidences which suggest you really had breached the agency agreement.

We understand that you want to push the sales of our products, but, to maintain the market order, we have no choice but terminate the agency agreement with you.

We thank you for your endeavor in the last two years in pushing the sales of our products and hope that you may understand our position.

Yours faithfully,

6.
(1) c (2) d (3) b (4) c (5) d (6) a (7) c (8) b

7.
(1) 政府机构之间的交易：由 A、B 双方政府机构之间所达成的交易不受本协议条款的约束，上述交易不被认为是由 B 方在此协议下所达成的。

(2) B 方有责任每三个月一次向 A 方提交一份有关本协议项下自行车的先行市场行情及客户对商品的质量、包装和价格等评论的书面报告。如果当地进口条例有什么特殊变化，B 方应该立即通知 A 方。

(3) 如果一方违反了本协议中的任何条款，另一方有权以书面形式通知另一方立即中止协议。

Exercise 15 Contracts and Agreements

1.

(1)包装：

货物需包装于新的适应长途海运(包裹/空运)和天气变化的牢固木箱,并具有防潮防震之功能。任何商品受损和因包装不当导致的花费及任何因卖方保护措施不足或不当而引起的生锈,卖方负有完全责任。应随箱附带全套有关维修及使用说明书。

(2)装运条款：

1)离岸价条款：

(a) 由买方租船订舱位。按合同规定,货物装运前45日,卖方应传真或电传通知买方合同号、商品名称、数量、金额、箱号、毛重、体积及起运口岸的装船日期。

(b) 买方或买方运输代理人应在货船到达装运口岸前12天,通知卖方船名、合同号及运输代理人名称。卖方应与运输代理人联系及安排货物装运。如买方因故需要变更船只或有船只提前或推迟到达情况发生,买方或船运代理人应及时通知卖方。

(c) 如买方所订船只到达装运港后,卖方不能按时装船,则空舱费及滞期费等均由买方负担。

(d) 卖方应承担货物未越过船舷及未脱开吊钩的一切费用及风险。

2)到岸价条款：

卖方应在合同规定的交货期内将货物由起运港运抵目的港,并按照本合同第12条规定通知装船日期以便买方及时洽办保险。

(3)商品检验及索赔：

货物到达目的口岸90天内,如发现品质、规格或数量或重量与本合同、信用证或发票不符合时,除属于保险公司或船运公司负责者外,买方可以凭广州商品检验局出具的检验证明书向卖方提出索赔(包括检验费)。

2.

(1) We suggest you ship your Stainless Steel Cutlery on consignment in future.

(2) If you accept our consignment offer you won't ran any risk, for we will bear all the expenses for the return of unsold goods.

(3) Please sell the consignment before the prices go down.

(4) We feel much disappointed at your delay of selling the consignment, and we hope to get news about it from you as soon as possible.

(5) We hope you are satisfied with our present business on your consignment and hope

you will give us more chances.

3.

(1) 条款和条件：

A. 寄售期限：自货物到达目的港起6月(180天)

B. 销售地点、方法及价格应由A方视情况而定，B方不得干预，不过B方可提出建议。双方应以适当的方式交流信息、共同研究，并解决在寄售期间所发生的任何情况。同时B方应以任何可能的方式促进销售。

C. 如果任何销售地点需做广告宣传或促销活动的话，A方应做出规划，B方应承担所有费用。

D. 当货物到达时，如果容器发生任何破损，其责任应由B方承担。或在寄售期限内发生任何质量问题，B方应根据A方的证明按照合同所规定的价格做出补偿，或以新货替换未达到标准的货物。

E. 在寄售期限内，如果A方要求增加上述商品的数量，B方应与A方合作以便扩大销售。

(2) 支付条款：

A. 在寄售期满之后15天内，A方应该按照合同规定的单价，根据实际销售的种类及数量向B方汇寄总金额。

B. 对于未出售的货物，A方应该列出清单交给B方。双方通过协商决定是将货物退还B方，还是将该货物自动转移到下一个寄售合同。

C. 变质或破损的货物的金额应从汇寄的总金额中减去，已经处理掉或解决了的变质或破损的货物除外，A方应向B方提交减除金额的详细发票。

4.

(1) Quality/Quantity&Weight Discrepancy and Claim: If the Buyer find the quality and/or quantity/weight of the goods are not in conformity with those stipulated in the contract after the arrival of the goods at port of destination, aside from those losses within the responsibility of the insurance company and/or the shipping company, the Buyers shall have the right to lodge claims against the Sellers on the strength of inspection certificates issued by the inspection organization accepted by both parties. In case of quality discrepancy claim should be filed by the Buyers within 30 days after the arrival of the goods at port of destination, while of quantity/weight discrepancy claim should be filed by the Buyers within 15 days after the arrival of the goods at port of destination.

(2) Arbitration: All disputes in connection with this contract or the execution thereof shall be settled by amicable negotiation between two parties. If no settlement can be reached, the case in dispute shall then be submitter for arbitration in the country (district) of defendant in accordance with the arbitration regulation of the arbitration organization of the defendant country(district). The decision made by the arbitration organization shall be take as final and binding upon both parties. The arbitration expenses shall be borne by the losing parties unless otherwise awarded by the arbitration organization.

5.

(1)

1) 除得到卖方同意之外,买方应通过卖方所能接受的第一流银行开立保兑的、不可撤销的及无追索权、可分割、可转让、全部货款凭即期汇票支付的信用证付款。买方应保证信用证最迟于合同规定装运月份前15天到达卖方,否则,不能按期装运者,卖方不负责任。如超过装运期仍未开来者,卖方有权取消合同并向买方提出索赔。

2) 凡按"成本加保险费、运费价"成交者,由卖方按发票金额的10%投保,如信用证规定货物需转运内陆或其他口岸者,由卖方代保至内陆或其他港口。但此项额外保费应由买方负担。

3) 索赔应在货到目的地后30天内提出,并须由买方提出充分证明供卖方参考以便通过友好协商解决。

4) 买方在收到本合同后即行签署,并将正本一份寄回卖方存查,如本合同到达买方后10天内买方尚未签回,应视为买方已接受本合同所规定之全部条款。

(2)

1) 本行向根据本信用证并按照本证内条款开出汇票的出票人、背书人和合法持有人保证,在单据提交本行办公室时,本行即应以电汇方式承兑该汇票。所有根据本信用证议付的汇票金额必须在本证背面批注。

2) 单据处理办法:本证条件之一是所有单据应分两次连续以航邮寄交本行。第一次邮寄包括所有各项单据,但如某项单据不止一份,则留下一份由第二次邮寄。

3) 本行一旦收到此信用证要求的各项单据,并审核无误后,即可以即期电汇的方式偿付。请将此证通知受益人。

Exercise 16　Invitation for Bids and Advertisements

1.(1)凡是合格的公司愿参加此项目投标者,请按下列地址了解详细情况及查询招标文件。全套招标文件将于1998年2月16号开始在下列地址四层出售或用快件寄送。出售时间为每日上午9:00—11:00(星期日和节假日除外)。招标文件每册售价为200美元,邮寄费另收50美元。

(2)上述招标文件的招标截止日期为1998年3月22日16:00,并由中国石化实业公司在1998年3月23日上午9:00公开开标。每份投标文件都需分别装入密封信封中呈交并缴投标保证金。未交缴投标保证金的招标文件不予接受。

(3)招标在下列地址 A0401 会议室开标。

2.上海玩具进出口公司,由中华人民共和国批准的第一家工业外贸联合公司,是一家企业公司。该公司专门经营玩具进出口业务。所经营的玩具有金属与塑料变通玩具(摩擦型和发条装置玩具、电池控制玩具、无线电控制、声控制和光控制电子玩具)、手推玩具、布娃娃、木制玩具、音乐玩具、可膨胀玩具、儿童车辆、玩具芯子和发动机等。产品品种齐全,在国内外市场享有盛誉。

3.获特权在中国任何地区均可以用书面出口报关单报关的一家外贸公司。由对外经济贸易合作部特别批准在中国任何地区均可报关的海南省外贸总公司是该省第一家地方外贸公司。该公司在过去的12年为海南省少数民族经济和文化发展起了积极作用。该公司经营进出口业务、房地产开发,以及建立合资企业和合作管理企业。

Exercise 17   Memorandums

1.

Monthly Sales Meetings

2.

To	All department managers at HDC
From	Jerry Fisher, Training Manger
Subject	Business English training program
Date	November 12, 2022

3.

Arranging Seminars on Negotiation with Japanese

4.

	Memo
To	All representatives of Dunn's
From	Helen Black, Office Manager
Subject	Order your headed paper and embossed ballpens
Date	(suitable date)

New supplies of the following will be available on Thursday:

- Headed notepaper
- Embossed advertising pens as gifts for customers

Order the amounts you need from me:

- In writing
- By Monday

It will be very helpful if you keep to the dates set.

5.

Memo	
To:	Peter Henderson, the Maintenance Department
From:	Jenny Gibson, Section "B" Leader
Date:	20th May, 2022
Subject:	Maintenance in our new office

As you know, our department moved into our new office on Wednesday. Unfortunately, the previously agreed maintenance has not been completed. The following problems are outstanding:

Word processors require wiring to printers.

Metal bookshelf requires to be built.

The fire door is sticking.

Filing cabinet drawers need to be fixed.

I would be grateful to know when you will be able to complete the work.

6.

Memo

To: All staff

From: Jack Dawson, HR Department

Date: May 23, 2022

Subject: Li Chen Promoted

I'm pleased to announce that Mr. Li Chen has been made Director of the Human Resource Department.

Mr. Li has been with our firm for five years. Before that he was the Director of the Human Resource Department for the Great Wall Industries, with such responsibilities as organizational planning, executive selection and management development.

7.

Memo	
To:	All grade B staff and lower
From:	Jenny Anniston, Manager
Date:	14th May, 2022
Subject:	Safety Precautions at Work

Last Thursday, when "B" shift were leaving work, one of the men struck his head against a safety ladder, which had carelessly been left in a lowered position. As a result, he had to have stitches in his head.

I have had cause to tell you about this type of accident on many occasions before. At some time, a serious accident will occur, and then it will be too late. Unless I see a great improvement in your attitude towards basic safety precautions, I shall be forced to punish offenders.

Exercise 17 Memorandums

8.

Memo

To: Dan Lee, the Personnel Manager
Division A
From: Jack Hill, the Managing Director
Date: March 3, 2022
Subject: Installation Of Coffee Machines

The Board is thinking of installing automatic coffee machines in the offices of each division. Before we do this we need to know:
How much use our staff will make of them?
How many we would need?
Can you provide us with your views?
How the staff will react to the idea?
Whether time now used for making coffee would be saved?
Should we install the machines?
If possible, I would like to receive your report before the next Board Meeting on 2nd September.

Exercise 18　E-mails

1.
(1) We have received your payment.
(2) We are looking forward to hearing from you soon.
(3) Thank you for your inquiring about our products.
(4) Could you please respond to this questionnaire by April 30?
(5) Please send me a price list for your M-series.
(6) Would you please sign both copies of the contract and return?

2.

Subject: Billing Error, Invoice NO. A-28250
Dear Mr. Jones,
Thank you for your message of April 10. We have confirmed that the invoice should read as US $ 300 instead of US $ 350.
We are sorry for this error and have attached a corrected invoice for US $ 300.
Thank you!
Yours sincerely,

3.

Dear Sir or Madam:
We have your name and address through the introduction of Mr. A. G. Topworth of Swanson Bros., of Hamburg, is one of our old clients. We wish to inform you that we specialize in exporting chinaware and shall be pleased to enter into business relations with you.
If our above desire coincides with yours, please let us know and also keep us informed of your specific inquiries. Then we can send our illustrated catalogue and price list for your reference without delay.
In the meantime, we would appreciate it if you could send the name of your bank before the conclusion of an initial transaction between us.
We are looking forward to your first inquiry.
Yours sincerely,

Exercise 18 E-mails

4.

Because of shortage of space, employees have put heavy boxes near fire doors. There should be access to fire doors as workers must leave the building quickly if there is a fire. Fire doors should be unblocked and obstructions should be removed.

According to a report submitted by Mr. Burton, our Sales Manager, sales have fallen recently. The reason is that our packaging is unattractive although it is functional. I think we should develop new and appealing designs. Could you please attend a meeting in the boardroom at 10:00 am tomorrow to discuss this matter?

There are twenty vacancies on training courses being given in May and June. The courses provide useful training for junior staff in computers, time management and other aspects of modern office work. Could you recommend suitable staff before the end of the week?

5.

Dear Mr. Ho,

Thank you for your E-mail of November 23. We are happy to know that your customers find our machines really useful. We'd like to confirm the following with you:

➢ The inclusion of business terms is an excellent idea, and we shall develop this idea.

➢ We shall produce special cards, which can be fitted into the translators to provide more languages in the next model.

➢ However, the inclusion of a leather case would add considerably to the price of our machines and might not be necessary as the casing is very strong.

➢ We are sending you 200 electronic dictionaries and 300 language translators by the end of this month.

Thank you for your valuable suggestions. We are looking forward to your new orders.

Yours sincerely,

Wang Luen Fung

General Manager

6.

Dear Mr. White,

Thank you for your February 23 E-mail expressing an interest in the Arrowhead Conference Center. This E-mail will confirm our plans for your meeting.

We understand that you company would like to reserve two rooms from March 15th to 17th. Approximately eighty people will attend your meeting.

As you requested, we will provide twenty tables — ten in each room. We also have a television and DVD available in one room. We will serve lunch on the 16th.

If you have any questions or need to make any changes, please contact me immediately.

We look forward to seeing you on March 15th.

Yours sincerely,

William Bush

Meeting Planner

7.

Dear Ms. Wilson,

Thank you for your E-mail of April 6 expressing an interest in Click Camera's new camera, the XL-Lite.

The camera will be available this May, and the cost will be approximately three hundred and fifty dollars.

I have attached a brochure on the camera. If you have any questions, please feel free to contact us or your local Click Camera dealer.

Again, thank you for your inquiry.

Yours sincerely,

Michael Smith

Customer Service

8.

Dear Mr. Dobson,

We are attaching you our price list and catalogue for the new season. From the catalogue, you will notice that every single one of our products is made from 100% natural ingredients. We don't use artificial additives at all.

This year, for the very first time, we have included BHJ samples of our ten most popular aromas. I think you will agree that our range of well over 200 natural flavours and aromas is second to none and is outstanding value for money.

If you need more information, do please get in touch with me. If you are telephoning, please ask to speak to me personally or to my assistant, Ms Jenny Lee, and we will be very pleased to help you.

I look forward to hearing from you.

Yours sincerely,

Jack Williams

Sales Manager

Exercise 19   Notices and Instructions

SECURITY FOR YOUR BELONGINGS
At the Hospitality Hotel we are very conscious of the need for the security of our guests and their property.

PLEASE HELP US.
LOCK YOUR ROOM WHEN YOU GO OUT.
Please bear in mind that unless our staff is negligent we cannot be held responsible for any loss or damage.

Check that you have left nothing important in your car.
WE HAVE A SAFE FOR YOUR VALUABLES.
Ask at reception.

ALL OUTSIDE DOORS ARE LOCKED AT 11 pm.
- After this time use the key you were given when registering.
- If you should forget it, ring the bell to the right of the front door.

Remember that there have hardly been any problems at Hospitality.
LET US KEEPIT THAT WAY!
Micheal Hill, Head of Guest Services, Hospitality Hotel, Bath Road, Harrogate HG23NF
Telephone 01423 - 505861

Exercise 20　　Agendas and Minutes

North Travel Agency
Minutes of a meeting of the marketing department
At 3:00—3:30 p.m. 26 April, 2022

Present:

Chairperson: Richard

Marketing Manager: Lily

Mark, Peter and Tom

This meeting was held to discuss whether or not this was the right time to expand the company's business, particularly whether they should open more agencies next year. Richard presided over the meeting.

Lily said they should set up agencies in new areas by looking at their sales figures over the past years. Besides, she thought they had better grasp the opportunity because Peter said that the Youth Tourism Corporation was planning to expand their business in the southwest of the country. Tom was strongly in favor of them.

Mark had a different view by suggesting expanding present agencies rather than setting up new ones by considering new overheads.

Richard concluded the meeting with his agreement on presenting their ideas to the Board of Directors.

Exercise 21 Business Reports

1.
Generally, staff think that the present layout is not satisfactory. Opinion is divided as to what "good" furniture should be. By and large, staff think the company should be projecting a modern image.

2.
(1) The objective of this sales report is to present an update of product progress, and to survey the week's events in the market.

(2) The aim of this report is to investigate television viewing preferences among the public.

(3) The purpose of this report is to assess the feasibility of the company's expansion into the European market.

3.
(1) findings   (2) recommendations   (3) conclusions   (4) findings

(5) recommendations   (6) conclusions

4.
(1) Financial statements and notes   (2) Selected financial data

(3) Management discussion   (4) Board of directors and management

(5) Stockholder information   (6) Letter to stockholders

(7) Corporate message   (8) Financial highlights

5.

Report on Increasing the Company's Business

Introduction:
The purpose of this report is to identify ways to increase our business on the basis of the comparison of our company's tractors with BBF's.

Findings:
Although BBF Tractors are average in price, the people in the survey considered our tractors cheaper. They also commented highly on the standard of servicing we provide. However, the quality and reliability of BBF Tractors were rated much higher than ours. Moreover, BBF tractors were considered more attractive in appearance, and above all, people were impressed by the availability of BBF Tractors.

Conclusions:
BBF Tractors have achieved a great success due to the higher quality and reliability, attractive appearance and availability of their tractors. Their strengths, however, are our weaknesses.

Recommendations:
➢ Methods should be worked out to make our tractors stronger and less prone to mechanical failure.
➢ New designs should be created for next model.
➢ It's suggested that we examine ways of increasing the availability of tractors, particularly in the northern region.

6.

Report on Choosing a Paint Supplier

Introduction:
The report aims to recommend an appropriate paint supplier for our company. There are three suppliers for us to choose: ASP Paints, SDF Paints and HIJ Paints.

Findings:
ASP Paints can complete the painting in 10 days. It has the widest color choice of very good quality and fast-drying paints. However, their wash resistance is only fair and the costs are the highest (RMB 450).
SDF Paints (RMB 400) has a smaller choice of colors and its paints dry only slowly. However, the quality of paints is good with very good wash resistance. Above all, the company can complete the work in 12 days.
HIJ Paints is the cheapest and has a wide range of colors with good wash resistance but with average drying speed. Unfortunately, it can only guarantee completion within 3 weeks.

Conclusions:
The paint of SDF Paints is the best choice for us, as we need products with very good wash resistance.

Recommendations:
It is recommended that the paints of SDF Paints be used.

7.

Report on the Introduction of New Practices

Introduction:
The report sets out to describe the most attractive features of staff management policies of the HVC Garden chain restaurants and to suggest the introduction of some items into the restaurant department of our hotel. The presented information has been obtained during the Assistant Manager's visit to the HVC Garden.

Findings:
It was found that one of the HVC restaurants is exposed to an exceptionally innovative management, and it has recently developed a new policy in order to maintain high standards in all aspects of the service provided to its guests. The two successful practices of the policy are as follows:
➢ All the waiting staff are exposed to a check-up before starting their lunch and dinner shifts so as to ensure maintenance of hygiene and compliance with the company's dress code.
➢ The evening briefings conducted on a regular basis in order to inform the staff of the basic changes in the menu and wine supplies have proved effective.

Conclusions:
It is clear that a successful introduction of the two procedures is sure to reflect on the waiting staffs better awareness of good service and an improvement in the hotel's image.

Recommendations:
It is suggested that these two procedures (staffs check-up and regular evening briefings) should be applied in the restaurant department of our hotel.

Exercise 22 Resume (CV), Application Letters, and Follow-Up Thank-You Letters

1.

July 3, 2022

Dear Sir or Madam:

Having noticed the enclosed advertisement in today's *Yangcheng Evening Newspaper*, I wish to apply for a part-time job as a salesgirl for the direct selling of your beauty products.

I am a junior student at Guangdong College of Commerce. My major is marketing. The courses I have taken in marketing include Marketing, Marketing Techniques, Psychology of Consumption, Psychology of Women, Business Law, Labor Law, Business Ethics, Communications, Public Relations, etc.

I have gained some work experience in marketing over the last two years. During the summer vacation and winter vacation of 2021, I served as a salesgirl at the Beauty Products Counter in the Taibai Department Store. Last year I worked as a part-time salesgirl on Sundays for Procter and Gamble (Guangzhou) Ltd. I went from house to house to sell Rejoice 2-in-1, and Head and Shoulders shampoos.

I think my educational background and work experience in marketing will enable me to offer services for your sales promotion. Should you give me a trial, I would do my best to give you every satisfaction. I will wait for your answer.

Sincerely yours,

Kay Jin

2.

4th November, 2022

Dear Sir or Madam:

Application for the Post of Assistant Sales Manager

I haves seen your advertisement for the post of Assistant Sales Manager in today's issue of the *Daily News*, and would like to be considered for it.

I am pleased to provide full details of my personal information, educational qualifications and work experience set out in the enclosed resume.

As you will see from my educational qualifications, I studied Textile Engineering and Product Engineering, so I feel that I am familiar with this branch of engineering. I am particularly anxious to work for a firm that is concerned with the manufacture of textile goods, and feel that my past experience showed in the resume will be of value to you in the sales field.

I will be able to attend an interview at any time that is convenient to you, though I would be grateful if you could give me two days' notice. If you do decide to appoint me, I can assure you that I will do my utmost in promoting the sales of your products.

Yours faithfully,
Wang Xu

Exercise 23 Letters for Social Purpose

Letters of introduction and recommendation

1.
(1) recommend (2) indicate (3) capable (4) opportunity (5) conscientious
(6) asset (7) hesitate (8) facilitate (9) appreciated (10) reservation

2.
(1) as (2) with (3) for (4) of (5) with; with
(6) to (7) with (8) in (9) about (10) for

3.
(1) my pleasure (2) her graduation (3) at the New York office
(4) As her immediate superior (5) shorthand (6) fulfilled
(7) helpful and conscientious (8) with her family (9) without reservation
(10) obliging

4.
(1) likes—like (2) on (deleted) (3) for—to (4) prepared (deleted)
(5) with (deleted) (6) for (deleted)

5.

Dear Mr. John,

My name is Jack Lee. I was one of your former students in the HKM College where I graduated in 2022. I was monitor of the class you taught at that time. I suppose you still remember me.

I was wondering if you could help me with an introduction. I am now trying to apply for an American university for my MA degree study. Could you recommend one school for me? I would be grateful if you could introduce a professor for me as well.

I plan to major in business administration and intend to start my study in America next semester. Therefore, I would appreciate it very much if you could provide me with a recommendation or other necessary information as soon as possible.

I am looking forward to your reply.

Sincerely yours,

Jack Lee

Letters of invitations and their reply

1.

(1) delegation (2) representatives (3) sponsor (4) accompany (5) schedule

(6) spare (7) reception (8) extend (9) participate (10) hearty

2.

(1) in (2) with (3) of (4) for (5) with

(6) at (7) to (8) for (9) from (10) for

3.

(1) thank—thanks (2) the (deleted from "in the honor of")

(3) to (deleted from "attend to the dinner party") (4) as (deleted)

(5) expand—extend

4.

(1) inviting me (2) on May 7 (3) delighted (4) confirm (5) projector

(6) available (7) look forward to (8) members (9) your conference

5.

Dear Mrs. Ellis,

Thank you very much for the kind invitation to your dinner party on Sunday, June 16. I would really love to come, but unfortunately my heavy schedule will not allow me to attend it.

On June 16, I will have to meet one of our most important customers in the airport. After that, I need to hold a reception for him. I hope you can understand this.

Thank you for the invitation again. I look forward to meeting you on another occasion.

Sincerely yours,

Paul Morris

Letters of thanks

1.

(1) informative (2) hospitality (3) mutual (4) cocktail (5) rewarding

(6) gracious (7) bouquet (8) reminder (9) enclose (10) memorable

2.

(1) for (2) to (3) of (4) about (5) in

(6) with (7) on (8) on (9) of (10) to

3.

(1) staying—stay (2) is—was (3) feeling—feel (4) number—amount

(5) than(deleted) (6) in(deleted)

4.

(1) my sincere appreciation (2) took (3) subsequent (4) informative

(5) take the time to (6) repay   (7) enclosing   (8) our discussions

(9) convey   (10) your fine staff

5.

Dear Mr. Peterson,

Thank you very much for accompanying me and making all the arrangements for me during my visit to Huston.

I have learned a lot from the visit, which was very informative and enjoyable as well. I think there will be a lot of opportunities for us to cooperate in the future.

Thank you again for everything you did for me, and I am looking forward to meeting you soon.

Yours sincerely,

Jeff Nicholson

Letters of goodwill

1.

(1) adapt   (2) president   (3) promotion   (4) heartfelt   (5) grieved   (6) beloved

(7) colleagues   (8) achievements   (9) acquaintance   (10) resign

2.

(1) of   (2) in   (3) to   (4) in   (5) on   (6) of/about

(7) by   (8) from   (9) for   (10) with

3.

(1) of (deleted)   (2) at—on   (3) need—needed   (4) ever—very

4.

(1) deeply distressed   (2) served   (3) firm   (4) passing away   (5) a great loss

(6) his associates   (7) knew him   (8) grateful   (9) unreservedly

(10) our sincere sympathy

5.

(1) We would like to convey our best wishes and congratulations to you on your promotion.

(2) I hear that he is very proud of your achievement.

(3) I was surprised to learn that you will resign the post of vice-president after April 1.

(4) If there is anything I can do to help you, please do not hesitate to let me know.

(5) May your Christmas be filled with good times and good cheer, and may the New Year bring you every joy.

(6) Your success is obviously the fruit of your hard work and intelligence.

(7) We are sure that many business people will be inspired by your success.

(8) I am confident that your experience here will be valuable to you in your future career.

(9) I know how much he meant to you and your family.

(10) Your tragedy brings back to mind the pain and grief I experienced several years ago when I lost my father.

6.

Dear Mrs. Roberts,

I would like to extend my warmest congratulations on your promotion to Market Manager of your company. You have been serving in this company for many years, and now it is time for you to be rewarded. My colleagues join me in wishing you a bright future and a fruitful career.

Yours sincerely,

Benjamin Stevenson

Managing Director

Exercise 24   Letters for Other Purposes

1.

Dear Mr. Jackson,

I regret that I shall not be free on 14th May to lecture on your company's training program.

Could we postpone the lecture to Friday, 21st May, from 10:00 to 11:00 a.m.?

If so, could you book a room for me?

I should be most grateful if you could supply me with details about the fees and expenses.

I look forward to hearing from you.

2.

Dear Mr. Asano,

I'm writing to apologize for the faulty batteries we sold you. We recalled all the users when this fault was first discovered, and I am now wondering why you were not contracted earlier.

Please return the two faulty batteries to us and we shall repair them as an urgent priority. We guarantee to return them to you within 5 working days.

Sincerely yours,

3.

Dear Mr. Johnson,

As you know, I shall be attending the business meeting you are having on Thursday, 26th September.

This will be my first visit to Denmark, and I should also like to travel privately during the weekend following the meeting.

I wonder if you could give me some recommendations on coach and train trips.

I would appreciate any help you can give me in this matter.

I look forward to seeing you again on this occasion, and to meeting other members of your staff.

Yours sincerely,